Pueblos, Plains, and Province

Pueblos, Plains & PROVINCE

New Mexico in the Seventeenth Century

JOSEPH P. SÁNCHEZ

UNIVERSITY PRESS OF COLORADO
Louisville

© 2021 by University Press of Colorado

Published by University Press of Colorado
1580 North Logan Street, Suite 660
PMB 39883
Denver, Colorado 80203-1942

All rights reserved
First paperback edition 2024

 The University Press of Colorado is a proud member of the Association of University Presses.

The University Press of Colorado is a cooperative publishing enterprise supported, in part, by Adams State University, Colorado State University, Fort Lewis College, Metropolitan State University of Denver, Regis University, University of Colorado, University of Northern Colorado, University of Wyoming, Utah State University, and Western Colorado University.

ISBN: 978-1-64642-083-4 (hardcover)
ISBN: 978-1-64642-672-0 (paperback)
ISBN: 978-1-64642-095-7 (ebook)
https://doi.org/10.5876/9781646420957

Library of Congress Cataloging-in-Publication Data

Names: Sánchez, Joseph P., author.
Title: Pueblos, plains, and province : New Mexico in the seventeenth century / Joseph P. Sánchez.
Other titles: New Mexico in the seventeenth century
Description: First edition. | Louisville : University Press of Colorado, [2021] | Includes bibliographical references and index. | Summary: "Offers an in-depth examination of sociopolitical conflict in seventeenth-century New Mexico, detailing the effects of Spanish colonial policies on settlers', missionaries', and Indigenous peoples' struggle for economic and cultural control of the region. Explores the rich archival documentation that provides cultural, linguistic, and legal views of the period's values"— Provided by publisher.
Identifiers: LCCN 2020045769 (print) | LCCN 2020045770 (ebook) | ISBN 9781646420834 (hardcover) | ISBN 9781646426720 (paperback) | ISBN 9781646420957 (ebook)
Subjects: LCSH: Indigenous peoples—New Mexico—17th century. | New Mexico—Discovery and exploration—17th century. | Spain—Colonies—History—17th century. | New Mexico—Civilization—17th century. | New Mexico—History—17th century.
Classification: LCC F799 .S266 2021 (print) | LCC F799 (ebook) | DDC 978.9/02—dc23
LC record available at https://lccn.loc.gov/2020045769
LC ebook record available at https://lccn.loc.gov/2020045770

Cover illustration: "Taos Pueblo, New Mexico," c.1921, by Nicholas Roerich. Public domain image from wikiart.org.

For
Maximiliano Francesco and Orazio Federico Luciano

Contents

1 Introduction — 3
2 Between Continuity and Change: Pueblos, Plains, and Early Spanish Explorers — 18
3 Strangers on New Mexico's Eastern Plains — 39
4 The Land of Disenchantment: New Mexico's Starvation Period, 1598–1609 — 51
5 Death on the Great Plains: Jusepe and the Ill-fated Leyba de Bonilla Expedition — 67
6 The Big Clash: Acoma and the Jumano War, 1599–1601 — 72
7 Oñate's Exploration of the Great Plains — 87
8 The Case against Juan de Oñate and Vicente de Zaldívar — 98
9 Pedro de Peralta and the Founding of Santa Fe, 1609–13 — 112
10 Showdown in Santa Fe: The Peralta-Ordóñez Feud, 1613–14 — 126

11 La Custodia de la Conversión de San Pablo: Early New Mexico
    Missions, 1614–25   154

12 Benavides's Halation of New Mexico: Pueblo and Great Plains
    Evangelists   173

13 Governors, Missionaries, Kachinas, and the Holy Office of the
    Inquisition, 1634–59   197

14 El Alemán and the New Mexican Inquisition of 1668   227

15 Revolt and Reconquest: New Mexico, 1680–92   237

*Appendix A: An Overview of Salinas Pueblo Missions
National Monument*   255

*Appendix B: Contested Lands in Perspective: Acoma, the Jumano War,
and the Pueblo Revolt*   265

Notes   275

Bibliography   313

Index   319

Pueblos, Plains, and Province

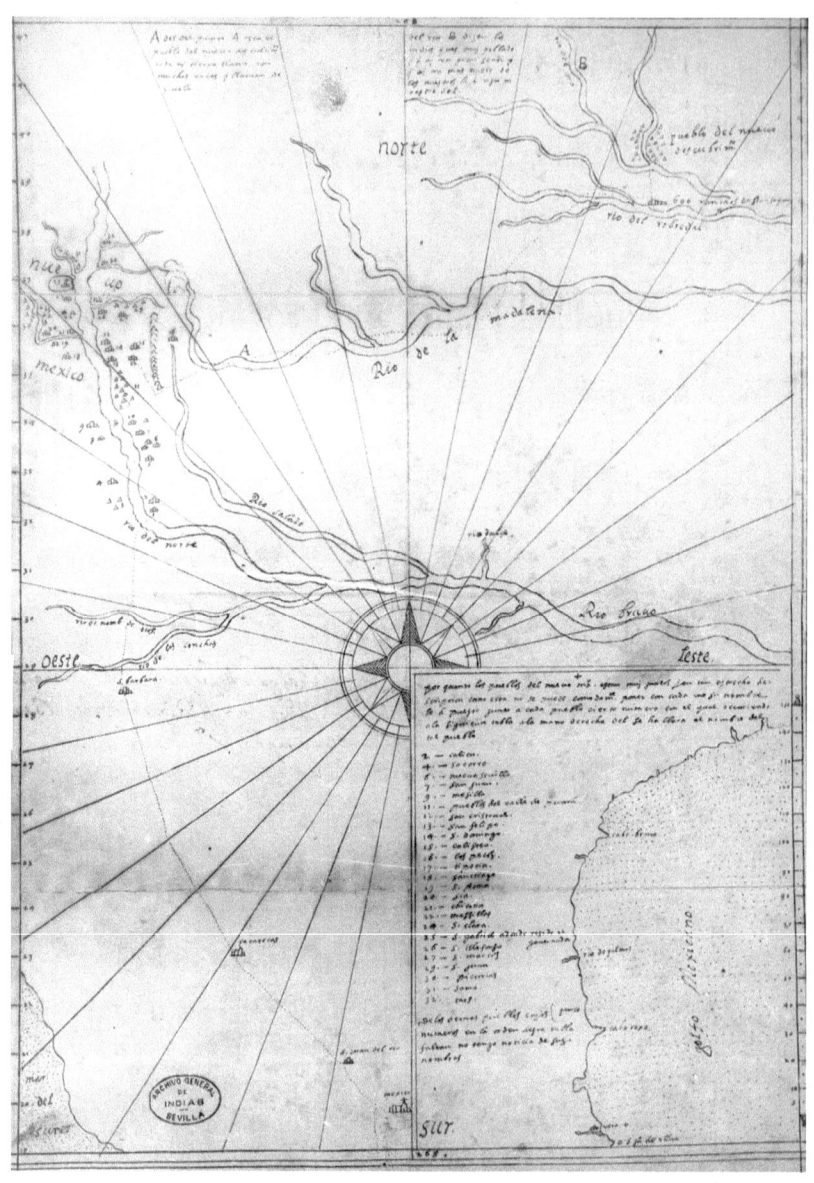

FIGURE 0.1. Enrico Martinez map, 1602, Center for Southwest Research Collection, Zimmerman Library, University of New Mexico.

1

Introduction

> The historical and cultural foundations of the Nation should be preserved as a living part of our community life and development in order to give a sense of orientation to the American people.... [Furthermore] the preservation of this irreplaceable heritage is in the public interest so that its vital legacy of cultural, educational, aesthetic, inspirational, economic, and energy benefits will be maintained and enriched for future generations of Americans.
> —*National Historic Preservation Act, Pub. L. 89-665, §1, as amended by Pub. L. 96-515*

The history of New Mexico between 1598 and 1680 is truly one of a contested frontier region between Spanish settlers and Indigenous peoples over political, economic, and cultural control of the region. In that regard, Indigenous territoriality clashed with European notions of sovereignty. Colonial policies throughout the Spanish empire were based on age-old European practices of claim of certain regions as well as control of resources and people within them. In many ways, colonial policies regarding Indigenous groups aimed

DOI: 10.5876/9781646420957.c001

to control and replace their political loyalties and social structures to fit the imperial paradigm and change their religious beliefs and rituals to comply with a Christian world view. Viewed comparatively, the history of European colonialism was replicated many times throughout the Americas as well as other places, such as Africa, India, the Philippines, and Australia. Yet the development of nation-states associated with the expansion of Spain, England, France, and Portugal, particularly, resulted in the evolution of today's world.[1] Today the native response to colonialism on a worldwide basis is "indigenization," a concept that in essence drives the hope that the Indigenous world can recover from the effects of colonialism and take back its cultures.

European sovereignty challenged concepts, traditions, and practices of tribal territoriality, especially as it revolved around defense of homeland. For thousands of years, prior to European contact, tribes spread throughout the Americas and differed linguistically and culturally as well as in identity. Since time immemorial, tribes in the Americas had carved out the boundaries of their homelands and prohibited any trespass. Their territorial claims marked their separate and distinct homelands. For tribes living within their territorial boundaries, unwanted and unwelcomed intrusions were a reason for war, as were issues associated with the predominance of European sovereignty. Such acts were met with open warfare between trespassing and defending tribes.[2] As Europeans expanded throughout the Americas, enemy tribes who allied with European cohorts were, indeed, trespassers onto their lands. To them, such unwelcomed intrusions were acts of war.

After 1492, tribal lands were continuously challenged by Europeans who would assume sovereignty by performing acts of possession in the name of their king and would issue land grant charters (England), *seigneurial* (France), the *sesmaria/sesmeiro* (Portugal), and *mercedes* (Spain) as well as the Dutch patroon system under their laws. The European claims disrupted and violated the norms of Indigenous practices and traditions tied to territoriality. Thus, the experiences of English, French, and Portuguese explorers and their Indian allies were no different from those of Spanish expeditions that made early contact with Indigenous peoples. From the earliest times, Indian alliances made by English, French, and Portuguese colonials, Spanish alliances had violated tribal territorial traditions.

Given the heritage and legacy of past European colonial powers, New Mexico, at the far edge of empire, was no different during those early centuries.

Indeed, the broader history of New Mexico is more than a narrative in a history book. History, on the other hand, is a living memory of places and events of the cultures that created them. Commemorating past cultures and people and their significance as a part of the march of humankind requires an understanding of historical processes and the values of the period under consideration.[3]

Along with that of Western Europeans that settled the New World, particularly North America, Native Americans are a part of the heritage that needs to be commemorated as a part of our national story and its shared histories with England, Spain, France, Portugal, Mexico, and Latin America. The prehistory and history of early New Mexico is of epic proportions in regard to the people who settled and developed the land and places that grew into towns and cities.

To study solely the narrative accounts of New Mexico's past without analysis of the historical cultural values at play during a given period is to deny the cultural dimensions of time, place, and the people who pioneered its founding, in this case, both Native American and Hispanic New Mexicans. The triad of pueblos, plains, and province is an integral part of the history of New Mexico, for it defines the complexity of the concept of homeland. In that regard, the word *culture* has many meanings, but one thing is sure: at its very least, culture is the way a group of people define their environment. It is done through language and practices that turn into customs, traditions, laws, and institutions. It is done by defining the homeland and its institutions as well as how they are governed, protected, and preserved for future generations.

To that end, the United States Congress, concerned with preserving and protecting our national heritage for future generations, enacted the National Historic Preservation Act in 1966.[4] The application of the philosophic tenets of the act clearly apply to state and local justifications in preserving and protecting historical places and structures related to New Mexico's history.[5] The National Historic Preservation Act rekindles the notion that historical significance is at the heart of the criteria for determining authenticity. Without doubt, wonderment, investigation, and analysis are building blocks for authenticity, preservation, and protection of New Mexico's history inclusive of many places, such as the Camino Real de Tierra Adentro National Historic Trail, the Northern Rio Grande National Heritage Area, the Old

Spanish Trail National Historic Trail as well as numerous New Mexico state monuments, such as early settlement and mission structures with their associated acequias, nineteenth-century fortifications, Indigenous archaeological sites, and other cultural resources. Similarly, the National Park Service preserves seventeenth-century Spanish Colonial heritage sites at Salinas Pueblos Missions National Monument (see appendix A), El Morro National Monument, and Pecos National Historical Park.

Our national story runs deep, especially in New Mexico. The native tribes that met the Spaniards in 1540 had long defined their environment and had learned to live in it. As First Peoples, they had, for centuries, lived their lives in a perilous land, which throughout time had become even more dangerous as events that were not within their control unraveled before them. Despite that they had been attacked, and sometimes entire settlements were wiped out, by other warring tribes, the Pueblo people of New Mexico had managed to recover and hold on to what mattered most to them. In the long haul of history, the historical process of modern times proved unforgiving and harsh in their regard. While many tribal languages have survived into modern day, others have long since disappeared and, along with them, their conceptual world view and their traditions. While many tribes survived both the prehistoric and Spanish colonial periods in North America, the nineteenth-century American westward movement, along with the Indian Wars on the Great Plains and California's gold rush period, proved to be the harshest of all tests they would face. Between the founding of Jamestown in 1607 and the massacre at Wounded Knee in 1890, the Indigenous world in North America was forever changed.

During the last half of the nineteenth century, Native American cultural values were further pushed aside under US military rule under policies ordering removal from their homelands onto reservation lands. To be sure, the missionization of native groups did not end with Spanish colonialism; it came west along with boarding schools with Anglo-Americans whose ministers continued to missionize Indians, Pueblos and Plains, along their paths. Sites such as Whitman Mission National Historic Site in Washington State, for example, reflect that part of our national story. In the process, many Native American ancient ways were further despoiled, while numerous cultural threads that held them together were torn apart and probably lost forever. Throughout the Western Hemisphere, the Indigenous world was similarly turned upside down.

Aside from policies of removal, wars of extermination were waged as Americans expanded westward. Attitudes toward Indians were deeply engrained in US culture and lore. Indeed, in the 1890s, such feelings were expressed by many Americans, among them L. Frank Baum, author of *The Wonderful Wizard of Oz* and editor of the *Aberdeen Saturday Pioneer* in South Dakota. Baum, for example, called for the extermination of the Sioux.[6] One can go further with a discussion about the disruption of Indian cultures, but the main point herein is that the theme is a part of our national story, and not relegated to a single European power of the past. Yet the story of the Indigenous world is also about its legacy of survival and cultural continuity.

Historically, in regard to the history of New Mexico, ethnographic details describing the homelands of Indigenous people on the Great Plains and of the Puebloans emerge as a descriptive window to the past that might have been historically forgotten were it not for the earliest Spanish colonial documentation. Today the historical documentation of the Spanish colonial period can, in today's world, be supported by Native American oral histories and traditions along with archaeological findings and ethnographic studies. Modern-day tribes in New Mexico retained a memory of their past, but their role in forging New Mexico's history is a part of this study, which adds to the reconstruction of an Indian perspective that is a part of our national story. As First Peoples, native groups deserve recognition and credit for their role in defining the history of the United States inclusive of its positive and negative effects on Indian America.

Spanish exploration, claim, and settlement of North America were extensive. The Spanish presence in what came to be called the Greater Southwest, which includes Texas, New Mexico, Utah, Colorado, Arizona, California, and Nevada, begins in the 1530s with Alvar Núñez Cabeza de Vaca's travels that included the southern plains. Cabeza de Vaca's odyssey touched on vague but real stories about the existence of Indian pueblos far to the north along the Rio Grande. Once established, nonetheless, the geographic limits of Provincia de Nuevo México defined the northernmost point of New Spain in the interior of North America. The New Mexico frontier stretched eastward to the western portion of the Great Plains of Kansas, Oklahoma, and Texas and from southern Colorado to the Great Salt Lakes in northwestern Utah. The Colorado River, which defines today's Arizona-California boundary, originally formed the western extension of New Mexico. By the end of the seventeenth century, such an expanse combined to form New Mexico and define the Spanish claim to North America. Still, the Spanish expansion that formed the triad of pueblos, plains, and province was constantly checked by Indigenous resistance.

Eventually, a land route known as El Camino Real de Tierra Adentro along the interior of New Spain connected Mexico City and the capital of the Province of New Mexico. As such, the Camino Real, forged and modified from Indigenous trails, combined with other trails in New Spain to facilitate other established patterns of exploration, migration, trade, and war. At first glance, the Camino Real formed a conduit for immigration and trade, but a closer view presents the trail as a linear frontier, running from south to north. Along that line towns, haciendas, ranches, mines, missions, and other aspects of an occupied line of places evolved and connected each other on a south-to-north basis. Indeed, the seventeenth-century towns aligned along later eighteenth- and nineteenth-century settlement patterns that criss-crossed along the long and linear Camino Real de Tierra Adentro, forming a braided trail. Shooting out from the Camino Real, spur trails connected isolated places on either side of the Royal Road.

Significantly, the Camino Real was a transmitter of Spanish heritage and practices associated with culture, lore, language, Spanish law, governance, religion, and a host of many institutional and cultural values that form the history and heritage of New Mexico and the Greater Southwest. Indeed, Indian ways, language, and customs also traveled along the Camino Real. Spain, Mexico, and regional Native American tribes share in that history and heritage that ties to the national story of the United States. The story begins in a prehistoric setting and evolves along the lines of a historical process that binds the triad of pueblos, plains, and province to the modern day.

The Spanish frontiersmen who ventured into New Mexico after blazing a portion of the Camino Real de Tierra Adentro from Santa Bárbara in present Chihuahua to New Mexico in 1598 were keenly aware that they were not the first settlers of New Mexico. They came, however, with a broader purpose than merely settling the area. They were part of a worldwide defense plan for the Spanish empire that included the establishment of civil government and the spread of Christianity. In that regard, the settlers of 1598 introduced a new system of governance and a new economy based on ranching, farming, and trade, combined with a new technology that allowed them to build on the land. On a cultural level, they introduced a new language, religion, lore, music, food stuffs, and other amenities.

Governance of the land required a political, legal, and organizational infrastructure that emanated from the king of Spain, who delegated executive power to a viceroy down to the governor and an *alcalde mayor*, a chief municipal administrator who worked with a *cabildo*, the town council, of a given area. The *cabildo*, composed of elected and appointed officials, made decisions for each province and town. Property rights, such as those that governed land grants, as well as contractual and judicial procedures were established through the Laws of the Indies. Their lives were not easy, for the first settlers suffered deprivation of the comforts of life, medicine, and security. The establishment of New Mexico, basically as a backwater area of the empire, which experienced its own "starvation period," depended on their sacrifice during the first years of its existence.

One aspect of Spanish culture allowed them to plan for the future, for they could, through the written word, record and secure the corporate memory of their endeavors, and, through architectural sketches, plan and construct the vertical world they would develop. In 1598, Spanish officials envisioned a braided corridor of the Camino Real de Tierra Adentro, which stretched from Mexico City to San Juan de los Caballeros, the first capital of New Mexico. In time, an infrastructure of forts, missions, towns, and ranchos evolved. Over time, the early pathways of the Camino Real de Tierra Adentro, forged from Indian foot trails, expanded into corridors for horse, mule, and wagon that eventually became modern-day corridors for motorized vehicles along a series of local, state, and regional roads, along with interstate highways.

Eventually Spanish towns grew into large cities with growing populations as the Camino Real faded into the romanticism of the past. Soon its pathways were overrun by paved streets, roadways, buildings, parkways, concreted arroyos, and every other imaginable land use pattern in modern times. Eventually the corridors gave way to Interstate 40 and Interstate 25, just as did historic Route 66 and Highway 85, which formed a part of New Mexico's historical highway system. Thus, colonial trails, based on Indian pathways, formed the corridor established by the Camino Real de Tierra Adentro and its many spur roads and trails that traversed New Mexico's landscape in all directions. Indeed, the significance of the Camino Real de Tierra Adentro to the history of New Mexico and our national story was clearly acknowledged in 2000, when the US Congress designated the Camino Real de Tierra Adentro National Historic Trail. That section of the Camino Real totaled 404 miles within the United States, starting at the Mexican border through El Paso, Texas, and New Mexico. Internationally, in 2015, UNESCO designated 1,200 miles within the Republic of Mexico as a World Heritage Site. Such honors pay tribute to the significance of the early Hispanic settlers of northern Mexico, New Mexico, and Texas, who developed towns, ranches, fortifications, and missions along a corridor that supported such enterprise. In that way, they touched the future of New Mexico and our shared national story with Spain, Mexico, and regional tribes.

Buried beneath today's New Mexican urban-rural infrastructures is the historical legacy and heritage of its native and Spanish colonial past. Education is a part of the remedy to salvage its patronage and promote the effort and commitment to preserve and protect New Mexico's early history and heritage as a part of our national story for future generations.

The early years of New Mexico's history, inclusive of the little-mentioned "starvation period," have, in many ways, been short-changed by historians who have concentrated on Spanish-Indian relationships without interpreting or analyzing the dynamics and values of the period. Indeed, Stan Hoig, in *Came Men on Horses* (2013), is one of very few researchers who have touched on the subject of the "starvation period" without necessarily ascribing causation when he writes, "Despite the provisions the relief expedition brought, both the New Mexico colony and Oñate's army fell into dire straits during the winter of 1600–1601."[7] Other historians have similarly mentioned the lack of food on both sides, Hispanic and Pueblo Indian, but have not gone far enough in specifically ascribing such analysis to it as a cause affecting relationships between both groups. Historiographically, historical narratives, told from a deficiency of analysis, have resulted in a retelling of historical events through the lens of nineteenth-century historians who subscribed to the "God, Gold, and Glory" school of thought and used "cruelty" as a theme to describe Spanish colonial motives. Oddly, the same formula was never applied to the first chapters of US history, which described Anglo-Americans as the builders of "the city on the hill" and as the sole presenters of the concept of democracy. Yet the question remains about the telling of reasons for the "starvation period" in Virginia's history or what happened to native tribes between the founding of Jamestown in 1607 and the long history of the Indian Wars, leading to the massacre at Wounded Knee in 1890. Among other wars, part of that early history is tied to the violent Powhatan "Uprising" of 1622, led by Opecancanough against the English settlers at Jamestown. The overall Powhatan War, caused by European trespass onto Indian lands and demands on Indian food resources, ran intermittently between 1609 and 1646.

New Mexico in the seventeenth century appeared no different from any other settled area established by Spain or, for that matter, by any of the European powers of the period. Thematically, between discovery, exploration, and conquest, New Mexico's early history is similar to events that were in progress in other parts of the Spanish Empire. Columbus's first voyage and the subsequent expansion of the Spanish Empire follow two important and relevant thematic periods: the so-called "Age of Discovery" and the "Age of Faith," in which a Church Militant emerged. Both were significant factors in the early period of expansion by Spain, England, France, and Portugal, the top four colonial powers of the period. Each, in its own way, utilized religious conversion and acculturation of the Indigenous peoples as part of their expansion efforts.

With exception to style, Spain appeared no different in its motives for expansion than those of the other powers; yet their stories are told from different vantage points. As colonial powers, the mother countries were interested in the exploitation of resources and the occupation of certain territories. In the end, the colonial penchant for exploitation of resources resulted in the exploitation of native peoples to work the land for every valuable asset found. All, however, had to deal with the tribes they encountered. Each European power evolved dual Indian policies to deal with peaceful or warring tribes. Under Spain, for example, tribes within the fold of Spanish sovereignty were treated as vassals of the crown with legal standings under the Laws of the Indies. Similarly, as in European feudal societies, vassals and their lands were protected from common enemies and paid a tribute in support of such protection. In 1598, for example, Governor Juan de Oñate met with all the pueblos in New Mexico and exacted their loyalty to the Spanish sovereign, which, in effect, resulted in a semblance of vassalage to the crown. The Pueblo people and their lands were protected under the Laws of the Indies. Warring tribes were dealt with militarily, and peace was maintained with them by treaty.

Within the scope of the historical process European colonials created a social hierarchy with strong racial overtones that allowed them to justify their treatment of native peoples and colonial minorities. Each contributed to a vestigial colonialism that affected the modern world in its struggle between "Jim Crow" types of practices and jurisprudence that clashed with our modern concepts of human and civil rights. To that end, the legacy of African slavery, too, speaks of those colonial values and its tragic aftermath that affected a given people. Thus, twentieth-century notions of democracy and human rights differ from seventeenth-century values across time, language, and culture. Although such values are different from today's American values, both evolved from the same historical fabric ingrained in European antecedents and notions of colonialism.

In New Mexico as elsewhere in the Spanish Empire, societal boundaries evolved that tied to Spain's mission to spread Christianity, to establish governance, law, and associated institutions, as well as to occupy the land for whatever it could yield either in agriculture, trade, or exploitation of resources. Had one walked into a Spanish settlement with its plaza during the colonial period, one would have heard the sounds of dogs barking, horses neighing, mules braying, along with those of cattle, goats, and sheep. At certain hours of the day, church bells made their clanging sounds announcing a moment of prayer. On a human scale, a given mix of people representing all colors and walks of life would have met the eye, and their voices expressing laughter, conversation, or heated discussions would have been heard at once. Spaniards, mestizos, mulattos, Indians, Asians, old and young, busily occupied the streets and marketplaces within a given plaza.

In the center of a given town, a plaza housed the institutions of church and state. Their structures formed the vertical cultural landscape of a given place. Each town had its *cabildo* (town hall) and its chief politicians: the *alcalde mayor* and his *regidores* (regents) of the cabildo. From time to time, the governor of the province would visit the outlying towns. The business of the cabildo was to attend to the *res publica*, the affairs of the people. The cabildo voted on policies in conformity with the Laws of the Indies on all matters that affected the town, colony, or province. Inescapable to the eye would have been the interactions of the cabildo with the people within the colonial society of the place. Beyond their social status, political leaders, the clergy, the laymen or the laity, itinerant traders, drovers, scribes, soldiers, and others in colonial societies seemingly had much in common as citizens of the empire.

Surrounding a given town, farmlands dotted the landscape with apple, peach, and apricot orchards as well as cultivated fields of melons, wheat, corn, chiles, and other assorted vegetables. Between the adjoining settlements were open ranges for pasturing herds of cattle, sheep, oxen, horses, and mules. In general, aside from stables or storage sheds for farm products, in corrals or within fences with small hutches near the homes of the settlers, one would have seen smaller numbers of domestic animals such as chickens, turkeys, milk cows, and goats, along with a few sheep and hogs for consumption. Farmlands with their attended acequias (irrigation ditches) would have dotted the landscape along rivers. Outlying settlements would have been, according to the Laws of the Indies, located near such necessities as water, wood, and pasturage. Other food sources, as available, included fish, wild birds, and foraging mammals.

On the outskirts of Spanish settlements, or not far from them, were Indian pueblos, which like their Spanish counterparts were farming communities, and rancherias (settlements of non-Pueblo tribes—in the case of New Mexico, Apache, Navajo, Ute, and Comanche communities), which lived off the land and trade. The dual Indian policy of dealing with peaceful tribes such as the pueblos and the warring tribes, especially those who lived on the eastern plains and woodlands to the north of New Mexico, affected both civil and religious entities. Spain dealt with the tribes as *"naciones,"* or nations. Yet the dual Indian policy defined the *"Gentiles,"* or those who had not yielded their sovereignty to Spanish authority and those, like the pueblos, who at least placated Spanish authorities by saying they accepted Spanish sovereignty. For them, coexistence was a means of survival. On the other hand, colonials preferred the object-lesson approach rather than the destruction of native groups. Indeed, control of native groups functioned as the preferred alternative. Groups or individuals who resisted coercion accordingly suffered the consequences of colonial European justice. Throughout the seventeenth century in New Mexico, for example, the pueblos, for the sake of survival, were submissive and obedient to Spanish authority and intimidation. Yet from time to time, the pueblos would "rebel" against Spanish sovereignty, but were defeated in their efforts until they succeeded in 1680.

Another element of Spanish Indian policy toward those who submitted to Spanish authority dealt with mission and non-mission Indians. Missionaries would have liked to have had control over an entire pueblo community, but Spanish law drew the line. Those Indians in the missions were under the authority and protection of the missionary priests. Those Indians in the pueblos who had not submitted to the mission process were not subject to the demands of the Spanish priests, but were a part of the population controlled by the civil authorities. Therein lay a three-pronged problem between missionaries, civil authorities, and the Indians themselves. The legal fight over authoritative boundaries between the priests and governors over control of Indians seemed, in the context of the times, to be a fine line. While priests tended to use Indian labor drawn from their charges, they could not demand work from non-mission Indians. That privilege was reserved to the governor and his chosen *encomenderos*, that is, those with the privilege to exact a yearly tribute (the *encomienda*) from non-mission Indians. If the tribute could not be paid in kind—that is, in blankets and *fanegas* (a fanega is equivalent to 1.6 bushels) of corn—then the value of the owed tribute would be paid in labor. The contractual aspects of the *repartimiento* outlined the guidelines for such work. For example, under the *repartimiento*, the *encomendero* had to pay one *real* a day to each laborer. Additionally, the type of work required and the number of days to do the work had to be specified.

The church-state feuds over Indian labor spilled into litigation brought before the Holy Office of the Inquisition, which dealt with issues such as the obstruction of the mission program. Governors and *encomenderos* were usually subjected to such investigations as a measure of control and intimidation by the clergy, which often led to their arrest, trial, and ouster from New Mexico. The laity, that is, the settlers, were often caught up in such fights and were literally forced to take sides, usually with the priests, who had the power to excommunicate dissidents. Too, in order to control the settlers in their choice of whom to side with, the priests would withhold the sacraments or not say mass on holy days, thus depriving the settlers of their religious practices. Such denials of the sacraments were frequently suffered in Santa Fe during the seventeenth century. Social conformity through such denials became the rule. Indeed, the struggle between church and state reflected the missionaries' passion to impose the supremacy of the church on the governor and Spanish settlers who stood in their way.

Spanish settlers, too, were subject to different forms of taxation. For example, despite their poverty, they paid a yearly tithe from their agricultural products, principally, wheat seeds collected by the church. They also paid a donation (alms) to the Santa Cruzada (the Holy Crusade) aimed at financing the fight against the "infidel," that is the fight over the Holy Land occupied by Islam. The Santa Cruzada alms had to be paid in specie, something of which New Mexican settlers had very little. If they did not pay, the total owed would be charged in arrears and, if still not paid, the debtor would be excommunicated from the church. Between 1633, when the Santa Cruzada policy was instituted, to the end of the seventeenth century, New Mexico settlers, through their *cabildo* representatives, argued that if the Santa Cruzada policy prescribed a special church tax collected to be used for the defense of the holy faith in a traditional war against "infidels," then instead of paying the tax, could they carry out a "holy crusade" against the unconverted Apaches and Navajos? Other taxes, such as the *quinto real*, or royal 20 percent for subsoil mineral resource, as well as the *diezmo*, a tithe amounting to 10 percent of their yearly earnings, were also charged the settlers.

Still, the goal of missionization of the natives had two diametrically opposed propositions. The crown, for example, utilized the missionaries to pacify the frontier so that expansion could be made without the cost of military force and manpower. Governors throughout the empire were keenly aware that mission fields served that purpose. Civil authorities saw pacification as a means to accomplish their goals dealing with the expansion of claim and sovereignty. They, like all investors, were motivated by personal economic gain. The second is that the missionaries were, indeed, imbued with the passion to serve their God by saving the souls of native peoples. In that regard, such religious fervor, compounded by a zealous drive, motivated the missionaries in the New Mexican mission field, known as the *Conversión de San Pablo*, to protect at all costs their work against the intrusive attitudes of civil authorities. Their fight to achieve their goals often resulted in extreme consequences.

One theme in New Mexico's history bears discussion because it formed the center of the Pueblo Indian resentment and antagonism that led to conflict with the Spanish settlers. The many pueblo rebellions of the seventeenth century, including the much misunderstood battle of Acoma in 1599 and the much ignored "Jumano War" of 1602–3, are tied to New Mexico's "starvation period" (see appendix B). The history of that period explains the issues that are usually presented as "Spanish brutality" against the pueblos without any interpretation regarding the events and values of the period. That subject is treated in a number of chapters concerning events during the period 1598–1603.[8] Certainly, earlier expeditions between 1540 and 1592 added to the history of such resentments by the pueblos that had experienced demands by Spanish expeditions for food.

Interpreting the early history of New Mexico is not without its dangers in making general statements, or, for example, utilizing single-factor analyses to reach conclusions, or misrepresenting the cultural values of the period. Thus, an effort has been made herein to reconcile or at least call attention to the need to balance preconceived notions of historical events as they are applied to interpretations of events of another era across culture, language, and time as they apply to New Mexico's history.

Despite the issues revolving around European sovereignty and tribal territoriality, Spain idealistically strived to respect tribes at peace. Aside from treaties made with nomadic tribes, pueblos were accorded a legal status, under the Spanish *Recopilación de Leyes de Indias*, a compilation of laws dating to the Middle Ages. While countless laws concerned the Spanish settlement of the Americas, other laws pertained to tribal lands, particularly those regarding Pueblos. By means of the Laws of the Indies, Spain strived to respect Native American lands. Settlers, for example, were not allowed to live in pueblos, buy Pueblo lands, or graze livestock on Pueblo lands, nor could they have livestock ranches within eight miles of a Pueblo mission. The laws also stated that no ranches could be established near an Indian pueblo and any lands taken from Indians living on them must be returned to them.[9] Spanish land grants conceded to Pueblos in New Mexico serve as a legacy noted today in Pueblo lands litigation.[10]

New Mexico's history is a strong regional force, as it has influenced the early histories of neighboring states. Its history, moreover, is part of a broader story shared on a national and international stage. In that regard, other places and people significant to the history of the United States, Mexico, and Spain share that stage. To that end, the history behind Salinas Pueblo Missions National Monument inspired the writing of this book (see appendix A). While this study focuses on Spanish New Mexico between 1598 and 1680, some light is shed on the history of the sites at Salinas Pueblo Missions National Monument and its ties to the history cited herein.

Insights to the early history of New Mexico, as seen through the Salinas Pueblos Missions National Monument story, can be gleaned from the pioneer writings of France V. Scholes, Charles Wilson Hackett, Herbert E. Bolton, and Hubert Howe Bancroft.[11] So, too, the archives of Spain and Mexico as well as those in the Vatican are filled with data that reflects on the history of the Provincia de Nuevo México, the pueblos, and the Great Plains during the seventeenth century. Their story lay hidden in the timeless mists of history.

The historiography of the exploration and settlement of New Mexico is rich in early Spanish colonial documentation. In addition to sources in the archives of Spain and Mexico as well as documentary depositories in the United States, this study utilized printed documentary sources such as those by George P. Hammond and Agapito Rey, whose monumental work translated and edited all available documents that they collected of the life and times of Juan de Oñate as well as those concerning early explorers of New Mexico. Similarly, Herbert Eugene Bolton's edited translations of correspondence, diaries, and reports regarding New Mexico's early history are essential for the study of Spanish colonial exploration and settlement of the Greater Southwest. Another major contributor to the history of seventeenth-century New Mexico, France V. Scholes, pioneered the use of ecclesiastical documents to unravel a deeper understanding of New Mexico's rich history. Among his many studies are *Church and State in New Mexico, 1610 to 1630* (1936) and *Troublous Times in New Mexico, 1659–1670* (1937). Additionally, sources extant in various national and international depositories were utilized in the present study. To that end, the author is indebted to the staffs of the following archives who aided him in locating related documents: the Archivo de Indias, Seville; the Real Academia de Historia, Madrid; the Biblioteca Nacional de Madrid; the Archivo General de la Nación, Mexico City; and the Bancroft Library, Berkeley, California; as well as the Center for Southwest Research, Zimmerman Library, at the University of New Mexico. Special thanks to Dr. José de la Cruz Pacheco Rojas, professor at the Universidad Juárez del Estado de Durango, who shared documents with me related to early New Mexico, which he located in the Biblioteca Nacional de Antropología e Historia, Mexico City.

2

Between Continuity and Change

Pueblos, Plains, and Early Spanish Explorers

The inhabitants of the buffalo region . . . lived by hunting and ate nothing but buffalo meat during the winter; . . . during the rainy season they would go to the areas of the prickly pear and yucca; . . . they had no houses but only huts of buffalo hides; . . . they were enemies of our informants, but nevertheless came to the pueblos of the latter in order to trade such articles as deerskins and buffalo hides for making footwear, and a large amount of meat in exchange for corn and blankets.

—*Hernán Gallegos, 1582*[1]

As the settlers bound for New Mexico gathered their families, belongings, wagons, and herds to move northward from Santa Bárbara in the last week of January 1598, they were unaware of the historical significance of their actions. Indeed, two major historical events occurred in 1598 that would affect both pueblos and plains. The first, the establishment of the Provincia de Nuevo México by Governor Juan de Oñate and his settlers, ushered an era of the Spanish occupation of the area among the pueblos and the exploration of the

DOI: 10.5876/9781646420957.c002

Great Plains. The second, the opening of the Camino Real de Tierra Adentro (Royal Road of the Interior) beyond Santa Bárbara, the northernmost outpost in Nueva Vizcaya (Chihuahua), facilitated expansion, immigration, and trade. Although used as a migration and trade trunk trail, the Camino Real, with spur trails emanating from it along its length, also served as a transmitter of Spanish cultural and legal practices. Along its braided pathway it introduced Spanish governance, law, religion, language, technology, ranching and farming techniques, as well as a host of cultural practices that played a major influence in establishing and perpetuating a Spanish culture along its path. Within the scope of change and continuity, such an infusion of cultural values and practices greatly influenced and, to an extent, changed aspects of native culture throughout the pueblo world. Similarly, the cultural values and practices spread by means of Spanish exploration and settlement throughout North and South America as well as the Caribbean proved equally pervasive. Once Hispanic New Mexico came into being, the triad of pueblos, plains, and province became the evolutionary catalyst for change and continuity. In that region the ambiguous lines between Indigenous territoriality and European sovereignty would soon be tested.

The Spanish presence in what came to be called the Greater Southwest, which includes Texas, New Mexico, Utah, Colorado, Arizona, California, and Nevada, began in the 1530s with Alvar Núñez Cabeza de Vaca's travels that included the southern Great Plains. Between 1540 and 1592 other explorers had been in the region and wrote about the people and the land they had seen, particularly the Indian pueblos far to the north along the Rio Grande. Once established, the Provincia de Nuevo México encompassed all three geographic entities—pueblos, plains, and province—and expanded, by dint of occupation, the Spanish claim to North America. Eventually a land route known as El Camino Real de Tierra Adentro along the interior of New Spain connected Mexico City and the Province of New Mexico.

At first glance, the Camino Real formed a conduit for immigration and trade, but a closer view presents the trail as a cartographic, vertical, south-to-north frontier and a transmitter of culture, lore, language, Spanish law, governance, religion, and a host of many institutional and cultural values that form the history and heritage of the area. Spain, Mexico, and regional Native American tribes share in that history and heritage, which ties to the national story of the United States. To that end, the Camino Real is much more than a line on a map. The story begins in a prehistoric setting and evolves along the lines of a historical process linking the pueblos, plains, and province of yore to the present.

Forged from Native American foot trails, the Camino Real de Tierra Adentro became an important transportation corridor during the Spanish colonial period of New Mexico and the Republic of Mexico. Cart caravans along with large herds of cattle, horses, mules, sheep, and goats wended their way along the route where towns, missions, and ranches were established. Seeking level land for better passage, pasturage, and water, wagon masters and scouts adjusted the trails from Native American pathways and, in many cases, blazed new routes that formed larger and longer trails. By 1610, the Camino Real de Tierra Adentro, which traversed nearly the entire length of the interior of present Mexico, connected presidios (forts), towns, mines, ranches, and missions between Mexico City and Santa Fe in New Mexico. Along the entire length of the trail were hundreds of *parages* (stopping places or campsites), where travelers set up campsites. Some *parages* became towns; others became ranches and mission sites. Utilized as the main road to transport people and things, the Camino Real de Tierra Adentro in the sixteenth century took on significance as the first step in the northward expansion of Spanish settlements, forts, farms, ranches, and missions.

Between 1540 and 1821, the Camino Real corridor formed a braided trail that resulted from differing and overlapping routes in which new towns, as destinations, were established during the sixteenth, seventeenth, and eighteenth centuries. Along a south-to-north axis varied patterns of newly developed towns, missions, forts, mines, and land grants marked the directions of each step taken during the period of expansion. The campsites along the Camino Real, themselves often overlooked in the evolving pattern of the braided corridor, are an integral part of the Camino Real and its heritage. Rivers influenced the route. From Santa Bárbara travelers often went north to the Rio Florído, a tributary of the Rio Conchos, which, in turn, was a tributary of the Rio Grande near where it makes its eastward turn toward the Big Bend. There, at La Junta de los Ríos, travelers veered north following the Rio Grande to New Mexico. That route was long, dangerous, and time consuming.

In 1598, Oñate and his settlers blazed a new segment of the route between Santa Bárbara and New Mexico. The new direct route to New Mexico ran about 600 miles in length.² It became known as La Ruta de Oñate (Oñate's Route), which ran from Santa Bárbara directly north, across the Río Florído, to a place that became known as El Paso del Norte. From there the route went due north to the area of Las Cruces. Once across the Rio Grande, hundreds of settlers, led by Governor Juan de Oñate, drove herds of cattle, horses, mules, and other animals along with their eighty-three-cart caravan northward along the new route. Near present Las Cruces, the winding river north through steep canyon lands proved difficult for the wagon train and animals to follow. Blazing a new route northward to suit their needs, the settlers went eastward along the route known later as La Jornada del Muerto (Dead Man's Journey).³ The nearly waterless route ran northward for nearly eighty miles. At the northern end of the Jornada, near present San Marcial, the route veered westward toward Socorro. Following the Rio Grande northward, the caravan eventually reached the area of present Albuquerque, thence past the pueblos and the area of present Santa Fe until it reached a place called Caypa, near present Ohkay Owingeh (San Juan Pueblo; Ohkay Owingeh means "Place of the Strong People").⁴ Caypa sat on an escarpment overlooking the Rio Grande. At the time, it had been abandoned "because of our coming," wrote a settler.⁵ Today a historical marker outside of Ohkay Owingeh marks the location of Caypa, also known as San Juan de los Caballeros, the first capital of New Mexico. On July 11, 1598, the exhausted members of the caravan, consisting of nine Franciscan missionaries, over 500 soldiers and colonists,⁶ accompanied by an unknown number of Tlaxcalan Mexican Indians, herders, and camp tenders, arrived at San Juan de los Caballeros. Their herds of horses, oxen, and mules included cattle, sheep, and goats, many of which had been consumed during the six months of travel. Of the eighty-three wagons, twenty-two were left along the wayside of the Jornada del Muerto because they were so laden with provisions, military accouterments, and munitions that the jaded oxen could not pull them. Later Juan de Zalivar returned to get them.⁷ Thus La Ruta de Oñate opened a new chapter for the history of New Mexico.

Spanish interests in New Mexico, with its attendant Indian pueblos and its bountiful resources of the Great Plains beyond the mountain ranges to the east, began long before 1598. Oddly, the earliest Spanish interests in New Mexico and its Indian pueblos began when castaways from a shipwreck made their way west along the southern edge of the Great Plains. The survivors were members of the expedition led by Panfilo de Narvaez to Florida that wrecked off its west coast in 1528. Making to the shore, the survivors followed the Gulf Coast on foot until they reached the Mississippi River, which blocked their path. Hoping to reach New Spain to the south in makeshift boats made from hides, they were drawn out to sea by the mighty rush of the river emptying into the Gulf of Mexico. Additionally, the survivors were hit by storms that scattered their boats so that only five men survived. The survivors made their way to islands off the coast of present southern Texas, where they were enslaved by local tribes.[8] Once on the mainland, one man chose to stay and live among the natives of the area. Meanwhile, Cabeza de Vaca and three of his companions, one of them a Moorish slave, Mustafa Zemmouri, known as Estebaníco the Black, decided to make their escape and reach whatever Spanish settlements they could find along the frontier areas of northern New Spain. They traversed the land within the southern plains of Texas, sometimes as free men, other times as slaves to different Indian groups.

They were the first Europeans to catch a glimpse of North America's interior. They had seen the rolling plains of East and South Texas to the Rio Grande and the arid prairies on the edge of the Chihuahua Desert. Once past the Edwards Plateau, they had made contact with different Indian bands and may have crossed and recrossed the Rio Grande where it makes its sweeping "Big Bend" on its way eastward to the sea, hundreds of miles away. Somehow the four castaways survived the hot summer months on the northern edge of the Chihuahua Desert as they migrated westward toward the setting sun. Somewhere along the Rio Grande, probably in southern New Mexico, they learned about the pueblos of the north. By the time they crossed the northern tip of the Sierra Madre Occidental, they realized that they had undergone a tremendous change.

After eight years on the run, they admitted to themselves that they had become Indian-like. Later, in 1536, once safe among the Spaniards in northern Sonora and later in Mexico City, they became vocal opponents of the Spanish Conquest. In crossing along the southern tier of North America, Cabeza de Vaca and his companions were the first Europeans to cross the edge of the Great Plains that extended into southern end of West Texas. Indeed, Cabeza de Vaca's report, given in his *Relación* (account) about the land to the north,[9] referred to as the *tierra adentro* (the interior), and its people, inspired later

Spanish exploration of the mysterious north country. Cabeza de Vaca and his companions were not only the first Europeans to make contact with various tribes of the southern Great Plains; they were the first to hear about the pueblos of the upper Rio Grande.

A year after their dramatic rescue, Spanish officials in Mexico City authorized a small expedition to reconnoiter the *tierra adentro*. Viceroy Antonio de Mendoza offered Cabeza de Vaca and his companions the opportunity to lead the expedition, but they declined to go north again. Estebaníco on the other hand, quickly agreed to guide a small party led by Friar Marco de Niza beyond Culiacán, the last Spanish outpost in northwestern Sonora. Niza, a Franciscan missionary who had served in the Caribbean at Santo Domingo (present-day Dominican Republic) in 1531 as well as later in Peru and Guatemala, was no stranger to exploration in the New World. In the spring of 1537 the Bishop of Mexico, Juan de Zumárraga, brought Niza to the viceregal palace in Mexico City. Recently arrived from Guatemala with tales the bishop desired to hear and share with Viceroy Mendoza, Niza said that he had spent time in Peru and had conversed with Francisco Pizarro, then engaged in winning new kingdoms for the crown of Spain. At first Zumárraga hoped to assign him as a missionary to Nueva Galicia, a province north of Mexico City, but, based on that interview, a plan to explore and conquer the *tierra adentro* evolved that included the participation of Fray Marcos de Niza.[10]

On November 20, 1538, Niza met with don Francisco Vázquez de Coronado for the first time at Tonalá, a village near Guadalajara. Coronado presented Niza with the viceroy's instructions that ordered him "to find a way to go on and penetrate the land in the interior" and to make careful observations about the people, the land, the rivers, and the flora and fauna of the interior.[11] More importantly, wrote Viceroy Mendoza,

> If God, our Lord, should will it that you find some large settlement which you think would be a good place for establishing a monastery and for sending friars who would devote themselves to conversions, you are to send a report by Indians, or return yourself to Culiacán. Send back reports with utmost secrecy so that appropriate steps may be taken without disturbing anything.[12]

Later, at Culiacán, on the edge of the Spanish frontier, Niza assembled his expedition. The reconnaissance party included Estebaníco, Fray Onorato, a Franciscan priest, and Indian friends of Estebanico who had accompanied him during his lost years. By spring of 1539, Fray Marcos de Niza and his retinue were on their way. On March 21, Passion Sunday, Fray Marcos made a fateful decision. Restless over the slow progress of the expedition, Estebanico proposed to go ahead as an advance scout and send back messages in the form of crosses regarding his finds. Estebanico promised to wait for Niza near the pueblos, and together they would proceed to Cíbola, the large kingdom they sought. Niza would never again see Estebanico, for he was killed by the people at Háwikuh, a Zuñi pueblo in the province of Cíbola.[13]

Meantime, Niza continued to receive messages in the form of crosses in varying sizes from Estebanico's Indian messengers. When Niza received a cross larger than the previous one, he quickened his pace in anticipation that Estebanico had discovered a rich city of gold. Niza's progress was not rapid because, aside from gathering information about the terrain and people, as instructed, he had to determine his proximity "to the sea." To do that, Niza claimed he took a side tour, away from Estebanico's trail, which caused him further delay.[14] He hoped the information he gathered would be useful, as the Spaniards were not clear on the coastal geography. They were unaware that Baja California was a peninsula, not an island, and that the body of water that formed the Sonoran coastline was actually a gulf, not an ocean. Yet Niza's new information failed to shed any light on the subject and appeared useful only to determine the distance from the Sonoran coast to wherever Niza's trail lay in the interior. Still, Niza wondered about the meaning of Estebanico's large crosses.

Once out of the Valle de Sonora, Niza entered the *despoblado* (uninhabited desert) of southeastern Arizona. There, in one of his lonely camps, Niza learned that Estebanico had been killed.[15] What happened next has baffled historians for centuries. Apparently, most of Niza's retinue deserted him about that time, but despite the desertions and the ill tidings regarding Estebanico's death, Niza continued northward until he got within sight of Cíbola. What did Niza see? In his account of the reconnaissance Niza wrote that he proceeded to see the "city of Cíbola." Accompanied by a small entourage of Indians and interpreters, he proceeded "until coming within sight of Cibola, which is situated in a plain at the base of a round hill."[16] Of Cíbola, Niza noted,

> The pueblo has a fine appearance, the best I have seen in these regions. The houses are as they had been described to me by the Indians, all of stone, with terraces and flat roofs, as it seemed to me from a hill where I stood to view it. The city is larger than the city of Mexico.... When I told the chieftains who were with me how well impressed I was with Cíbola, they told me that it was the smallest of seven cities, and that Totonteac is much larger and better than all seven, that it has so many houses and people that there is no end to it.[17]

Upon his return to Compostela on Mexico's western coast, Niza reported what he had seen to Governor Vázquez de Coronado. Later, on September 2, 1539, Friar Marcos met with Viceroy Mendoza in Mexico City and reiterated his story, this time with some exaggeration. Convinced by Niza's stories, Mendoza decided to explore the north in hope of discovering another Tenochtitlan.

Confident of the existence of "another Mexico" in the interior of the north country, Mendoza pushed forward with his plans. Determined that Francisco Vázquez de Coronado, his protégé, should lead the expedition, Mendoza pushed to get his nomination approved by the king. Sanction from the king arrived on January 6, 1540, while Vázquez de Coronado was making confidential plans to proceed with the expedition. By late February 1540, the expedition stood ready for Viceroy Mendoza's review of the troops at Compostela. In 1540, Vázquez de Coronado began his march at the head of a large expedition consisting of over 1,100 men and nearly 5,000 sheep, goats, cattle, and horses from Compostela. Among the men of the expedition were 800 Indian allies. Three women listed as wives of foot soldiers also accompanied the force. Fray Marcos de Niza accompanied the soldiers, as did several other priests, among them Fray Juan de Padilla.[18] In northern Sonora Coronado divided his force so that an advance guard could move faster to the pueblos of New Mexico. Along the San Pedro River valley, Vázquez de Coronado veered northward through the mountain ranges of eastern Arizona until they reached Háwikuh.

The expedition's reports gave Europeans their first glimpses of places and people in the interior of North America. Among the marvels seen by Coronado's men were the Grand Canyon, the southern Rocky Mountains, the Continental Divide, the western edge of the Great Plains, the Rio Grande, and the many Indian pueblos along it from Taos to Socorro, and others from

Zuñi and Jémez to Pecos and Las Humanas. In West Texas, places visited by the expedition included Blanco Canyon and Palo Duro Canyon, near Amarillo in the Texas Panhandle, and across present Oklahoma beyond to the Great Bend of the Arkansas River in Kansas. On the Great Plains they saw buffalo numbering in the thousands and Plains tribes who lived off the land, seasonally following the herds from sunrise to sunset.

Thus, the far-ranging expedition of Francisco Vázquez de Coronado, became the first major European exploration to penetrate the interior of the present western United States. A contingent of Coronado's men explored northward along the western coast of Mexico and beyond the mouth of the Colorado River. While the main expedition traveled northeastward toward the New Mexico pueblos along the Rio Grande and beyond as far as the Great Bend of the Arkansas River in central Kansas. There, near present Lyons, Kansas, a small party of his expedition led by Father Juan de Padilla and Andrés Ocampo, chose to remain to evangelize the tribes there after Coronado began his retreat to Mexico.

The significance of the expedition is based on the vast lands explored and claimed as well as the first contact made with Indigenous people a mere forty-eight years after Columbus's first voyage. The expedition began a literary history of the area explored along with the first ethnological descriptions of tribes from Plains to Pueblo Indian peoples. Scientifically, the explorers wrote about the flora and fauna, especially the large buffalo herds, as well as other marvels they saw. The reports of the Coronado expedition by Juan de Jaramillo and Pedro de Castañeda, in particular, as well as Coronado's letters to the king form the earliest literary descriptions of the Greater Southwest and are part of the national stories of the United States and Mexico.

At the same time, between 1539 and 1543, two other explorations sallied forth. The first was led by Juan Rodríguez Cabrillo, who, seeking a route along the Pacific coastline to China and the Philippines, explored the California coast from Baja California by sea, reaching the southern coast of Oregon. His expedition showed that California was not an island. Far to the east, Hernando de Soto led the second expedition from Georgia to the Mississippi River, crossing through states known today as Florida, Alabama, Mississippi, Tennessee, Louisiana, and Arkansas. Some of Soto's men crossed into eastern Texas. As a result of their efforts, Europeans grasped the large extent of the continent, measuring at least 3,000 miles across. Coronado's expedition inspired subsequent exploration of the interior, including the founding expedition of New Mexico led by Juan de Oñate in 1598.[19]

Some of the contacts made by the three expeditions were friendly; others were antagonistic. For Native Americans those expeditions left another legacy. In New Mexico the pueblos at Tiguex along the Rio Grande took the brunt of warfare against Coronado's expedition that had intruded upon them with demands for food and other items that, given their limited resources, they were not prepared to share. Coronado, on the other hand, had extended his supply line, and the expedition, in the state of starvation, desperately needed food. Hoping to protect its food supply, Zuñi Pueblo became the first to experience the impact of the Spanish *entrada* ("approachment" or "entrance"; usually the first expedition into an area). At that moment in time, the belligerency on both sides, each with their own reasons, affected Spanish-Pueblo relationships throughout the latter sixteenth century.

Forty years had passed since the Coronado expedition had explored the pueblos and the Great Plains. In that time the Indians of the *tierra adentro* had almost forgotten their encounters with Cabeza de Vaca, Marcos de Niza, and Francisco Vázquez de Coronado, or had at least given them the form of a vague oral tradition with a portent. So too had the Spaniards forgotten much about the explorations of the past and what lay in the *tierra adentro*. For the most part, the settlement pattern had expanded the Spanish frontier line northward along the silver-mining districts of the central Mexican corridor. From time to time, however, rumors of mysterious cities in the *tierra adentro* flitted among Spanish frontiersmen. Occasionally Vázquez de Coronado was remembered, or someone claimed to have heard of an "account given . . . in a book" concerning the lands to the north. To remind them of the details, the archive of the viceroy, filled with diaries, reports, and correspondence, described the pueblos and Great Plains of North America. The written word possessed by Europeans had salvaged the past. There was yet another source for inspiration. As the frontier extended from Nueva Galicia, north of Mexico City, to southern Chihuahua, Spanish slavers crossed the Rio Grande chasing "thieving Indians," they said.[20] Looking northward into the *despoblado*, they wondered about what lay beyond them. At Santa Bárbara, on the edge of the Spanish northern frontier, they told tales about the *tierra adentro*.

In 1581, an expedition led by Francisco Sánchez Chamuscado continued upriver for the next twenty days. Finally, the men reached a settlement near present-day San Marcial, which they called San Felipe.[21] In the next century the mission of Senecú would be built there. At that time, explorers saw an abandoned pueblo. Hernán Gallegos, a member of the expedition, noted that "[it] had been inhabited by a large number of people, who must have been very advanced." He wrote, "The said pueblo was walled in; and the houses had mud walls and were built of adobes, three stories high, so it appeared, though they had crumbled from the rains and seemed to have been abandoned for a long time."[22] The next day they continued their march northward along the Rio Grande. Shortly, they came upon another pueblo which and been abandoned the previous evening. Of the pueblo, Gallegos wrote,

> we found many turkeys and much cotton and corn. Although we did not see any people in the pueblo on entering it, we did find in the valley many cornfields like those of Mexico, and also fields of beans, calabashes, and cotton. We did not dare to take any of the goods, for we wanted the people to know we did not intend to harm them. We found the houses very well planned and built in blocks with mud walls, whitewashed inside and well decorated with monsters, other animals, and human figures. There were many curious articles in these houses, more neatly wrought than those of the Mexicans when they were conquered. The inhabitants have a great deal of crockery, such as pots [ollas], large earthen jars, and flat pans all decorated and of better quality than the pottery of New Spain.[23]

Gallegos's description, written through Spanish colonial eyes, would provide Spanish officials with a glimpse of the typical pueblo in the *tierra adentro*. They named the pueblo San Miguel.

They spent the day trying to make contact with the inhabitants. Finally, some of them returned, whereupon the Spaniards explained their peaceful intentions, hoping that the rest of the people would come out of hiding. "We sent them away in peace," reported Gallegos, "telling them to make the sign of the cross with their hands as an indication that we did not wish to harm them. The news that we were coming in peace spread so widely that there was not a day when we were not surrounded and accompanied by more than twelve thousand people."[24] Later the people of San Miguel would be known as the Piros. From them, the Spaniards learned of another nation farther north, "with which they are at war."[25]

All along the Rio Grande, the Spaniards encountered people who lived similarly, yet spoke different languages. The Piros of the southern Rio Grande in New Mexico and the Tiguas, or Tiwas, in the area of present Albuquerque whom Sánchez Chamuscado encountered were only subtly different to the Spaniards. Yet to modern-day ethnographers the differences in material culture and other features are specifically noted. Gallegos did notice that all of the pueblos grew corn, beans, calabashes, and cotton. The Indians also made corn tortillas and atole as well as pottery and blankets.[26] Although the pueblos they described were generally two, three, and four stories high, the distinctions they made were generally based on their size. "The further one goes into the interior," wrote Gallegos, "the larger are the pueblos and the houses, and the more numerous the people."[27] Gallegos did leave behind a fair description of how the Pueblo Indians constructed their fortified houses:

> The way they built their houses which are in blocks is as follows: they burn the clay, build narrow walls, and make adobes for the doorways. The lumber used is pine or willow; and many rounded beams, ten and twelve feet long, are built into the houses. The natives have ladders by means of which they climb to their quarters. These are movable wooden ladders, for when the Indians retire at night, they pull them up to protect themselves against enemies since they are at war with one another.[28]

Moving north beyond the Tigua country, they passed several pueblos of a different nation. Somewhere north of the Tiguas they heard of other pueblos to the east of them, including a place they called San Mateo in the present-day Galisteo Valley south of Santa Fe. Before taking the side trip to San Mateo, Sánchez Chamuscado made Puaray, one of the Tigua pueblos, his headquarters. The friars remained there while the soldiers made their explorations to the east, beyond the purplish Sierra de Puaray (present Sandia Mountains), which the tribes in the area held to be a sacred mountain. Moving southward, they crossed into the Manzano Mountains, which they called the Sierra Morena.

Once at San Mateo, they learned of mines with "coppery steel-like ores."[29] The Puebloans, however, were quick to add that similar ores could be obtained from Indians "in the region of the buffalo," for they "had given them a part of the ore." It seemed that the people of San Mateo hoped the Spaniards would go to the plains and, wishfully, they would get lost and never return. Sánchez Chamuscado and his men would go, but as sage travelers, they would return unharmed.

The soldiers went to the Plains people because the Puebloans had told the Spaniards that the Plains Indians had a knowledge of mineral wealth. They were to be disappointed. Gallegos wrote that the Plains Indians lived by hunting and that during the winter ate mostly buffalo meat. In spring they migrated south to areas where cactus, for its prickly pear, and yucca could be found. He wrote that

> they had no houses but only huts of buffalo hides; . . . they were enemies of our informants, but nevertheless came to the pueblos of the latter in order to trade such articles as deerskins and buffalo hides for making footwear, and a large amount of meat in exchange for corn and blankets.[30]

In their exploration of the plains east of Galisteo, the soldiers took note of the people and the natural resources such as water, the fertility of the soil, and the large buffalo herds. Having ventured onto the plains, the Spaniards returned to San Mateo.

Once back among the pueblos in the Galisteo area, the curious Spaniards wondered why the people at San Mateo lived away from the Rio Grande and so far from the buffalo herds. Pondering the question, Gallegos wrote: "We asked them why they lived so far from the herds, and they replied that it was on account of their cornfields and cultivated lands, so that the buffalo would not eat their crops."[31] They learned that during certain times of the year, the buffalo were two days' journey away. The Puebloans were keenly aware that the Indians who followed the buffalo were brave hunters and able bowsmen who would kill them. Too, the Galisteo basin had enough water to sustain them and their cornfields, which did not require as much water as other crops. Thus, the Spaniards gained insight into the delicate relationship between the Pueblo Indians and the Plains Indians. There were other pueblos in the mountains and ridges on the western edge of the Great Plains beginning at Taos in the north to Picurís, Cicúye (Pecos), and the Salinas pueblos to the south.

While in the Galisteo region, Sánchez Chamuscado learned that one of the priests, Fray Juan de Santa María, had departed for Santa Bárbara to report to his superiors the wondrous opportunities for missionization of the *tierra adentro*. Fray Santa María took the shortcut south on the east side of two great mountain ranges (present Sandia and Manzano mountain ranges) in the hope of reaching the ford of the Rio Grande at El Paso in less time. Later, other natives informed the Spaniards that the priest had been killed by the Indians "in the mountain."[32] Meanwhile, at Puaray, Fray Rodríguez and his friars had made little progress in his attempt to convert the natives there. When Sánchez Chamuscado and his men returned to Puaray, the priests were still hopeful that they could convert the Tiguas. Restless and determined, the explorers attempted to go to Acoma and Zuñi, but the freezing temperatures and snow forced them to turn back to Puaray. Meanwhile, they explored behind the present-day Manzano Mountains southeast of Puaray, where they "discovered" some pueblos and salt beds.

While at Puaray, in December 1582, while exploring behind the Manzano Mountains, they found five more pueblos, which they named Zactula, Ruiseco, La Mesa, La Joya, and Francavila. These pueblos were probably located between Tajique, Chililí, and Quarai. While there, the explorers heard reports about other pueblos, probably Abó and other pueblos in the area.[33] Moving onto the plains, the explorers discovered the salt beds, from which historic Las Salinas would take its name, near present Estancia and Willard, New Mexico. Of them Gallegos wrote, "The salt is found in some lakes measuring more than five leagues in circumference. They are, in the opinion of this witness, the best salines he has ever seen."[34]

The freezing temperatures and a heavy snowfall forced them back to Puaray.[35] There they recovered from the numbing cold and waited for the weather to lift. The salt beds and the pueblos would later be governed from Spanish Santa Fe and known as the Jurisdicción de las Salinas. Today the history of Las Salinas is interpreted at Salinas Pueblo Missions National Monument in Mountainair, New Mexico.

Having explored along the Rio Grande and the edge of the Great Plains, the soldiers had seen enough of the land and its people. In council with the priests, the soldiers informed them of their decision to return and bade the priests come with them. The Franciscans, ever hopeful of their spiritual conquest over the Tiguas, decided to stay, even if it meant martyrdom. Amid prayers, hugs, and handshakes, Sánchez Chamuscado and his men headed south without the priests. Somewhere on the northern Chihuahua prairieland, the old Spanish leader took ill, died, and was buried.[36]

Nearly a year after the expedition had begun, the fatigued and dust-covered soldiers returned to Santa Bárbara. In May 1582, two of the men, Hernán

Gallegos and Martín de Pedrosa, presented their reports of the *tierra adentro* to the viceroy's notaries in Mexico City. Their testimony, although sparse in its mention of riches in the north country, caused speculation that the priests who had remained among the pueblos could still be alive and should be rescued. Soon curiosity gave way to rumors that the land of the pueblos contained rich mineral deposits if one only knew where to look. To the fore stepped several who would risk life and fortune for permission to go forth to rescue Friar Rodríguez and his subordinates. The rescue mission, of course, served only as a pretext for eager prospectors to go north with the blessings of the Spanish government.

Padre Bernardino Beltrán presented the justification for a rescue mission to his superior, who also believed that a party should go north to help Brother Rodríguez. Permission given, Friar Beltrán prepared for the undertaking. At his side stood a willing supporter, don Antonio de Espejo, who promised to outfit a small military escort, provided he would be permitted to explore the *tierra adentro* for signs of mineral wealth. Espejo had been in New Spain since 1571. During that time he had become a wealthy cattle rancher north of Mexico City and even held a position of *familiar* or lay officer of the Inquisition. As an entrepreneur, Espejo owned a mercantile business in Mexico City and Texcoco as well as a stockyard in Tacuba. Espejo had an additional motive to volunteer his assistance. Despite his success as a wealthy cattleman and as an official of the Holy Office of the Inquisition,[37] he was a wanted man. In 1581 officials charged Antonio de Espejo with murdering two people at his ranch in Celaya. According to the charges, Espejo and a crew of fifteen cowhands were preparing to round up a herd of cattle at his ranch in Celaya. Four of the cowboys walked off the crew, saying that they did not want to do the work. They encouraged the rest to refuse to work. Later, in the proceedings, they testified that they had refused to work because of Indian raids in the area of the roundup and because their horses were too weak for that kind of work.[38] At that point in time, however, Espejo stood in their way, even though they threatened to hogtie him. The problem was that Espejo had already paid the men to round up and brand the cattle and had supplied them with his horses. Espejo argued with them not to take his money, horses, and saddles. Espejo said they threatened to kill him. In the fight that ensued, the combatants, including Espejo's brother, Pedro Muñoz de Espejo, fired their weapons at each other, wounding Espejo and one of the cowhands. Two other cowhands were wounded by Espejo's brother.[39] In that fight Espejo had stabbed one of the cowboys, who died of his wounds. After the fight, everyone scattered. An informant said that Espejo had tracked down one of the men and found him miles away with an harquebus bullet through the head, apparently fired at close range.[40]

As an official of the Inquisition, Espejo attempted to claim immunity from criminal prosecution but failed. In 1581 a warrant had been issued for his arrest on a murder charge. He quickly named his uncle, Francisco de Santiago, as his legal representative to handle his affairs, and then he fled northward to Santa Bárbara.[41] Meanwhile, his brother, Pedro de Espejo, was tried and received a heavy punishment. Sentenced to five years imprisonment in the Fortress of San Juan de Ulúa, he was exiled from his land holdings for ten years. Pedro Muñoz de Espejo was convicted of having fired the fatal shots in the murder. Antonio de Espejo, who had already fled, was convicted in absentia as the accomplice and ordered to pay a fine. However, no one was willing to testify that they had seen Antonio de Espejo fire any of the fatal shots.[42] Refusing to appear in court and failing to pay the fine levied against him, he fled northward with whatever assets he could take.[43]

At Durango, Espejo heard of Fray Bernardino Beltrán, the resident priest of the convent there, and offered to underwrite the expedition. "As I was in the area at the time," explained Espejo, "I made an offer—in the belief that by so doing, I was serving our Lord and his Majesty."[44] Using his influence with the mayor of Cuatro Ciénegas, south of Santa Bárbara, and hoping for a pardon, Espejo, the former cattle rancher and fugitive, gained authorization in the name of the king to accompany, at his own expense, the good Brother Bernardino Beltrán.

In certain ways, the second expedition resembled that of Sánchez Chamuscado. On November 10, 1583, Espejo, Father Beltrán, fourteen soldiers and servants carrying quantities of munitions and provisions left Valle de San Gregorio on their rescue mission to the land more frequently called "New Mexico." They also drove a large herd of 115 horses, mules, and cattle before them. Soon after departing the Valle de San Gregorio, one of the members, Miguel Sánchez Valenciano, departed the party and returned to Santa Bárbara to escort another priest who wanted to join the party. There Casilda de Anaya, Sánchez's wife, confronted him and also demanded to go on the expedition. Two days later, Sánchez and his small party caught up with the expedition. A surprised Espejo saw that Sánchez had brought his family: his wife, his oldest son Lazaro, and two younger sons, Pedro, who was almost four years old, and Juan, then twenty months old. Two others of the family came along as well. Although Casilda became pregnant during the expedition, the hearty frontierswoman and her children stayed with the expedition until it returned to the northern outpost of San Bartolomé on September 10, 1583, eleven months later.[45] Casilda's story offers a glimpse of the resolve, role, life, and times of women on a sixteenth-century frontier far from the metropolis of Mexico City.

Heading north to the Rio Florído, the expedition bore eastward toward La Junta de Los Rios, where it would pick up the Rio Grande, which would take them to the pueblos. After several weeks and hardships the expedition reached the Rio Grande in mid-December, which they named El Río Turbio "because it is exceedingly muddy." Overgrown with cottonwood and willow groves, the river flowed through a plain miles to the south of present-day El Paso. By mid-January they had followed the river to a place near El Paso that they called Las Vueltas del Río "because here it starts to wind as far as the settlements."[46] There in the vicinity of El Paso the party camped for a week, recovering from the hard marches they had undertaken to that point. Leaving their camp, they moved northward for eight days, reaching a place they named El Peñol de los Cedros. They wrote that at that place "there is a large black rock and all the ranges and gorges are covered with juniper groves and, in some parts, oak groves."[47] At that point they were near the site of present-day Elephant Butte Reservoir, one day's journey from the first pueblo, which Sánchez Chamuscado named San Felipe.

After a few days' rest, Espejo, his men, Sánchez Valenciano's family, and their livestock were on the western edge of the volcanic malpais near present-day Carrizozo. Marching northwest toward present-day San Marcial, they reached the Rio Grande and the abandoned pueblo of San Felipe. From there, they proceeded upriver to the Piro villages described earlier by members of the Sánchez Chamuscado expedition. Espejo's men noted details of Piro life that had escaped the previous expedition. Although the Spaniards noted the Indians' pottery, they also pointed out that "they have earthen jar stands on which they keep their water jars."[48] In regard to the doorways, the Spaniards remarked that they were "shaped like a U so as to allow only one person to go through at a time." As if gathering military intelligence, Diego

Pérez de Luján, the chronicler of the expedition, reported: "These people do not seem to be bellicose, because they fight with flint-edged clubs and hide-wrapped stone bludgeons about a half a yard long. They have few and poor Turkish bows and poorer arrows." Noting their footwear, Luján observed that "they wear shoes of tanned buffalo leather and tanned deerskins fashioned like boots."[49] Observing the pueblos structures, they noted significant features of the pueblo. They described the multistory design, the plaza, and its attendant kivas, which the Spaniards called *estufas*, meaning assembly chambers. Of the *estufas*, Luján wrote, "In each pueblo, in the center of the plaza are some very large cellars two and one-half *estados* [an estado measures six feet deep] deep, with an entrance in the shape of a trap door and a stepladder. They are all whitewashed and provided with stone benches all around. Here the people perform their games and dances. On one side are their *temascales* [sweathouses] where they bathe."[50] In every pueblo they visited, Espejo's men could not help but notice the kivas, the plazas and the native weaponry.

By mid-February of 1583, the small Spanish party, after several side trips from the river, had reached the valley of the large Sierra Morena. Soon after, as they proceeded north, they entered another long valley with a large mountain (the Sandia Mountains) within present Albuquerque. There, after three months of travel, they entered Puaray, a large Tigua settlement of several pueblos along the river valley. Puaray had been abandoned, wrote Luján. Fearing that the Spaniards would avenge the dead priests, Luján noted, "The inhabitants of all these settlements had fled to the sierra because all had taken part in killing the friars. Some Indians soon came to find out what we wanted to do and we sent them to bring the others in peace. There was one among them playing an instrument resembling a flageolet."[51] The memory of Vázquez de Coronado's attack on Moho and Arenal forty-one years previous still burned fresh in the lore of the pueblos of the Rio Grande. Espejo and seven men went to the mountain, which they called the Sierra de Puaray, to bring the people back. Some came down, and by means of signs they agreed to return to their pueblos because their families were suffering greatly from the cold. Still, many refused to return for fear of Spanish reprisal. At Puaray the Tiguas confirmed that they had killed Father Agustín Rodríguez and Father Francisco López. They also stated that Fray Juan de Santa María had met his death farther south in the Sierra Morena.

At Puaray, the Spaniards inspected many of the abandoned pueblos and provisioned themselves with corn, beans, green and sundried calabashes, and other vegetables as well as cocks and hens. They also took some pottery, which they needed. Still, the people of Puaray would not come down from the sierra, for they were "very frightened." Perhaps hoping to draw the Spaniards away from Puaray, Indians from other pueblos came with gifts and offered information about other provinces far away. Finally, at the end of February, Espejo and his men departed Puaray and headed north to the Keres country. They stopped at a pueblo called Cachiti (modern San Felipe Pueblo) and traded hawk-bells and small iron articles for buffalo hides, corn, tortillas, turkeys and pinole. As for the pueblos north of Puaray, the Spaniards observed that, while they were linguistically different, "they are similar to the people of Puaray."[52]

Venturing westward from the Rio Grande, the expedition visited the pueblos of Zia and Jémez. Meanwhile, a disconsolate Father Beltrán continued to pray for his fallen brethren, Rodríguez, López, and Santa María. From Jémez the party moved in a southwestward direction to Zuñi by way of Acoma. Crossing on the east side of the Sierra de Cebolleta, today's Mount Taylor, the small group picked up the trail to Acoma and pushed westward until snow forced them to camp on the malpais, volcanic rock east of present-day El Morro. Once out of the malpais, they came to a large pine forest that protected them from the snowfall. "We slept in the woods because it snowed so much that we were unable to proceed," recalled Luján. They drank snow water that they melted in their pots and pans, and they called the area El Helado (The Freezing Place) because of the extreme cold they suffered. On March 11, 1583, they reached a place they named El Estanque del Peñol (The Waterhole of the Rock).[53] There, in the shelter of El Morro, they camped, as many Indians and probably some of Vázquez de Coronado's men had also done. Espejo and his party were the first Spaniards to see it since 1540 or 1542, when Alvarado passed by there on his way to the "Río Nuestra Señora," and likely when Vázquez de Coronado and his army retreated to New Spain after two years of exploration. After a short rest, Espejo and his people continued their march west past Acoma, and a few days later they stood on the edge of the Province of Zuñi. Throughout Zuñi, in the villages of Háwikuh, Alona, Cana, Quaquina, and Mazaque, they found "very well built crosses." There they found Mexican Indians, a number of them from

Guadalajara, whom Vázquez de Coronado had left behind. Some of them spoke Spanish with difficulty, as they had been absent forty-one years from New Spain. "Here," wrote Luján, "we found a book and a small trunk left by Coronado."[54] The influence of Vázquez de Coronado's Mexican Indians was evident in the crosses and other signs that the Spaniards perceived among the Zuñi. They served as translators, and two of them, Andrés and Gaspar, who had not seen a Spaniard in four decades, gave Espejo information about the land and its people.[55]

At Zuñi Fray Bernardino and Espejo argued over continuing the expedition. The priest argued that the expedition's purpose—to rescue Friar Rodríguez and his companions—had ended at Puaray when it was learned that they were dead. But Espejo had other plans. Although Fray Bernardino threatened to leave without Espejo, the argument settled little else. Espejo, hoping to find mineral wealth, left Zuñi with four soldiers to explore west into present-day Arizona. Father Beltrán and the rest of the expedition refused to go any farther and remained among the Zuñi. After a few weeks of wandering, probably as far as present Prescott, Arizona, Espejo and his men returned to Zuñi, where he found Friar Beltrán and his party still there. The rift between the two proved irreconcilable as the two men continued their arguments. Some of Espejo's soldiers took sides and split his force. Soon after, Friar Beltrán and his followers returned to Mexico by way of the Rio Grande.

Meanwhile, the indefatigable Espejo with eight loyal soldiers returned to the Rio Grande, where, in early July 1583, he found that many of the people had fled to the mountains. About thirty warriors from Puaray confronted Espejo and refused to give them food, whereupon Espejo attacked them and the situation became deadly.[56] After the skirmish at Puaray, Espejo marched northeastward toward the Galisteo pueblos and Cicúye (Pecos) on the edge of the Great Plains. At several pueblos along the way, including Cicúye, they asked for food, but the Puebloans said that because of the lack of rain, they had none to spare. Preparing for the worst, they pulled up their ladders, armed themselves, and watched the Spaniards from their walls. In some cases, Espejo and his men walked away. At other places, they threatened to burn down the pueblo if their demands were not met. Thus, Espejo and his men had offended a number of pueblos with their brazen actions. As a result, Espejo and his soldiers realized that they could neither remain in that area nor could they return to the Rio Grande in order to get back to

Santa Bárbara. In all cases, a dangerous situation awaited them. They decided to march southeast, beyond Cicúye and Galisteo. The march proved quite difficult as they made their way to the Pecos River. It was their only safe way out. Vázquez de Coronado had named the Pecos El Río de Cicúye; Espejo called it El Río de las Bacas (The River of the Buffalo) because of the buffalo that roamed near it. It sharply contrasted with the Rio Grande, according to Luján, who described it as "a medium-sized river with very good water, surrounded by numerous trees, vines, roses, roseberries and pennyroyal."[57]

Fleeing down the Pecos to where it joined the Rio Grande, they turned westward toward La Junta de los Rios. Once there, they knew the way back to Santa Bárbara. After two months of travel, they reached the valley of San Bartolomé in Nueva Vizcaya. It had been a long year for the explorers, who, lucky to escape the *tierra adentro* with their lives, had nonetheless come home empty-handed. As autumn gave way to the winter of 1584, these explorers had many tales to tell of their adventures and many descriptions of the people of the north. Such tales would only stimulate the imaginations of those who would dream of conquering the *tierra adentro*. It was only a matter of time.

By 1575, the frontier line of New Spain had moved as far north as the Santa Bárbara–Parral in present Chihuahua. Since 1540, mining camps and towns as well as presidios dotted the road between Querétaro and Durango and defined the importance of protecting the settlement pattern. By 1600, for example, presidios between Querétaro and Guanajuato at Maxcala, Jofre, and Atotonilco and beyond to Zacatecas and Durango marked the beginning of the route known as the Camino Real de Tierra Adentro. Beyond Zacatecas and Durango, the presidial garrisons at San Martín and Llerena for a while marked the northernmost end of the Camino Real de Tierra Adentro. Off the beaten path, away from the northernmost extension of the Camino Real, along the eastern edge of the Sierra Madre Occidental, a lonely outpost, Santiago de Janos, stood like the Roman God Janus, facing two directions: one, westward toward northern Sonora, and the other, southeast to the Santa Bárbara–Parral frontier. Although New Mexico's pueblos on the Rio Grande attracted the vision of Spanish officials as an area of settlement, the Great Plains, teeming with thousands of people and resources, beckoned.

3

Strangers on New Mexico's Eastern Plains, 1590–1601

The charges against the defendant being the invasion of the lands inhabited by peaceful Indians, raising troops, entry into the provinces of New Mexico, and other acts cited in the suit: We find that, by reason of the guilt proved against the said Captain Gaspar Castaño in these proceedings, we should and do condemn him to exactly six years of exile from the jurisdiction of New Spain, during which period he shall serve his Majesty in the Philippine Islands.

—Judicial Orders, October 7, 1593[1]

With a shout, the Indian sentries of Cicúye, the fortress pueblo on the edge of the Great Plains, alerted the pueblo to a small band of ten helmeted Spanish horsemen who stood outside their walls. On that cold, snowy December morning in 1590, starving and nearly half frozen Spaniards stood shivering below the walls of the pueblo, hoping that they would be let in. Through signs, the warriors learned that the thin, bearded Spaniards asked only for food. The Indians gave them a small quantity of maize. Fatigued and malnourished from their journey across the southern plains of present Texas, they had followed the Pecos River, past present Carlsbad, New Mexico, to Cicúye. There the Spaniards spent the day at the pueblo, and the Indians lodged them in their plaza for the night. The next morning the soldiers went among the people unarmed so as not to alarm them and asked for more food. Suddenly, the warriors let out a great outcry, "and at the same time much stone and arrows were shot" at the unsuspecting visitors. Quickly, the Spaniards scurried about for their weapons, but pueblo warriors had come down from the roofs and carried off most of their arms. In the melee, the Spaniards grabbed what they could to defend themselves and dashed to their horses. Riding bareback, they fled down the Pecos River. Luckily, the warriors did not pursue them into the snow-packed mountainous terrain leading to the southern plains. Afterward the Pecos Indians divided up the booty and disassembled the assortment of harquebuses, swords, saddles, armor, bedclothes, and other apparel for their own use.[2] Knowing that the Spaniards would return, the people of Pecos prepared to defend themselves against a larger force. For now, they could only wonder, whence came the Spaniards? Pecos stood on the edge of both time and geography, for its inhabitants not only faced the Great Plains and its tribes; they now faced a new intrusion onto their land that would change their world.

Following Antonio de Espejo's expedition, New Mexico had been all but ignored except for a few traders, prospectors, and slavers who crossed the Rio Grande into the *tierra adentro* beyond the north Mexican frontier of Nueva Vizcaya (Chihuahua), Coahuila, and Nuevo León. The accounts of the Sánchez Chamuscado and Espejo expeditions had portrayed New Mexico as a land with potential mineral wealth. During the period following their expeditions, speculators hoped to gain concessions from the crown to monopolize whatever mineral wealth existed, while Franciscan friars prayed that they, too, could return and convert the Puebloans to Christianity. By the 1590s, Spanish officials in Mexico City had, once again, begun to turn their attention toward the *tierra adentro*. As the Spanish crown pondered the pacification of New Mexico, bidders for the contract to settle New Mexico, subdue the pueblo world, and explore the Great Plains played a political game to influence their chances in the competition for royal favoritism.

Meanwhile, in Nuevo León, on the northeastern Mexican frontier, far to the southeast of New Mexico an unexpected situation unfolded that would result in the premature, unauthorized, but temporary settlement of New

Mexico. Under the able leadership of Gaspar Castaño de Sosa, a large colony of nearly 200 settlers wended their way northwestward toward New Mexico. The arrest and incarceration of Luis de Carbajal, governor of Nuevo León, by the Holy Office of the Inquisition on charges of being a Jew prompted Gaspar Castaño de Sosa, his lieutenant governor, to assume the leadership of the province.³ Castaño de Sosa, on the other hand, had a plan of his own.

Despite the efforts of the crown to stop Indian slaving, the slavers from Nuevo León continued to cross into South Texas as well as onto the southern plains of the Big Bend country. For years Carbajal's men had crossed the Rio Grande into the *tierra adentro* and brought back Indian slaves. Sometimes Puebloans were among the captives. They also brought back information about the land and the way to New Mexico from the town of Saltillo in Coahuila. Possibly some slavers had reached as far as the mountains of New Mexico and had heard about the pueblos on the edge of the plains. Armed with such knowledge and based on privileges implicit in the king's original concessions to Carbajal, which implied an extension of his rights to colonize beyond his grant in Nuevo León, Castaño de Sosa decided to colonize New Mexico.

As soon as word reached Mexico City of Castaño de Sosa's projected expedition, Spanish officials charged that his actions were illegal. In the debate that ensued, the lieutenant governor persisted in what he believed to be right and just. Castaño's argument soon took on a history of its own, as the files on the case accumulated in the office of the Viceroy Marqués de Villamanrique in Mexico City. When Castaño de Sosa sent agents to the capital to argue in his favor, the viceroy ignored their petitions. In 1590, when a new viceroy, Luis de Velasco, took office, the outgoing Marqués de Villamanrique informed him that Castaño and his followers were nothing more than

> outlaws, criminals and murderers—who practice neither justice nor piety and are raising a rebellion in defiance of God and king. These men invade the interior, seize peaceable Indians, and sell them in Mazapil, Saltillo, Sombrerete, and everywhere in the region.⁴

The new viceroy took heed. He sent Captain Juan Morlete with a message for Castaño to cease his slaving activities and cancel his expedition to New Mexico. On a warm June day in 1590, the two men met in the dusty mining town of Nueva Almaden and exchanged words in a heated debate. Castaño took Morlete's warnings with a grain of salt. As quickly as he had arrived,

Morlete and his escort departed.[5] The two men, however, would meet again on the Río Abajo twenty months later. Next time Morlete would hold the upper hand.

Unmoved by the warnings, the charismatic Gaspar Castaño de Sosa addressed his followers of Nueva Almaden about his well-known intentions to settle New Mexico in the *tierra adentro*. He reasoned with them that a grateful king would reward their efforts to expand the area of pacification and settlement at no cost to the crown. Convinced of his righteousness, nearly 200 men, women, and children packed their belongings on carts and prepared for the new opportunities promised them by their confident leader.

On Friday, July 27, 1590, the slow, creaky, oxen-pulled *carreta* caravan pulled out of Nueva Almaden amid a great cloud of dust, as men, women, and children driving large herds of goats, pigs, cattle, and other livestock waved farewell to their friends and relatives. Six weeks later they arrived at the Rio Grande east of the Big Bend near present-day Ciudad Acuña on the US-Mexico border. After several more weeks of traversing the dry and barren land of the *tierra adentro*, their Spanish scouts and Indian guides led them to the waters of the Pecos River, which, because of its brackishness, they called El Río Salado (The Salty River).[6] Throughout the fall months, the caravan followed the Pecos River northwestward, and by early December they passed the sandy hill country near present-day Carlsbad, New Mexico.

Somewhere, at one of their camps on the remote plains of southeastern New Mexico, don Gaspar called a council of his men. He told them that they were not distant from one of the first pueblos. In anticipation of making contact, he instructed them not to enter any Indian town.[7] First, he would send scouts to gather information, even if they had to capture Indian informants, about the strengths and weaknesses of the pueblo. The first pueblo, however, was still far from them.

On December 2, 1590, the first scouting party departed the caravan. Led by Cristóbal de Herédia, the ten-man detachment, which ranged far in advance of the expedition, had to return twice in two weeks for food. They reported that no pueblo had been sighted. On December 13 a messenger reported that the advance party had found an Indian trail that they hoped led to the pueblo. Another week passed with no word from the scouts. As snow had recently fallen on the plains, Castaño became concerned lest some disaster had befallen his men.[8]

Two days before Christmas, as a cold wind swept the plains, Castaño de Sosa and Andrés Pérez, his administrative secretary, stood on a hill and, peering into the distance, saw a man "on foot with his harquebus across his shoulders and a horse in front, tired, without a saddle." They rode out to him and recognized Juan Rodríguez Nieto, one of their scouts. Bruised, cold, hungry, and exhausted, Rodríguez told them of the surprise attack they had suffered at a pueblo they would later identify as Pecos. Somehow the men, having lost their capes and bedding in the fight, had survived three days and two nights in freezing temperatures. They had been saved from starvation by an Indian woman along the way who had given them each a handful of cornmeal to eat. Fortunately, the pueblo warriors had not pursued them. Shortly, the rest of the battered soldiers, with three wounded men, arrived to tell their tale of woe. Undaunted, don Gaspar decided to go soon to the large pueblo and recover their property,[9] which, unknown to him, had already been taken apart or destroyed by the Pecoseños. A few days later the Spaniards camped outside of the walled pueblo.

Before dawn of December 31, the men were up and slowly saddled their horses in the cold winter air. While some of their servants prepared breakfast, others packed up the camping gear. Standing near the campfires to warm themselves, the soldiers ate, with little conversation between them. Approaching his men, Castaño de Sosa spoke, pausing periodically to gather his thoughts about how to approach the pueblo without provoking the Indians. The Spaniards intended "to do them no harm at all." After the plan had been explained, the orders were given and the soldiers set out for the pueblo.[10]

Castaño de Sosa and the main corps marched with banners flying high, while two men, Martín de Salazar and Diego de Biruega, ran ahead of them to the pueblo with a message of peace, which the warriors refused. At a safe distance from the pueblo, Castaño de Sosa halted his army and ordered the trumpets blown. The sound pierced the cold, still air as the warriors and their women looked on.

Galloping their horses, the scouts reported to Castaño de Sosa that the entire pueblo appeared armed, "men and women on the roofs and below, with great preparation." Sizing up the situation, don Gaspar ordered a new camp established at "an harquebus shot from the pueblo, on the side where it seemed to be strongest." Two bronze cannons were brought up, placed, and readied for firing. He ordered all to be prepared in case of "some effrontery like the previous one" against the advance party the week before.[11] For all intents and purposes, the siege was on.

After deploying his troops, Castaño called to the Indians, but none were willing to leave the security of their pueblo to parley with him. One of the longest days in Pecos's history began at eight o'clock in the morning. The battle began as a standoff.

From where they stood, the Spaniards could see the pueblo's defenses. Ramparts complemented the defensive walls and narrow passages, which were staggered so that attackers could not easily gain entry to any of the long passageways to the pueblo's interior. Typical of pueblo Indian warfare, the Pecoseños were armed with slings and stones as well as bows, arrows, and clubs. Later the Spaniards learned that the pueblo had been at war with other tribes and that the fortifications had been up for some time.[12]

Wondering what thirty-eight men could do against the pueblo, Castaño hoped to avoid an assault against the heavily protected walls. With five men, he again approached Pecos to convince the warriors to "understand that we did not come to harm them." Instead they jeered at him as their women hastily carried up more stones to the roofs "because the men were all armed at their posts and giving loud cries in high spirits." Several times don Gaspar and others rode their horses around the whole pueblo holding up ornaments for them to see, giving signs of peace, and shouting words of friendship for the pueblo to hear. Each time they went around, the Indians slung rocks and shot arrows at them. All the while the din from the pueblo grew louder as the Indians taunted and jeered at them from behind the walls and roofs. After five or six hours of rejection, Castaño pulled back to discuss with his officers the perplexing situation before them. He reckoned that there was still time in the day for an assault on the pueblo. Pondering the situation, he said, "If the victory is God's to give us, we have time and more to spare."[13] Vacillating in his decision, Castaño considered the attack, but only if his small army did not shoot to kill. He hoped only to intimidate his enemy.

The Indians watched the sun between the clouds as it began its descent toward the western sky. The Spaniards took their positions for the assault on Pecos about two o'clock in the afternoon. From the pueblo rooftops the warriors could see two Spaniards move around the north side of the pueblo. Then lookouts saw the Spanish leader ride up to one of the walls and shout something they did not understand. Suddenly, one of the Pecos women threw some ashes mixed with embers at him, and the Puebloans gave a loud shout. Meanwhile, on the west side of the pueblo, warriors counterattacked five armored men who had attempted to scale the wall of an isolated building that the soldiers later managed to gain. Next they pulled up a small field gun, moved it into position, loaded it, and fired it and their harquebuses in an effort to intimidate the warriors. But the fearless warriors hurled stones at them and shot a volley of arrows to the roof that the Spaniards had captured. Meanwhile, Castaño, on the opposite side of the pueblo, called out to them again; they did not understand him.[14] Besides, it was too late; their pueblo was under attack.

Castaño withdrew and rallied his men to attack the strongest point of the pueblo in order to dislodge the defenders. But the warriors held their positions. Suddenly, the warriors who had fought so valiantly lost their resolve. The Spaniards, sensing a victory, took advantage of the situation and gained the main plaza of the pueblo. With that, the firing and the fighting stopped. don Gaspar surveyed the quieted pueblo. As he walked about the plaza, the Indians watched him from their houses. Not a shot was fired nor a stone thrown. Some of the Pecoseños emerged from hiding, making the sign of the cross with their hands and saying, *"amigo, amigo, amigo"* as they signaled surrender.[15] The mighty pueblo had fallen, and word spread quickly throughout the pueblo world. The pueblos of the Rio Grande, which had hosted three previous expeditions and had tasted defeat at the hands of the Spaniards years before, realized that the fall of Pecos meant their conquest as well.

Castaño de Sosa's settlers and the people of Pecos began the European New Year with an uneasy truce. Once the rest of the wagon train had arrived and rested at Pecos, they were ready to depart the pueblo. Such a move is what the Rio Grande pueblos feared most. After mass on the Feast of the Epiphany, January 6, 1591, Castaño de Sosa and his settlers departed Pecos, bound for the Rio Grande pueblos, which their scouts had, by that time, reconnoitered.

Traveling through Glorieta Pass, the Spaniards took time to search for possible mines. At a place they called Urraca, twenty-five to thirty miles south of Pecos, they left the wagons and set up their temporary headquarters. From Urraca, Castaño de Sosa and a small party marched through the area of present-day Santa Fe and likely went on to visit some of the Río Arriba (the upper Rio Grande) pueblos at Tesuque, Cuyamungue, Nambé, Pojoaque, and Jacona. It is possible that the expedition got as far as San Juan Pueblo at the confluence of the Chama and the Rio Grande, despite heavy snows "a yard in depth by actual measure . . . so deep that the horses could not travel."[16] Near the confluence of the two rivers, the Spaniards set up a camp below a small pueblo that refused to pledge allegiance to them. Castaño de Sosa became concerned when he saw men and women hurriedly moving baskets of stones to the roofs. By January 27, 1591, Castaño de Sosa's small force had reconnoitered the Río Arriba and had returned to Urraca with some provisions from the pueblos.

February brought warmer temperatures, and the Spaniards returned southward to the Galisteo Basin. By mid-month they were camped at a pueblo in Galisteo that they called San Marcos. Near there they discovered some mines, but the elusive silver mine they sought was nowhere to be found. During that time, Pecos, now out of sight and but not out of memory, refused to send supplies to the Spaniards. In March 1591, after a Spanish show of force, the people of Pecos sent supplies along with some of the weapons that had not been taken apart and clothing that they had stolen from the hapless scouting party in December 1590.[17]

Sometime in the first week of March, Castaño de Sosa and his settlers moved from Galisteo, one of the gateway pueblos to the Great Plains, to the Rio Grande. They settled at a pueblo they called Santo Domingo. As the weather warmed, signs of spring could be seen everywhere along the river. The Spanish settlers began working hard to set up their farms and to begin planting their crops.

Santo Domingo quickly became the "center of operations" for the Spaniards. "While we were in this pueblo of Santo Domingo," wrote a colonist, don Gaspar "and a party of twenty men went out to look for mines and a certain pueblo which he had not visited before. As they went along, taking possession of various settlements, they crossed some mountains where they found two pueblos that had been deserted only a few days earlier on account of wars with other pueblos which forced the inhabitants to leave their homes."[18] There were signs of many having been killed in those towns. The referenced pueblos were likely those in the San Pedro Arroyo between the high Ortíz and Sandia Mountains, which were constantly exposed to attacks from the Plains Indians. Returning to the Rio Grande, Castaño de Sosa and his men attempted to stop the natives from abandoning their pueblos. "Then the governor and all the rest of us crossed the river, although it was in full flood, and forced some of the people who were fleeing to turn back."[19] Before crossing the river, Castaño de Sosa and his men found two abandoned pueblos on the east bank. Once across the river, the Spaniards tried to forestall the exodus. An informant told the Spaniards that their pueblos "had been abandoned by the inhabitants due to fear and that they had sought refuge in the mountains or in other pueblos."[20]

The common practice of abandoning pueblos to find refuge elsewhere had been done for centuries. This time, their past experiences with Spanish explorers and missionaries were enough to make Puebloans distrust and fear Castaño de Sosa and his settlers. This time, however, they had reason, especially those from puebos that were over twenty miles south of Santo Domingo, and feared the return of Spanish troops. They had felt the sting of Spanish military might. The informant very likely referred to the pueblos of Puaray, which formed the ancient province of Tiguex and had been attacked by Vázquez de Coronado. In addition to their lore, which contained the details of the Spanish attack on Moho and Arenal fifty years earlier, the people of Puaray, who had killed Fray Agustín Rodríguez and Fray Francisco López and their companions in 1582, lived in fear of a returning punitive army. In order to allay their fears, Castaño de Sosa withdrew his troops and remained with five men to assure them of his peaceful intentions.

Over the next few days, Castaño de Sosa and his men visited the semideserted pueblos. Hoping to convince them that the Spaniards meant no harm, "He assured the natives with kind words, gave them some small trinkets, and asked them to go and call back all the other Indians."[21] In his tour of the pueblos along the Río Abajo, he noted that some were abandoned, while others were fully occupied; yet others contained only a few people. His settlers noted, "He treated the natives generously and reassured them so convincingly that he induced large numbers to return to their pueblos. In fact, his attitude was so kind and friendly that they felt very safe, for he gave them to understand that we would not harm them at all. As a result of this treatment, we saw large numbers of Indians returning from the fields to their homes."[22]

Regarding the pueblos where the priests had been killed in 1582, Castaño de Sosa took pains to be especially conciliatory. At one pueblo of Puaray, he told the people "not to be afraid . . . and that they should call back the people where the padres were believed to have been killed."[23] At the last pueblo he visited, "a large one with many inhabitants," they were received well. With a handful of men, Castaño de Sosa achieved more with diplomacy than with force of arms. He had, at least temporarily, pacified the pueblos of the Río Abajo. As wary as they were of the Spaniards, the Puebloans, on the other hand, knew and feared the capabilities of the conqueror of Pecos.

Before leaving the Tigua pueblos of Puaray, Castaño de Sosa appointed an Indian governor and an Indian *alcalde mayor* for those pueblos in the name of the king of Spain.[24] About three miles north of Santo Domingo, the returning Spaniards met an Indian captain. In his hands he carried "the bowl from a silver chalice," its stem having been removed. The broken chalice obviously belonged to one of the martyred priests who had been with Sánchez Chamuscdo. The Indian also gave Castaño de Sosa some alarming news He said that "many other Spaniards had arrived. . . ." With dread, Castaño de Sosa hastened to return to his headquarters at Santo Domingo. Not far from there, he, met with some of his settlers who had ridden out to meet him on the trail. They confirmed the arrival of another force. Puzzled by the fact that he did not recognize any names from Nueva Almaden, Castaño de Sosa tried not to show his concern. But when he heard that "Captain Juan de Morlete" commanded the new force, his heart sank. He knew that Morlete had come to arrest him. "When our leader realized the situation, he asked that not a word be said, adding that if they wanted to arrest him, they were welcome to do so, although he was serving his Majesty and had ample authorization for what he was doing. If it was the king's will to have him arrested, he would gladly submit."[25] Time had run out on Castaño de Sosa's enterprise. His time in New Mexico had ended abruptly.

Twenty months had passed since the two men had met on the dusty streets of Nueva Almaden in Nuevo León. Now they met in the dusty plaza of Santo Domingo just before dark. Of their meeting, the author of the *Memoria*, an account of Castaño de Sosa's expedition, wrote:

> When Don Gaspar arrived at the pueblo, he went to one side of the plaza while Captain Juan Morlete was passing through the center, on his way to his quarters; and as they met they greeted each other. After dismounting, the lieutenant governor walked toward Captain Juan Morlete and his men; the captain, seeing him approach, drew near with his men closely grouped about him. They greeted each other again and embraced; and then many of the others who were friends of the governor embraced him also.[26]

Greetings exchanged, Morlete presented a royal decree from Viceroy Luis de Velasco and read it to Castaño de Sosa, who submitted to the order of arrest. As they walked to Morlete's camp outside of Santo Domingo, he ordered Castaño de Sosa shackled. Although Governor Castaño de Sosa was a prisoner, Morlete considered his official rank. The author of the *Memoria* wrote that Morlete "honored him and treated him in the manner due his rank and merits."[27]

For his violations of the Laws of the Indies regarding unauthorized conquest and settlement of the king's lands, Gaspar Castaño de Sosa was tried in Mexico City and found guilty. On March 5, 1593, sentence was imposed by the Criminal Court in the Royal Audiencia and Chancellory of New Spain. Nicolás Escoto, the royal notary, stood before don Gaspar and his lawyer, Diego de Paz, and read aloud:

> The charges against the defendant being the invasion of the lands inhabited by peaceful Indians, raising troops, entry into the provinces of New Mexico, and other acts cited in the suit: We find that, by reason of the guilt proved against the said Captain Gaspar Castaño in these proceedings, we should and do condemn him to exactly six years of exile from the jurisdiction of New Spain, during which period he shall serve his Majesty in the Philippine Islands, with salary, performing such duties as may be assigned to him by the governor of the Philippines, receiving his pay from this city like the other soldiers, and liable to the death penalty if he defaults from that service. By this definitive sentence we so rule, ordering that it be executed, with costs, and that the decision shall not be subject to appeal.[28]

In the end, his impressment into service in the Philippines under penalty of death ended tragically. Castaño de Sosa lost his life in the first year of his sentence during a mutiny of 250 *sangleyes* (Chinese) galley rowers in 1593. Fifty-two soldiers and the Spanish governor of the Philippines also died in the attack.[29]

As for Castaño de Sosa's settlers, who numbered some 200 men, women, and children, in the attempted settlement of New Mexico (1590–92), they were all ejected from New Mexico by Captain Juan de Morlete and forty soldiers.[30] Although the settlers complained bitterly about the loss of their work and farmlands they had left behind, Morlete saw it differently. Of that sentiment, Morlete wrote, "If your grace had not remedied the situation," he wrote to his viceroy, "those who stayed would have been slaughtered by the Indians." In the context of the time, Morlete's conclusion would likely have proven correct. With Gaspar Castaño and his followers gone, the pueblos of New Mexico kept a wary eye to the south. They knew their respite would be temporary.

On October 4, 1593, Viceroy Luis de Velasco informed the king that legal preparations were underway for a sanctioned expedition to settle New Mexico. Five years would pass before the next wagon train would roll its creaky wheels northward beyond Santa Bárbara. While preparations and contractual negotiations were underway with Juan de Oñate, one other intrusion into the pueblo lands and the Great Plains occurred. On the heels of Castaño de Sosa's ill-fated attempt, Francisco Leyba de Bonilla went beyond the bounds of legality. Commissioned by the governor of Nueva Vizcaya to track down and punish Indian raiders, Leyba de Bonilla went beyond his orders.[31] Once on the northern edge of Nueva Vizcaya, he and his men ventured into New Mexico and beyond to the Great Plains where they met their fate. Details regarding Leyba de Bonilla's doomed expedition, however, were not known until 1599, the year after Governor Juan de Oñate established New Mexico. At that time, Oñate met the lone survivor of the Leyba de Bonilla expedition, a Mexican Indian named Jusepe, and interviewed him. But there was more to the story, and Oñate, obligated by his contract to investigate the whereabouts of Leyba de Bonilla and his men, would have to wait until 1601, when he himself explored the Great Plains and learned about the tragic end of the expedition.[32]

Between 1540 and 1590, glimpses of the coming changes to both pueblos and plains could be seen. Indeed, the Puebloans kept a wary eye on events and rumors of events to the south of them that reached their ears. They had, with the Coronado expedition as well as those led by Francisco Sánchez Chamuscado, Antonio de Espejo, Francisco Leyba de Bonilla, and Antonio Gutiérrez de Humaña, seen a disconcerting vision of the future. Tribes on the Great Plains also retained similar stories of intrusions into their territories. Indeed, Jusepe's account narrated the most recent intrusion into the heart of the Great Plains. Yet the expedition led by Castaño de Sosa and his settlers presented a new and possible reality as they witnessed yet another intrusion, this time Spanish settlers who came by way of the Great Plains. The next intrusion into their worlds would forever bind the early history of the triad that evolved between pueblos, plains, and province.

4

The Land of Disenchantment

New Mexico's Starvation Period, 1598–1609

I bind myself to carry out the said discovery to the best of my ability by peaceful means, friendliness, and Christian zeal.

—*Juan de Oñate, 1595*[1]

We find ourselves in extreme need of food and see the natives starving to death, eating whatever filth there is in the fields, even the twigs from the trees, dirt, coal, and ashes. . . . If we stay any longer, the natives and all of us here will perish of hunger, cold, and nakedness.

—*Francisco de Sosa Peñalosa, 1601*[2]

Sitting at a desk in 1595, Juan de Oñate, newly appointed *adelantado* and governor of the Provincia de Nuevo México, dipped his plume in the sepia-filled inkwell and wrote a letter to his viceroy, Luis de Velasco. With flowing penmanship, he wrote, "I bind myself to carry out the said discovery to the best of my ability by peaceful means, friendliness and Christian zeal." That year, Viceroy Velasco and Oñate agreed on a formal contract for the settlement of New Mexico.[3]

DOI: 10.5876/9781646420957.c004

Under terms of the contract, with certain prescribed privileges granted by the sovereign, Oñate would receive a salary of 6,000 ducats a year and would have almost unlimited power, accountable only to the Council of the Indies. In that sense, the sovereign claim would be known as the Reyno de Nuevo México (Kingdom of New Mexico) instead of the Provincia de Nuevo México. He would also hold the title of *adelantado*, the only person in New Mexico's colonial history to receive the privilege to advance the frontier line of settlement. Additionally, he would serve as governor and *capitán general* in command of all troops within his jurisdiction, collect taxes from the settlers for the defense of the province, and administer the *encomienda*, a feudal collection of tribute from Indians under Spanish control. Generally, if Indians could not pay the tribute, the amount due was converted to payment in labor.[4] Mission Indians, however, were exempt from paying the tribute. The Oñate years in New Mexico, 1598–1609, would bring many changes to the pueblos along the Rio Grande, the western pueblos such as Acoma and Zuñi, and those pueblos that faced the Great Plains, particularly Pecos and Las Humanas. While Spanish sovereignty dominated over Indigenous territoriality, individual boundaries of the pueblos would be recognized. In time, Spanish land grants issued to each pueblo would confirm their boundaries. With Spanish settlement, the triad of pueblos, plains, and province would, in the seventeenth century, be set in motion.

Significantly, Viceroy don Lorenzo Suárez de Mendoza y Figueroa's report of the Francisco Sánchez Chamuscado expedition inspired the Spanish crown's interest in the settlement of New Mexico. In March 1583, King Felipe II issued a royal *cedula* (decree) approving the viceroy's recommendation and authorizing the settlement of the *tierra adentro*. By the time that Antonio de Espejo returned from New Mexico, the wheels to settle New Mexico had begun to turn. Espejo's report, nonetheless, did stir up considerable interest among prominent investors in Old and New Spain who vied for the privilege of leading the expedition northward. Indeed, Hernán Gallegos, who had been with Sánchez, and Antonio de Espejo were among the prospective applicants. Gallegos quickly fell out of competition for lack of wealth to support the expedition, and Espejo, on his way to the court in Spain, fell ill and died unexpectedly in 1586 in Havana, Cuba.[5] Meanwhile, the viceroy searched for a leader with wealth as well as experience in such matters.

Twelve years passed before the viceroy and the Council of the Indies finally selected Juan Pérez de Oñate of Zacatecas. Viceroy Luis de Velasco knew the Oñate family well and appreciated its willingness to underwrite the cost of the expedition. But there were other factors that prompted the selection of Oñate. Too much time had elapsed since the authorization to settle New Mexico had been announced. Already on the restless frontier of Mexico there were others who would dare to strike out on their own and possibly ruin conditions for the royal enterprise.

Before the contract could be executed, Viceroy Velasco was transferred to the Viceroyalty of Peru and replaced by a new viceroy, Gaspar de Zúñiga, Conde de Monterrey. The new viceroy asked to review Oñate's contract. For the next three years, the viceroy held up the contract while he scrupulously reviewed all provisions of the contract and had it reviewed and analyzed for its legal and practical merits. Meanwhile, Oñate's expeditionary force in the field underwent additional inspections to assure that all parts of the contract were fulfilled by the contractor.[6] Finally, three years later, after much consideration and time, the viceroy issued a new and greatly modified contract, giving himself greater control over the expedition than he would have enjoyed under the previous contract. Doubtless Oñate was not happy with the new contract, but because he had invested so much money and time in the expedition's organization, he agreed to the new terms. Once in New Mexico, he hoped to recover his losses.

On January 26, 1598, after much delay and great expenditure to Oñate, the expedition received authorization to leave for New Mexico. Too, everyone on the expedition knew that the delay had caused the food supply and the herds to dwindle even before the march began. The two- to three-year wait caused some settlers to change their minds about going north. Oñate would later accuse them of desertion. In a great cloud of dust, the slow-moving, eighty-three *carreta* caravan pulled by oxen creaked out of the Valle de San Bartolomé in Nueva Vizcaya (Chihuahua). Driving thousands of sheep, pigs, goats, cattle, mules, and horses, the soldiers, settlers, servants, herders, Indian allies, and others began their six-month trek to their new homeland far to the north.[7] Sargento Mayor Vicente de Zaldívar, nephew of Oñate, and his scouts rode far ahead of the wagon to find water and pasturage as well as an easier route to the Rio Grande.[8] Heading north, they crossed the Río Florído where, a few days beyond, light snow fell in the area as a cold wind swept the desert of northern Chihuahua.

For months on end, the sound of sharp cracks made by the whips of drivers pushing the oxen-pulled *carretas* forward punctuated the air as the caravan made its way farther into the *tierra adentro*. Similarly, the air of northern Chihuahua resounded with human voices amid the creaking *carreta* wheels, neighing horses, braying mules and oxen, and barking dogs herding noisy cattle and sheep. Sometimes the caravan, in the flat terrain of the northern Chihuahuan prairies, spread out nearly a mile wide to avoid the choking dust that kicked up in the arid terrain.

By the end of April 1598, they had reached the Rio Grande. Of the event, the author of the Itinerario, the main diary of the expedition, wrote:

> On April 30, 1598, day of the Ascension of our Lord, at this Río del Norte Governor Don Juan de Oñate took possession of all the kingdoms and provinces of New Mexico, in the name of King Felipe [II], our lord, in the presence of Juan Pérez de Donis, royal notary and secretary of the jurisdiction and expedition. There was a sermon, a great ecclesiastical and secular celebration, a great salute and rejoicing, and in the afternoon, a comedy. The royal standard was blessed and placed in charge of Francisco de Sosa Peñalosa, the royal ensign.[9]

Following the river to a point where the mountains came down to form "the pass of the river and the ford," they forded the wide stream at a place they called "Los Puertos."[10] At that point, the land formed a geographic gateway leading north that would later be known as El Paso del Norte (The Pass of the North). There they stopped to camp and give thanks to their God for bringing them safely to that point in their travel northward. The event at the Rio Grande augured one of the first European thanksgivings in that part of North America.

The warm spring sun of May 4, 1598, upon that desolate spot witnessed the activity of Oñate's army and forty local Indians, who helped them move their cargo, carts, and livestock across the river. Near there, on the other side of the river, they met the first Indians from New Mexico.

Gazing northward into the *tierra adentro* beyond the river crossing at El Paso del Norte, Oñate noted the winding river moving southward from the distant north and the rough terrain it flowed through. He concluded, "There is no other road for carts for many leagues."[11] From a point beyond the crossing, the Spaniards would have to blaze their own route. He asked the friendly Indians about Cíbola and how long would it take to get there. They responded "very clearly by signs that the settlements were six days distant, or eight days along the route of travel." Still, the cart caravan must find a more navigable terrain away from the river. Oñate's opinion about there being "no other road" was soon contradicted. Late that day, according to the Itinerario, "we passed the ruts made by ten carts that Castaño [de Sosa] and Morlete took out from New Mexico"[12] about six years earlier. That caravan traveling southward from New Mexico had encountered the same problem and found a route along flatter land away from the river. Indeed, some of Oñate's men had been with Morlete, and they recalled the route they had followed in 1592.

Scouts were sent out to retrace Morlete's route. Ten days later the caravan moved up the desolate trail, now stopping to repair their carts; now stopping to observe a holy day of obligation; now stopping to wonder about the place "where it is said that Captain Morlete hanged four Indians because they had stolen some horses."[13] The summer rains and heat alternated as often as the thirst and hunger that afflicted the slow-moving wagon train that passed below the present-day Organ Mountains, with their craggy spirals that rose a short distance to the east of the Río del Norte. At that time the Organ Mountains were dubbed "Sierra del Olvido" (Mountain of Forgetfulness) because Oñate's men who had been with Morlete could not remember ever having seen them. Eight decades later, the Sierra del Olvido, named for the memory lapse suffered by Oñate's men upon entering New Mexico, would be renamed Los Organos by Spaniards fleeing the province in the Pueblo Revolt of 1680, who saw the topographic spirals as resembling a pipe organ. More realistically, it could also be that the Organ Mountains were probably named for the similar-looking Sierra de los Organos near Sombrerete in the state of Zacatecas, Mexico. The Sierra de los Organos, a well-known topographic feature for travelers passing along the Camino Real de Tierra Adentro, could be seen in the distance. Indeed, both sites, Parque Nacional Sierra de los Organos and Organ Mountains Desert Peaks National Monument in New Mexico, are sisters in the heritage of the US Camino Real de Tierra Adentro National Historic Trail and Mexico's Camino Real de Tierra Adentro World Heritage Site.

Having entered New Mexico, the scouts continued to search for a flatter route for the caravan to follow. Still, the advance proved extremely slow as the wagon train moved away from the river and slowly northward toward the faraway Indian pueblos of the Rio Grande. Approaching the vicinity of present Las Cruces, Oñate, along with the Father Commissary Friar Cristóbal de Salazar, Juan de Zaldívar, Vicente de Zaldívar, and a complement of sixty horsemen, decided to set out in advance for the Indian settlements far to the north. They rode ahead of the slow-moving caravan to prepare the pueblos for their coming.[14] And as the expedition was in need of provisions, Oñate hoped to replenish their supplies.

Meanwhile, the caravan continued its journey. Earlier, the scouts had reported that to the east of the river lay a plain that stretched northward and that would be easier for the carts to travel on despite its lack of water. Taking the recommended route, the caravan took a chance and moved into the waterless route for a few days without sighting any water holes or streams. Wondering if they could find water, the almost despairing settlers seemed to have been miraculously saved by a small dog. The writer of the Itinerario wrote, "We all fared badly on account of the river [being] toward the west. On this day, when a dog appeared with muddy paws and hind feet, we searched for some water holes. At a place commemorated as El Perrillo [The Little Dog], Captain Gaspar de Villagrá found one and Cristóbal Sánchez another, not far from where we were, toward the river."[15] Moving slowly, the caravan, still a distance from the river, followed the route through the arid terrain. Overcome by much hardship to man and beast and low on provisions, they realized that they were almost out of the flat land. They noted, "We were exploring and feeling our way along the entire route for the first time, and we suffered a great deal because of not knowing it. . . . We went six leagues to the marsh of the *mesilla guinea*, so-called because [the rock on] it was black."[16] By May 27, 1598, not far from the Rio Grande, they passed a point near present San Marcial on a flat, marshy plain below a round top of black rock. The long trail across the waterless plain, later known as the Jornada del Muerto (Dead Man's Journey), is about eighty miles long.[17] After one more day, they camped at a pueblo called Qualacu on the northern end of the *jornada* and at the southern end of the Río Abajo, a relative geographical reference meaning the lower Rio Grande between Cochití Pueblo in the north to a point near Socorro in the south.

The cart train had finally reached the river. Crossing it to the west bank, the caravan proceeded northward. By mid-June the caravan had arrived at the pueblo of Teypana, which the Spaniards called Socorro because there they had found relief from their distressing situation. Noticing the kindness of the people who recognized their plight, the settlers wrote that the people of

Teypana had "furnished us with much *maiz*." One of the leaders of Teypana, Letoc, spoke Piro and told the Spaniards about the other pueblos they would pass on their way northward. Many of the people in those pueblos, having seen earlier Spanish explorers with their terrible weapons and war horses, feared them and abandoned their homes. Nonetheless, passing by several abandoned pueblos north of Socorro, the settlers left them undisturbed as they pushed their caravans past them. Somewhere north of Socorro the settlers recrossed the river and traveled along the east bank on the slightly flatter terrain. Soon afterward they reached an abandoned pueblo they called Nueva Sevilla, which later Spanish maps would show as Sevilleta. There, in the abandoned pueblo, the settlers camped for a week as they recovered from their arduous march northward.[18]

While the settlers rested and repaired their *carretas*, Oñate and his men pushed on toward the area of present Belen. Just south of there, Oñate's nephews, the Maese de Campo Juan de Zaldívar and the Sargento Mayor Vicente de Zaldívar, left the main groups to scout ahead. Traveling northward from the camp, they explored the nearby pueblos along the river. Still, they could not avoid looking eastward to a large mountain range that intrigued them. Before long, the Zaldívar brothers were soon lured eastward by curiosity to the large mountain they called the Sierra Morena, present Manzano Mountains. Looking eastward toward the mountain, they could discern present-day Abo Pass, later called *el portuelo* (the little gateway) by the explorers. Wending through the pass, they encountered other pueblos at the southern end of the Manzanos, doubtless some of which were seen by Sánchez Chamuscado in 1582 and Antonio de Espejo in 1583. Soon after, the Zaldívars returned and reported to Oñate that they had seen other pueblos on the other side of the mountain. One of them they identified by the intriguing name "Aboó."[19] The Zaldívar brothers saw the ancient pueblo around June 22, 1598.

Breaking camp, Oñate and his men pushed northward once again. Passing through the Valley of Puaray, they saw many pueblos and planted fields on both sides of the valley within the area of present Albuquerque. Along the river, most of the pueblos of Puaray had been abandoned in fear of Spaniards coming to avenge the deaths of missionary priests seventeen years previous. Even as late as 1598, the murders of Friar Agustín Rodríguez and his missionary companions in 1581 seemed to loom over Puaray like a curse. Almost every time a Spanish expedition passed by, the people fled to the Sierra de Puaray (present-day Sandia Mountains) or to nearby pueblos. Although Oñate had no such intentions of attacking them, the people of Puaray and those of other pueblos believed that the Spaniards would seek revenge for the deaths of the missionaries.

Oñate and his horsemen rode past the abandoned pueblos of Puaray to a Keres pueblo known as Santo Domingo.[20] They knew of the pueblo because of the eventful arrest of Gaspar Castaño de Sosa by Juan de Morlete in 1592. There the Spaniards sought out two of the Mexican Indians, Tomás and Cristóbal, who had been with Castaño but had decided to remain at Santo Domingo. Oñate needed them as translators. Although Spanish activities along the Río Abajo between Nueva Sevilla and Santo Domingo had been peaceful, Tomás and Cristóbal were taken by surprise and quickly impressed into service as interpreters.[21]

Although the people of Santo Domingo looked on with guarded distrust, they soon realized that Oñate intended them no harm. Through his Mexican Indian interpreters, Oñate called a general council at Santo Domingo and invited the seven nearby pueblos to send representatives. Once assembled, Governor Oñate, speaking to them through Tomás and Cristóbal, explained the purpose of the new Spanish presence among them and asked each leader to pledge obedience to the Spanish crown, an act that he believed they comprehended.[22] Then he announced that Santo Domingo would be the site of a Franciscan convent dedicated to Nuestra Señora de la Asunción and that the patron saints of the pueblo would be Peter and Paul.[23] Indeed, throughout the seventeenth century, Santo Domingo served as the ecclesiastical capital of New Mexico. Convinced that peace had been established among the pueblos of the Río Abajo and the Spaniards, Oñate departed Santo Domingo in a northward direction.

Seeking a place to settle, Oñate and his men pushed their horses along the Río Arriba, the geographic reference of the upper Rio Grande between Cochití and Taos pueblos. En route, Oñate passed the pueblo called Bove, which he named San Ildefonso in honor of the expedition's father commissary, Fray Alonso Martínez.[24] Having passed much of the land described by Castaño de Sosa, they reached the confluence of the Rio Grande and the Rio Chama. There on July 4, 1598, at a small pueblo called Caypa, Oñate set up camp. He renamed the pueblo San Juan de los Caballeros, which served as the first capital of New Mexico. During the early years, San Juan de los Caballeros was also known as San Juan Bautista.

Once at San Juan de los Caballeros, Oñate ordered the Maese de Campo Juan de Zaldívar and a small contingent of soldiers to return to Nueva Sevilla and bring up the settlers.[25] By mid-August the settlers and sixty-one carts had arrived at San Juan. Of the eighty-three wagons that had begun the expedition, twenty-two had been left along the trail between El Paso and Nueva Sevilla. Because of their value to colonial transportation, they would be retrieved at a later date.[26] The long distance and the time to reach northern New Mexico had resulted in the depletion of their food stores as well as in the reduction of their herds, either by consumption, accidents, or preying wolves and coyotes along the way.

The expedition to settle New Mexico had taken nearly eight months. Beyond Santa Bárbara, Oñate's settlers had blazed a new route directly north stretching nearly 650 miles long to the Rio Grande at El Paso del Norte. The Camino Real de Tierra Adentro from Mexico City, with its winding pathways, to San Juan de los Caballeros now stretched nearly 1,600 miles long. It would become the major immigration and trade road connecting the New Mexican outpost with the rest of the Spanish Empire for the rest of the colonial period. The newly blazed segment of the Camino Real from Santa Bárbara to San Juan de los Caballeros became known historically as La Ruta de Oñate (Oñate's Route).

As the settlers were establishing themselves at San Juan de los Caballeros, their new capital, Governor Oñate, as required by the Laws of the Indies that each governor must tour the province under his charge at least once during his tenure,[27] busied himself with the first phase of his reconnaissance of the pueblos of the upper Rio Grande as well as the eastern pueblos that faced the Great Plains. While at Taos Pueblo, which the Spaniards knew as Braba, Tayberon, and San Miguel,[28] and at Picurís Pueblo, Oñate got his first glimpse of the Plains Indians, who had come to trade there. Moving southward through the mountains, the party traveled to Galisteo, where the plains were quite visible to the east of a small mountain range that the Spaniards later called the Sierra de San Lázaro (present Ortiz Mountains).[29] At the pueblo of San Cristóbal, Oñate released a young Indian woman named Doña Inés to her pueblo friends and relatives.[30] Doña Inés, born at San Cristóbal, had been taken as a child by Castaño de Sosa to be trained as an interpreter.

"Her parents and almost all of her relatives were already dead, and there was hardly anyone who remembered how Castaño had taken her away,"[31] wrote a colonist. Doña Inés, however, had resisted her role as interpreter for the Spaniards and had refused to become "a second Malinche [that is, doña Marina, the translator for Hernán Cortéz, conqueror of Tenochtitlan], but she does not know the language or any other spoken in New Mexico, nor is she learning them,"[32] lamented a Spaniard.

Intrigued by pueblo relationships with the Plains tribes, the Spanish governor visited Galisteo and the great fortress pueblo of Pecos. At Pecos the Spaniards had better luck with their Indian interpreters, Juan de Dios, who had learned to speak their tongue from Pedro Oróz, a captive from Pecos who had spent many years living in Mexico. Traditionally, Spanish explorers throughout the Americas either took natives to train them as translators or exchanged them with Spanish boys, who would remain behind to learn their languages. Between 1540 and 1690, Vásquez de Coronado, Antonio de Espejo, and Castaño de Sosa had followed the common practice throughout the New World of taking natives like Doña Inés and Pedro Oróz to teach them Spanish; they, in turn, taught others their native language so that whenever they returned to a given area, they could be used as translators. For example, in 1582, Antonio de Espejo, hoping to return and conquer New Mexico, abducted two men from Pecos. One of them managed to escape, but the other, closely guarded, was taken southward to Santa Bárbara. Espejo, meanwhile, convinced authorities there to place the native under the tutelage of Fray Pedro Oróz. At baptism, the native took the name of his tutor and became known as Pedro Oróz, *indio*. Before the New Mexico expedition got underway, Pedro died at Tanepantla, north of Mexico City, without ever again seeing his homeland.[33] Prior to his death, however, Pedro taught the Pecos language to a Mexican Indian, Juan de Dios, who served as a Franciscan lay brother on the Oñate expedition. Once at Pecos, Juan tested his linguistic skills and learned valuable information about Pecos and the Great Plains that Oñate found useful. Thus, when Oñate arrived in New Mexico, he already had a cadre of translators as well as certain Indians, whom he sought out, who had been with recent explorers and had remained among the pueblos. What he had learned about the plains after his visits to Taos, Picurís, Pecos, and Galisteo piqued his curiosity, and he soon made plans to go out to the Great Plains and see that wilderness for himself.

Meanwhile, having spent four days at the fortress pueblo of Pecos, Oñate resumed his reconnaissance of the pueblos, particularly those immediately west of the Rio Grande. Leading his men westward from the Rio Grande, he proceeded toward present Santa Ana and Zia pueblos on his way to Jémez. Pulling their horses over a steep hill to get to "the great pueblo of the Emes," they lost two of their mounts, which rolled down shortly before getting to the top.[34] Jémez impressed them. Ever diligent, the observant Spaniards took note of everything they saw. At Jémez a "petty chieftain" wearing around his neck a paten with a hole drilled through the center caught their attention. Oñate's men discerned that it had belonged to one of the priests who had been martyred seventeen years earlier at Puaray. Determined to retrieve the sacred paten, they approached the man. "He traded it for hawkbells," wrote one Spaniard, "but even if he had not accepted them, he would not have been allowed to take it away."[35] They noted the date, August 3, the feast day of San Estévan, when they recovered the paten. Later the Spanish priests kept it in the ciborium of the convent at San Juan Bautista. Doubtless when the Spaniards moved their headquarters to San Gabriel, they took the paten there along with the ciborium.

Oñate's men explored Jémez and its environs. The "other Emes pueblos" numbered eleven, but the Spaniards saw only eight of them, reported Oñate. The terrain proved to be exceedingly rough, and the descent to the other pueblos was so steep that two horses were killed when they tumbled down a precipice. On the way to one pueblo, they saw the "marvelous hot baths" with their cold and hot waters and many deposits of sulfur and alum.[36] The hot springs at Jémez were frequented many times by Spaniards throughout the colonial period. Jémez was the last place visited during the summer explorations of 1598. Having seen almost all of the pueblos and made their presence known, Oñate and his men returned to San Juan by way of Santo Domingo and San Ildefonso.

As the summer of 1598 came to a close, the settlers at San Juan organized their village and prepared for winter. Between August and the end of September, they organized their new homes and their fields and began to harvest their first crops. Certainly by the end of August, they had commenced work on the *acequia madre*, the main irrigation ditch, and had planned their fields for the following spring. Low on provisions and the long, cold winter that followed, the settlers would depend on nearby pueblos to share their food supply with them. Between August 23 and September 7, the church at San Juan, with the help of "some 1,500" Indians, was constructed. Although small, the church "was large enough to accommodate all of the people in the camp,"[37] wrote a settler. Once completed, the church, San Juan Bautista, was dedicated on September 8. Following a procession around the church, the priests blessed the church and consecrated the altar and the chalices. Father Salazar delivered the homily before the packed congregation. Amid great rejoicing after the mass, the small village celebrated the end of their long trip in the wilderness of North America. In the afternoon the settlers reenacted the pageantry of the sham battle *Moros y Cristianos* for the entertainment of all.[38]

To the natives looking on, the scenario appeared somewhat perplexing, yet distressingly familiar. It may have disturbed them to remember what they had retained in their lore about the Europeans, who had come to their land in the past with terrible weapons, war dogs, and horses. As in the past, they had again begun to resent that they would be obligated to give or trade their stored food with whatever Spanish expedition came their way. In the next few months, as the settlers survived their first winter, they began to rely on the pueblos for food or face starvation. At that point, Hispanic settlers and Pueblo Indians were unaware that New Mexico's starvation period was at hand and, especially in the short term, would become a leading factor in damaging relationships between them. Whatever the natives' prophecies may have warned concerning the coming of the white man, they now stood witness to the fact that the pueblo world, indeed, the Indian world, would never again be the same.

The next day Oñate presided over a general assembly, which he had planned days earlier.[39] Under a canopy of cottonwood trees at San Juan de los Caballeros, the settlers and Indian leaders of the pueblos of the Río Arriba and the Río Abajo watched and listened as Governor Oñate addressed the assembly. Speaking through his interpreters, the governor gave an account of the country he had explored and the pueblos he had visited on his way to establish San Juan de los Caballeros. As the translators presented what Governor Oñate said next, the pueblo leaders looked around in quiet astonishment. Oñate told them that the pueblos of New Mexico would be divided among the eight Franciscan friars in the expedition. The divisions would be called *conversiones evangelicas*, and the entire evangelic conversion of New Mexico would eventually be called the Conversión de San Pablo de la Provincia de Nuevo México.

As the assignments of the priests were announced, Governor Oñate explained that he had come to this land to bring them the knowledge of God, on which depended the "salvation of their souls, and to live peaceably and safely in their countries, governed justly, safe in their possessions, protected from their enemies."[40] He told them that he had come in peace. It was fitting, he told them, that they should "render obedience and vassalage to God and king, and in their stead, to the most reverend father commissary in spiritual matters, and to the governor in temporal matters and those relating to the government of their public affairs."[41]

After Oñate had given the pueblo leaders his explanation through interpreters, they acknowledged that they understood what he had said. The governor repeated his message, and the pueblo leaders, wise in the ways of survival, pledged to render obedience to God and king, and did so voluntarily, in the names of their respective pueblos.[42] At least, that is what Oñate understood they had said.

In a ritualistic manner, Governor Oñate accepted their pledges and asked them to stand up, for they had been seated on the ground for quite some time. Then he bade the Indians approach him and Friar Martínez, kneel before them, and kiss their hands as a sign of submission. In tandem, the pueblo leaders did so as the two Spaniards, representing the duality of church and state, received the homage as a sign of obedience and vassalage.[43] Through the act of possession that Oñate had performed at El Paso del Norte in which he ceremoniously claimed New Mexico for Spain, so too did this act of homage and obedience represent an act of subsumed sovereignty that had been practiced since Christopher Columbus planted the Spanish flag and claimed the lands in the Americas for Spain. Similar acts in the Western Hemisphere were practiced by all colonial powers such as England, France, Portugal, Germany, and Holland through their charters that claimed Indian lands from sea to sea.

As planned, the governor and the commissary assigned the friars to the *conversiones evangelicos* of the pueblos. "Take the priests and ministers of God," Oñate told them, "so that they might learn their languages and so that the natives may be instructed about God's law." He told them that they "should be baptized so that they might go to heaven and escape going to hell."

Somewhat intimidated, based on what Oñate said next, the pueblo leaders replied that they would accede. "Look after the padres," he said, "treat them well, and support and obey them in every respect." This he repeated three times with the admonition that if they failed to do so they and their pueblos would "be put to the sword and destroyed by fire."⁴⁴ That they understood under duress. Although they must have had second thoughts about their agreement, they also realized they were powerless to resist. The safety of the pueblos came first.

Patiently and courteously, the leaders of the pueblos sat as they waited for assignments of the Franciscan ministers to be read aloud, and the friars were presented. The long, detailed list indicated the precision of Oñate's intelligence gathering. He left no question that he knew every pueblo in the entire province of New Mexico by its Indian name. Then their attention focused on two Franciscans who stood before them as the assignments regarding the Río Abajo were read:

> To Father Fray Juan de Rozas, the province of the Cheres, with the pueblos of Castixe called San Felipe, and Comitze and the pueblo of Santo Domingo, and Olipoti, Cochiti, and the pueblos of the Ciénega of Carabajal and San Marcos, San Cristóbal, Santa Ana, Ojana, Quipacha, and El Puerto, the burned pueblo [el pueblo quemado]. . . . Father Fray Juan Claros, the province of the Chiguas, or Tiguas and the pueblos of Napeya and Tuchiamas, Pura, together with the four next in order down the river, Popen, Puarai, Tziymatzi, Guayotzi, Acacagui, Henicoho and Viareato, with all those subject to Puarai, both up and down the Río del Norte; and the province of Xala, the province of Atzigues down the river, with all its pueblos, which include Puguey, Tuzahe, Aponitze, Vumaheyn, Quiapo, Cunguili, Pinoe, Calziati, Aguiabo, Emxa, Quiaguacalca, Tzelaqui, Puquias, Ayqui, Yanamo, Teyaxa, Qualacu, Texa, Amo, on this side of the river, and on the opposite side, the pueblos of Pencoana, Quiomagui, Peixoloe, Cumaque, Telytzaan, Puguey, Canocan, Geydol, Quiubaco, Tohol, Cantemachul, Tercao, Poloaca, Tzeyey, Quelquelu, Atexua, Tzula, Tzeygual, Tecahan, Qualahamo, Piloque, Penjeacu, Teypama, and lastly Tenaqual de la Mesilla, which is the first settlement in this kingdom toward the south and New Spain.⁴⁵

The list went on. It also included the pueblos of Las Salinas, namely Las Humanas, Quarai, and Abó, to the southeast within and behind the Manzano

Mountains and the desert pueblos of Zuñi and Hopi to the west. After hearing the assignments, the pueblo leaders present were instructed to kiss the hand of the friar chosen for them. The Indians rose and "kissed his habit and embraced him."[46] The missionization of New Mexico's pueblos had begun, albeit on a very small scale, for the friars were too few and the distances between many of the pueblos too great to administer their assignments.

Oñate's tour of the pueblos of New Mexico presaged his exploration of the Great Plains (1601) and his final projected exploration westward to find a port to supply his settlement from the sea. The first attempted expedition to the Colorado River in December 1598 was interrupted by the death of his nephew, Juan de Zaldívar, at the hands of the warriors at Acoma. Subsequently, Oñate did not resume his old plan of exploring westward toward the Pacific Ocean until October 1604.[47] Although the expedition proved insignificant in terms of accomplishing its objective, it was Oñate's last westward exploration of the region in which he left a lasting mark by engraving his name, seen at today's El Morro National Monument. According to Zárate Salmerón, "Oñate took 30 soldiers, most of them being raw recruits; and they took only 14 pairs of horse armor."[48] Along with Fray Francisco de Escobar and a lay brother, the expedition traveled southward before veering westward. Moving south from San Gabriel, Oñate and his men visited pueblos along the Rio Grande, Galisteo, Salinas, and west from Isleta to Zuñi, where they traded for provisions. From there, the expedition went northwest to Oraibi and the Hopi pueblos.

Once beyond the Hopi pueblos, the expedition followed a series of mountain valleys and rivers, some of them seasonal, to the Bill Williams Fork and the Colorado River. From there they went southward to the confluence of the Gila River and the Colorado River, thence southward to the mouth of the Colorado River where it flows into the Gulf of California. Along the way they met various Indian tribes who told them about the metallic resources of the area, largely copper and tin, but not valuable minerals such as silver and gold. They learned about coral, concha shells, and colorful stones, but not anything of value.

On that expedition Oñate found no mines, saw no gold or silver; and, once on the Colorado River in western Arizona, they moved southward to the Gulf of California. Disappointed in his final hope to find a worthwhile port or at least any sources for mineral wealth, Oñate pointed his men eastward toward the rising sun and began the long, toilsome journey back to San Gabriel. On passing El Morro (present Inscription Rock), Oñate paused long enough to leave a message for posterity: "Pasó por aquí el Adelantado don Juan de Oñate del descubrimiento de la mar del sur a 16 dia de abril año 1605" (Through here passed the Adelantado don Juan de Oñate from the discovery of the South Sea on the 16th day of April, year 1605). Oñate's inscription is the oldest Spanish inscription on the rock; only the Indian petroglyphs are older.

5

Death on the Great Plains

Jusepe and the Ill-fated Leyba de Bonilla Expedition

This deponent saw that after going three days beyond the said Great Pueblo, discord arose between captain Leyba and Antonio Guriérrez de Umaña. The latter remained alone in his tent and entire afternoon and morning, writing, and at the end of this time he sent a soldier named Miguel Pérez to call Captain Leyba, who came, dressed in shirt and breeches. Before he reached the tent, Antonio Gutiérrez de Umaña went out to meet him, drew a butcher knife which he carried in his pocket, unsheathed it, and stabbed Captain Leyba twice, from which he soon afterward died. He was buried at once.

—*Jusepe Gutiérrez de Humaña, 1599*[1]

As the pueblo leaders broke camp to return to their respective pueblos after learning the names of the Franciscan ministers assigned to them, Juan de Oñate turned his attention to another order in compliance of his contractual instructions from the viceroy: the Great Plains and the mystery surrounding the Leyba de Bonilla expedition. The whereabouts of Leyba de Bonilla, Antonio Gutiérrez y Humaña, and their men remained unresolved. Oñate, under orders of the viceroy, had to investigate the unauthorized expedition led by Leyba de Bonilla, find him and his men, and, assuming they were still alive, arrest them for their illegal entry into New Mexico.[2] Indeed, no one could violate any area the sovereign's claim by exploring it without permission. On the other hand, Leyba y Bonilla's men failed to understand the norms of territoriality practiced by Great Plains tribes. Reporting on the status of his mission in 1599, Oñate wrote to the viceroy, the Count of Monterey, saying, "I reached these provinces on the twenty-eighth day of May [1598] . . . to pacify the land and free it from traitors, seizing Humaña and his followers, to obtain full information, by seeing with my own eyes, regarding the location and nature of the land, and regarding the nature and customs of the people."[3] At that time, the fate of the Leyba de Bonilla and Gutiérrez Humaña expedition was unknown, but there were rumors of a lone survivor.

In summer 1598, Juan de Oñate found the lone survivor, a man named Jusepe, living at San Juan Pueblo.[4] On February 16, 1599, Oñate interviewed Jusepe in regard to Leyba de Bonilla's expedition. Jusepe Gutiérrez Humaña, a native of Culhuacán, a village about fifty miles north of Mexico City, told Oñate how he had joined the ill-fated expedition.[5] Jusepe (sometimes referred to as Jusepillo) said that he had met Antonio Gutiérrez de Humaña and became his servant on an expedition led by Leyba de Bonilla. As his servant, Jusepe had added the surname Gutiérrez Humaña.

From Jusepe's interview, Oñate pieced together a narrative of the fated expedition. In 1593, as the story went, Captain Leyba de Bonilla and his second-in-command, Antonio Gutiérrez de Humaña, led a company of soldiers out of southern Chihuahua on a punitive expedition against marauding Indians who had fled northward. Somewhere on the edge of the northern Chihuahua Desert, after the soldiers had completed their mission, Leyba de Bonilla told his men of his desire to penetrate the *tierra adentro*. Six soldiers refused to join the party, but the rest of them were intrigued by what lay ahead. The horsemen led by Leyba de Bonilla and Antonio Gutiérrez de Humaña crossed the Rio Grande and followed the pathway along the Rio Grande to the pueblos of New Mexico.

After some months among the pueblos of the Rio Grande, particularly San Ildefonso, they decided to visit Pecos Pueblo, a gateway to the Great Plains. There Leyba de Bonilla and Gutiérrez de Humaña made another decision.[6] They would dare to go eastward from Pecos onto the Great Plains. Perhaps the Pecos people, as they had Coronado in 1540, told them about the wonders of the plains and Gran Quivira, or maybe Leyba de Bonilla and his men had arrived at the northern pueblo in time for the annual trade fair attended by Plains Indians, for they mentioned that they had met vaqueros (literally, in this case, plains buffalo "cow" herders), warriors from a Plains tribe.[7] In any event, Leyba de Bonilla and Gutiérrez de Humaña learned about the plains and were determined to go there in the hope that some great civilization, like the legendary Gran Quivira, similar to the Aztec kingdom, existed. After all, they may have reasoned, Vázquez de Coronado, Sánchez Chamuscado, and Espejo probably did not go far enough in the correct direction to find it. Leyba de Bonilla and Gutiérrez de Humaña headed northeastward into the plains toward what is now Kansas.

Proceeding in a northerly direction, they marched for fifteen days and reached two large rivers, and beyond them were many rancherias with a large population. They called it the "Great Pueblo." The houses, they said, were built on frames of poles, covered with grass or straw. They were built very close together with very narrow streets. Between the structures were crops that included corn, calabashes, and beans. The natives there seemed friendly. Departing the settlements, they proceeded northward, amazed by the flat land covered by thousands of buffaloes. They traveled through a stretch of land with no settlements until they came to a very large river. Somewhere in the lonely llano beyond the Great Pueblo, Leyba de Bonilla and Gutiérrez de Humaña had a falling-out. In the brawl that followed, Gutiérrez de Humaña stabbed his captain to death.[8] He now found himself in command of the troops in the midst of a very hostile land.

Following the burial of Leyba de Bonilla somewhere on the flat plains of Kansas, Gutiérrez de Humaña led his men northward for many days on end. Still shocked by the death of Leyba de Bonilla, Jusepe and five other Indians, likely camp tenders, promptly fled. In their attempt to return to New Mexico, they reached the large river, lost their bearings, and soon became lost.[9] Jusepe and another man reached the Great Pueblo, where the people there killed his companion. Jusepe escaped from them but was taken prisoner by Apaches and held for a year. Finally, he escaped from them and made his way back to Pecos. Soon afterward he settled at San Ildefonso on the Rio Grande. At the time, Jusepe did not know the whereabouts or the fate of Gutiérrez de Humaña and his men. Based on Jusepe's testimony, Oñate's next step would be to see if any traces of that unauthorized expedition could be found.

In September 1599, as a preliminary step to his planned expedition to the Great Plains, Oñate ordered Sargento Mayor Vicente de Zaldívar and a contingent of soldiers to go to the plains and locate Leyba de Bonilla's campsites to determine the route of their expedition. Oñate also instructed Zaldívar to report about the land and its people, resources, and great buffalo herds on the plains. Indeed, Jusepe, the known sole survivor of the Leyba de Bonilla expedition, served as one of Zaldívar's guides. Their route to Galisteo east of the Rio Grande pueblos was uneventful. At San Cristóbal, Zaldívar turned southward, past present South Mountain behind the Sandias, and headed toward the Salinas pueblos in the Manzanos. Zaldívar and his men, who had been gathering foodstuffs from the pueblos for their march to the plains, were rebuked by the people of Salinas. Later Oñate would make one of the Salinas villages serve as an object lesson to those who would disobey Spanish authority over them.[10]

Once on the plains, somewhere near the Canadian River beyond the Texas Panhandle, Zaldívar and his men found large herds of buffalo. Hoping to capture some of these "monstrous cows," they spent several days constructing a large corral from the cottonwoods along the river. Then they tried to herd the buffalo into it, but the wild animals could not be penned. In the attempted roundup, three horses were gored to death by the stampeding buffalo. When the Spaniards roped some calves, the animals were severely injured in their attempts to break loose. Finally, Zaldívar decided that the buffalo could not be captured. Instead, he had some killed for their meat.[11]

During his fifty-four days on the plains, Zaldívar located several of Leyba de Bonilla's campsites. Along the way, Zaldívar located Leyba de Bonilla's first camp beyond the Pecos River, about twenty-four leagues (about sixty-three miles) from Oñate's headquarters at San Juan de los Caballeros.[12] All that remained of the sites he found were burned-out campfires and dried horse dung throughout the areas of the camps.[13] Days into the buffalo plains, Zaldiver and his men met three Indians who had come "from a mountain, and, being asked where their ranchería was, they said that it was a league from there, and that they were very much excited because of our being in that land."[14] Taking precautions not to agitate the natives, he left his soldiers in the camp and accompanied the three warriors with only one of his men and Jusepe, as translator, to the rancheria. As they approached the settlement, some Indians came out to meet him in friendship, which, as Zaldívar reported, they did by extending "the palm of their right hand to the sun and then to bring it down on the person whose friendship they desire." In return, Zaldívar gave them trinkets. That done, the Plains Indians bade him visit their settlement, which he did so that they would not think he feared them.[15] He returned to the Spanish camp later that night.

The next day, they traveled farther into the plains, meeting many Indians, men and women, who brought them food. Zaldívar described them, writing, "Most of the men go naked, but some are clothed with skins of buffalo and some with blankets. The women wore a sort of trousers made of buckskin, and shoes or leggings, after their own fashion."[16] That particular tribe hoped Zaldívar would help them attack their enemy, the Jumanos, but he declined. His primary mission—to trace the path traveled by Leyba de Bonilla and his men into the *tierra incognita*—remained a priority over gathering information about the land and its people, albeit some intelligence was similarly gathered. Moving deeper into the plains, Zaldívar reported, "In this region and on this road were found some camps and sleeping places made by Leyba and Humaña when they left this land."[17] After nearly two months on the trail, Zaldívar began his slow return to San Juan de los Caballeros, where he presented his report to Governor Oñate. The death of Leyba de Bonilla was clear, but what about that of Antonio Gutíerrez de Humaña? Not until late summer of 1601, when Oñate led an expedition to the Great Bend of the Arkansas River, would they learn about Gutíerrez de Humaña's fate.

Perhaps, the most significant information that Zaldívar reported dealt with the population of thousands of natives on the Great Plains, which would later be confirmed by Oñate when he went out to the Great Plains in 1601. The threat to New Mexico's survival was evermore evident. Zaldívar and Oñate would later agree that, if provoked, the Great Plains tribes could overrun and destroy the Spanish settlements in New Mexico. For the next two centuries, Spanish governors, following Oñate's orders, prohibited any Spanish settler from trading with those tribes, fearing that a deal gone bad would lead to the annihilation of New Mexico's nascent settlements.

6

The Big Clash

Acoma and the Jumano War, 1599–1601

They hurled many insulting words asking what we had come for, why were we waiting, and why we did not fight, since they were ready for battle and [they] were waiting for nothing but to kill us and then kill the Queres and the Tiguas and everyone at Zia because they failed to kill the Spaniards.

—*Spanish witnesses at Acoma, 1599*[1]

Asked why, when [Zaldívar] offered . . . peace, he and the others did not come down to accept but shot many arrows and threw rocks and cried for the Spaniards to come and fight, he said that the old people and other leading Indians did not want peace, and for this reason they attacked with arrows and stones.

—*Testimony of Taxio from Acoma, 1599*[2]

When [Zaldívar] came by that pueblo [of the Jumanos] with some soldiers and asked the inhabitants for provisions and tortillas, as his men were hungry and exhausted, the Indians refused to furnish any. On the contrary, this witness was told that they offered them stones to eat.

—*Ginés de Herrera Horta, 1601*[3]

The threat of the annihilation of the Spanish settlement, however, did not come from the Great Plains; it came from an unexpected quarter within New Mexico. While Pueblo Indian resentment had slowly seethed throughout the land, their displeasure with the Spanish presence grew stronger as summer 1598 came to a close. The main issues that brought the matter to a crux centered on the Spanish settlers' intrusion onto Indigenous territories and the dwindling food supply on both sides. The double-edged issues formed a chasm between the Spanish settlement and the pueblos. Having arrived in mid-summer 1598, the Spanish settlers had barely enough time to plant their fields and have a ready supply of food to get them through the winter, much less the following springtime. Thus, food shortages were evident throughout the land.

Since time immemorial, the natives had gathered all the produce they could during the planting season and stored it for the winter and the succeeding spring. Bad times followed whenever early frosts damaged their crops or scant rainfall scorched their fields during the late-summer months. When droughts occurred, the pueblos, and later Spanish settlers, had barely enough to get them through until springtime. Some of the more prosperous pueblos, in good times, stored corn "for as many as six years at a time."[4] Still, given the situation, the strain of sharing their food supply was not a viable option for the pueblos. Likewise, in the early years of establishing New Mexico, the Spanish settlers, for the sake of survival, did not have much choice. The dilemma overpowered both groups.

In his correspondence to the viceroy in 1601, Fray Juan de Escalona reflected on the early years of the establishment of the Spanish settlement at San Juan de los Caballeros. Of the situation he wrote that "there has not been a week since we came here that we have not used up fifty to sixty *fanegas*[5] of corn, and when the governor and the rest of the people were here we consumed upwards of eighty *fanegas*. As a result of this, the Indians have reached the state of famine.... Reflecting on this situation and that we were all in danger of perishing, Indians as well as Spaniards, the entire army, in a body, resolved to move to some other place where it could find relief of its wants."[6] As a solution, in early 1599, Governor Oñate moved the Spanish settlement from San Juan de los Caballeros to San Gabriel at the confluence of the Rio Grande and the Chama River, an area more suitable for farming, fishing, and hunting. Still, while the settlers struggled to survive with what they had at hand, a caravan with relief supplies did not reach the New Mexican settlement at San Gabriel until late December 1600.[7] Scarcely had the settlers lived in their newly founded settlement at San Juan de los Caballeros four months, between August and December 1598, when they met their first unwanted challenge emanating from Acoma Pueblo.

In the wake of Pueblo Indian resentment and discontent, Oñate, in fall 1598, departed San Juan de los Caballeros to explore westward to the Pacific Ocean to find a harbor from which to better supply New Mexico by sea. Following the Rio Grande southward from San Juan de los Caballeros, the Spaniards, as usual, expected the pueblos along the route to trade their food for Spanish goods in order to supply their expedition. On this journey, Oñate took a roundabout route to Galisteo and then southward to the Salinas pueblos. By mid-October, when Oñate and his men left the Salinas pueblos, they traveled westward and passed through El Portuelo, present-day Abo Pass. They crossed the Rio Grande at Isleta and traveled north toward Puaray. Having picked up provisions at those pueblos, they turned west to Acoma.[8] There the Spaniards traded for food with resentful natives who watched their food supply dwindle as winter approached.

At Acoma, some warriors plotted to kill Oñate. Politely the Acomans invited Oñate to their pueblo atop a *peñol*, a promontory some 220 feet high. Climbing the footholds carved into the rock, Oñate and some of his men made the precarious ascent. The plan of the Acomans, made against the better judgment of some among them, was to isolate Oñate from his men and kill him.[9] When they invited the Spanish governor into one of their kivas, he declined. Again they tried to persuade him to enter another one, telling him that he would see something wondrous inside. Peering through the entryway of the kiva, the wary Oñate sensed a trap. His men urged him to decline, which he politely did. Unknown to him at the time, a dozen or so armed warriors were inside ready to kill him the moment he entered. The Acomans would have to wait for another opportunity.

Before he departed Acoma, Oñate sent a message for his nephew, Juan de Zaldívar, to join the expedition to the Pacific Ocean. Some Acomans were relieved to see Oñate leave. Others persisted in their belief that it would be necessary to drive out the Spaniards, while others warned that if they did not succeed in their attack the pueblo would surely be destroyed.[10] The warmongers at Acoma, however, argued that they had much to gain and were confident of a successful attack against the Spaniards. The decision to attack the Spaniards caused much debate among the Acomans. As Oñate and his men marched away, the Acomans looked on with mixed opinions.

Meanwhile, Oñate reached Zuñi and awaited his nephew to join his force. Sending out scouts to determine Juan de Zaldívar's whereabouts, Oñate had begun to wonder about the delay. Then he moved his camp to a place near Tusayán,[11] a Hopi village within present Arizona. There he waited a while longer. Still no word from Zaldívar. Meanwhile, Oñate sent Marcos de Farfán ahead to explore northern Arizona. Farfán reached as far as present-day Prescott. Before turning back, he noted copper deposits in the mountains of western Arizona. The weather had begun to turn cold. Oñate, still at Tusayán, decided to return to San Juan de los Caballeros for the Christmas holiday.[12]

At that time, the situation at Acoma turned deadly. As the cold winter months set in, the people of Acoma relied on their storage of food as they had since time immemorial. When the Maese de Campo Juan de Zaldívar and his men stopped at Acoma and asked to trade for food, the Acomans took offense. Later, after the battle of Acoma, which ensued as a result of the killings, Caoma, an Acoma warrior, explained that when the Spaniards stopped at "the pueblo and asked the natives to furnish them with the maize and flour which they needed, and because they asked for such large amounts, they killed them."[13] Other warriors, among them Cat-Ticati, confirmed that they "had killed them because they asked for maize, flour, and blankets."[14] Xunusta, on the other hand, contrarily added that "the Spaniards first killed an Indian, and then all the Indians became very angry and killed them."[15]

Once beyond Zuñi Pueblo, Oñate and his men were overtaken by a heavy snowstorm in which they lost many horses. While they were camped near El Morro, which the Spaniards called El Estanque del Peñol (The Water Tank at the Large Rock), a messenger from Zaldívar's command rode in from Acoma to tell the governor of the deaths of his nephew and others in an ambush at the pueblo. In mid-December a grieving Oñate and his men rode back to San Juan de los Caballeros. There he would learn more details about the murderous fight at Acoma. Shortly, Goveror Oñate would make a momentous decision that would affect Spanish-Indian relations in New Mexico for the rest of the colonial period.[16]

From survivors of the skirmish, Oñate learned details about the death of his nephew at Acoma. It seems that while Maese de Campo Juan de Zaldívar and his men were camped near the bottom of the *peñol*, some Indians came down and invited a few Spaniards to ascend and visit their pueblo.[17] Leaving part of his troop below to guard the camp and horses, Zaldívar and his men climbed the "stone ladders" to the top. The Spaniards began to trade for food, as usual. This time, however, the Indians led them about so that the Spaniards were divided.[18] The Indians rapidly fell on them, killing the *maese de campo* and twelve others and throwing their bodies from the cliffs.[19] The guard at the bottom of the mesa was helpless to come to their aid. In desperation, three men survived by leaping from the escarpment. In the melee, one other plummeted to his death from the pueblo's edge.[20] No matter the causes or the warnings from within the pueblo not to do so, the Acoman warriors had cast the first blow that would lead to the battle that would cost them dearly.

After attending to the wounded, the troop divided into three squads of less than a dozen men each. One group retreated to San Juan de los Caballeros to warn the settlers, a second party hurried to warn the friars at the various pueblo missions, and the third squad hastened to report the attack to Oñate.[21]

While the Indians at Acoma gloried in their victory over the Spaniards, the settlers at San Juan de los Caballeros tried to come to terms with an uncertain future. Fear gripped the Spanish settlement, for the settlers believed that the successful revolt at Acoma could signal a rebellion of all the pueblos. When Oñate and his men arrived at San Juan de los Caballeros, they found the settlement heavily guarded.[22]

Amid the mourning for the dead soldiers, Oñate called a council of war and heard testimony from those who had been with Juan de Zaldívar at Acoma. Prompt action would be necessary to show Acoma and the rest of the pueblos that defiance of Spanish authority would not be tolerated. From a military point of view, the Spaniards knew they could not permit Acoma to get away with the attack or leave an enemy at its back, lest the other pueblos interpret Spanish inaction as a sign of weakness. At the council of war, Oñate consulted his captains and the friars about their course of action.[23] All agreed that Acoma should be attacked and punished for its aggression if the Spanish settlement hoped to survive. One priest wrote that "peace was the principal end for which war was ordained." In order to reestablish peace and control, they believed, Oñate had no alternative but to attack Acoma.[24]

Although Oñate had planned to command the seventy troops selected for the mission, Sargento Mayor Vicente de Zaldívar, whose brother had been slain at Acoma, asked to lead the punitive expedition. Some Spaniards believed he had the right to avenge his loss.[25] Oñate gave him instructions to proceed to Acoma, "plant your artillery and musketry," and deploy the troops in "battle formation."[26] That done, Zaldívar, with the aid of Mexican Indians, particularly the interpreters, Tomás and Cristóbal, or other suitable interpreters among their Nahua-speaking allies, had to "summon the Indians of Acoma to accept peace, once, twice and thrice, and urge them to abandon their resistance, lay down their arms, and submit to the authority of the king, our lord, since they have already rendered obedience to him as his vassals."[27]

Zaldívar's instructions explicitly stated that he demand that the people of Acoma "surrender the leaders responsible for the uprisings, and the murders, assuring them that they will be justly dealt with." The bodies of the dead Spaniards, along with their accoutrements, must be returned. If the Acomans should resist, then Zaldívar should decide whether to attack them or postpone the fight. The attack should be called off, warned Oñate, if the Indian strength is too great, "for there would be less harm in postponing the punishment for the time being than in risking the people with you."[28]

If the Acomans wanted a fight, then the Spaniards would oblige them; after all, they initiated the conflict. Oñate's instructions to Zaldívar were clear. "Inasmuch," he ordered, "as we have declared war on them without quarter, you will punish all those of fighting age as you deem best, as a warning to everyone in this kingdom." The orders that covered the possibility that the Indians would surrender those responsible for the attack called for a restrained effort in the punishment of Acoma, but left open the possibility of a war of "fire and sword" if they refused to meet the Spaniards' demands. Dipping a quill in ink, Oñate signed the instructions to Zaldívar before his secretary, who notarized the document.[29]

When Zaldívar and his troops arrived at Acoma on January 21, 1599, they were greeted by taunts, jeers, insults, and obscene gestures from the defiant warriors of the mighty pueblo. Undaunted, Vicente de Zaldívar deployed his men and artillery with an odd calm. With an experienced eye for siege warfare, his scouts collectively ascertained the best point for the assault on the *peñol*. Standing around a campfire, the members of the council of war formulated a plan. The main tactic, to feign an assault on the pueblo by climbing up the main ladderways on one side of the escarpment, called for a detail of men to pull up an artillery piece on the opposite side of the pueblo the night before the battle and catch the warriors in a crossfire.

Meanwhile, as the Spaniards planned their attack, Zaldívar and his interpreters offered the prescribed peace gestures "once, twice and thrice."[30] Despite warnings from some of their leaders, the Acomans rejected Zaldívar's peace offerings. Jeering, shooting arrows, hurling wooden spears, and throwing rocks at the Spaniards, the Acomans made clear their intentions to fight.[31]

That night the Spaniards camped below the pueblo and rested; the Indians spent the night "in huge dances and carousals, shouting, hissing . . . and challenging the army to fight."[32] Zaldívar reported that "the Indians all shouted loudly, raised their swords on high, and presented themselves in the coats of mail and other pieces of equipment they had taken from the dead Spaniards, boasting that they had killed ten Spaniards and two Mexicans [Spanish Indian allies], and that we were a pack of mongrels and whoremongers."[33] Throughout the entire encounter, reported the Spaniards, the Indians, "in their own language" as well as in "Mexican" (that is, Nahuatl), kept shouting that they wanted to fight.[34] The Indians, Zaldívar said, asked in defiance, "why were we waiting, and why we did not fight, since they were ready for battle and [they] were waiting for nothing but to kill us and then kill the Queres and the Tiguas and everyone at Zia because they failed to kill the Spaniards."[35]

At three o'clock in the afternoon of January 22, 1599, the attack began. Under cover of darkness the previous night, twelve Spaniards had dragged a small cannon around the rear and hid themselves. The next day, when the attack began, the main body of troops, as a diversion, climbed up the front ladderways. The Acomans engaged the intruders, leaving the rear of the pueblo unprotected. Soon the twelve Spaniards had reached the top and fired their cannon into the pueblo.[36] Meanwhile, Zaldívar, seeing a warrior wearing his brother's uniform, fought his way toward him, finally killing him with his sword. Night ended the first day's battle to take the pueblo. Many Indians had surrendered, but a large body of warriors had hidden themselves in the chasms.

The next day the battle continued from early morning until five o'clock that afternoon. Zaldívar again asked them to surrender. The Acomans refused, and the battle resumed. Escaping from the Spaniards, "The Indians ran from house to house and killed each other without sparing their children, however small, or their wives."[37] Zaldívar ordered that "all Indian women and children who could be found should be taken prisoners to save them from being killed by the Indian warriors."[38] About 500 young and old men and women were taken for that purpose. The *sargento mayor* ordered the soldiers to proceed without quarter, setting fire to all of the houses and even the provisions. Spanish arms and assault tactics were too much for the courageous and most feared warriors from Acoma. Zaldívar "ordered them [the Indians in the houses] taken out one by one, and, at least one Indian (likely a Nahua-speaking Mexican Indian ally among others who had accompanied the expedition) stabbed them to death and hurled them down the rock."[39] The fall of Acoma shook its inhabitants but did not break them, for most of them would escape and rebuild their pueblo and continue to defy the Spaniards and challenge other pueblos to resist Spanish control of the area. Years later, in 1601, it was reported that the Acomans were still living in their pueblo. In 1602 Zaldívar testified that Acoma "remains peaceful to this day."[40] Indeed, in 1613 Acoma warriors, back to full strength, successfully defended Acoma against a Spanish attack.

The 1599 defenders of Acoma had been subdued for the moment, and they were taken to Santo Domingo Pueblo for trial. There Captain Alonso Gómez Montesinos served as their appointed attorney and guardian. On February 9, 1599, Spaniards and Indians gathered to hear the testimony of those who had taken part in the battle of Acoma. Statements were taken from Acoman warriors named Caoma, Cat-Ticati, Taxio, Xunusta, Excasi, Caucachi, and others.[41] Statements made by the Acomans were sometimes contradictory. For example, when asked why they killed Juan de Zaldívar and his men, Xunusta replied that "the Spaniards first killed an Indian, and then all the Indians became very angry and killed them." Caucachi, on the other hand, said they killed Juan de Zaldívar, ten men, and two servants because they had wounded an Acoma Indian and for this reason his people became angry and killed them. Excasi responded to the same question by saying that "they killed the Spaniards because a soldier either asked for or took a turkey."[42]

Asked why they did not accept peace when Sargento Mayor Vicente de Zaldívar asked them not to fight, they basically gave the same response: "some wanted peace, others did not; but because they could not agree, they would not submit."[43] Similarly, they added that they did not accept peace because they had already killed Spaniards and that "the old people and other leading Indians did not want peace, and for this reason they attacked with arrows and stones."[44] The next day, Captain Gómez Montesinos presented a petition to Oñate in behalf of the Acomans. He declared:

> I, Captain Alonso Gómez Montesinos, defense attorney for the Indians, state that I have frequently explained to them through the interpreter that if they have any pleas to offer or any witnesses to present in their defense, they should have them appear so that the appropriate inquiries may be made. They replied that they had no witnesses or defense pleas to offer for having killed the Spaniards. This being the case, their only defense was that many of them were not guilty as they were absent when the Spaniards were killed, and they were unaware of the crime the others had committed. For this reason and from what was learned in the testimony that your lordship took from some of the Indians, you should acquit them, set them free, allow them to go wherever they wish, and order that they be compensated for the expenses resulting from their arrest. Wherefore, I beseech your lordship to grant this petition and show clemency to the Indians in view of the fact that they are uncivilized.[45]

Gómez Montesinos pleaded the case in colonial terms, expressing his compassion for the Acomans as well as revealing his Eurocentric view of the natives under his charge.

After other pleas for clemency, the three-day trial at Santo Domingo came to an end. On February 12, Oñate read out the sentence that would harshly punish the Acomans for "having wantonly killed don Juan de Zaldívar Oñate, two captains, eight soldiers, and two servants, and for having refused the peace offered them by Vicente de Zaldívar. I must and do sentence all of the Indian men and women from the said pueblo under arrest."[46] Boys and girls under twelve years of age whose parents were involved in fighting against the Spaniards were placed under the guardianship of the missionaries.[47] Those between twelve and twenty-five years of age were sentenced to twenty years of servitude. The elderly men and women were freed but entrusted to the Querechos, Indians from the Great Plains, who "may not allow them to leave their pueblos."[48] Then Oñate read the sentence that brought protests from the colonials themselves. "The males," ordered Oñate, "who are over twenty-five years of age, I sentence to have one foot cut off and to twenty years of personal servitude."[49] According to one settler, Captain Luis Gasco de Velasco, the sentence would be carried out against twenty-four Acoma males at Santo Domingo and at other nearby pueblos on separate days. In opposition, some of the Spanish settlers helped as many Acomans as they could to escape. Still, the swift and severe punishment of Acoma had evidently served its purpose. Agitated by the battle at Acoma and its aftermath, other Pueblo Indians continued to defy Spanish rule in New Mexico, but Oñate's force was sufficient to quiet them.

The battle at Acoma should also be seen against the travails of Oñate's settlers. If, in 1599, the settlers protested the Acoma sentences, they vented their anger at Oñate's excesses against them as well. When, for example, four soldiers deserted Oñate's force, he, under the authority granted him by the viceroy to hold the colony together, sent two captains, Gaspar Villagrá and Gerónimo Márquez, to track them down as they fled along the Río Abajo and to execute them for desertion. Somewhere in Chihuahua, the deserters were surprised, captured, and executed. As proof that they were dead, their right hands were cut off, preserved in salt, and presented to Oñate.[211] Resentment among the settlers began to build against Oñate. In time, the settlers brought charges against him and Zaldívar in 1613 for their excesses against them. Both were found guilty, heavily fined, and banished from New Mexico.[50] They lost all of their landholdings and investments in the establishment of New Mexico, a heavy price for a colonial to pay.

Historiographical writings, in this case, the collective literature about the battle at Acoma and its aftermath, are often based on earlier historical literature and are sometimes repeated verbatim without question. The study of history is, indeed, an academic discipline, which, by extension, evolves into a body of historical literature on a particular subject. The writing of history should be based on a critical analysis, not only regarding the immediate event, but also the related broader story in order to achieve a multifactor analysis. The achievement of such a critical analysis includes the use of authentic sources, which may include archival documents, archaeological reports, and, to an extent, lore. Linguistically, as the documents were written in seventeenth-century Spanish, early historians were limited in their abilities to interpret accurately the information in them. Often much was lost in translation. In many cases, research opportunities in the distant Spanish and Mexican archives were also limited. Researchers, thus, were left to use the scant documentation available to them at the time. Still, while today many more of the facts surrounding the battle at Acoma and its causes and aftermath are known from the historical documents of the period, they often suffer from interpretation biases of narrators. Yet the more accurate historical perspective is that the battle at Acoma was not an isolated case and should be interpreted as part of the broader story associated with the European expansion throughout the Indian world of the Americas well into the nineteenth century (see appendix B).

About six months after the battle at Acoma, a second major altercation led to a deadly confrontation between Indian warriors and Spanish soldiers. The resulting provocation, known by historians as the "Jumano War," was deeply rooted in the region's Indigenous struggle for survival. The stored native foods, for example, never had a surplus that could have supplied Spanish exploring parties. At the same time, Oñate and his soldiers expected obedience, as representatives of the sovereign, based on their belief that the pueblos had indeed sworn sovereignty. If blind obedience was expected, it would not be easily forthcoming from the pueblos, unless under duress and as a way of survival. To the pueblos, the thought of giving up their provisions from their food supply was antagonistic. Especially, the pueblos that faced the Great Plains, such as the Salinas pueblos, depended on trade for a portion of their food supply. Supplemented by hunting, gathering salt and piñon nuts for trade, and dry farming, the Salinas pueblos, such as Las Humanas, Quivira, and Abó, far from the water sources of Rio Grande, had reason to resent having to share their stores. Still, to Oñate and his men, aside from the denial of their need for food, such disobedience and insolence toward Spanish sovereignty was subject to a military corrective. To not commit to action was, as seen in the case of Acoma, tantamount to leaving an enemy at one's back. In the Spanish colonial mind, it could only lead to annihilation of their settlement. Both sides were caught in a conundrum that in the context of the times could have only one outcome. Each side viewed such moments in terms of survival. Still, the pueblos throughout New Mexico watched the Spaniards with growing animosity.

In July 1599, Sargento Mayor Vicente de Zaldívar and twenty-five men explored westward toward the mountains of present-day Arizona. Following the familiar trail from the provincial headquarters to the Galisteo pueblos, the troop marched southward behind the great Sandia-Manzano mountain range toward the Salinas Salinas Pueblos. There he visited "a pueblo of the Jumanos," probably today's Gran Quivira, to collect provisions for his expedition.[51] At that place lived a group of Indians known to the Spaniards as *indios rayados*, Indians who "wore a stripe painted across their nose."[52] Beset with hunger and exhaustion, the Spaniards asked them for food, but the Indians, feigning ignorance, instead gave them stones. Outnumbered by the warriors, Zaldívar and his men moved on, but not before sending a messenger to Oñate about the insult. The Spaniards were not likely to forget this affront to Spanish authority.[53]

At first opportunity to avenge the insult, Governor Oñate set out with fifty men to collect "what they call in that land the 'tribute of the mantas [blankets].'"[54] Before he set out to collect the tribute, Oñate remarked to an acquaintance that he wanted to punish the Jumanos for their insolence toward his nephew.[55] The army headed toward the saline pueblos. When they arrived at the "pueblo de los Jumanes," the governor (through an interpreter who spoke their language) asked for the required blankets. Quickly the Indians gathered twelve or fourteen and gave them to him. Speaking through an interpreter, they said they had no more to give him.[56] The Spaniards withdrew to a watering place not far from the pueblo and camped for the night.

That night at camp Oñate and his men discussed the meager tribute that to them seemed analogous to Zaldívar's treatment. The next morning the governor and his army stood outside the pueblos walls. Through an interpreter he told them that he was "going to punish them because they had refused to furnish the sargento mayor with provision, and those who submitted peacefully he would treat kindly."[57]

At the governor's signal, the soldiers set fire to certain groups of houses.[58] Whereupon the warriors took to the rooftops and terrace to defend themselves with stones and arrows. Oñate then ordered that they be showered "with a volley of harquebus shots."[59] In seconds five or six Indians fell dead, and others clutched at their wounds as they looked for safe quarters. A soldier who thought the interpreter had incited the Indians reported him to the governor. After the battle, Oñate ordered the interpreter and some warlike Indians hanged.[60] One colonial, who believed the resistance had been quelled, wrote, "The Indians of that province are all orderly, peaceful and timid, and live in great fear of the Spaniards."[61] But even as the Spaniards rode away, resentment among the Jumanos grew stronger against them.

The Jumanos bided their time. In late December 1600 five soldiers attempted to abandon New Mexico,[62] bound for *tierra de paz* (land of peace), as New Spain was sometime called. On their way, they "passed by the Pueblo of Abo," where, for some reason, they were attacked and two of them, Juan de Castañeda and Bernabé Santillan, were killed. Three men escaped the melee and reported the attack to Oñate.⁶³ Word of the violence at Abó spread quickly, and the entire land, Indian and Spanish, was aroused.

Anxiously, the Spanish settlers met at San Gabriel, New Mexico's second capital, established in 1599, to discuss the gravity of their situation. From the survivors' reports, they viewed the attack as having been unprovoked. Rumors abounded that the Indians at Salinas were organizing and preparing for war.⁶⁴ The province was imperiled. Petitioning the governor to punish Abó, the settlers hoped to make their attack an object lesson for the rest of the pueblo world that would dare to conspire to kill Spaniards. The friars and the leading colonials went to the governor's home to rationalize their request to attack Abó. They explained to him the laws and defined what constituted "just and unjust war." To them the Indians had provoked Spanish antagonism; therefore, Oñate would be within his rights to order a punitive expedition against them. As the governor had planned to leave on an expedition to the South Sea (Pacific Ocean), the settlers petitioned him to postpone his trip until the matter with Abó had been settled. Furthermore, they asked that Vicente de Zaldívar, on account of his high birth and proven valor, be appointed to conduct the operation.⁶⁵ Don Juan agreed to both requests and ordered Zaldívar to pick seventy men to attack the pueblo of Abó.⁶⁶

By now the horse trail from the provincial capital to Salinas had been worn to a visible trace on the ground. Zaldívar, one of the discoverers of Abó, or at least one of the first Europeans to realize its Indian name, must have winced at the irony that he should also be its destroyer. For some unknown reasons, the expedition delayed its march until spring 1601.⁶⁷ Swinging southeastward around the Sierra de Puaray (present Sandia Mountains), the small army stopped to camp. At that point, they were less than one day's ride from Abó.

The next day before they reached Abó, "many Indians . . . with arrows" attacked the Spanish vanguard.⁶⁸ Zaldívar brought up the rest of the troops and with a swift charge forced the Indians to retreat to a nearby pueblo—"Agualagu," someone called it, one of the lesser-known Indian towns near the salines. The Spanish scouts reported that they were attacked by a mixed group of warriors from the nearby Jumano, Tompiro, and possibly Tiwa settlements. The ambush had brought the Spanish army to a halt.

Through "two or three" interpreters, Zaldívar called out to the warriors.⁶⁹ He wanted to talk peace with them and promised justice. But the memory of Oñate's earlier attack on one of their pueblos remained vivid.

The warriors were unwilling to trust Zaldívar. Instead, they responded with a daring volley of arrows and stones.[70] Undaunted, the *maese de campo* waited for the offenders to settle down, and then he approached them again and repeated his offer. The warriors looked at him from behind their walls and made no response. To no avail, Zaldívar tried to talk peace with them several times.

Within the first moments of the Indians' retreat into Agualagu, the Spaniards had laid siege to the pueblo. The Spaniards estimated that 200 Indians—old men, women, and children, aside from the warriors—were in the pueblo. The siege lasted six days and five nights. By day the warriors demonstrated with arrows and stones (and clubs), and at night some tried to escape through the tight cordon of Spanish troops around Agualagu. The soldiers fought back and, at one point, set fire to a block of houses in the pueblo. From time to time Zaldívar called out to negotiate peace, but the Indians refused to listen. Once when Zaldívar came too close to the pueblo, the warriors were ready. They took dead aim and clobbered the *maese de campo* with a barrage of rocks and arrows. Badly injured, Zaldívar escaped death. Although he continued the battle, he was unable to mount his horse throughout the siege without assistance from his men.[71]

On the fifth day of the siege, a large number of old men, women, and children tried to escape. The injured Zaldívar rallied his men and led the maneuver to apprehend them. Realizing that they were noncombatants, the Spaniards moved the terrified Indians away from the pueblo and gave them water and food. Then Zaldívar addressed them. Sternly he told them how they should live and that they should not kill Spaniards. The soldiers took a count of "four hundred or more of them," and then Zaldívar released them. But the siege had also worked a hardship on the Spaniards, and their supplies were running low.

The warriors had watched it all from the pueblo. They also knew that Zaldívar suffered greatly from his wounds. Emboldened by what they saw, the warriors decided to break the siege. The warriors sallied out from behind the wall, shooting their arrows and slinging rocks at the Spaniards. Limping to his horse, Zaldívar mounted it with difficulty and turned to lead the charge against them.[72] Seeing Zaldívar's resolve, the warriors ran back to the pueblo. They had had enough. They knew they could not defeat the Spaniards. They surrendered.[73]

One of the Spaniards, Captain Gerónimo Márquez, opined that the peace was not harsh.[74] After the Jumanos had surrendered, he said, Zaldívar "pardoned all the Indians, men and women, and set many free; and that he assigned one of the most guilty to each soldier as compensation for the hardship he had endured; and that this assignment was without title of any kind, so that of the Indians brought here hardly one is left who has not returned to his land."[75] Another soldier, Captain Francisco de Rascón confirmed Márquez's statement, by noting that Zaldívar had "set them all free, admonishing them to be loyal or he would have them all killed." Accordingly, he released all but seventy warriors, of which, in the European tradition of "just war," one was given to each of his soldiers to compensate them for their service. One soldier reported, "Of the Indians that he distributed among the soldiers, this witness does not believe that four are left, as all ran away and returned to their land."[76] Rascón reported that most of them had "run away by now."[77] Some likely had escaped or been allowed to escape by the soldiers in route to San Gabriel.

Although the siege of Agualagu was a terrifying experience to those who withstood the Spaniards, the Indians could point to a sort of victory. They had stopped the Spaniards before they could reach their objective. Short of supplies and energy, the injured Zaldívar turned his troops around and headed home. Abó went unpunished. As for Agualagu, the portion of it that had been burned by the Spaniards was rebuilt when the Indians returned. Still, resentment and fear of the Spaniards ran deep. With the departure of Zaldívar and his troops, the Jumano War came to an end. The Indians of Salinas never again raised arms against the Spaniards and in their own way submitted to Spanish rule.

7

Oñate's Exploration of the Great Plains

> After meeting these people, we saw some of their *rancherías*, which consist of small tents made of tanned hides which they pitch and dismantle very easily; they pack them on small dogs like ours, which have sores from their packs. When they travel an Indian woman leads the way, followed by the laden dog; then the other pack dogs follow in a single file, followed by the women and children. The men travel at a distance to one side within sight, in battle array, scouting for the enemy, or game such as buffalo or deer. The never stay long at any one place, because they always follow the cattle.
>
> —Juan de León, 1602[1]

Just before the battle at Acoma, Vicente de Zaldívar had returned from his reconnaissance of the Great Plains in search of the route taken by Leyba de Bonilla. He reported his findings to Oñate. Still, unanswered questions remained. Were there, for example, any survivors? After the battle at Acoma, Oñate turned his attention to the mystery regarding Leyba de Bonilla's expedition. Indeed, Oñate's mission was far from over; after all, he had been ordered by the viceroy to investigate the whereabouts of Leyba de Bonilla and his men and, assuming they were still alive, to arrest them for illegal entry into New Mexico and return them to Mexico City for trial. Reporting on the status of his mission in 1599, Oñate wrote to the viceroy, the Count of Monterey saying, "I reached these provinces on the twenty-eighth day of May [1598] . . . to pacify the land and free it from traitors, seizing Humaña and his followers, to obtain full information, by seeing with my own eyes, regarding the location and nature of the land, and regarding the nature and customs of the people."[2] At that time, after talking to Jusepe, Oñate learned of the fate of Leyba de Bonilla, but he wondered what had happened to Gutíerrez de Humaña.

Having received the viceroy's blessings to venture beyond the newly established Spanish settlement at San Juan de lo Caballeros, Oñate and his men were soon to be tested by Great Plains tribes and their notions of intrusions onto their land. Pursuant to his viceregal instructions, Governor Oñate, on June 23, 1601,[3] led eighty soldiers eastward, stopping to gather provisions from the pueblos along the way before moving eastward beyond Galisteo to explore the plains and its resources and people. Additionally, he hoped to verify and find out more about the fate of Leyba de Bonilla and Gutíerrez de Humaña. Oñate motioned his men to move out alongside the eight-*carreta* caravan loaded with munitions, provisions, tools, artillery, and arms.[4] Besides his soldiers, Father Francisco de Velasco, Fray Pedro de Vergara, Jusepe, as guide and translator, and a number of camp tenders also accompanied him. Maese de Campo Vicente de Zaldívar led a scouting party in advance of the main body. Oñate explained that he went there "both because of the splendid reports which the native Indians were giving of this land, and also because of what an Indian named Joseph [Jusepe], who was born and reared in New Spain and who speaks the Mexican tongue, saw while going with Captain Umaña."[5] Amazed by the large buffalo herds, Oñate and his men recognized that once on the plains, "no one can die of hunger because of the innumerable buffalo herds that are there; the plains are so extensive that no one has seen their end and conclusion."[6]

The resources that the land bred up were evident to them as they moved northeast across the plains. Probably near the land traversed by Leyba de Bonilla and Gutíerrez de Humaña, as Jusepe had said, Oñate and his men saw "quantities of plums" and called the place "Las Ciruelas." In 1599,

Zaldívar had also passed by there.[7] In that area Oñate and his men "saw great grazing grounds, beautiful fields, a great deal of water, fertile land for farming, and a good climate. . . . traveling in a straight line they reached the fertile promised land, where the fields [grew] without any cultivation, produce grapes, plums in great abundance and many other fruits. Although there are Indians on the plains they are not settled in any definite place. . . . they sustain themselves with this livestock."[8] The explorers noted that the Indians, whom they called vaqueros, followed the herds and lived off the land and did not farm or harvest crops. Generally, they tanned hides and traded them to the pueblos and other Indian settlements for corn and corn flour.

Days later, as they approached the settlements closer to the Arkansas River, they noted unattended fields of corn growing wild on the Plains, which supplemented the diets of the inhabitants. Similarly, Oñate noted that as they went farther northeast into the interior, they soon found themselves "surrounded on all sides by fields of maize and crops of the Indians. The stalks of the maize were as high as that of New Spain and in many places even higher. The land was so rich that, having harvested the maize, a new growth of a span in height had sprung up over a large portion of the same ground without any cultivation or labor other than the removal of the weeds and the making of holes where they planted the maize. There were many beans, some gourds, and, between the fields, some plum trees. The crops were not irrigated but dependent on the rains, which, as we noted, must be very regular in that land."[9] The Spaniards were aware that while buffalo herds sustained the large populations on the plains, there were other food resources that they were surprised to see and that contributed to their diets.

Traveling farther into the Great Plains, Oñate and his entourage moved northeastward where they met Plains tribes and exchanged the traditional greeting of raising the palms of their hands toward the sun as a sign of peace. At one rancheria south of the Arkansas River, they encountered the Escanjaques, a warring tribe that "was at war with the people [of Quivira] eight leagues distant toward the interior, and they, thinking that we were going to avenge the murder of the Spaniards who had entered with Umaña, of course took the opportunity to throw the blame upon their enemies [the Quiviras] and to tell us that it was they who had killed them."[10] Meanwhile, the Spaniards learned that the Quiviras, on the other side of the Arkansas River, had hoped to meet them, "but since they saw them in the company of their enemies the

Escanjaques, they were afraid."[11] The Escanjaques hoped that Oñate would ally with them against the Quiviras, but he wisely chose not to get involved.

In 1626, Fray Gerónimo Zárate Salmerón wrote his *Relaciones de todas cosas*, in which he noted that the Escanjaques informed Oñate that Gutiérrez de Humaña and his men had met their deaths in the land of the Quiviras. Zárate Salmerón noted, "In this place they say that they killed Humaña and his companions when they were returning loaded with gold; here were found remains of this, for some articles of iron were found, some *botas*, and the bones of the horses; the way they killed them was to set fire to the camp while they were resting. Only one Spanish boy, named Alonso Sánchez, and a partly burned mulatto woman escaped. When this expedition was made, they say she was alive and that she was three days' journey from this pueblo.[12] This Alonso, the Indians told me, was alive a few years ago and because of his great courage, was a captain, and very feared by the Indians." They also learned that near there, were "seven small hills on a plain, from where the Ahijados take out the gold which they refine. Nothing was done about any of this."[13] The Escanjaques, noted Oñate, thought "that we were going for this purpose only, they were much pleased and offered to accompany us, and as we were unable to prevent it, lest we should cause them to make trouble, they went." The Indians guided them seven leagues northward to the Arkansas River, filled with "wonderful banks, and, although level, so densely wooded that the trees formed thick and wide groves."[14] Still, Oñate did not trust those who accompanied them. Later, he reported, "they threw off their disguise and shamefully made war on us."[15]

Meanwhile, some Escanjaque warriors guided Oñate and his men northward to the "large river." After crossing the Arkansas River, the Spanish expedition traveled four leagues into hostile territory where they were challenged to battle by other Plains Indians, probably the Quiviras, who "inviting us to battle and war, shouting and throwing dirt into the air, which is a sign used in all of this region to proclaim cruel war."[16] Finally, they were able to meet peacefully and exchanged gifts as the tribe declared friendship. Oñate learned firsthand "that in this region they had murdered the Spaniards, surrounding them with fire and burning them all, and that they had with them one who had escaped, injured by the fire."[17]

Oñate proceeded northward, reaching the Little Arkansas near present-day Wichita, Kansas, where they met a new informant. There, wrote Oñate,

We took new information from the Indian, who appeared to be one of the caciques or lords of the land, regarding what there was further ahead, and he informed us that up the river were settled people like these in large numbers and that at one side was another large river which divided into six or seven branches, on all of which there were many people, and that the people whom Umaña had brought had been killed eighteen days' journey from here. We compared the statements of these Indians with those of Indians of the rancheria who had remained in our company, and without discrepancy in any point they said the same, adding that down the river also, going due east, it was all settled by people.[18]

Oñate, according to Zárate Salmerón, "ordered some soldiers to go inland. They traveled one full day and returned to say that they had not come to the end of the settlement, and the Indians had said that it was very large and that further to the north there were other larger ones."[19]

Oñate's men argued that his objectives had been met in terms of reconnoitering the land and learning about the people. They stressed the dangers they faced by continuing to explore the area. They had, moreover, learned about the fate of Gutiérrez de Humaña and his men. Listening to their sage advice, Oñate ordered the expedition to return to New Mexico. Besides, their horses and mules were jaded, and his men, desiring to return, were similarly tired after having traveled many leagues through hostile territory. They had already spent nearly five months on the trail. At that point, Oñate deemed it foolhardy to continue exploring the area.

Turning the expedition southward, Oñate and his men knew that they would have to pass through the land of the Escanjaques. Warned by the people of Quivira, Oñate realized that he could not trust them. They warned him, wrote Oñate, that "under no circumstances should we proceed, saying that the people who had withdrawn from the settlement had done so in order on the third day to assemble their friends, who were so numerous that in the course of a whole day they would not be able to pass by their houses, and that undoubtedly, our number being so small, they would soon put an end to us, not a single person escaping."[20]

Meanwhile, Oñate ordered Zaldívar to press forward to see what awaited them. Moving about three leagues through the populated area, Zaldívar noticed that a great assembly of people in the extended settlement had rapidly increased. He quickly discovered that the trap set by the swarming warriors would easily envelop them if Oñate and his men moved forward. Just then, some warriors approached Zaldívar's scouting party. At first, the Indians showed him signs of peace as they walked forward. Then suddenly, "on the run [they] began to surround him and his companions, with bows and arrows in their hands; but he, like a good soldier, did not give them a chance to do so, for, retreating in good order, he emerged from among them with no more damage than the loss of a horse or a couple of arrow wounds."[21] Oñate would soon taste the violence of Plains Indian warfare.

Noting the hostility around them and fearing an ambush, Oñate ordered his men to put on protective armor for themselves and their horses. He also issued express orders that "all should enter in peace."[22] Then the Escanjaques, estimated at 1,500 warriors,[23] set up a battle line in a semicircle and attacked with great fury. Still, Oñate hoped that the warriors would back off.[24] The warriors pressed for an all-out attack and let a shower of arrows fall on the Spaniards. Only then did Oñate give "the signal to his people to defend themselves. . . . The brave soldiers showed an excess of courage and spirit, and in a short while repelled the attack of the people, killing and wounding many of a group who were stationed at an arroyo, whereas only two of our soldiers were wounded."[25] But the warriors regrouped and furiously attacked again. By now, the greater part of the Spanish soldiers were wounded. Seeing that many warriors were dead as a result of Spanish firepower, Oñate ordered a retreat and returned to a safer campsite. After two hours, Oñate's men repulsed the offensive. Although the Indians suffered many casualties, dead and wounded, they were unafraid of the firepower of the Spaniards. Cautiously, the expedition left the land of the Escanjaques with some captives, including an Indian the Spaniards called "Miguel." Two decades later, Zárate Salmerón, in his *Relaciones*, repeated the story of the Escanjaques' costly attack on the Spaniards. He wrote that "much to their sorrow . . . about a thousand died, and of the Spaniards, not one was dangerously hurt, although many were wounded."[26]

Escaping the land of war on the plains, Oñate and his men warily crossed back into New Mexico. They had explored far into the interior of the Great Plains, reaching as far northeast as present Wichita, Kansas. The expedition had yielded much information for Spanish officials in Mexico City as well as Oñate's settlers at San Gabriel, New Mexico's second capital, which had been moved a half mile from San Juan de los Caballeros to the confluence of the Chama River and the Rio Grande in 1599. While the resources were described, the cultures of the various Plains tribes they had encountered were also noted. Oñate's fear of the large populations of Plains tribes, which he had seen firsthand, clearly alarmed him about the clear and present danger to the Spanish settlement in New Mexico being overrun by them. His report and accompanying affirmation by his men documented that singular fact. Testimony given by the Spanish soldiers confirmed the large populations and the numerous settlements they saw on the plains. They said that according to Indian informants, some of the rancherias contained "more than five or six thousand souls, [which] they represented by making a circle with seventeen kernels of maize; and for many of the settlements beyond they placed in the circles many grains of maize; and for one in particular they placed seven hundred and twenty-seven kernels of maize, which, in the opinion of all or most of those who were present, meant two hundred thousand people and more, and this in but one of the many settlements which they indicated."[27] Thus, the Spaniards had reason to respect the power of the Plains tribes.

After five months of exploration, fifty-nine days of which they had spent in the interior of the Great Plains, they returned to their new settlement at San Gabriel at the confluence of the Chama and Rio Grande. By Oñate's count, they had indeed traveled "more than two hundred and twenty leagues [approximately 624 miles]" from San Gabriel.[28] Oñate's absence from San Gabriel during his five-month exploration of the Great Plain, however, had cost him the total political control over his settlers that he had previously enjoyed. He returned to San Gabriel to find that some of settlers had deserted the colony, and others, resentful of his leadership, had sent damning reports about him to Mexico City.

Meanwhile, Spanish officials in Mexico City tended to one order of business that involved the captive named "Miguel," taken in the battle with the Escanjaques. Indeed Zárate Salmerón noted that "two Indians of the Aijado nation [were captured] . . . one was a little boy, and the other was a lad; when they baptized those two, they gave them the name of Miguel, because the battle had been on the día de San Miguel."[29] On April 29, 1602, Miguel, who had been taken to Mexico City by Vicente de Zaldívar, answered questions posed to him by Spanish officials. They met at the home of the factor don Francisco de Valverde y Mercado, who was in charge of investigating the situation of

New Mexico following complaints against Governor Oñate. In this instance, Miguel, communicating through signs, answered their question as best he could about his country and people. Of his homeland, Miguel said that he was born in Tancoa. By signs, he indicated that as a boy around age twelve he had been taken as a prisoner in a battle between his people and those of Aguacane.[30] He said he was "held a captive there until the Spaniards came and the Indians of Aguacane and its district went to war against the Spaniards near the Great Settlement, and that he was taken prisoner and brought to San Gabriel and then to the city by the maese de campo, Vicente de Zaldívar."[31] One of Oñate's men, Baltazar Martinez, had earlier verified Miguel's story that in the midst of the battle "the governor, in order to avoid killing the women and children, halted the attack. Eight or ten boys and girls were taken in the skirmish, including the Indian Miguel. This put an end to the fight."[32]

Hoping to learn more from Miguel about the Great Plains in terms of people, land, and resources, Valverde y Mercado organized a list of examples to direct the answers given by young Plains Indian. Assembling a number of Mexican Indians, some daubed with war paint, others striped (*rayados*), dressed in battle array or different costumes, Valverde y Mercado brought them before Miguel to see what he could identify from their presence. Some wore blankets called *tilmas*, such as those worn on the Great Plains. They were presented to Miguel in order that he might see them and identify where on the plains they could be located.[33] Miguel looked over the Mexican Indians in the room. By signs he indicated "that in his land and in others reached by the Spaniards there were Indian like these, daubed and striped, although they were all naked except for deerskins, to which he pointed, each Indian wearing two, and they also had hides from the native cattle."[34] They showed him arrows, with and without flint points. Miguel said "that where he was born and reared they have large bows with long flint-headed arrows, and he pointed to the largest bows and arrow that the Indians had. He said that at the Great Settlement reached by the Spaniards, the Indian used small bows and short, black arrows."[35]

One other exhibit of metals brought to Valverde y Mercado's house included a large ingot of gold, small ingots of silver, copper, brass, and low-grade gold trinkets with ancient designs found in New Spain. They asked Miguel to show which ones he could identify and tell if they could be found in his land. He indicated that there was no silver, copper, or brass in his land.[36]

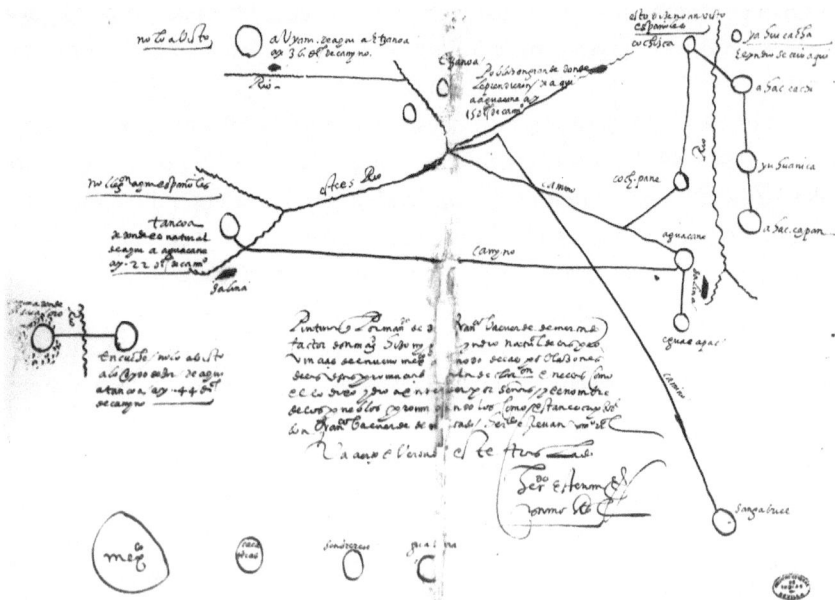

FIGURE 7.1. Miguel's map of the Great Plains, 1602, Center for Southwest Research Collection, Zimmerman Library, University of New Mexico.

As for the large gold ingot, Miguel pointed to the map that, although he had not been there, he had heard that gold could be found at Encuche. The people of Encuche traded their gold at Tancoa and other places to obtain meat and hides.[37] The Spaniard showed him gold dust. Miguel said that he knew of gold only in the form of ingots. Pressed for information, Miguel said that the Indians obtained gold from the river at Encuche. He said that he had heard that there was a lake beyond Encuche that contained gold dust, from where it was taken "to Encuche where it was made into ingots."[38] He said he had twice seen gold ingots made from dust at Tancoa. "They placed the gold dust in some vases that had a hole in each of the four sides," he said, "and that at each hole a man put in wood and fanned the fire with some fans made of buffalo hide. Keeping the vase covered three or four days, they melted the gold and made the ingots of the size stated."[39] Miguel marked the location of the lake on his map.

The Spaniards showed Miguel other items such as green turquoise, which he did not recognize as being on the Great Plains. Another exhibit consisted of skins of tigers, lions, and deer for him to identify.⁴⁰ Apparently, Miguel knew only about turkeys, mountain lions, wolves, bears, buffalo, coyotes, and deer.

Hoping to identify other resources on the Great Plains, they showed Miguel "a bunch of flowers (*suchil*) . . . containing roses, poppies, and camomiles." Asked if any were found in his land, Miguel examined them and only identified what appeared to be "a carnation plant and flower," of which he said there were many in his land.⁴¹ Miguel said that corn grew plentiful in his land, the *metates*, or grinding stones, were smaller than those in New Spain, but there was "corn in his land and in the Great Settlement reached by the Spaniards, but there was none at the place he was held captive, because there are cattle and deer meat."⁴²

Next, by signs, they asked Miguel to indicate the location of Indian settlements in his land by marking them on a sheet of paper with a plume pen. He marked the paper with circles, some larger than others in a way that spatially, in a geographic way, made sense to him. In that way, with the aid of translators, Miguel made a map leading from Mexico City to Zacatecas, New Mexico, and the Great Plains. According to his testimony, he next "drew lines, some snakelike and others straight and indicated by signs that they were rivers and roads; they were given names, according to his explanation."⁴³ The distances between places on the Great Plains were great. Miguel said that "from the pueblo of Tancoa, where he was born, to the place he was taken captive and grew up, it was twenty-two days' travel, counting the days with kernels of corn. From the Great Settlement where the Spaniards took him prisoner to the place where he was held captive by the Indians, it was fifteen days' travel. From his pueblo of Tancoa to Encuche, where gold is found, it was forty-four days; from the pueblo of Tzanoa to Vyana, shown on his map, he heard that it was thirty-six days. He did no know how far it was from his pueblo of Tancoa to Vyana."⁴⁴

Skeptical but wanting to believe what Miguel had told them, Valverde y Mercado noted, "This Indian Miguel was not asked regarding his contradiction when he said he was taken captive in his land when he was a boy and carried to Aguacane and had never returned to it again and then said that he twice saw gold ingots made in his land when he was a man; moreover, he had also said that he had never seen gold dust brought to his land, but only ingots and cups. There was no way of explaining this contradiction to him."⁴⁵

The story of Miguel did not end there. After his testimony, the Spaniards took Miguel to the house of the chief *alguacil* until a decision could be made regarding where to take him next.[46] It was said that later Miguel was taken to Spain.[47] Miguel accordingly lived the rest of his life there.

Although nothing ever came of the proposal made by officials in Mexico City recommending that the king outfit at least a 1,000-man expedition, of which a donor offered to outfit another 500 men, to go to the Great Plains to look for the mineral wealth that Miguel had mentioned. Father Zárate Salmerón quipped, "That is how things were left concerning this trip until God moves the heart of some rich man who wants to spend the money as a legacy."[48]

8

The Case against Juan de Oñate and Vicente de Zaldívar

In life, Juan de Oñate was never the hero of his own story, but rather the victim of his personal catastrophes.
    —*Marc Simmons, 1991*[1]

Historians, by helping to define "us" and "them," play a considerable part in focusing love and hate, the two principal cements of collective behavior known to humanity. But Myth making for rival groups has become a dangerous game . . . and we may well ask whether there is any alternative open to us.
    —*William H. McNeill, 1986*[2]

In his biography of Juan de Oñate, *The Last Conquistador: Juan de Oñate and the Settling of the far Southwest* (1991), Marc Simmons concurs with other historians who maintain, unapologetically, that Oñate's downfall resulted from a combination of factors, including "the vacillation and dalliance of royal officials, by the jealousy of rivals, and by the poverty of New Mexico [as well as] for the sake of completeness, that some of the blame doubtless could be traced to don Juan's own flaws."[3] Although Simmons is careful not to inject modern-day judgments in place of the sixteenth-century values of the period, his multifactored analysis points out that Oñate was, indeed, a controversial figure in his day for reasons not always understood in today's world. Oñate's legacy is beset by misconceptions, biases, and misinterpretations of the historical events surrounding his governorship of New Mexico. Yet Oñate in his day, as today, had both his defenders and detractors.

Recognition of the incongruity associated with chronology, language, cultural values, and a tradition of sovereignty that differ from our modern-day perceptions enhances our understanding of history and the historical process of how our modern day evolved. Indeed, in her editorial of November 10, 2017, Patricia Ortiz, although disapproving of any violence that occurred historically, similarly questions the unfair use of today's values in judging events that took place across time and culture. Given the diatribe by Oñate's detractors, Ortiz advocates balance and fair play with this sober reminder as follows:

> One cannot compare today's psyche to that of humans living during the time of exploration and European settlements. Life as we know it, today is pretty civilized. Back in Oñate's day, life was dreadfully cruel. The Indian was considered savage by Europeans but life across the ocean was just as savagely cruel. King Henry VIII had one of his wives brutally beheaded. Beheading was not unusual; centuries earlier, John the Baptist was another victim; Jesus was atrociously crucified, a common practice in some societies; people were horrendously skinned or burned alive. Violent scalping, human sacrificing and inhuman cannibalism were not unknown in the Americas by indigenous Indians. And in some societies, feet were unbelievably cut off. Why would Spanish Oñate be atypical in a ruthless world? Oñate was no more ruthless than the enemy holding a position parallel to his, an Indian Chief, or Popay for that matter, who became enemy to the Pueblos after the Revolt.[4]

Still, the general concern within the Hispanic community is that the attack against Oñate sometimes plays out in a generally toxic anti-Hispanic atmosphere.[5]

Notwithstanding such a criticism against Oñate, Simmons, basing his analyses on historical documentation, concludes that while Oñate "was disappointed with the way events in New Mexico turned out, he did not view his effort there as a failure. Even in the end, when every one of his projects had soured and his funds were exhausted, he was eager to stay on the Rio Grande and continued trying to develop the new but floundering realm he had hewn from the northern wilderness. Such dogged persistence was a hallmark of the conquistador's irreducible individualism."[6] Yet his single most notable accomplishment, establishing a Spanish colonial settlement in 1598, redefined the cultural landscape that, through a historical process, became modern New Mexico.

Because of the modern-day emphasis on the battle at Acoma, which is often seen in isolation in contrast to the world around it, the accomplishments of Oñate and his Hispanic settlers have often been overlooked or pushed aside. Long before the founding of Jamestown in 1607 and the establishment of the Virginia's General Assembly (1619), later known as the House of Burgesses, and the New England Town Hall (1620), Oñate and his settlers, in 1598, established the first capital and government institutions, including the cabildo, at San Juan de los Caballeros in New Mexico within the interior of North America. Accordingly, the Laws of the Indies specifically required a governing institution in the form of a *cabildo* or town council presided over by a mayor (*alcalde mayor*) as the executive officer, who reported to the governor. Such a requirement, based on Greco-Roman tradition, became part of the European practice as well as a standard of government throughout the Spanish Empire. Practice and tradition merged in New Mexico in 1598.

In 1599, Oñate and his settlers moved to a new settlement at San Gabriel at the confluence of the Chama River and the Rio Grande. Subsequently, in 1610, Governor Pedro de Peralta moved the *cabildo* of San Gabriel to Santa Fe. Once built in the Plaza de Santa Fe, Governor Peralta firmly situated the Cabildo de Santa Fe in the Palace of the Governors, where it remained for the next 211 years. Later, during the Mexican territorial period (1821–48) under Mexico, the *cabildo*, known as the *ayuntamiento* or *asamblea* of Santa Fe, remained in the Palace of the Governors. Finally, during New Mexico's territorial period (throughout the late nineteenth century leading into statehood), the Palace of the Governors housed the Territorial Legislature under the United States. Today, a mere few blocks from the Plaza de Santa Fe, the New Mexico State Legislature is housed at the "Round House."

Oñate's settlement of New Mexico, furthermore, introduced new possibilities for the future that included a new spoken and written language, the

Spanish culture with an oral tradition, a new religion, an agrarian economy based on livestock such as horses, mules, oxen, sheep, and goats as well as farming techniques inclusive of a legally regulated watering system that utilized acequias (irrigation canals) and new produce such as apples, peaches, wheat, and chiles, mining techniques and associated ordinances, a European technology and medicine, and, among other important contributions, a genealogical pool that continues to reach into the future. Importantly, the connecting route of the Camino Real de Tierra Adentro (Royal Road of the Interior), based on Native American footpaths, changed over time to suit horse, mule, oxen, and wagons. The part blazed by Oñate and his settlers from Santa Barbara in present Chihuahua to El Paso del Norte connected with the stretch of trail along the Jornada del Muerto.[7] From there, the Camino Real followed the Rio Grande northward past present Albuquerque and Santa Fe to San Juan de los Caballeros. That portion of the Camino Real is known as "La Ruta de Oñate." Today, the Camino Real de Tierra Adentro is a binational trail, part of which lies in Mexico as a World Heritage Site and the other part in the United States as a National Historic Trail.

Yet their successes did not come without hardships, suffering, and tragedies, which, for a brief moment in history, were tied to the successes and failures of Juan de Oñate. Between 1598 and 1610, New Mexico remained a small, isolated backwater area known as the Reyno de Nuevo México—the Kingdom of New Mexico. Following Oñate's departure in 1608, the crown reduced New Mexico's status to that of a province, known as the Provincia de Nuevo México.[8] Thus Oñate's world was that small "kingdom," which he governed and hoped to make prosper in his lifetime. Instead, New Mexico and its early settlers were poor. They had suffered through a "starvation period," during which time they depended on support from the the Native American population, which, in itself, was barely surviving from year to year. By the end of the first year, the settlers of New Mexico had been reduced to conditions approximating starvation. Nor did they expect the winters to be unbearably frigid in New Mexico, for it was the middle of the Little Ice Age. The land was basically sterile during the cold winter months, and farming was limited. The decades between 1560 and 1660 were among the worst years.[9] Similarly, the cold, frigid spell caused droughts and famine in the succeeding years around the world. New Mexico's history during that period is well-documented, for during the 1660s New Mexico and the Great

Plains suffered through devastating droughts and famines as climate changes affected the land.

Poorly nourished and ill-prepared for the severely cold temperatures and the snow-filled months of northern New Mexico, the settlers turned to the pueblos for food and blankets and for help. Unprepared to offer assistance, the pueblos became agitated by such demands to share their provisions, which in some cases were barely enough to sustain the native population during the hard months of winter. In 1601 Father Juan de Escalona wrote to the viceroy explaining how strongly the pueblos felt about sharing their most valuable resources: corn and blankets. He wrote, "This was the cause of the Acoma war, as I have clearly established after questioning friars, captains, and soldiers. And the war which was recently waged against the Jumanos started the same way."[10]

By 1601, New Mexico's settlers had fallen into despair. The complaints and laments of the settlers who sent messages to Mexico City officials predicted the collapse of the colony. Defections had taken place as some settlers had departed New Mexico even though their desertion was punishable by law. Survival dictated their actions. In 1601, there were an estimated 150 men-at-arms; about a third of them were married, and some had children and servants. Of the large herds brought into New Mexico in 1598, large numbers of the cattle had been consumed or had perished in winter storms. One observer reported that there were probably fewer than 400 head of cattle in the settlement and that no oxen could be seen, noting that the plowing was done mostly with horses.[11] In effect the shortage of cattle and oxen resulted when Oñate, in 1601, took all available oxen to pull the *carretas* and some of the cattle on his expedition to the Great Plains. The same was true of the mules that formed the mule train to haul provisions and military equipment for the expeditionary force. At that time, however, reports indicated that there were about 300 mules, in total, within the settled area.[12]

With Oñate's absence from the colony for several months during his expedition to the Great Plains, the situation among the settlers at San Gabriel worsened. While many of them had gone to New Mexico as farmers with their families and friends to start a new life, their morale had hit a low point, for some of them viewed the land as sterile and the pueblos were as poverty-stricken as themselves. They constantly felt threatened, especially after the battles at Acoma and Las Jumanas, as well as beset by warring Plains tribes around them. At the start of the Jumano War, for example, several soldiers, including Captain Alonso Conde de Herrera, Diego de Zubía, and Alonso de Quesada, "declared that unless the punishment was administered by the expedition they wanted permission to remove their women and children from the land, because otherwise they would not consider themselves safe."[13]

Many of the settlers were, moreover, disappointed in the authoritarian leadership offered by Governor Juan de Oñate. In Oñate's absence, the settlers met with members of the *cabildo* at San Gabriel and aired their grievances and sent reports to the viceroy in Mexico City. The *cabildo* convened with the traditional and formal announcement signifying "Sepan cuanto" (Know ye present) that they, as regents of the Villa de San Gabriel de Nuevo México, were forthwith gathered in council in accordance with the prescribed customary and collective voice to deal with local affairs and to accomplish their official duties.[14] After which they named the officials of the *cabildo*. Once convened, they heard the complaints of the settlers, who had agreed to put their grievances against Oñate in writing. Among the writers, Father Juan de Escalona posited that: "Your lordship should believe them and not certain other persons who have deceived your lordship and all of us by telling stories in New Spain of things that do not exist here. . . . If your lordship should wish to get the facts as to what there is in this land, you could hold an inquiry among the people who have gone back and those who are now returning and thus you could find out what has been going on here from the time the governor started this expedition."[15] Similarly, eighteen settlers who were loyal to Oñate addressed the *cabildo* and requested that an agent be appointed to investigate the accusations against the governor. They also suggested that they were willing to send Captain Gerónimo Márquez "to appear before his majesty or the viceroy of New Spain to inform him in our name of the present situation in this land, and also of our dire need for aid."[16]

Regarding the dissatisfaction and disappointment among the settlers who left New Mexico and were presently in New Spain, Viceroy Conde de Monterrey, in 1601, ordered Francisco de Valverde to interview them and investigate their grievances. To that end, he reported the following:

> The situation had reached such a point that [he] heard them say that they would run any risk in order to return to New Spain and appear before his excellency, the viceroy, to ask for mercy for their women and children. The

single men were eager and determined to flee.... The reason for this was the cold and harshness of the land, for the winter lasts eight months, and the cold is so intense that... the rivers freeze over and the Spaniards are always shivering by the fire. Moreover, there is a scarcity of firewood, which has to be brought six or eight leagues to the camp in wagons and carts.[17]

The summer months, they said, were so dry and hot that between the seasons there were "eight months of winter and four of hell."[18] Aside from such calamities, the settlers were starving, but they were equally dissatisfied with Oñate's leadership plus the fact that some of them did not trust him.

The situation was not much better for the Indian pueblos. Despite pressure from his settlers, Oñate had demurred about establishing the *encomienda*, a grant of specific pueblos to certain individuals for the purpose of collecting tribute that had been promised to his leading settlers because the pueblos were too poor. He argued that the tribute, in the form of the possible numbers of cotton blankets and *fanegas* of corn to be collected, was inadequate. Finally, he acquiesced and ordered, as was his prerogative under the Laws of the Indies, that tribute be collected from the pueblos under his jurisdiction.

As usual throughout the empire, if tribute could not be paid in kind, then the amount owed was converted to personal service—to work in the fields, harvest the crops, or do other necessary work in the settlement. Valverde, however, noted that the settlers had often been seen "plowing all by themselves without assistance from the Indians."[19] Valverde also reported that every month, the soldiers went out, by order of the governor, to collect the tribute payment in certain amounts of corn or cotton blankets. He commented that that the soldiers told him, "The Indians part with it with much feeling and weeping and give it of necessity rather than of their own accord."[20] In some cases, the Indians were able to trade back some corn in exchange for wood and water needed by the tribute collectors.

Despite the hardships tribute collection would cause, Oñate, on the other hand, knew that the situation, not unlike a double-edged sword, would cause both sides to suffer and create further resentment among the pueblos. He made sure that when such provisions were taken, they were distributed to the neediest of his settlers.[21] Similarly, from time to time, such provisions were collected from resentful pueblos along the route of his expeditions for sustenance. Valverde confirmed that "the Indians store their maize for three and four years to provide against the sterility of the land, for it rains very seldom, although there is much snow, which helps to moisten the ground so that they may harvest what they plant."[22] While the situation of the settlers in terms of the shortage of food was evident, the resentment among the Indians having to share their dwindling supplies grew with each incident.

During the early years of Spanish settlement, 1598–1600, in particular, the shortage of food among the settlers nearly devastated their hopes of survival and hurt their relationships with the pueblos. Yet as the situation seemed to have improved by 1601, other settlers testified that the shortage of food issue had been alleviated. Aside from farming and gathering what the land naturally produced, hunting and fishing were other ways to supplement their diet. One influential settler, Gerónimo Márquez, testified that the situation had changed for the better, acknowledging that "there have never been such abundant supplies as at present, for of the two thousand fanegas of corn that may be required at this camp each year, there is now a crop of fifteen hundred fanegas of wheat from our own harvest; and that this is also harvest time for the natives, who will gather much corn, so there is no fear of a famine; that there are more than three thousand head of cattle and sheep, and that the gardens are filled with fruits and vegetables, which we could support ourselves. . . . in the three years we have been here we have planted wheat and vegetables and that both the planting and harvests have increased."[23] Similarly, Captain Bartolomé Romero stated that "the first year the Spaniards harvested about two hundred fanegas of wheat; the second, some one thousand five hundred fanegas, which show that the harvest increases every year. This is true, also, with vegetables."[24] Optimistically, both men saw improvements with the harvest and, as a result, hopefully, with relationships with the pueblos.

It is a truism that Oñate was a controversial figure in his day. His settlers were divided on whether to support him: some did, others did not. The accusations leveled against him varied; some were supported, while others were not accepted by official investigators of the period. Countering the arguments and actions of dissident settlers, Oñate initiated proceedings against certain individuals, most of whom were men-at-arms who had met with the *cabildo* at San Gabriel during his absence to the Great Plains. Subsequently, before Oñate returned from the expedition, some of them fled the colony to New Spain. Angrily, when he returned, Oñate accused them of deserting their post in New Mexico without authorization and considered their mutiny to be derelection of their duties as soldiers, punishable by death. To that end, he sent Zaldívar with an armed escort to pursue them, capture them, and execute the leaders of the mutiny.

The pros and cons of the "mutiny" were part of the attacks and defense against Oñate's administration of New Mexico. Fray Juan de Escalona, for example, reiterated the arguments that "because this has been a bad year, without the usual rains, causing many grain fields to dry up and many of the pueblos to harvest no grain, and because the governor refused to sow a community plot so that his captains and soldiers might eat, the people at the camp came to a mutual agreement to return to the land of peace [i.e., New Spain], to prevent all, both Spaniards and Indians, from perishing, and to go as far as Santa Bárbara, there to await the viceroy's instructions whether they should move elsewhere or come back here, aided and reinforced with some supplies; or whether they should be allowed to settle at Indehe [a settlement near Santa Bárbara]."[25] While Fray Escalona made his point, Captain Bartolomé Romero questioned the motives of the missionaries and noted that they did not want to learn any of the Indian languages because "they did not care very much to stay in the land."[26] In another statement, he said that he knew "that the friars themselves strove to quit the land."[27] He also stated that Captain Diego de Zubía, Alonso Sánchez, Luis de Velasco, Bernabé de las Casas, Alonso Quesada, Gregorio César Antonio Conde, and Pedro Alonso Valles "were the main instigators in inciting the people to abandon the land."[28] The recalcitrant Quesada, for example, had earlier attempted to desert. Arrested and facing execution, Governor Oñate pardoned him at the intervention of the friars and other settlers. In Oñate's defense, Captain Alonso Gómez Montesinos, a supporter, stated that "he saw the captains and friars go about arousing the people, who were calmly and peacefully gathering their grains and tending their gardens."[29]

Meanwhile, Zaldívar and his escort pursued the "mutineers" southward. Although the runaway settlers were far ahead, the quick-moving escort under Zaldívar pursued them to Santa Bárbara. As Nueva Vizcaya lay in a different jurisdiction, officials there told Zaldívar that he had no authority there. The fleeing settlers were now securely under their protection. There the settlers quickly composed another series of letters that they sent to the viceroy, listing and expanding upon their grievances. Informing his uncle of the change in events, Zaldívar continued south by way of Sombrerete to Mexico City in hope of arranging an audience with the viceroy to explain the situation in New Mexico. Disappointed at the situation he faced in Santa Bárbara, Zaldívar commented that the entire situation could have been avoided had Oñate and his men returned sooner to San Gabriel from their exploration of the Great Plains. Writing to Oñate's familial agents in Mexico City on February 28, 1602, he explained how it came to be:

> When we arrived at our headquarters we found that this treason had been carried out, and that the few people who had remained there were on the verge of doing likewise, all of which had been done on the order, advice, and machination of the friars. It was a heavenly foresight that we arrived at this time, for otherwise the land would have been completely abandoned and it would have been impossible to repair the enormous harm that all of us would have suffered. The governor at once gave orders to proceed against these traitors, and after having tried the case, he pronounced sentence as their crime deserved, and he ordered me to set out in pursuit of them and to execute the sentence, which I would have done punctually, as the case required, had I been able to overtake them before they reached Santa Bárbara. There I found that they had been arrested by order of the viceroy and were being held and protected by Captain Juan de Gordejuela, and in order not to violate this charge I was unable to execute the governor's instructions, because it seemed to me that this procedure was proper for all of us and that any punishment of these people should be made with the approval of the viceroy.[30]

Meanwhile, the viceroy, having received the letters from Santa Bárbara, convened a council to determine whether the runaway setters should be punished for desertion. The council considered that the men-at-arms were primarily settlers and should not be charged with military desertion. The council also ruled that the runaway settlers should not be compelled to return to New Mexico. Later, in 1602, the king of Spain ruled that "the Spaniards there will remain willingly, and that others may be induced to go and settle there."[31] The ruling from the crown initiated a new migration from Spain and New Spain to New Mexico.

The complaints resulted in a case against Governor Juan de Oñate and his captains. After much investigation, Viceroy Marqués de Guadalcázar, on May 16, 1614, passed judgment for crimes and excesses taken during Oñate's administration of New Mexico. His crimes ranged from maltreatment of his captains and soldiers of his army to abuses and maltreatment of natives within the province and the executions of some of his settlers. One of the issues considered was that he took food from the pueblos to provision his expeditions. To the extent that the viceroy considered some of the charges against Oñate frivolous, the viceroy threw out certain charges against him, pronouncing, "Therefore, what I ought to absolve and do absolve: I declare the aforementioned adelantado, Don Juan de Oñate, to be free of the said charges and I acquit him of them. Among those charges, were accusations that he failed to pacify the tribes in the province; that he ill-treated and belittled the clergy and allowed others to do so; that he caused or ordered the deaths or murder of several of his settlers; that he allowed Vicente de Zaldívar to call him 'majesty'; that he seized the clothing and arms of deceased soldiers who died at Acoma, sold them, and gave the money to Zaldívar; and others."[32]

The more serious charges led to his conviction and sentence, the greatest of which was his permanent exile from New Mexico. Those charges pointed out that he allowed the attack on Acoma "with great severity, injuring many innocent people and causing the death of many natives; and . . . exercised the same severity with those taken alive in the said pueblo; that his lived scandalously with women of the army, married and unmarried; that he ordered the deaths of Captain Pablo Aguilar and Alonso de Sosa; that he ordered the execution of soldiers who deserted the colony; that he did not comply with royal decrees sent to him regarding the cost of the expedition"; that he "boasted that he was the mortal enemy of the Viceroy Conde de Monterrey and spoke ill of him"; that he reported that the land was fertile and rich when it "really was poor and sterile." In view of this report, Oñate's actions led to many expenses and costs in maintaining the colony. Furthermore, Oñate threatened and punished settlers "who spoke the truth in the matter." To those charges, the viceroy pronounced: "On the basis of those above charges, which have been proved against Don Juan de Oñate in this trial, I should condemn him and do condemn him, to perpetual exile from the provinces of New Mexico, and from this court and five leagues around it, for exactly four years; furthermore, I condemn him to pay six thousand Castilian ducats, half of which I allot to the court of the king our lord, and the other half for war expenses and pacification of the said provinces."[33] Thus, the viceroy ordered Oñate to pay all costs of the trial.

The charges related to the Jumano War and the battle of Acoma were made in the case against Vicente de Zaldívar, for which he was found guilty. While in both cases the pueblos had initiated the violence that followed, Spanish officials viewed Oñate's and Zaldívar's actions to be excessive. Others in Oñate's command were also tried and convicted for their involvement in those actions. In the end, Zaldívar's sentence was similar to that given to Oñate. Concerning the battle of Acoma, Vicente de Zaldívar bore the responsibility for ordering the attack against the pueblo "with great severity, injuring many innocent people and causing the death of many natives; and the adelantado exercised the same severity with those taken alive in the said pueblo."[34] Oddly, neither Oñate's sentence nor the proceedings against him specifically mention the part of the sentence that called for the severance of one foot of twenty-four warriors deemed responsible for the death of Juan de Zaldívar. The proceedings did not mention that such a sentence against the warriors was carried out.

The seemingly unanswerable question is: was the sentence to cut off the foot of twenty-four Acomans actually carried out? The ambivalence of the documentation leaves room for debate. At least one historian has raised the question of whether all or part of the Acoma sentence was ever carried out. In reviewing the work of eminent historian John L. Kessell, Colin Gordon Calloway writes: "Historian John Kessell raises doubts about whether the Acoma sentences were actually carried out, since Spanish strategy often involved sentencing Indians to death only to have the friars intercede and secure mercy."[35] Of the controversial part of the sentence whereby twenty-four Acoma warriors were to have their foot cut off, Kessell persuasively argues that it likely never happened. He writes clearly and perceptively that

> Only one brief mention in the record testified that Oñate's punishment was carried out. Elsewhere in colonial Spanish America, on similar occasions, while the conqueror maintained his stern countenance, churchmen knelt at his feet to beg that he show paternal mercy and commute so harsh a sentence. "In this manner," Oñate himself had instructed Zaldívar before the battle, the Acomans would "recognize the friars as their benefactors . . . and come to love and esteem them, and to fear us." The absence of any subsequent reference to a one-footed Acoma slave, *un cojo*, raises doubt that the Spaniards wielding axes or swords indeed followed through.[36]

Although the settlers supported the attack on Acoma as a defensive measure, they opposed the severe sentences to be served on some of the Acoma warriors. As Kessell writes, oddly, the amputations or references to a "one-footed Acoma slave" are not mentioned in any subsequent correspondence, reports, or other documents.[37] Such was normally the case where the Spanish corporate memory, enhanced by the written word stashed in the viceregal archives, were continuously referred to time and again. The shipwreck of the *San Agustín* in 1595 at Point Reyes, California, for example, was not only mentioned periodically in reports from time to time; it was recorded on maps as late as the 1790s, indicating "Aqui se perdió el nao Filipinas nombrado San Agustín en el año 1595 [Here is where the ship *Filipinas* aka *San Agustín* was lost in the year 1595]."[38] Kessell's argument would correspond to the query: why mention the shipwreck of 1595 repeatedly for two hundred years in the documentation of the California coast and not the Acoma sentences of 1599 in early New Mexico? Were the Acoma sentences forgotten, for they seem not to be mentioned again in later testimony? Even after the subsequent battle against the Jumano pueblos east of the Manzano Mountains, Acoma was not brought up. After the "Jumano War," Zaldívar set free 400 captured men women and children.[39] About seventy other captive warriors that Zaldívar allotted to his men never got to San Gabriel for punishment because the soldiers let them escape. An inquiry into that situation noted that "all of them except three or four have escaped to their land."[40] Regarding Acoma, Ginés de Herrera Horta stated in 1601 that most of those who had been enslaved had runaway to reestablish Acoma and that Governor Oñate "neither authorized nor prevented this."[41] Indeed, in 1602, Zaldívar reported that Acoma "remains peaceful to this day."[42] Again, opportunity to mention the Acoma sentences in recollection of the event presented itself when, in 1613, Spanish soldiers attacked Acoma and were driven off by the pueblo's warriors.[43] Oddly, not one mention of the 1599 victory at Acoma or the punishment of the Acomans is found in these or other known accounts. Thus, Kessell not only raises questions about past historiography of one of history's conundrums; his analysis calls attention to the shortcomings of previous histories written about the battle and its aftermath. The condemnation of this episode as well as others in the history of Spanish colonial New Mexico should be measured against certain events in our national history. By way of comparison, dare one ask: what happened to Native American tribes in North

America between Jamestown in 1607, the nineteenth-century Indian Wars on the Great Plains, and the massacre at Wounded Knee in 1890?[44]

Both Oñate and Zaldívar lived out the rest of their lives as citizens of the Spanish Empire, seemingly with the experience of New Mexico behind them. As for Oñate, he returned to Spain and served as an inspector of mines at Guadalcanal, Spain, where he died in the first week of June, probably June 3, 1626. He was about seventy-four years old.[45] On the day of his death, he had entered an inundated mine to try to pump out water when he collapsed and expired soon after. Ten years later, in the third week of February 1636, his nephew, Vicente Zaldívar, about sixty-four years of age, died in Zacatecas. On February 21, Agustín Barroso, a royal scribe, witnessed the body of Vicente de Zaldívar lying in state. Barroso noted that he had been laid in a coffin dressed in the uniform of the Orden de los Caballeros de Santiago. Later that day Zaldívar was buried.[46] As a wealthy *hacendado* (landowner), he had, years earlier, been inducted as a knight of the Order of Santiago, as was his uncle, Juan de Oñate. So ends the history of the life and times of both men.

9

Pedro de Peralta and the Founding of Santa Fe, 1609–13

We feel that our greatest service to his majesty has been to wait all this time, for it looks as if the governor [Oñate] maintained the expedition miraculously for so many years, which he did. He treated us as if we were his children, and we looked upon him as a father.
—*Members of the Cabildo de San Gabriel, 1607*

Although I have such good intentions, an evil star follows me.
—*Pedro de Peralta, (1613)*[1]

Look with eyes of pity on us and aid our cause, for on our part, there is little malice, and pardon us if we have been in error.
—*Francisco Pérez Granillo (1613)*[2]

After the desertions that occurred during and after Governor Oñate had returned from his exploration of the Great Plains, it seemed clear that the New Mexico colony teetered on the verge of collapse. Much later, in 1607,

DOI: 10.5876/9781646420957.c009

members of the Cabildo de San Gabriel still wrestled with the issue and hoped "to prevent the abandonment of this land."[3] Authorities, nonetheless, supported the idea that New Mexico would remain as a settlement and a mission field.[4] Having implored Spanish authorities in the viceroyalty of Mexico to assure that the deserters would be arrested and punished for violating the sovereign's instructions regarding the establishment of New Mexico, Oñate saw that nothing had been done. He argued that they continued to spread falsehoods about his administration of the province and ruin his reputation. Furthermore, he posited that the falsehoods were made to justify their treasonable actions against his leadership as governor and their disloyalty to their promised obligations of establishing the settlement of New Mexico.[5] To those settlers who remained in New Mexico, Oñate said that he would, pending a positive response from the viceroy, hold them there until the summer of 1608.[6] Still, mutinies, battle casualties, camp deaths and diseases, plus a major desertion from the colony plagued Oñate's enterprise.

Meanwhile, he, his brother Pedro, and Zaldívar did as they had done as early as 1602: they sought to reinforce their numbers with a new migration of settlers and resupply their needs.[7] Hoping to keep alive his dream of establishing the Provincia de Nuevo México, Oñate requested that the king evaluate the continuation of the settlement and argued that the province not be abandoned, as had been suggested. In late 1607, after a discussion with the officials of the Cabildo de San Gabriel, Oñate submitted his resignation as governor of New Mexico.[8] By early 1608, he had received the reply from the viceroy and the Audiencia de México stating that they had accepted his resignation.[9] Sternly, Viceroy Luis de Velasco commanded that Oñate remain at San Gabriel until further notice and that he not "leave those provinces during this time or to abandon them without my express authorization."[10] The settlers, moreover, were also warned that if they or Oñate were to leave during this time, they would be "committing the crime of *lese majeste*," that is, treason against the sovereign.[11]

About that time, Viceroy Velasco appointed Captain Juan Martínez de Montoya, one of Oñate's officers, to serve as interim governor.[12] Martínez de Montoya had been in New Mexico since 1600, when he arrived with a relief caravan. He also served as a member of the Cabildo de San Gabriel. As *alcalde ordinario*, or magistrate, he sat in the council and had experienced the political atmosphere that pervaded the colony as well as issues related to defense and the economy. Although Martínez de Montoya had not sought the office of interim governor, his tenure was never validated by the Cabildo de San Gabriel, which refused to accept his governorship. Instead, the *cabildo* appointed Cristóbal de Oñate, the deposed governor's eighteen-year-old son, as the duly elected interim governor. In the tradition dating to Greco-Roman days, the *cabildo* called a *cabildo abierto*, an open town meeting, in which all adult male property owners voiced their opinions and, in this case, approval of Cristóbal de Oñate's nomination. Why was the selection of Cristóbal de Oñate made with little or no consideration for Martínez de Montoya or no other opposing candidate? This unanswerable question may lie in the possibility that the *cabildo* had been instituted by Governor Oñate, who likely chose members who had remained loyal to him. In the end, such a conclusion may be a part of the plausible answer.

During that time, probably about 1607, settlers had been moving southward and extending their farms south of San Gabriel. It appears that some settlers had made their way toward a small valley along today's Santa Fe River, a tributary of the Rio Grande. There, probably with some acquiescence from Juan de Oñate, a new settlement began to take root about 1608. Soon after, in 1609, the viceroy ordered former governor Juan de Oñate to leave New Mexico,[13] ending an eleven-year struggle, albeit successful, to establish New Mexico. The new place, settled sometime after 1605 by the settlers from San Gabriel, was within the Santa Fe River Valley and referred to as *"el puesto de Santa Fe."*[14]

In 1609, the status of the area along the Santa Fe River changed when Governor de Peralta received instructions to establish "La Villa Real de la Santa Fé de San Francisco de Asís" (The Royal Villa of the Holy Faith of St. Francis Assisi) as the new capital of New Mexico. Unlike a *puesto*, which designated a place, the Villa de Santa Fe, established in 1610, bore a given status and prescribed privileges, as were all *villas* under the Laws of the Indies. In effect, the Villa de Santa Fe, as the seat of government, had the traditional rights, as stated in Peralta's instructions, to establish a *cabildo* (town council with elected officials) and be recognized as the capital of New Mexico.[15] Privilege-wise, by dint of its status, the Villa de Santa Fe, for example, was the terminus of the Camino Real de Tierra Adentro, a privilege no other town or pueblo in New Mexico enjoyed. As a legal entity, the prestige of the *villa*, in particular, as defined in and governed by the Laws of the Indies, lay in its authority to impose legal jurisdiction within its entire territory.

On March 30, 1609, Viceroy Luis de Velasco handed don Pedro de Peralta a list of instructions to follow in establishing his administration as royal governor and captain-general of the Provincia de Nuevo México and in strengthening defenses within his jurisdiction.[16] According to his instructions, the viceroy ordered Peralta to establish a *villa*, a *cabildo*, and to allot land to the settlers. The viceroy also authorized him to allot *encomiendas* to certain settlers and expected him to protect the pueblos and settlers from their enemies. Upon receipt of his orders, Peralta organized his expedition and, picking up the path of the Camino Real de Tierra Adentro, left Mexico City for New Mexico sometime that summer.

A company of soldiers, Fray Alonso Peinado, the newly named *comisario* of the New Mexican mission field, and eight friars accompanied the newly named governor and bade goodbye to their friends and relatives. Laden with supplies, the slow-moving *carreta* caravan, drawn by oxen, pulled out of the ancient capital. Wending their way northward along the Camino Real de Tierra Adentro in a cloud of dust, servants and teamsters drove a large herd of livestock before them, as a mounted escort scouted the trail ahead for water and safe resting places. Peralta and his entourage arrived in New Mexico after several arduous months on the trail just as the weather had begun to turn cold.

His instructions from the viceroy empowered him to found a new capital for New Mexico and to establish the appropriate governing institutions and appoint or elect officials to them. Most explicitly, Peralta was to "found and settle the villa that has been ordered built."[17] The establishment of the Villa de San Francisco de la Santa Fé came about because the old capital at San Gabriel had been founded in an unsatisfactory location, difficult to reach and easily preyed upon by raiding nomads. The settlers desired a more centrally located capital in the pueblo country. After passing the winter at San Gabriel, Peralta and the settlers moved to the newly selected site along the Santa Fe River beneath the Sangre de Cristo Mountains. The governor and the four councilmen, who had been elected by the residents, began to implement the viceregal plan. Six *vecindades* (districts) were marked out for the *villa*, with one square block being set aside for government buildings and other public works.[18]

The body politic comprised the governor, four elected councilmen, two *alcaldes ordinarios* (municipal magistrates), an *alguacil* (constable), and a notary. Under the watchful eye of the governor, the *cabildo* issued ordinances for the administration of the province. In general, the council's jurisdiction was limited to the affairs of Spanish settlers. The two *alcaldes ordinarios* held a one-year term during which time they heard civil and criminal cases that arose in and near the *villa* "for five leagues around."[19]

As regards the Indians, Governor Peralta was authorized to allot them *encomiendas*, "as many as he . . . thinks suitable . . . without interfering with those granted by Don Juan de Oñate, since they must be preserved." The viceroy also instructed Peralta to regulate the tribute levied on the natives, which "is excessive, and . . . is collected with much vexation and trouble to them." On Indian affairs, Peralta's orders had been clearly stated by the viceroy: "no one shall have jurisdiction over Indians except the governor or his lieutenant."[20]

The viceroy had hoped that the natives could be dealt with fairly under the Indian policies long prescribed by Spanish colonial law. Enemy Indians were to be subdued, driven out, or brought under Spanish rule by peaceful means. The viceroy felt that the enemy Indians who attacked the Spanish and their Indian friends did great damage to their positive relationship. "It will be important," wrote the viceroy, "to pay close attention to this matter in order to establish prestige with friends and enemies, because this is important for the protection of the converted." Such provisions of Peralta's instructions would be difficult to achieve, for Navajo and Apache raids had increased and consequently many Indians had been "intimidated" and were "disinclined" to communicate with Spanish missionaries.[21]

The friars would also play a role in Peralta's reorganization of New Mexico. Pueblos and nations "on the frontiers of the Apaches," which served as shelters for enemy Indians and as places for them to hold meetings and plot against the Spaniards, would have to be moved "to more appropriate and peaceful locations." To that end, Peralta's orders obligated him "to establish these reductions in the most suitable places, in consultation with the friars and persons of practical experience . . . This plan must be carried out with such mature counsel as to forestall any uneasiness or dissatisfaction among the Indian."[22]

New Mexico needed a lingua franca, or at least so Spanish officials in Mexico City believed. They explained that "the land is inhabited by various small nations, in each of which they speak different and barbarous languages, which gives rise to many problems of administration and much concern to both friars and natives."²³ The viceroy instructed Peralta to concentrate this effort on "the children and young people . . . but in case they have no aptitude for it, efforts should be made to teach them the language most widely spoken in the land."²⁴ A common language for New Mexico seemed a good idea, but perhaps it was too soon.

The governor had his hands full reorganizing the provincial government after Oñate's departure. Before he could permit any expeditions against hostile Indians, before any expedition for exploration would be allowed, he had first to establish the Villa de Santa Fe. In the interim, the only people allowed to travel to the lands of unfriendly Indians were the friars.²⁵ They could go out to spread the word of peace and the holy faith, but only if sufficient priests remained behind to care for Spanish settlers and Indians who were at peace. For the moment, Peralta turned to establishing a new capital for New Mexico.

In the meantime, Fray Alonso Peinado had some reorganizing to do himself. He established the first church in Santa Fe and expanded the mission field, which previously had served only the Tewas, to include the Tanos and the Rio Grande Tiwas and Keres as well. When Peinado arrived, only two or three friars from the Oñate period resided in New Mexico. Peinado and his new group added nine more, bringing the total Franciscans to twelve. Next Peinado established a new mission and *convento* at Santo Domingo Pueblo as the ecclesiastical capital of the province. Centrally located, Santo Domingo, on the upper end of the Río Abajo, at the beginning of the lower portion of the Rio Grande in New Mexico, ideally served the Río Arriba missions and the Villa de Santa Fé. As the prelate of the missionaries in New Mexico, Fray Alonso had taken a major step in initiating the intensive missionization of the pueblo world that followed. In 1611 the aged friar sent Fray Isidro Ordóñez to Mexico City to recruit eight new friars and to procure more supplies and equipment for the mission work. The work that Peinado had begun would prove significant in the long course of New Mexico's colonial history.²⁶

On August 25, 1612, another supply caravan arrived at San Francisco de Sandia, and with it was Fray Isidro Ordóñez. Aside from large quantities of supplies for the clergy already in New Mexico, the twenty-*carreta* caravan consisted of a military escort and new Franciscan recruits. Even before the caravan had reached Sandia Pueblo, at that time the southernmost pueblo on the Río Abajo that had a *convento*,²⁷ word had spread that Ordóñez would replace Peinado as the *comisario* of the missions. The first inkling anyone had about Ordóñez's takeover of the missions occurred on the trail. About three or four days before reaching Santa Fe, Ordóñez appointed Fray Luis Tirado as guardian of the church at the Villa. The act "caused us to murmur amongst ourselves," wrote Father Francisco Pérez Huerta, one of the new recruits, who later wrote the anti-Ordóñez *Relación verdadera* (True Account).[28] As the Franciscan notary, Pérez Huerta attended almost every meeting held by his fellow Franciscans. When he writes about Ordóñez's perfidious actions, he also serves as a witness of events narrated in his *Relación verdadera*. Where did Ordóñez get the power to appoint anyone? The new recruits were suspicious of him. Meanwhile, Fray Tirado traveled ahead of the group to announce Ordóñez's arrival. The Peralta-Ordóñez affair would leave long-lasting scars on New Mexican society. Peralta, Ordóñez, and several others, as Pérez Huerta revealed, preyed upon one another. After both men had openly clashed, Pérez Huerta spoke out against Ordóñez.[29] The Pérez Huerta *Relación verdadera* is a biased account against Ordóñez, albeit the only complete account of the Peralta-Ordóñez period that survived the seventeenth century with other related extant documents and that verifies the events that took place.

When Governor Peralta, who had previously experienced poor relations with Ordóñez, learned about the appointment of his nemesis, those nearby heard him exclaim, "Valgame Díos! [God save us!] Better that the devil were coming instead of that friar."[30] Doubtless, in Peralta's view, Ordóñez was not the best choice to head the New Mexico missions. While Peralta and Peinado had worked harmoniously for two years, Ordóñez's abrasive and arrogant attitude toward all civil authorities became widespread and well known. Many of the friars questioned his credentials. Some believed that the *comisario* had forged his papers.[31]

When Peralta, as required by law, asked Ordóñez for the documents, he refused to present them. Instead, he presented the governor with a *real provisión*, an order from the viceroy in the name of the king, directing that all soldiers and settlers who so desired be permitted to return to New Spain.[32] Peralta read the order incredulously. To him it seemed unbelievable that such an order would emanate from either the king or the viceroy, when shortly before he had been instructed to reorganize the province and its defenses. But despite qualms that he had been given a forged paper, he submitted to the order. Much later, when Pérez Huerta examined Ordóñez's papers, he determined that they were indeed forged.[33]

If Ordóñez sought to gain control of New Mexico by weakening the civil authority's political and military base, he had succeeded. Within five years the Hispanic population dropped significantly and New Mexico became a weakly held outpost. Ordóñez viewed the settlers as troublesome and incidental to the mission program. Most of them were farmers with an obligation to military service; others were retired soldiers with their families.

Disliked by the governor and the settlers as well as by most Franciscans in New Mexico, Ordóñez had breached the fine line of protocol that had bound the church-state arrangement on that remote frontier. The ensuing controversy between Peralta and Ordóñez hurt the mission program, created a malaise between civil and ecclesiastical authorities, and set the pattern for Spanish-Indian relations for the rest of the century.[34] As civil control diminished and ecclesiastical power grew, New Mexico in the seventeenth century came to be viewed by king and viceroy primarily as a mission field. Between Ordóñez's tactics and Peralta's submission to his chicanery, Spanish New Mexico had been subverted.

Ordóñez's relations with his fellow Franciscans during his first assignment in New Mexico (1607–9) were cool, but after 1612 dissatisfaction with him became widespread. Some of the new recruits who came with him learned to suffer his unkind manner. Even before they had reached New Mexico, he had alienated most of them by failing to make proper provisions for their journey. And when they complained, he harshly criticized and disciplined them. At one point, after one lay brother had deserted the caravan, the other discussed turning back. Friar Pérez Huerta noted that Ordóñez had persuaded them to go forward to New Mexico, where "God had greater labors for them." They did so thinking that when they reached New Mexico they would submit to Fray Alonso Peinado.[35] Once at Sandia Pueblo, however, Ordóñez presented a letter purportedly written by the commissary general ordering Peinado "to obey the said Fray Isidro Ordóñez."[36] Although some of Peinado's friends suspected the letter to be forged, the good padre himself accepted the document as genuine and turned over the administration of the missions to Ordónez.

A few days later, Ordóñez called a chapter meeting of the friars at Santo Domingo. At the meeting he named Friars Cristóbal de Quirós, Andrés

Bautista, Alonso Peinado, Estéban de Pérea, Pedro de Haro de la Cuesta, and Juan de Salas to head each convent. The rest of the friars would serve as their subordinates. After he read out the new assignments, dissension grew anew among the missionaries. Some of the newly recruited friars voiced dissatisfaction at having been named as subordinates to other missionaries rather than being given the independent appointments they had expected. Furthermore, Ordóñez's arbitrary distribution of the mission supplies tended to favor the brethren friars who sided with him. The rift among the Franciscans widened when Fray Luis Tirado, assigned to the church at Santa Fe, complained bitterly about his appointment. Tirado called a meeting among his supporting clergymen, and they voted to return to Spain.[37]

Instead of opposing Ordóñez, Father Peinado quietly surrendered his authority to him and acquiesced to his demands.[38] Almost all who knew him thought Fray Alonso Peinado, a native of Malaga on Spain's southern Mediterranean coast, to be a saintly man. By the standards of his day, the friar, probably in his middle to late fifties, was considered elderly in 1609. He entered the Franciscan novitiate on June 15, 1574, at the Convento Grande in Mexico City, and a year later, on June 16, 1575, he professed the vows of chastity, poverty, and obedience.[39] It seems Peinado had been in New Mexico as early as 1603 but had temporarily returned to Mexico. In 1609, Peinado was appointed commissary of New Mexico, then returned there in 1610 with Governor Pedro de Peralta. With Peinado were Friars Isidro Ordóñez, who had previously been in New Mexico in 1601, Lázaro Ximénez, Andrés Bautista, Agustín de Burgos, Bernardo de Marta, Estéban de Pérea, Cristóbal de Quirós, and Alonso de San Juan, a lay brother. Alongside Governor Peralta, Peinado witnessed the establishment of the Villa de Santa Fe in 1610.

Between 1609 and 1612, Fray Alonso Peinado, as *comisario* of the missions in the province, ordered the assignments of the twelve Franciscans in his charge. Under Peinado the construction of Santa Fe's first church had begun,[40] and Santo Domingo had been selected as the ecclesiastical capital of New Mexico. Peinado's contributions to the Provincia de Nuevo México also included the expansion of the mission field to the Tano, Keres, and Rio Grande Tiwas.

Among the most widely resented of Ordóñez's actions was his shabby treatment of Fray Peinado. At that first chapter meeting at Santo Domingo, over which Ordóñez presided, he began his dominance over Peinado. Ordóñez tried to take away his quarters (*la casa y su rincón*) at Santo Domingo but met with some initial resistance from the old priest. However, once Ordóñez reminded the elderly padre of his vow of obedience, Peinado had little argument against his prelate. Finally, Fray Estéban de Pérea, with Ordóñez's indulgence, "conceded" Peinado a house at Galisteo and apparently escorted him there. Fray Alonso remained at Galisteo a short while, for after a few days Ordóñez angrily recalled him. When Fray Alonso reported to his prelate, Ordóñez ordered him to go to the convent at San Ildefonso as the subordinate to Fray Andrés Bautista. Under Ordóñez's orders, Bautista housed Peinado in extremely barren quarters. A few months later, Peinado's health broke down and, infirm, he was taken to Santa Fe. Later he returned to serve again at Galisteo.[41]

Because of such odious treatment from Fray Isidro Ordóñez, his replacement as commissary, the elderly priest, after serving a stint at the Tano mission at Galisteo, chose to exile himself from Ordóñez's dictates. Peinado virtually fled south to the Tiwa pueblo of Chililí in the Manzano Mountains. Some time around 1613, Peinado established the first of several missions that would serve the Salinas pueblos. Between 1613 and 1620, missionary endeavors along the Manzano Mountains moved slowly but steadily.[42]

Meanwhile, Ordóñez persisted in his plan to control New Mexico by discouraging the governor, his lieutenants, and the settlers from becoming influential. New Mexico in his view would be a Franciscan mission field. Everyone in the province knew that Ordóñez and Peralta did not like each other. Now Peralta would feel the scourge of Fray Ordóñez.

At first the governor sought to befriend the Franciscans for the purpose of enlisting them as partisans in his struggle against Ordóñez. Often they would dine at his house and occasionally would come to drink chocolate with him. Fray Luis Tirado and his brethren friars seemed to enjoy his company. On Easter Day, 1612, he presented them with gifts. To Fray Tirado, he gave a fine pistol (*pistola muy rica*). Two days later Peralta loaned Fray Pedro de Haro his favorite harquebus. On April 23, the governor gave Fray Tirado a marvelous hunting knife, inlaid with silver, which the priest had admired and for which he had dared to ask him. Tirado also asked Peralta for a piece of steel, a valuable commodity on any frontier, which he gave him. In his effort to keep good relations with the priests, Peralta would, at the request of the friars, discipline soldiers who were accused of "excesses." The friars, at least, had become the beneficiaries of his friendship.[43]

Ordóñez watched Peralta. He took careful note when, the following year, Peralta sent a hunting party to the Great Plains. As Easter approached, Ordóñez knew he could use the holy day to declare the bad timing of the expedition against Peralta. On April 25, 1613, the governor sent Captain Gerónimo Márquez, an old-timer who had served with Juan de Oñate, with six soldiers and their servants to the "Llanos de Cíbola," the Great Plains, to capture buffalo calves, some of which would be sent to Spain for the king to enjoy hunting on his preserves. The rest would be used by the governor and his captains. The meat, the hides, and the fat would be put to good use. Márquez, an experienced hunter, had been to the Great Plains many times since 1598. This time he would be gone for Eastertide, and Ordóñez would later question him and his men on how they had observed Holy Week without a priest. He plotted to make Peralta appear insensitive to the religious needs of his soldiers.[44]

Another activity that Ordóñez observed was the collection of tribute from Pueblo Indians, a routine colonial practice throughout the Spanish Empire. As royal governor, Peralta relied on his empowerment by the king and viceroy to uphold the Laws of the Indies. One of them included the prerogative to send *encomenderos* to collect tribute in Indian products such as corn, bread, some crop, or other things such as blankets, which the pueblos made.[45]

On May 16, 1613, Peralta sent a detachment of soldiers to collect the tribute owed by Taos Pueblo. This time the collection of tribute went awry. Within five days they returned empty-handed with a report that the Indians of Taos were rebellious and refused to pay the tribute. Disturbed by this news, Fray Luis Tirado sent word of it to Ordóñez at Santo Domingo. Ordóñez traveled to the Villa de Santa Fé, arriving there on May 15 to confer with Peralta. The priests were agitated by the disobedience of the Taos Indians, and they demanded that the governor punish the pueblo even if it meant war by fire and blood (*a fuego y sangre*), for it was justifiable in this instance.[46]

Peralta, the cooler head in this situation, calmed the priests' fears by telling them that "such news had no more of a basis than the faint heartedness of the aforesaid captains who had gone to collect the tribute." At any rate, he would send the same captains back with four others to ask again for the tribute. If the Taos Indians refused to pay it a second time, he would punish them. First, however, he decided to send two Indian allies to Taos as spies, one named Anda, a captain from the pueblo of San Cristóbal, the other named Cañasola from Pecos Pueblo. On the pretext of trading they would enter the pueblo and note the disposition of the Taos Indians. Anda and Cañasola asked for a few days to gather trade items.[47]

Satisfied that the governor had a worthy plan, Ordóñez left Santa Fe on Friday, May 17, for San Ildefonso to attend to some repairs and other work at the church there. The next day, some Indians from Picurís, a pueblo near Taos, arrived to deliver a message to the governor. Peralta received them. They explained that the Taos Indians had asked to be excused for not having paid the tribute to the Spaniards because many of the tribute payers were not in the pueblo at the time. They asked the governor not to be angry at them, as they had collected all the required *mantas* (blankets). Apparently word had spread about the Taos Indians' omission, for another Indian leader, Lorenzo, "capitán del pueblo de Pojoaque," friend of the Spaniards, and Alferez Simón de Abendano, a Spaniard among the Tewas, also reported that the Taos Indians were repentant. As Peralta weighed the gravity of the situation against the decision of Taos to comply, Ordóñez assumed a wait-and-see posture.[48]

If Taos should rebel, what would the other pueblos do? The Spanish policy had always been to respond with a military attack to keep recalcitrant pueblos in line. It was their only means of defense, as natives outnumbered the colonials. Peralta must act quickly and deliberately, for if he tarried, the Taos might think that the Spaniards were planning an expedition against them. Concerned that the Taos, fearing Spanish reprisals, would join with their Apache allies and start an "inexcusable war," the governor decided to send a detachment of soldiers to collect the tribute as soon as possible. On May 24, 1613, without waiting for Anda and Cañasola to report, Peralta sent two captains, one of them Pedro Duran, and six companions to collect the *mantas* from the Taos.[49]

Meantime, Ordóñez had finished his inspection of the church at San Ildefonso and began his journey back to Santo Domingo by way of Nambé Pueblo. At Nambé, Ordóñez met Gaspar Pérez, a member of the detachment going to Taos. Pérez, a rugged frontiersman, had gone to Nambé to visit the priest there. Just as he dismounted from his horse, Comisario Ordóñez, as if out of nowhere, appeared before him. Acknowledging him, Pérez kissed Ordóñez's hand. The father commissary quickly asked him about his destination, and the soldier responded that he and a detachment were bound for Taos to collect the tribute as ordered by the governor.[50]

In disbelief that the soldiers had been sent by the governor as a church holy day, the Feast of Pentecost (May 26), approached, the father commissary remarked, "But now is the eve of the holy day." He asked him, "How many are with you?" Pérez answered, "Two captains and six soldiers." As if speaking to a child, Ordóñez asked, "Pues donde estan?" (Well, where are they?). Pérez replied that they had taken another route and that he had left them to visit his priest friend at Nambé. Looking him in the eye, Ordóñez said, "Well, Señor, I order you under pain of excommunication to return to Santa Fe." The father commissary then turned to his young Indian servant, Joseph, and said, "Hurry, boy, run and tell the soldiers that I order them under pain of excommunication to return to the Villa as I am going there too."[51]

Then Ordóñez, taking the unfortunate Pérez with him, departed for Santa Fe. When they arrived at the Villa, Ordóñez rested at Fray Tirado's *convento* and told him about Peralta's disregard for the upcoming holy day. A little over an hour after his arrival, one of the soldiers of the detachment rode in ahead of the others, sought out the father commissary, and asked him to confirm the order. Ordóñez responded affirmatively that he had ordered their return so that they might celebrate the Feast of Pentecost in proper fashion.[52]

Upon their return, Captain Pedro Ruíz de Rios and two companions went to the governor's house and reported that they had not been able to speak to Father Ordóñez because he was taking his late-afternoon rest (*dormía la siesta*). They had been greeted at the door of the convent by Joseph Velasquez, a *retraido* (a person who had taken refuge or sanctuary in the church), who told them that Ordóñez had ordered their return so that they could hear mass on the Feast of Pentecost. At any rate, they had gotten as far as San Juan Pueblo, where they had left their remuda, and they asked why they could not have heard mass there instead so that they could continue on their way to Taos the next day. The captain now feared that because of a small herd of mares near San Juan his stallions would escape from their corral and be scattered. It would cost them extra time to round them up and consequently, he reasoned, the trip to Taos would be further delayed. Impatiently, Peralta heard of Ordóñez's unreasonable demands. After all, Ordóñez had openly pushed for a punitive expedition against the Taos. Time was of the essence, and Peralta hoped to get his soldiers to Taos before they rebelled.[53]

Having heard his captain, Peralta ordered the soldiers back on the trail to Taos, some of whom went grudgingly. First, he instructed them to return to

San Juan and round up their horses. Next he ordered them to continue to San Ildefonso and hear mass, then proceed to Picurís and spend one night there before going to Taos. The eight soldiers again made preparation to leave, some complaining that they had returned because they had not wanted to go in the first place. The commissary's order was merely convenient for them. Other soldiers said they had returned because they wished to attend mass in the Villa with their families. Whatever their sentiments, Ordóñez had used the church calendar to countermand Peralta's orders, and the governor now exercised his powers as captain-general to override his prelate's wishes.[54] In this contest of wills, trouble brewed furiously that Friday afternoon of May 24, 1613.

10

Showdown in Santa Fe
The Peralta-Ordóñez Feud, 1613–14

> The more he [Governor Peralta] tries to afflict and incriminate them and shed their blood, the more trouble will rain down on him.
>
> —*Fray Andrés Perguer, 1613*[1]

"Some said that the trouble actually began on Saturday, May 23, 1613," wrote Fray Pérez Huerta in his *Relación verdadera*, "when Governor Peralta stood on the Plaza de Santa Fe with Juan de Tapia, a soldier who served as the scribe of the Cabildo and one of the four encomenderos of Taos, and a few soldiers. The men were standing around indulging in small talk regarding the recently arrived herd of twelve buffalo calves from the plains." However innocuous this social occasion seemed, it turned out to be the spark which set the rhythm, tone and tempo of the church and state conflict for the rest of the seventeenth century. "'Téngolo por patraña' [Take it as fiction], but it could be true"[2] regarding what was said at that gathering started the fight between Peralta and Ordóñez. The events that followed continued to strain relationships between pueblos, plains, and province. Spanish sovereignty

DOI: 10.5876/9781646420957.c010

would be challenged within the province by this question: who governed the Provincia de Nuevo México—civil or ecclesiastical authorities?

It seems, according to Pérez Huerta, that the conversation at the plaza turned from admiring the twelve buffalo calves to the question of the collecting party going to Taos instead of observing Pentecost in Santa Fe. In all probability, Juan de Tapia first raised the question. After all, he was one of the eight ordered to go to Taos. He had expressed that he and the soldiers could leave soon after Pentecost so that he could stay with his wife, Francisca Robledo, and children and enjoy a holiday repast with them.[3] Sarcastically, Peralta, singling out Tapia's comment, snapped that he should "kill a couple of chickens, cook them with a piece of bacon, spice them with salt and take them in his saddle bag and go wherever he is sent, with that he should pass the holiday . . . besides . . . it is never a lousy holiday when one serves the King."[4] Rebuffed and humiliated before his peers, Tapia reportedly approached the father commissary about Peralta's attitude and insolence toward the prelate's orders that the Taos tribute collectors should observe their religious obligation for the Feast of Pentecost in the Villa. Others of the detachment went before Ordóñez and supported Tapia's accusation. "I believe," wrote Pérez Huerta, "that from what this soldier said the father commissary formed his Inquisitorial case" against Peralta.[5]

Father Ordóñez now pulled another surprise document from his robe: one that named him as the agent for the Holy Office of the Inquisition. Angrily, he called upon the notary Aséncio de Archuleta to take "ink and paper" (*tinta y papel*) and deliver the following summons to the governor:

> I, Friar Isidro Ordóñez, Apostolic Commissary and Judge Ordinary by the [authority of] Señor Licenciado Bernardo Gutiérrez de Quiros, Chief Inquisitor of New Spain, order the governor, Don Pedro de Peralta, under pain of major *excommunication late sententie ipso facto incurrendo* to recall the soldiers who are going to Taos within two hours and have them appear before me for investigations of matters pertaining to the Holy Office.[6]

Perplexed by Fray Isidro's newly found authority, the governor replied that he had not previously understood that Ordóñez had brought any commission from the Holy Office. Furthermore, as governor, he alone administered judicial affairs in the name of the king, and any changes of his duties should have been presented to him in a formal manner. Peralta added that if Ordóñez presented the document authorizing him as the Inquisition official, he would promptly obey his order to recall the soldiers bound for Taos. Displeased with Peralta's response, Ordóñez waited for the two hours to expire and then pronounced the governor excommunicate and posted (*poner en tablilla*) the declaration of excommunication for all to read on the door of Santa Fe's church.[7]

Fray Isidro pulled no punches in his fight with don Pedro. Next he wrote instructions concerning the steps to be followed should Peralta seek absolution and presented them to the guardian of the Santa Fe church, Fray Luis Tirado:

> If the governor wishes to be absolved, he shall pay fifty pesos fine in the manner I may wish to apply them. At door of the church let him be absolved with the Psalm De Miserere in conformance with the Manual. Later let him be taken into the church where he shall swear to be obedient, and there, barefoot and a candle in his hand, in the presence of all the people let him hear mass.[8]

Fray Luis read the order carefully, especially the part that instructed him not to "modify nor do anything else" as regards the form of absolution prescribed.[9] At mass, on the Feast of Pentecost, Father Tirado publicly denounced the governor from the pulpit and declared that any persons who might speak to Peralta or, upon seeing him, take off their hats in his presence would also suffer excommunication. The Spanish settlers, some stunned by Ordóñez's recent power and demand for retribution, were shocked by the event.

Tirado showed compassion for the governor. Through Captain Bartolomé Romero, a dark-complexioned, black-bearded Spaniard from Corral de Almaguer near Toledo, who had been in New Mexico since 1598, Fray Luis secretly informed the governor that Ordóñez had returned to Santo Domingo after lunch and urged that absolution should be made before Ordóñez's next visit to Santa Fe. Tirado, as a friend, offered to say the mass two hours before sunrise and said that the governor's penance need only be made in the presence of three or four of his friends. Should Peralta delay until Ordóñez returned, "things would not take place with the impartiality and secrecy that he offered."[10] Tirado had given Peralta a way to save face, but the governor argued that the excommunication was not justified and he refused to accept absolution in that form.

In the next few weeks the situation worsened for Governor Peralta. During that period Tirado for some reason withdrew his secret friendship with the governor. Perhaps he feared reprisals from his prelate, or perhaps Ordóñez had, through his unpleasant contacts with the governor, somehow intimidated Fray Luis. Nonetheless, Tirado henceforth would be unwilling to aid Peralta in his dilemma. When Peralta, convinced of the injustice of his excommunication, tried to obtain a written statement concerning what had occurred, Tirado refused to cooperate. Peralta demanded a copy of the terms of excommunication and a written statement of Tirado's order that no citizen should speak to him under pain of excommunication, doubtless to include in an official report he was preparing to send to Mexico City; Fray Luis refused that too. Peralta then summoned Aséncio de Archuleta, the ecclesiastical notary, and demanded the written statements, but Archuleta refused to comply with the request. The governor felt he had no alternative but to imprison Archuleta in the jail of the *casas reales*, the governor's residence and office.[11]

Tirado put great social pressure on Peralta. From the pulpit, Fray Luis, moved by passion and vengeance, denounced Peralta as "a heretic, a Jew, a Lutheran and man of low and vile lifestyle."[12] Tirado and Ordóñez sought to destroy Peralta, not so much because he insisted on performing his gubernatorial duties but because it served as a means to establish the supremacy of the church over the civil government in provincial New Mexico. As if their accusations against Peralta were not enough, the two priests conducted an investigation of the governor by questioning witnesses in a partial and partisan manner regarding his conduct. Peralta responded by convening his own fact-finding commission. Father Ordóñez had made his investigation in the name of the Holy Office of the Inquisition. Witnesses often left Ordóñez's interrogation terrified (*salian todos espantados*). If they did not respond as he wished, he would correct their language (*corregía el lenguage*) with the admonishment that the "Señores" of the Holy Office would be offended if what the witnesses stated were not couched in certain terms.[13]

Between the decree of Pentecost Sunday in which Tirado forbade anyone to speak to Peralta and the inquisitorial interrogations that some of the settlers underwent, Ordóñez and Tirado had succeeded in making the governor a virtual outcast in a land he had sworn to govern in the name of his king. All who testified against him were obligated by Ordóñez to swear under penalty of excommunication that they would tell no one what they had stated. Each swore on a missal that he had told Ordóñez everything truthfully. The New Mexico settlement at Santa Fe was split between the vocal Ordóñez faction and the intimidated Peralta followers. By June rumor spread beyond Santa Fe of the scandalous governor who had told Juan de Tapia "to take the holy day and stuff it in his saddlebag" in a most sacrilegious manner.[14]

Peralta asked that the information of Ordóñez's inquisitorial investigation be released so that it could be made public. In order to clarify his position, he convened his own investigatory body, hoping to expose the innuendo created by Ordóñez's secrecy. The governor's inquiry was quickly interrupted when Tirado ordered Peralta's notary, Juan Donayre de las Misas, not to serve the governor. Donayre obeyed the priest, but when he refused to work for Peralta, he was arrested. Even after arresting him, the governor asked Donayre three times to act as his notary and scribe, but he refused.[15] Under colonial justice such civil disobedience amounted to treason punishable by strangulation. Unmoved, Donayre, threatened by a friar he believed represented the Holy Office of the Inquisition, valued his soul much more than his life.

The Donayre affair was far from finished. As soon as word reached Tirado that Donayre had been sentenced to death, the priest sent some boys who lived in the *convento* to call the alcaldes, councilmen, captains, and whomever else they encountered to come quickly to the *convento*. When all had gathered before him, Fray Luis appealed to them by saying that if they wished to be favored and helped in their needs by God, they should rid themselves of a certain tyrant who would commit a crime before them. "Know ye," he continued, "that the governor has Juan de las Misas unjustly imprisoned, and I am told that he wants to garrote him because he did not wish to be a scribe to the unjust cause which he would perpetrate."[16]

The citizens, now a mob encouraged by Tirado's rhetoric, marched on the *casas reales* where Peralta resided. When the governor appeared before them, they demanded Donayre's release. The mob was adamant; Tirado's words still rang in their ears. If they failed to gain the release of Donayre, the friar had said that they were forcibly to free him and kill the governor. He had told them "that if they did not dare do this, he, the said father guardian, and friars would come and release him and kill [the governor], and if this could not be done, he would consume the Holy Eucharist, seal the doors of the Santa Fe church, and he would go to the convent of Santo Domingo where the father commissary was and see to it that no religious went to the Villa."[17]

Hoping to avert such a tragedy, the councilmen begged Peralta to release Donayre. Prostrating themselves before Peralta, some with tears rolling from their cheeks, they implored the governor to pardon Donayre. Peralta heard them out and wisely released the prisoner, but not before he declared that he based his decision on his desire to avoid "a disaster," for he was otherwise unmoved by their pleas and promises.[18] He did, however, refuse to release Asencio Archuleta.

The Archuleta case, too, added to Peralta's woes. On June 7, Father Tirado sent another communiqué to the governor, demanding the release of the ecclesiastical notary on the grounds that he was exempt from civil jurisdiction. Peralta, however, refused to acknowledge that Archuleta enjoyed the privilege of ecclesiastical immunity, arguing that Archuleta was a soldier first and an ecclesiastical second. As a soldier, Peralta questioned how Archuleta could subordinate himself to Tirado and assist in writing excommunication announcements against his commanding officer, a title that the governor held as captain-general of the province.[19]

After reading the latest excommunication decree, which stipulated a greater fine and more severe penance, Peralta wrote a response to Tirado that he gave to a messenger to take to the convent late that afternoon. He viewed the situation as tragic yet amusing. After all, how many times could he be excommunicated? In his reply he asked Tirado not to try to quiet him with so many excommunications and rigorous penances because the extreme passion with which they were made was so evident. Both sides were flustered to the point that their only form of communication was legal petitions, uncomplimentary epithets, and threats. Tirado now created a new form of insult. He reached over, took the paper from the messenger's hands, tore it to pieces, stepped on it, and gave him a message filled with contumely and "ugly and indignant words" for the governor.[20]

By mid-June 1613 the situation had reached a stalemate. The father commissary had returned to Santa Fe, and third parties moved quickly to mediate between the governor and the prelate. Peralta, in the meantime, had received copies of all the summons and announcements against him from Father Pérez Huerta, the Franciscan notary. Pérez Huerta explained to Ordóñez that he had given the documents to Peralta in order to get him to answer in writing to the charges against him. Ordóñez wanted copies of church documents returned by the governor, and Peralta wanted the excommunication lifted, but not under terms of penance because of the humiliation it would cause him and the principle involved. Ordóñez stubbornly handed Peralta an ultimatum: within twenty-four hours Ordóñez would convene his twenty friars, who would seize the governor and bring him before the prelate; he would be humbled and made to submit. Those were the prelate's terms for absolution. Naturally, Peralta refused.[21]

In the end, certain friends of the prelate arranged a compromise. The original terms in the first excommunication decree would be modified if Peralta would return the copies of all documents given him by Pérez Huerta. Furthermore, Ordóñez agreed, Peralta would not have to attend a public mass, but he would have to pay the fifty-ducat fine and present himself at the door of the church and read the psalm of "miserere" (mercy) as prescribed by the manual of the Holy Office of the Inquisition. Peralta agreed.[22]

Accompanied by a few friends, the governor went to the door of the church with the prescribed psalm in hand. Upon being notified that Peralta was waiting, Ordóñez, dressed in a white surplice (*sobrepelliz*) over his religious garb, carried a rod in each hand. With him were Fray Tirado, the notary Fray Pérez Huerta, and two others. Quietly they passed through the interior of the church to the front door. The two men, governor and prelate, faced each other. Ordóñez spoke first. "Do you have the report you have made against the priests?" he asked. Peralta responded with a simple "No." The father commissary retorted, "Well, if you wish absolution, you must present it." Peralta started to respond, saying, "Padre, of what importance is it . . ." But before he could finish his sentence, Ordóñez quickly interrupted him. "I will not absolve you," he retorted, "if you do not bring the report and give it to me." A brief silence followed as Peralta thought about the demand. The confrontation became increasingly tense. Turning to his secretary, Peralta said, "Take this key and bring the report we made."[23]

The secretary returned with the papers shortly and handed them to the governor. Peralta hesitated, then instead of handing them over to the commissary, he tore them up, saying, "Pardon me if I not do give them to you."[24] When he had finished, he fell to his knees. Commissary Ordóñez stood over him and began the absolution. For each verse of the psalm, Ordóñez would hit Peralta with the rods he held in each hand. When the absolution was finished, he ordered Peralta into the church so that he could swear obedience to him. With great humility the governor did so by signing a paper presented to him by the prelate. As for the fifty ducats, Peralta said he did not have them at the moment, and it was agreed that he would pay them in the fall after the harvest. The governor went home and the priests returned to their convent.[25] The ordeal was over, or so it seemed.

Three or four days later, the fight between the two heads of the province began anew. Ordóñez fired the first shot. He and Tirado, perhaps to vex Peralta, conspired to take away the herd of buffalo calves that had been captured in May. They approached Captain Márquez to ask Peralta if he could take charge of the herd for him. Once he had gained possession of them, he should refuse to return them and hold them until the appointment of the next governor. Márquez refused. The governor was now apprised of the conspiracy.[26]

With impunity, Tirado sent Peralta a bill for the tithe (*diezmo*) he owed in arrears to the church. In it he asked the governor to pay the *diezmo* with the buffalo calves. Peralta responded that he did not owe the church the tithe, as he had already paid it. Tirado sent Peralta a second bill, and he again refused to acknowledge his debt. Next Tirado tried to convince Ordóñez that he would be justified in entering the governor's corral to kill the buffalo calves. But the father commissary realized that such a deed would be going too far and would result in a scandal that would hurt their public image.[27] Tirado's plan was dropped. Besides, Ordóñez only had to wait for Peralta to play into his hands, and he would have all of the governor's property.

Ordóñez did not have long to wait. At the end of June 1613, certain settlers of the Villa were about to depart for the countryside to round up their cattle and brand them. Before leaving they asked Peralta to appoint one of the *alcaldes ordinarios* to mediate the roundup of disputed cattle, which often resulted in quarrels over ownership. Peralta appointed don Juan Escarramad,[28] who seemed to be a good choice, primarily because at forty-five years of age he had good standing in the community and was one of the original members of Oñate's founding expedition to New Mexico. Short of stature with brown hair and hazel eyes, he was a native of Murcia in Spain.[29] As many of the vaqueros at the roundup worked for the founding families, Escarramad would be a man whom everyone could respect.

The appointment made, the roundup began. About four leagues from the Villa at a ciénega (spring), Escarramad became embroiled in an argument with one of the cattle owners named Simon Pérez. The argument intensified, and before anyone could stop it, swords were drawn and Escarramad was severely wounded. Witnesses said that if the sword had "penetrated him just a little more," he would have died.³⁰ Simon Pérez fled to the safety of his family. Escarramad appealed to the governor for justice and redress. By the time Peralta acted on the matter, Pérez had been hustled off by friends and relatives to the safety of the *convento* of Santa Fe where Fray Luis Tirado granted him sanctuary. Unwilling to violate the right of sanctuary, Peralta ordered those who had helped Pérez escape confined to their homes. This act raised the ire of Pérez's friends and relatives, who were among the leading provincial families. One of them, Captain Gerónimo Márquez, had earlier refused to cooperate with the prelate against the governor. They appealed to Ordóñez at San Ildefonso for protection of their rights.³¹

Ordóñez wasted little time in learning which of the leading citizens had been placed under house arrest. Márquez headed the list, followed by the Barela brothers, Captain Alonso and Alferez Pedro Barela, and Captain Alonso Baca.³² These men belonged to families who had participated in the conquest of New Mexico and the establishment of Santa Fe. Ordóñez immediately assessed their usefulness in his fight to get Peralta removed. All he had to do to win them over was to support their cause. He would find a way to help them.

Everywhere Ordóñez looked, trouble brewed for Peralta. As he read the names of leading citizens confined to their homes, he held in his other hand a letter from Fray Andrés Perguer, padre guardian of the *convento* of San Lazaro near Galisteo. Fray Andrés was disturbed about an order issued by Governor Peralta authorizing Alonso Gutiérrez to take a levy of Indians from the pueblo of San Lazaro to perform some personal labor under the system of tribute called the *tequio*. Apparently Gutiérrez had a field he wished cleared, and he requested a crew from Perguer. In defense of the Indians under his charge, Perguer wrote a letter to Ordóñez suggesting that Gutiérrez get his work crew from the Salinas pueblos near the Manzano Mountains because they were better rested. Perguer thought that the pueblos of Picurís and Jémez, which were also taxed, were not as often used as San Lazaro. But Gutiérrez, a true colonial, viewed the *tequio* as his right in return for the defensive assistance he had given these Indians against their enemies. Perguer noted that he had sent the same letter to Governor Peralta.³³

Meanwhile, Ordóñez decided to have another chat with the governor. As Perguer had raised the subject of the governor's treatment of the citizens in the Escarramad case, Ordóñez would add his own thoughts to both matters. "I believe," he replied, "that I must go to the villa this week for I imagine that this man must once more be put in a position from which he cannot escape . . . [for] according to what I am told, I believe that I must do [now] what I did not do in the past affair."[34] Perguer spoke for the Ordóñez faction: "The more he tries to afflict and incriminate them and shed their blood, the more trouble will rain down on him."[35]

Saturday, July 6, Ordóñez journeyed to Santa Fe to meet with Peralta over the Escarramad case and the *tequio* levied at San Lazaro. As he expected to be gone a long time, he left Fray Bernardo Marta in charge of Santo Domingo. The aged Fray Bernardo asked Ordóñez not to go, saying that he did not trust Peralta and feared that the governor would shoot the father commissary dead. Ordóñez laughed, saying, "Jesus, Father, a man as wise as he wouldn't do anything like that, would he?"[36] Father Marta sensed a showdown in Santa Fe between the governor and prelate.

Once at Santa Fe, Ordóñez challenged the governor by asking him for an escort to go to New Spain to give an account concerning the "serious matters" to the viceroy, the Audiencia, and the Inquisition. The governor replied that he would not only grant him the escort but that he would join the guard as well so that the commissary "would be better accompanied and served."[37] Ordóñez did not like the response and planned to reply in kind.

That afternoon, he and Father Tirado hatched a plan to embarrass the governor in front of the citizenry of Santa Fe. Closing the door behind them, they sat in one of the *convento* rooms and planned three Sunday masses; one of them, the *misa mayor* (main mass), would attract the captains, alcaldes, and *cabildo*. The next day, Sunday, Ordóñez and Tirado officiated at the main mass. They watched as the church filled with all the local dignitaries and waited until Peralta's servants had finished setting his chair on its platform in anticipation of the governor's arrival. Immediately, Father Tirado stormed from the sacristy and ordered the chair thrown out into the street as partisans of both factions and neutral citizens cringed or privately applauded the act, according to their convictions. When the governor arrived, he calmly ordered his chair placed just inside the door near the baptismal font, and there, among the Indians at the rear of the church, he sat while his political subordinates, friend and foe, sat nearest the altar. Meanwhile, Ordóñez joined the choir along with Father Pérez Huerta and the Indians who sang the mass.[38]

After Father Tirado had read the Gospel, Ecclesiastical Notary Aséncio Archuleta, who by now had been released by Peralta, ascended the pulpit and read an official notice ordered by the father commissary that under penalty of excommunication and a 500-peso fine, no one would be permitted to send, carry, or secretly take any dispatches to New Spain without first giving notice to the father commissary. After Archuleta read the notice, Ordóñez, wearing his habit instead of his altar vestiture, stood in the pulpit and delivered an impassioned speech against the governor, much of it emotional and scandalous:

> Do not be deceived. Let no one persuade you with vain words that I do not have the same power and authority that the Pope in Rome has, or that if his Holiness were [here] in New Mexico he could do more that I. Believe [ye] that I can arrest, cast in irons, and punish as seems fitting to me any person without any exception who is not obedient to the commandments of the Church and mine. What I have told you, say for the benefit of a certain person who is listening to me who perhaps raised his eyebrows. May God grant that affairs may not come to this extremity.[39]

The next day Peralta sent his secretary to Ordóñez with an official notification (*auto*) for him to prepare to leave for New Spain on August 1, 1613. Not wishing to hear the *auto*, the commissary sent him away. That same day, Ordóñez asked Captain Romero to go to the governor and to tell him that "I kiss his hand and that it would serve your lordship to grant license to the syndic, fiscal and notary to go about their ecclesiastical business."[40] In particular, the syndic needed leave from his military duties to collect the tithes. The governor's response was predictable. Ordóñez knew he had to ask the governor's permission to send his own ecclesiastical officials on assignment because the syndic, fiscal, and notary were also soldiers. Thus, Peralta refused to grant the request because the three men were men-at-arms who served the king, and as for the syndic, there were no tithes to be collected.

When Ordóñez heard the response, he flew into a rage, yelling that the governor was a Lutheran, heretic, Jew, a man of low and vile bearing. Making gestures with his beard (*echando mano a la barba*), the prelate threatened to convene the friars to arrest him and send him to Mexico for trial.[41] Captain Romero, the unfortunate bearer of the bad news, could only stand there, blinking in fright as the commissary carried on. Romero attempted to reason with the prelate and protested the name-calling, especially when he called the governor a "sly dog" and his followers "vicious animals at his side." Ordóñez replied, "If the governor is a dog then I say that those who consent to what the man does are vicious animals."[42] Without another word, Captain Romero wisely tipped his hat to Ordóñez and left.

Ordóñez sat at his desk and wrote out the letters calling friars at nearby missions to Santa Fe. As he planned to arrest the governor, the letters were sent out in secret. Peralta's luck still held. The next day, Juan Lujan, a Canary Islander, paid the governor a visit. Something was amiss, Lujan reckoned. He told the governor that his wife, probably Francisca Jiménez, a former Indian servant of his,[43] often cooked for Father Tirado. "Yesterday afternoon," he began, "they [meaning the Spanish servant boy and another] brought a large quantity of flour to my house so that she could bake bread and when my wife asked why they brought so much flour, they replied that many friars were coming."[44] Juan Lujan became curious and decided to look into the matter. From Aséncio de Archuleta, the notary, he learned that friars were coming to Santa Fe to arrest the governor. Ordóñez had lost the element of surprise, but he still held the upper hand.

Peralta, however, would strike first. He called on his followers to grab their guns and meet at his house. When all had arrived, he explained to them that the father commissary and some of his friars planned to arrest him. Peralta cited the incident at the church when Ordóñez claimed that he had the same authority as the pope, Perguer's letter questioning the governor's power to authorize the use of Indian labor, and Archuleta's recent comment to Lujan stating Ordóñez's intention to arrest the governor. Peralta now asked these frontiersmen to join him in ousting Ordóñez from Santa Fe. After the meeting they followed him to the *convento* of the Santa Fe church.[45]

Alarmed by the loud noise of men's voices, the priests had been watching the early-morning commotion in the plaza as the armed settlers spilled out from Peralta's house. As the men walked toward the *convento*, their wives, some of whom were crying in fear that the father commissary would excommunicate them, entered the church for morning mass. Inside the church Ordóñez had entered the sanctuary and stood at the altar, turned, and gazed at the congregation. Looking directly at doña Lucía López Robledo,[46] the wife of Bartolomé Romero, one of Peralta's supporters, he very unkindly told her to shut up (*callase*), "words that today still ring in the church."[47] With an odd calm Ordóñez turned toward the altar and said mass. The churchman knew the showdown with the governor was at hand.

Outside, near the *portería*, the gate to the convent, Father Pérez Huerta stood and watched Peralta's soldiers a few hundred yards away walk toward him. He asked passersby what were they doing, but no one dared answer him; some walked away lest they be associated with the rabble, others gave him a frown as if to blame the priest for the current sad state of affairs. As the noisy frontiersmen came closer, Fray Tirado and Father Andrés Suárez also went to the *portería* to see what was going on, but the lay brother Fray Gerónimo de Pedraza stayed in the garden and prayed. As the priests retreated to the patio near the convent library, the governor, wearing a coat of chain mail and armed with a sword in his belt and a *pistolet* (pocket pistol) in his hand, entered the *portería* with a large group of men.[48]

As Peralta had no quarrel with these priests, he courteously saluted them with his hat and asked to speak to the father commissary. Father Tirado responded that he was inside the church saying mass, quickly adding, "Perhaps he has already finished." The governor retorted, "May I ask you to call him." Tirado bowed, turned to the door of the library, and in a loud voice said, "Padre Comisario, the governor is here to see you!"[49] Ordóñez came out, saw the large group, did not like their disposition, and went back in to get a wooden cane that he found in one of the corners of the library. Then he came out again.

The two opposing groups stood quietly in the cool morning air waiting for their leaders to speak. Peralta greeted the prelate by tipping his hat. "What do you want?" asked the prelate. "Padre Comisario, on behalf of his Majesty, I require you to return to your convent [at Santo Domingo] this very day and to order your friars whom you have called here to remain in their missions," spoke the intrepid Peralta. Shaking his head as if Peralta had absolutely misread his intentions, Ordóñez replied, "It is true that I have called the friars here, but it is for business which interests us."[50]

Then Ordóñez abruptly turned around and angrily entered the library, moving around inside "as if looking for a weapon, and mumbling 'traitor dog.'"[51] Upon hearing the remark, the governor yelled back, "Aye, a dog devoted to God who knows how to kill a friar!"[52] Everyone's blood ran cold at that instant, for what happened next reflected the bitter passion of the preceding six weeks. Peralta raised his pistol and cocked it. Then he ordered his soldiers to enter the room and confiscate all the weapons they could find. Glaring at them, Ordóñez ordered them under pain of excommunication, "Do not enter."[53] But Peralta ordered his men in anyway. They searched the room but found no weapons.

The governor turned to the father commissary and said, "Understand that I require you to leave for your convento de Santo Domingo this very day. Do as I say and leave me and this Villa in peace."[54] Undaunted, Ordóñez replied, "I don't plan to do that, for I am already in my own house." Turning to the settlers, he said, "You who have come here don't you realize that you are the vassals of this church?"[55] Then he raised his cane as if to strike the governor, but Juan Lujan grabbed his arm in time to stop him. Ordóñez said, "Don't you know with whom you are toying?" Peralta replied, "It appears I toy with Father Isidro Ordóñez." With a sneer Ordóñez said, "No, you have taken on the whole [Franciscan] order," and placing his hand on his beard swore, "By the life of Fray Isidro I will destroy you, for it well appears that you do not know the trouble in which I have ensnared you."[56] The governor snapped back sarcastically, "What kind of trouble could you have me in that I don't already know?" Then he repeated his requirement that Ordóñez rescind the order to have his friars meet and asked him again to leave the Villa. If he did not leave, the governor would order him thrown out in a pair of shackles. "Bring eight pairs,"[57] Ordóñez dared him, meaning that the governor would have to shackle his friars also. Peralta intimated that he would have him arrested when a scuffle ensued.

The fight in the library was brief, but the whole affair had an irreversible effect in their relationship, hostile as it already was. When Peralta grabbed at Ordóñez's cape as if to arrest him, the prelate slapped away his hand. Standing at each side of the father commissary, Friar Suárez and Father Tirado moved to defend him. In the scuffle Tirado grabbed a sword from one of the soldiers and stabbed at the governor, ripping his cape. Father Suárez ran to his room to look for a weapon but could not find one so he returned with a bassoon (*saco un bajón con que se hace música*), a musical instrument.[58] In the meantime, the governor and the commissary were engaged in hand-to-hand fighting. Ordóñez raised his cane to strike the governor; Peralta held him by the wrist while he raised his pistol again. Witnesses thought the governor was trying to shoot the prelate just as Father Marta at Santo Domingo had predicted. Someone, probably the governor's secretary, grabbed Peralta's arm away from the prelate and the gun went off, wounding Fray Gerónimo de Pedraza and Gaspar Pérez, the armorer from Brussels.[59] At first no one noticed that Pedraza had been shot until he fell. Pérez, wounded and bewildered, fled the scene.

When everyone realized what had occurred, they stopped. A silence fell over the group in the library. The governor swore that he was unaware, because of the din throughout the fight, that his pistol had discharged. As Fray Pérez Huerta and Fray Tirado looked after Pedraza, the sound of women crying could be heard from outside. The soldiers drifted out of the room away from the governor. The fight was over.[60]

That afternoon, Father Commissary Ordóñez told all who had participated in the fracas to return to ask forgiveness and be absolved. All were absolved except the governor and Gaspar Pérez, the wounded armorer who had fled. Pérez, moreover, blamed Ordóñez for the whole affair. Even after Pérez had become dangerously ill as a result of his wound, Ordóñez refused to hear his confession and absolve him. When the general absolution of all the combatants was finished, the Host was consumed, the church and sacristy were closed, and their doors were sealed with mortar of mud (*lodo*) and stone. Ordóñez ordered his priests to leave Santa Fe and reunite at Santo Domingo. Before he left, he posted a notice of the excommunication of Governor Peralta on the sealed front door of the church.[61] Tuesday, July 9, 1613, would live in infamy in the annals of Santa Fe's history. The settlers in the Villa were thoroughly mortified.

At Santo Domingo the clergy convened to discuss future policy. Almost all attended the three-day meeting except for Fray Estéban de Perea, guardian of the convent at Sandia Pueblo, who arrived late. At the meeting, the father commissary presented his version of the incident at the Villa in which he blamed the governor for the whole affair. Pérez Huerta claimed that much of what his prelate had said was exaggerated.[62] He pointed out that only four of them had been present at the incident and the rest, having no contrary opinion on the matter, accepted his version. None of the three who were with Ordóñez at Santa Fe dared contradict him. Having explained the situation, Ordóñez proposed that the friars go as a group and arrest Peralta. Fray Alonso Peinado urged caution, for the arrest of a governor could endanger the friars. He recommended that the *padre comisario* go to the viceroy and the *audiencia* and make a report. He suggested, furthermore, that the friars pull out to Santa Barbara in Chihuahua. Ordóñez rejected his opinion and refused to let Father Marta, who seemed to support Peinado, speak.[63] Besides, Ordóñez's decision was final: Peralta would be arrested.

Ordóñez ordered the friars to prepare for the journey to Santa Fe. At about two or three in the afternoon of Saturday, July 13, they began their long walk toward La Tetilla, a prominent landmark along the old Camino Real near La Bajada on the plateau leading to the Villa by way of La Cienaga. The walk from Santo Domingo to the Villa took about nine hours. They arrived there about eleven o'clock that evening. Word spread throughout the Villa that the priests had returned and they had scheduled a Sunday mass.[64]

On Sunday morning Ordóñez issued a statement to the alcaldes and councilmen of Santa Fe that they should have the governor arrested after mass. The requirement, read to them from the foot of the altar by Pérez Huerta, demanded the arrest of Peralta for his attempted murder of the father commissary.[65] The provincial officials asked for a copy of the requirement so that they could respond to it. At two o'clock that afternoon, they returned with their response. After two hours of discussion, they announced their refusal to arrest Peralta.

Ordóñez decided to appeal to Viceroy Diego Fernández de Cordova, Marqués de Guadalcazar. He wrote a report explaining the causes of his complaint, with the most recent incident emphasized, and asked for the viceroy's authorization to arrest the governor. Four soldiers, one of them Simon Pérez, still protected under the right of sanctuary, accompanied a priest entrusted with the message. They left Santa Fe on July 23, and when they arrived in Mexico, the viceroy reprimanded them for having departed from New Mexico without license from Governor Peralta.[66] Since time immemorial it had been common knowledge, supported by the Laws of the Indies, that only the governor could permit travel out of his jurisdiction. The messengers Ordóñez sent were illegally in Mexico. Their illegal status tended to lessen their importance in the eyes of the viceroy.

Nonetheless, he listened to their petition. As he had already decided to recall Governor Peralta, the investigation of the matter was entrusted to Bernardino de Ceballos, next governor of New Mexico. The viceroy's appointment of Ceballos may have been based on the legal premise stated in the Laws of the Indies that each governor should serve a term of three years, a rule not always followed. At any rate, Governor Peralta had not been appointed for life and therefore was subject to recall.

Long before Ceballos arrived in New Mexico to investigate the matter and carry out the *residencia* (audit) of Governor Pedro de Peralta, Father Ordóñez had exacted his vengeance. Ordóñez's influence over the settlers loomed perniciously over them. When his messengers departed, Peralta tried to stop them by sending Alcalde Ordinario Juan Ruiz de Caceres, a forty-three-year-old relative of Juan Lujan who had come to New Mexico in 1600, and two soldiers after them. Before Ruiz and his escort departed, the father commissary persuaded him to let the messengers go. The commotion subsided once again, and the priests returned to their missions.

Ordóñez, with his loyal priests, returned to Santo Domingo to plan the arrest of the governor. From Santo Domingo, Ordóñez threatened to excommunicate anyone who would carry the governor's report to the viceroy. As the Camino Real from Santa Fe to Mexico City led directly south through Santo Domingo, Ordóñez had a number of people watch Peralta's movements so that he would know when to expect him as he rode past the pueblo. Like a gathering storm, Ordóñez persuaded certain Spanish settlers who had a grievance against Peralta to join him at Santo Domingo.[67]

On July 24, Captain Gerónimo Márquez, Captain Barela, and Captain Baca, who had been involved in the Simon Pérez affair, and Alferez Asencio Archuleta, the notary who had been held prisoner by Peralta, arrived, and the following day Juan Ruiz de Caceres joined them at Ordóñez's *convento*. Ordóñez promised them great rewards and unending gratitude from the king and the *audiencia* if they would arrest Peralta. All except one, Captain Alonso Barela, refused to carry out Ordóñez's request. Barela expressed his loyalty to the priest. The others demurred on grounds that they would not participate in an act that the "whole world would not hold well."[68] Father Tirado taunted them and called them "captains of chickens" (*capitanes de gallinas*). Still, Ordóñez's overpowering influence caused these leading captains to sit before him and consider his plan. If nothing else, they agreed not to interfere in it.

At the end of July, the father commissary sent for two Indians, probably Hopi, who were living in the *convento* at Zia Pueblo, to help him execute his plan. About that time, Captain Juan de Victoria Carvajal, who passed by Santo Domingo with seven soldiers to collect the tribute from Jémez Pueblo, visited Ordóñez. Carvajal, a native of the town of Ayotepel in southern Mexico, had been one of Oñate's original settlers in 1598, and had, in

1600, brought back reinforcements to settle the province.[69] As a member of Oñate's war council, he knew New Mexico well.

While his men watered their horses at Santo Domingo, brown-haired Carvajal told the prelate that Peralta was on his way to New Spain with many people and that the royal standard preceded the entourage. But conflicting rumors from other settlers indicated that Peralta instead proceeded to Santo Domingo for absolution. Ordóñez decided to take no chances in letting the governor proceed to Mexico City. He posted spies along the royal road from Santa Fe to inform him when the governor approached the pueblo. Armed with harquebuses, the two Indians, who came to the *convento* at Zia, were placed on the rooftop of the *convento* "like good soldiers," with instructions that "the first one which I point out is the governor."[70] It seems Ordóñez would stop at nothing to keep the governor from leaving New Mexico. But the plan fell apart when the spies, thinking Peralta approached them, misinformed Ordóñez. Instead, it was a troop of soldiers passing through the pueblo.

Apparently Peralta attempted to get a report through, but the wily Ordóñez let nothing escape his watchfulness. When a soldier and a Peralta loyalist, Juan Montero, passed near Santo Domingo, Ordóñez, thinking he was as messenger, ordered Alcalde Ordinario Juan Ruiz de Caceres after him. Ruiz found Montero asleep at Sandia Pueblo and took him to Santa Domingo as prisoner and jailed him there.[71]

In Santa Fe, Ordóñez kept a "double-dealing man" (*hombre que hacia a dos manos*) who professed loyalty to Peralta but who reported to the prelate all the governor's movements.[72] On August 10, the man sent word to Ordóñez that the governor had set out on a journey to New Spain at four o'clock in the afternoon. The prelate called all the friars to Santa Domingo, "but some excused themselves" and only certain ones came.[73] After midnight, the father commissary and his party, carrying arms, left for Sandia. Along with the friars were the captains and soldiers who had been with him at Santo Domingo. At Sandia they awakened a surprised Fray Estéban Perea, who did not expect their arrival. Ordóñez explained that the governor had left the Villa and was fleeing (*salia huyendo*) to New Spain. Turning to his followers, the commissary tried to persuade them to sign a petition justifying the arrest of the governor on the grounds that his flight indicated guilt. They refused to sign it.[74]

The party went on to Isleta Pueblo. There Ordóñez brought up the petition for their signature. After discussion, some of them signed it and stated falsely that it had been signed in Santa Fe, adding names of persons who were not even present.⁷⁵ They spent the night at Isleta waiting for the governor. The next day the father commissary left the *convento* at Isleta and retraced the trail that led to the governor's camp. Approaching Peralta, Ordóñez loudly announced his arrest in the name of the Holy Office of the Inquisition. After a brief struggle, the governor and his party, surrounded by Ordóñez and forty armed men, were arrested. Ordóñez took him to Sandia and there incarcerated him. Fray Estéban Perea did not want the governor imprisoned at his mission,⁷⁶ but Ordóñez convinced him that it was far enough away from Santa Fe. Besides, like it or not, Ordóñez, his superior, wanted the governor there. Held in chains and guarded by three soldiers and several Indians from the pueblo, Peralta sat in his cell at Sandia Pueblo. Another person arrested with the governor was the *alcalde ordinario*, Juan Escarramad. On August 17, Ordóñez had Peralta, arrested and shackled, transferred from Sandia to Santo Domingo and held there for two months under very poor living conditions.⁷⁷

Ordóñez had in his possession most of the governor's papers and reports. He read through them and familiarized himself with Peralta's arguments. A few days after the arrest of the governor, Ordóñez sent word to Fray Estéban at Sandia to go through the governor's belongings and find the keys to the trunks and boxes that the governor had left at the Villa.⁷⁸ On August 22, Ordóñez and Tirado entered the governor's house and rifled his trunks and boxes until they found his personal papers. Among the papers and effects, a book entitled *Practica Criminal Eclesiástica*, caught Ordóñez's eye.⁷⁹ He sensed that Peralta had prepared himself to complain to authorities in Mexico City. Convinced of the danger Peralta posed to his ego and ambitions, Ordóñez censured any communication by or with the governor. Peralta would be held incommunicado.

For now, Ordóñez appeared to be the unquestioned master of New Mexico. At a fiesta in Santa Fe on September 9, he unabashedly announced that he held the governor imprisoned, and he expected a great prize for this deed. Those who had helped him could expect no less. With impunity, the prelate moved to destroy the character of Governor Peralta. The campaign against Peralta took on new life when Ordóñez ordered Fray Gerónimo de Pedraza, the brother who had been wounded by the governor, to go from house to house and show the people what the governor had written about them, in particular, a letter addressed to a friend in Zacatecas expressing Peralta's negative attitudes about people of mixed ancestry.[80]

Shortly Ordóñez himself began to inquire about every facet of the settlers' lives. Before long, "excommunications were rained down," especially against supporters of the governor. Everyone feared that every little word they spoke would be used against them. Anyone who criticized the prelate would have an inquisitorial *proceso* started against them that would surely "send their souls to hell." Indeed, many felt that "it was hell to be in the Villa" (*era un infierno estar en la villa*).[81] An inquiry into the July 9 incident began, and those who had participated in it quaked in their boots.

Ordóñez's takeover of New Mexico appeared virtually complete, and the provincial government in the absence of a governor did as the prelate dictated. However, a new problem plagued the provisional government. On September 11, 1613, Ordóñez heard that the Indians from Zia Pueblo had abandoned their village to go to Acoma, "pueblo of the infidels."[82] Apparently Acoma, even after the punishment inflicted upon them by Oñate in 1599, had continued to resist Spanish rule and encouraged other pueblos to do the same. The Acomans may have offered Zia protection if they deserted the Spaniards, and maybe even threatened them if they did not. At any rate, Ordóñez approached the lieutenant governor, who had been left in charge of the province in Peralta's absence from Santa Fé, and demanded that an expedition be sent to attack Acoma in order to free the Christian Indians from Zia and wage war against the infidels (*infieles*).[83] The lieutenant governor argued that it would be dangerous to start a war against Acoma because so few soldiers remained in New Mexico, especially after Ordóñez in 1612 had given settlers license to leave the province. The prelate accused officials of being uncooperative and threatened to excommunicate them if they did not agree to the punitive expedition against the Acomans.

On October 2, 1613, the lieutenant governor, who could muster only a handful of soldiers, left the Villa de Santa Fé for Santo Domingo where they joined Ordóñez. From there they went to Sandia where they celebrated the feast of San Francisco. Within a week they were camped below Acoma. From their camp, they launched several unsuccessful assaults that resulted in some of the soldiers being wounded and some Indians killed.[84] Under such conditions, Ordóñez found their failure excusable, but the settlers and priests in the province were fearful that the attacks would cause a general uprising. Within eight days after the attempted assaults on Acoma, the war party returned to Santa Fe.⁸⁵ Their foray against Acoma, in which they were driven off by the warriors, proved to be foolhardy and patently unsuccessful from a military and an ecclesiastical point of view.

After the excitement of the expedition to Acoma, Ordóñez settled into his old pattern of harassing the Peralta loyalists. In November he learned that Juan de Escarramad and others planned to free the governor from his jail at Sandia Pueblo. The commissary ordered the *alcalde ordinario*, Juan de Vitoria Carabajal, to arrest Escarramad and bring him to Santo Domingo. From there, Ordóñez ordered him transferred to a cell at Zia Pueblo to be detained for three and a half months despite the suffering of his wife and children, who were unable to do the farm work without him. With the province under his control, Ordóñez spent December reading all of Peralta's papers and writing reports and letters against the governor.⁸⁶

In January 1614, Ordóñez resolved to send another report to Mexico City regarding the Peralta affair. He chose Captain Cristóbal Baca to do it. Baca, after all, had been the syndic and had played a role in the governor's arrest. The captain spent more that three hours with Ordóñez, who read him the entire report. Upon leaving Ordóñez, he encountered Fray Juan de Salas and Fray Agustín de Burgos, who asked him, "What has the father commissary written?" He stated, "I swear to God there is no truth in all this man writes." Ordóñez spent the rest of the month writing more about Peralta.

In early February, Baca returned to Santo Domingo to receive instructions for his journey to Mexico City with the new reports. Ordóñez also asked Baca to deliver a Black servant to a certain person in Santa Barbara for him to sell. Finally, on February 3, they left, Ordóñez accompanying them to Isleta Pueblo where they stopped to rest for two days. At Isleta Ordóñez discovered that one of Baca's soldiers carried a parcel of secret letters to the viceroy from the lieutenant governor and the *cabildo* of Santa Fe. The prelate, according to witnesses, took them and falsified the signatures.⁸⁷ Soon after, Baca, the soldier, and the Black servant departed for New Spain.

On March 18, Governor Peralta escaped from Sandia. On foot, with much difficulty and without food, the fettered Peralta crossed the rugged hill country east of Santo Domingo. Three days later he arrived in Santa Fe in a state of exhaustion. He went to the lieutenant governor's house to recover. Peralta, in poor health, had not eaten in three days. Badly bruised from the ordeal, he still had shackles on one of his ankles.[88] Father Tirado immediately summoned all the people he could gather and demanded that under pain of excommunication they go and arrest the fugitive. With Tirado they went and took Peralta to the *convento* of the Santa Fe church and put him in a heavily guarded cell for the night. The next day, March 22, the eve of Palm Sunday, dawned as an extremely cold day in Santa Fe with snow and wind. Tirado had Peralta dragged outside, put on a horse, and made to wear an Indian hide for his trip to Santo Domingo.[89]

In the meantime, Ordóñez, who had "wasted a week" looking for Peralta, also hosted another group of prisoners. It seems a gang of Jémez and Apache Indians had killed an Indian from Cochití, a *visita* (i.e., a mission without a resident priest), of Santo Domingo. Ordóñez sent a detachment of soldiers to capture them and bring them to Santo Domingo for trial. On Palm Sunday one of the Indians was sentenced to death by hanging. Despite the fact that he had no jurisdiction in the case, Captain Juan de Vitoria de Carabajal carried out the execution ordered by Ordóñez. More hangings were ordered, "with the result that the [Indians] from this nation wanted to rise in revolt."[90] Before transferring Peralta to Sandia for imprisonment, Ordóñez called the Jémez Indians together so that they could see him as he was being led away. At that point, everyone now clearly understood the father commissary's power.

Taken to the jail at Sandia Pueblo. Peralta remained there until April 6. He had been Ordóñez's prisoner for eight months, during which time Fray Estéban de Perea, guardian of Sandia, complained that he was tired of keeping him there. Finally, the commissary moved Peralta to Zia Pueblo under the guardianship of Fray Cristóbal de Quiros. One day in mid-April a group of Spaniards were at Santa Ana Pueblo to collect the tribute when Father Quiros saw them. He went over and spoke to them. They asked about Peralta. Quiros, an intimate friend of Ordóñez, remarked that all the people were talking about the imprisonment of the governor by churchmen. He countered by saying, "We don't have the governor imprisoned, the Spaniards [of the Villa] do."[91] When the soldiers returned to Santa Fe they told certain citizens who opposed Peralta's imprisonment what Quiros had said in terms of shifting the responsibility from Ordóñez to the settlers. As a result, a rumor began in the Villa in defense of Peralta. When Father Tirado heard about it, he called the soldiers who had spoken to Quiros on the matter and excommunicated them.[92] The whole thing died down quickly.

If any doubt existed in regard to the censure placed on the settlers at the Villa, it was soon erased. On April 20, Ordóñez prayed the Holy Mass in Santa Fe and from the pulpit declared, "I have the governor jailed by authority of the Holy Office of the Inquisition. No one may attempt correspondence with the lieutenant governor nor the alcaldes to stir up the situation. No one ought to meddle in the affair."[93] The congregation clearly understood the point. They would quietly suffer the Ordóñez regime.

Although Ordóñez dictated the affairs of the province as he wished and priests like Quiros and Tirado supported him, other friars disapproved of his actions. In 1614 some of them, including Fray Francisco Pérez Huerta and Fray Andrés Juarez, spoke of returning to Mexico. Convinced that "only God could remedy" the situation, Fray Andrés decided to risk the wrath of Ordóñez and leave. One of his brothers tried to stop him, but he explained that he could take no more. Fray Andrés had determined to leave lest he "hang himself or kill the commissary."[94] He gathered his belongings and finally set out. Ordóñez's spies reported Fray Andrés's plans to him. The prelate wasted no time and went after him. Lying in wait along the way, Ordóñez seized him and took him to Santo Domingo "where he was absolved and put in a kind of jail for four months."[95]

The Juarez affair caused difficulty for others who had sided with Fray Andrés. When the friar sought to escape New Mexico, he took with him a number of letters that were confiscated by Ordóñez. One of them, written by Father Pérez Huerta, was viewed by Ordóñez as damaging to his cause. Pérez Huerta had never been a willing ally of Ordóñez. He merely did as he was told. It seems that Pérez Huerta's differences of opinion with the prelate began during their journey to New Mexico in 1612. One incident that stood out in Pérez Huerta's mind, in which the father commissary showed his dictatorial tendencies, occurred on July 13, 1612, on the trail between Santa Barbara and New Mexico.[96]

While they were camped that day, a fight broke out between two members of the *escolta*, or military escort, Captain Pedro Durán, one of the founders of Santa Fe who had also been with Oñate in 1600, and a corporal. Durán drew his sword and threatened him with harm. Apparently the corporal also held a knife in his hand, and the two men went at it. When the fight finished, the corporal complained to Fray Tirado, and both began to form a case against Durán. Tirado wanted to have Durán garroted and Ordóñez agreed, stating that the royal provision he carried gave him authority to make that kind of decision. Pérez Huerta disagreed because he did not feel it was a serious enough crime. He and the others repeatedly asked the corporal to pardon the captain, but he refused. Ordóñez and Tirado threatened Pérez Huerta and the others and went so far as to arrest Durán and spoke of his death to the point of ordering one of the soldiers to stab the captain with a poniard, a small, sharp, three-cornered dagger. But Pérez Huerta intervened.[97]

Later, in the summer of 1613, Pérez Huerta served as notary for Tirado and Ordóñez when Peralta had been excommunicated and arrested. In many instances, Pérez Huerta did not agree with his prelate, and he seemed always at odds with Tirado.

In spring of 1614, Tirado denounced Pérez Huerta and those who had planned to leave for New Spain. Ordóñez summoned Pérez Huerta to Santo Domingo where he chastised him and sent him back by force to Galisteo where he served as missionary. Pérez Huerta's escort consisted of two brothers who each wore a coat of chain mail. One carried a machete, and the other a pistol. They had instructions to kill Pérez Huerta if he resisted.[98] Smarting from Ordóñez's acrimony, Pérez Huerta wrote a letter of complaint that he asked Father Andrés Juarez to deliver in Mexico City. When Ordóñez confiscated the letter from Fray Andrés and read it, he immediately summoned Pérez Huerta to Santo Domingo and publicly denounced him in the presence of his friars. Ordóñez, furthermore, accused Pérez Huerta of plotting to kill him. He had the friar searched, and they found a small knife on him. Pérez Huerta said it proved nothing as "all the friars carried knives and machetes for their everyday use."[99] Ordóñez sentenced Pérez Huerta to be held in seclusion for several months at Zia Pueblo.

On May 3, 1614, the new governor, Bernardino de Ceballos, a former admiral of the Spanish navy, arrived at Isleta Pueblo. Two days later Ceballos departed for Sandia and then for Santo Domingo. Part way there, Ordóñez came out to meet Ceballos, who had met him years before in Mexico City where he knew him as a friar living in poverty. This time when Ceballos saw him, he asked, "Are you the same *padre missionero* who represents himself as most powerful and exacting, whom I have met before?" He recalled four days prior at Isleta commenting to Padre Guardian Juan de Salas that he should throw Ordóñez out "in a pack saddle for all the things that he knew the father commissary had done." He said he had met Captain Baca on the way, who hardly dared to give him the papers Ordóñez had entrusted to him because of the "false and evil" statements made in them. The indignant Governor Ceballos said he knew that his predecessor was held captive, but he would "release him and honor him . . . as a governor deserves." Thus, Ceballos met Ordóñez once again.[100]

When they arrived at Santo Domingo, he was received by the pueblo amid the ringing of bells and cheers. Inside the church the tabernacle door was open, and organ music could be heard along with a chant the priests had prepared the choir to sing. Ceballos dismounted and went inside the church to pray and then proceeded to his quarters in the *convento* where he rested two days. On the third day, he proceeded to the Villa, accompanied by Ordóñez and some of the friars. Once at Santa Fe, Ceballos wrote a letter, unbeknownst to Ordóñez, telling him that he regretted Peralta's absence and would bring him to the Villa and honor him. Peralta, however, remained incarcerated at Zia for another month.

In the meantime, Ceballos learned of Friar Pérez Huerta's imprisonment. As he had known about the friar before coming to New Mexico, he inquired about him. Ordóñez and Tirado explained that Pérez Huerta, presently in disgrace, had been denounced and that he deserved to be defrocked for his disobedience and his attempted murder of the prelate. Actually, the prelate planned to keep Pérez Huerta incommunicado until after Peralta's departure from New Mexico, which did not occur until November 1614.[101]

Within fifteen days of his arrival, Ceballos began the *residencia*, the customary review and audit of his predecessor's tenure. Peralta's enemies lost little time in giving their testimony to Ceballos. As anyone could say what they wished in such proceedings, Ordóñez nervously attended each session in the hope that his censure of the settlers would still hold and that everyone would be careful about what they said in his presence. Although it seems that the testimony bore heavily against Peralta, it was nonetheless clear that Ordóñez did lack inquisitorial authority for his arrest. The record of the proceedings of the Peralta *residencia* are incomplete, as the actual document has not been found.

According to Pérez Huerta, Peralta did not testify in his own behalf after he arrived in Santa Fe on July 4, 1614. He explained his position and told about his attempts to notify the viceroy about the improper actions taken by Ordóñez. He realized that his *residencia* had been negative and that he could not receive a fair trial in Santa Fe, so he appealed the entire process to the viceroy and *audiencia*. Peralta further explained that Ordóñez had removed all of the papers but that he had taken some testimony from people who were still loyal and was sending them to the *audiencia*. All Peralta would say was that a man named Juan, probably Juan Escarramad, had already departed Santa Fe to deliver the papers to the *audiencia*.

When Ordóñez heard about Peralta's rider, he did all he could to stop him. Governor Ceballos cooperated with Ordóñez to stop Escarramad. Troops were sent after him to catch him; some said they had orders to execute him. A detachment of troops led by Captain Juan Ruiz de Caceres rode south along the Camino Real toward Santo Domingo. Another group of soldiers commanded by Captain Marin rode south and east of Santa Fe toward Galisteo, around the Sierra de Sandia past the Salinas pueblos, in their attempt to catch him. Both troops patrolled the area to the south but failed to find him.

The *residencia* continued into August, and Pedro de Peralta, former governor of New Mexico, and Juan Escarramad, his friend, soon found themselves outcasts. As the feast day of Nuestra Señora de los Angeles de Porciúncula approached, they petitioned Father Tirado for Father Alonso Peinado to hear their confession, as he had heard their confessions many times previously. Father Tirado responded by saying, "I do not believe that Fray Alonso Peinado must hear your confession, and that being the case, if they wish to confess themselves I am here to hear their confession." But before Tirado would even consider granting him absolution, Peralta first had to admit in public that all that he had written about him and Ordóñez was false. Furthermore, Peralta would have to surrender all papers and state in the confessional that he possessed no writings that bore false witness against the prelate. Tirado asked Peralta to make an examination of his conscience in writing and submit it to him before confession. Again Peralta sent the notice with the words, "Yo suplico me deje confesar" (I ask that you allow me to confess). Tirado and Ordóñez considered the request, but Peralta insisted he would only confess his sins to the "Santo Viejo" the old, holy man, Fray Alonso Peinado.

In early November Peralta was finally permitted to leave New Mexico, but not before Father Commissary Ordóñez and Father Guardian Tirado despoiled him of some of his property. Ordóñez kept six ploughshares, two coats of chain mail, and a set of leg armor (*escarcelas*). Tirado took the copy of *Practica Criminal Eclesiástica*, the book that he and Ordóñez had confiscated earlier. But Peralta had not yet suffered the final indignity. Far to the south on the Camino Real at a place called Agua del Perillo in the Jornada del Muerto, northeast of El Paso, four soldiers sent by Governor Ceballos and Father Ordóñez caught up with him and ransacked the cart in which he carried his personal property. They were looking for any papers he might try to smuggle out of New Mexico. There, practically in the middle of nowhere, they searched his *carreta* and his person but could not find the documents. He had hidden them well in a hollowed-out brace of the *carreta* frame.

What were the soldiers looking for? Before Peralta had left Santa Fe, some of the priests had rebelled against Ordóñez and had written a series of reports. Father Peinado led the rebellion. Letters and reports were written to important churchmen in Mexico by Peinado and Father Pedro de Haro. Prudently, Haro refused to send his to Mexico, but Peinado gave a copy to Peralta and sent another copy in the mission mail. Ordóñez found out and "with tears in his eyes" told Peinado that his comments would cause him and the Franciscan Order great harm. "For the love of God" Ordónez pleaded for Peinado to give the copies to him. The "Santo Viejo" heard Ordóñez and said, "I would not want my letters to harm anyone."[102] He wrote a note to the brother who carried the mission mail to return it. As for the second copy, Peralta would have to surrender it. He didn't.

Meantime, Ordóñez called a chapter meeting at Santo Domingo and tried to make "el Santo Viejo" recant whatever the letters contained. Ordóñez and Tirado attempted to disgrace Peinado before his peers and the settlers, but the old priest was too revered among them and the tactic did not work. Finally, the aged and infirm Peinado asked permission to leave for a convent "far from the Villa." About the time Peinado departed Santa Fe for Chililí and Tajique pueblos in the Manzano Mountains amid the tears shed by some of the settlers who loved him, Peralta had gathered his belongings and had left Santa Fe on his way to Mexico City.

Pedro de Peralta arrived in Mexico sometime in the spring of 1615 and doubtless reported to the *audiencia* as soon as he could. On October 6, 1617, after three years of deliberation, a final verdict on the *residencia* had been rendered. Peralta may have felt some sort of vindication in that Ordóñez was finally brought to Mexico. The Inquisition of Mexico in 1615 at least pronounced against Ordóñez' pretensions:

1615 Fray Ysidro Ordóñez, commissary of St. Francis in New Mexico; because pretending to have a commission from the Holy Office and *por causa de Inquisición*, he sought the aid of soldiers and citizens against the governor, Don Pedro de Peralta, seized him and held him in chains for nine months. On complaint of the said Don Pedro and [on the basis of] information which he gave, [Ordóñez] was brought to Mexico and confined to his convent. But nothing was done and [after] giving Peralta a statement that there was no *causa del Santo Officio* [as a basis] for his arrest, license was given to the friar to go as Procurator of this province [of the Franciscan Order] to the General Chapter in Rome.[103]

To a degree, Ordóñez was vindicated. Both men thereafter disappeared from the limelight, but not before their conflicts had opened the door to larger church-state issues, especially those regarding the mission, mission Indians, and the pueblos.

11

La Custodia de la Conversión de San Pablo

Early New Mexico Missions, 1614–25

The Indians received them with glad rejoicings; and, preaching to them through the interpreters whom they took along, they instructed and catechized them in the mysteries of our Holy Faith; those Gentiles begging for the sacrosanct water of Baptism [and] thirsting for it; wherein is seen how God giveth knowledge to souls through the Baptismal absolution.

—Fray Juan de Perea, 1631[1]

Fray Isidro Ordóñez's star faded slowly. For approximately two years after the departure of Peralta in November 1614, he continued to exercise the powers of prelate. Issues between civil authorities and the missionaries under Prelate Ordóñez plagued relationships between provincial officials, settlers, and Pueblo Indians. At first Ordóñez showed Governor Bernardino de Ceballos cooperation and friendliness, but as summer turned to autumn, he dropped all amicable pretenses. The reason for this change is unclear, but the pretext seemed to be disagreement over Indian affairs. The same arguments used by Ordóñez against Peralta surfaced against Governor Ceballos.

Reflecting on Ordóñez's tactics, Fray Francisco Pérez Huerta looked back on how Ordóñez had cleverly used Indian relations as a basis for his grievance against Peralta. Although Ordóñez dutifully kept watch on how Peralta administered Indian labor and paid close attention to any abuses or mistreatment of Indians by private individuals, "every little fault which occurred was insinuated and exaggerated in the extreme."[2] Ordóñez saw to it that the governor did not pardon any soldier for committing any offense against Indians. To placate Ordóñez, Peralta issued an order that he would levy a fine of "so many blankets and ten days in jail for whosoever mistreats an Indian." Presumably the blankets would be given to the offended Indian as damages.[3] The statement only reinforced the law and sentiment already codified in the Laws of the Indies.

The publicity given the subject tended to interfere with the traditional colonial business of tribute collection. Seeing that the governor actually executed the fines and punishments, the pueblos would cunningly bait the colonials to commit acts of violence in order to claim damages. The confrontations usually ran according to a pattern, explained Pérez Huerta: the colonial would ask for tribute in blankets, and the Indians would refuse to give them, whereupon the tribute collector would threaten to "strike them on their faces" if they did not give the tribute. The Indians, "greedy for blankets," played their game. Taunting, the Indians would say, "Go ahead, hit me, and you will pay me the blankets the governor orders."[4]

Somehow the *encomenderos* managed to collect the tribute, but not without hard feelings and frustration on their part and resentment on the part of the Indians. Nonetheless, many Spaniards had begun to lose patience with Peralta's scrutiny and strict observance of the rules that seemed to favor the Indians. Those concerned with the issue, for example, took notice after Peralta ordered Aséncio de Archuleta, *encomendero* of Cochití, to "pay fifty mantas and fifty fanegas of maize to those he had abused over a period of three years."[5] Apparently, through some privilege, Archuleta owned a house (*casa de asiento*) at Cochití; otherwise, pursuant to the Laws of the Indies, Spaniards were prohibited from owning property inside any Indian town.[6] Archuleta's family, nevertheless, were aghast at the tremendous fine imposed on their kin "as they were not accustomed to such judgment being made against them."[7] Peralta made many enemies among the settlers as a result of his policy, but also made Indian friends. As a result, during his *residencia* in

Santa Fe, many Indians came to testify in his behalf. Ordóñez knew well the dynamics and intricacies of Spanish colonial society in the empire, and Santa Fe was no exception.

When Ordóñez and Tirado tried to persuade Governor Ceballos to follow the same policies, he refused. Having seen that Peralta's problems were partially due to lack of support from the settlers, Ceballos reckoned that he could not afford to alienate the leading citizens and soldiers of the Villa with such a policy. He learned of the animosity between Ordóñez and Peralta from many Santa Feans and slowly began to realize his mistake in not having sent the prelate with Peralta to New Spain when he had the chance. The father commissary placed so many complaints at the governor's doorstep that one day Ceballos, having had enough, went with two soldiers to the *convento* to threaten him with his life, but they could not find him. For eight days, armed with harquebuses, they looked for him to shoot him on sight. Apparently Ordóñez left the convent only at night to do his business. "So great were the scandals," wrote Pérez Huerta, "that it would require another large memorial or account like this one to tell about them."[8]

Ordóñez's influence among his clergy deteriorated to the point where he nearly lost his ability to administer them with confidence. On February 8, 1616, Friar Agustín de Burgos went to Chililí to assist Peinado in baptizing the Indians he had converted. Burgos spoke many times with Peinado about Ordóñez, and on one occasion he learned that Peinado still had the letter Ordóñez had presented to him in 1612 to replace him. After Friar Burgos left Chililí, he returned to Galisteo to rest for a few days and passed that information to Pérez Huerta. He added that he and Peinado had looked at the letter "with attention and discovered that it was false from the first letter to the last, [even] the seal."[9] Curious to see it, Pérez Huerta asked that Peinado send him the letter, which he did. When the letter arrived in Galisteo, four priests read it and determined itsinauthenticity. Pérez Huerta challenged Ordóñez several times to show him the patent authorizing him to be father commissary, but Prelate Ordóñez at first refused, or at least delayed doing so.[10]

A debate ensued between Ordóñez's loyal followers and the dissident group led by Pérez Huerta. Soon debate led to confrontation. Ordóñez ordered Pérez Huerta and two others to come to the Santa Fe convent. Pérez Huerta had hoped to avoid a confrontation, but it occurred anyway. Ordóñez called him in and showed him the "patent." "I saw it and I read it," said Pérez Huerta, "but to this day I am in disbelief that he was [truly] my prelate."[11] Ordóñez ordered him into seclusion and took him, the next day, to Santo Domingo where he placed him and two others in two cells.

Friar Estéban de Perea traveled there from Sandia Pueblo to write the report against them. The friars were divided in their support for Ordóñez, but blamed Pérez Huerta for the latest incident. Ordóñez circulated a petition against Pérez Huerta, but many of the friars refused to sign it. After a meeting in which the report and Pérez Huerta's insubordination were discussed, the friars decided to expel him from New Mexico. As he prepared to leave, Fray Juan de Salas had him unpack his belongings and sent him on his way without them. By the time he got to the last convent, probably Isleta, he was, for some unexplained reason, ordered back.[12]

Pérez Huerta ended his report with the events of spring 1616. His description of events to that point are the only record of the period 1612–16. By 1617, Ordóñez had been recalled to Mexico City, and Ceballos's term of office would expire within the following year.

Sometime in 1616 a new prelate for New Mexico was appointed with the title of custodian (*custos*), which signified greater authority and local autonomy for the missions than that enjoyed under a commissary, a title that implied delegated, temporary authority. As prelate, the *custos* exercised general supervision of the work of the missions, administered the rule of the minor friars under his charge, and acted as their spokesman. Although Ordóñez went beyond his jurisdiction and crossed the line of authority to assume his power, the work of prelates generally included assigning priests to the missions, attending to church affairs such as the general administration of tithes to be collected from the settlers, approving the creation of *confradias* (brotherhoods), presiding over the missionaries in their chapter meetings, distributing the mission supplies, and, in general, watching over the administration of the church calendar and of Indian policy as it concerned Indians in their charge.

The New Mexico mission field was, at this time, named the Custodia de la Conversión de San Pablo, adopting St. Paul as its patron because of the many incidents associated with him in its already full but brief history. The church calendar in the province maintained "the celebration day" (January 25) of the conversion of St. Paul as the "day the glorious saint is honored as the general patron on account of the marvelous things he has done in this region."[13]

The Spaniards often claimed that St. Paul had divinely aided them at the battle of Acoma, thus saving the Christian settlement from certain destruction. In particular, they claimed they saw, an apparition in the sky representing the blessed Virgin Mary, St. Paul. or Santiago.[14] Wherever New Mexicans went, they celebrated the feast day of their patron. When in 1604–5, Oñate led an expedition to the head of the Gulf of California, they camped there on January 25. There he performed an act of possession. As part of the ceremony, the priest prayed the Holy Mass, and, soon after, don Juan took formal possession of it in the name of his king and God. "With his sword in his hand [he] went into the water to his waist and, striking the sea, said that he took possession of those countries for the King of Spain, and the friar, too, entered the water with a crucifix and said that he took possession of it for God, for the holy Catholic faith, and for the holy mother church of Rome." They named it Puerto de la Conversión de San Pablo and described it as a large harbor where "a thousand vessels can anchor in it."[15]

In 1616 the new *padre custodio* arrived in New Mexico. Friar Estéban de Perea was about fifty years of age when he succeeded Ordóñez as prelate. A native of Villanueva de Fresno in Extremadura, Spain, he was of Portuguese ancestry.[16] His father, Rodrigo Alonso, was from Beja, and his mother, Inez Núñez, was born in Moncaraz, just across the border from Villanueva. Born and reared in southern Spain, Perea doubtless had been influenced by the many tales of the Americas he had heard as a child. He entered the Franciscan Order in Spain and went to Mexico in 1605. There he affiliated himself with the missionary work in the vast Provincia del Santo Evangelio. Four years later, he joined the Peinado group, which set out for New Mexico. Under Peinado, he worked among the Tiwa of the Río Abajo along the middle Rio Grande Valley. In 1612, when the Ordóñez group passed by Sandia Pueblo, Friar Pérez Huerta remarked that it was the "primer convento de este Nuevo Mexico" (the first convent one comes to in New Mexico).[17] The *convento* at the mission of San Francisco de Sandia seemed obviously large enough to hold a jail for such prisoners as Governor Peralta.

During the four years under Ordóñez, Perea did not always appear sympathetic toward his prelate, but he was considered "zealous in the propagation of the faith, fearless in denunciation of error, and unrelenting in defense of ecclesiastical jurisdiction and immunity."[18] He served in New Mexico from

1609 until his death in the winter of 1638–39. During the years 1617–21 he served as *custos* of the missions in the Conversión de San Pablo.

When Perea took over the New Mexican mission field in 1617, the friars were scattered over an area along the Rio Grande from San Ildefonso in the north to Isleta in the south, and from Jémez in the west to Galisteo in the east. A series of missions dotted the Spanish map around Galisteo and south of there to the Salinas group of missions at Chililí, Tajique, and Quarai. The pattern of the mission field had been heavily influenced by Fray Alonso Peinado, who expanded the *doctrinas* by assigning priests to work in the areas that had been rarely visited by priests since the Oñate period. Under Fray Alonso, the mission field was still in its incipient stage; Perea would intensify the effort somewhat, so that by 1635 the missionization of New Mexico would be in full bloom.[19]

Before Perea assumed the prelacy of New Mexico, the mission priests were distributed around a greater area than they had been during the Oñate period. Fray Luis Tirado, a protégé of Ordóñez who along with Peinado had established the church in Santa Fe, served the Villa from 1612 to 1616. North of the Villa, Fray Andrés Bautista, who arrived with the Peinado group in 1609, founded the permanent mission at San Ildefonso, which he served from 1610 until 1631. Fray Pedro de Haro de la Cuesta, who came up from Mexico with Ordóñez in 1612, established the mission at Nambé and was still there in the early 1630s. Fray Andrés Suárez of the 1609 Peinado group succeeded him. Suárez served as guardian at Nambé from 1635 to 1647. The San Juan mission was probably a *visita* of San Ildefonso or Nambé, as were other Tiwa pueblos during the period.[20]

Although Fray Alonso Peinado assigned a priest to Galisteo about 1610, he himself is the first known guardian of Galisteo in 1612. In 1613 he was subordinate to Fray Andrés Bautista at San Ildefonso, and in 1615 the aged Fray Bernardo de Marta served as guardian at Galisteo. By 1616, Fray Francisco Pérez Huerta, the author of *Verdadera relación*, had replaced Marta. It is possible that in 1613 Fray Andrés Perguer established the Tano mission at San Lazaro near the Ortiz Mountains, then known as the Sierra de San Lazaro.[21]

In late 1613 Peinado decided to "banish himself" as far from Santa Fe as he could and still be in the province. As a result, he established the mission at Chililí, a Tiwa pueblo in the Manzano Mountains, no later than 1614. In 1616 Fray Agustín Burgos went there to assist in the baptism of the newly converted Tiwas. Peinado probably remained at Chililí until his death on November 16 of 1622 or 1623. He was believed to have been buried at Chililí. Other friars who served at Chililí include Fray Francisco de Salazar (1634 and 1636), Fray Fernando de Velasco (ca. 1660), and Fray Gomez de la Cadena (1671–72). Peinado dedicated the church at Chililí that he established to La Natividad de Nuestra Señora. Perea was the first guardian of Sandia; the convent at Zia Pueblo had as its first guardian Fray Cristóbal Quiros, who came with Peinado in 1610 and became a staunch supporter of Ordóñez.[22]

Fray Juan de Salas founded Isleta, the southernmost mission, during the early period, late 1612 or early 1613. Father Salas remained there until 1630. In 1629 Fray Diego López came to live at Isleta, which continued to grow in importance as a stopping place for weary travelers coming up from Mexico or leaving. Fifteen mission sites were scattered throughout the Province of New Mexico. Along the Camino Real, which stretched from Mexico City to the Villa de Santa Fe, there were by 1616 six New Mexican missions: Santa Fe, Santo Domingo, Cochití, San Felipe, Sandia, and Isleta. Cochití (1614) and San Felipe (1615) were *visitas* administered from Santo Domingo. The other missions of New Mexico lay west of the Rio Grande at Zia, Santa Ana, and Jémez, east of the river at San Lazaro, Galisteo, and Chililí, and north of Santa Fe at San Juan, San Ildefonso, and Nambé.[23] With Ordóñez gone, sixteen Franciscans administered them.

In his first term as *custos* (1617–21) Perea appointed Sebastian de Noboa y Castro syndic and procurator general of the *custodia*. Noboa y Castro lodged a formal complaint against Juan Escarramad for having made scandalous remarks about certain friars. Escarramad was out of favor with most people in the Villa because he had been a strong supporter of Peralta. Although it is uncertain, it appeared that he was probably the person who had made the daring run to Mexico City to deliver Peralta's dispatches to the *audiencia* and made the report against Ordóñez. When Escarramad returned with the mission caravan in 1616, his troubles began. The following winter he went to Sandia for confession with Friar Cristóbal Quiros, a friend of Ordóñez. Quiros showed Escarramad a report containing his statement against the clergy. Before he could absolve him in the confessional, Quiros asked Escarramad to recant. He refused to take back his remarks, and soon after Noboa y Castro presented the charges against him to the ecclesiastical judge delegate.[24]

In the trial eight witnesses testified that Escarramad had said that Fray Pedro de Escolar had been an outlaw in New Spain before he became a priest; that Fray Alonso de San Juan was a licentious person; that Governor Peralta was a better Christian than all the friars; that Ordóñez had lied to the viceroy and the *audiencia* about Peralta; and that in New Mexico only three friars were "worthy of the name, for all the others were devils who wished to disturb the land."[25]

Escarramad's trial dragged on. The intrepid frontiersman refused to have a lawyer represent him and he refused to testify in his own behalf. He asked Quiros to bring forth the paper that he claimed to have shown him at Sandia when he refused to hear his confession. Quiros said that after Escarramad had refused to recant, he had destroyed the paper. Escarramad denounced the validity of his trial, which went on despite his protests. On July 1, 1617, he was found guilty as charged, fined fifteen *mantas*, and ordered to make a public confession of his crime against the priests. The defendant appealed the decision of the *audiencia*, but the court refused his plea.

Despite his sentence Escarramad refused to pay the fine. The priests appealed to Governor Ceballos to make him comply. At first the governor refused, but did so after he had aroused the wrath of Fray Cristóbal Quiros, who had him excommunicated.[26] During the end of his administration, Ceballos underwent the same embarrassment of the public penance and unhappy relationship with the priests as had Peralta. Meantime, he gave in and forced Escarramad to perform his penance. "In irons and gagged he [Escarramad] was taken through the streets of [Santa Fé] to the parish church where, in the presence of assembled citizens, he heard mass and made a formal retraction of the libels and slanders he had made against the clergy,"[27] wrote Pérez Huerta.

The Peralta affair had indeed traumatized New Mexican society. The Peralta-Ordóñez episode carried over into the Ceballos-Perea administrations. The Escarramad case showed that the traumatic Peralta-Ordóñez affair could not be forgotten by that generation of New Mexicans. Later Perea had a falling out with Captain Gerónimo Márquez, a leading frontiersman and a supporter of Ordóñez who assisted in the arrest of Peralta. Perea's disdain for Márquez, whom he considered a troublemaker, reached a point where he asked officials in Mexico City to expel Márquez and his family from New Mexico. In the end, the sad state of affairs from 1610 to 1621 set the pattern for church-state relations, which ran its course to 1680. In many ways, the church-state feud formed one of the many complex causes of Indian dissatisfaction with Spanish colonial rule.

During the period, the New Mexico mission field markedly expanded. As new missions spread to the far reaches of New Mexico, so too, by the same token, did Spanish control over the area expand. Under Custos Perea, the mission field extended to Pecos, Picurís, and Taos on the eastern frontier facing the edge of the Great Plains, the Tompiro pueblo of Abó in the Manzano Mountains facing the southern plains, and Jémez to the west of Santa Fe.

At the end of December 1616, another supply train prepared to leave Mexico City bound for New Mexico. With the caravan were seven Franciscans who brought a patent confirming Fray Estéban Perea as father *custos* of the New Mexico missions. At their first chapter meeting, Perea assigned some of them to serve as guardians of newly established *conventos* and others to work at some of the missions that had been in existence for some time.

By 1619 the mission at Pecos had a permanent guardian assigned there. In 1609, Fray Pedro Zambrano Ortiz, a Canary Islander, had, at age twenty-three, received the Franciscan habit at the Convento Grande in Mexico City. Seven years later, Fray Pedro and some of the Franciscan brethren dedicated the new *convento* of Nuestra Señora de los Angeles de los Pecos on August 2 of 1617 or 1618. Zambrano served at Pecos until 1621, when he was assigned to Galisteo. He became an active opponent of Governor Juan de Eulate.[28]

Meanwhile, sometime between 1614 and 1621, the missionaries abandoned Mission San Lazaro in Galisteo because of interference by *encomenderos*, who discouraged conversion. The priests complained that the *encomenderos*, who, by law, could not collect tribute from mission Indians, actively encouraged the persistence of the native religion. The *encomendero* at San Lazaro told the newly converted Indians that they did not have to give up their idols or concubinage. As a result, Fray Pedro de Ortega had difficulty maintaining the mission discipline at San Lazaro and the other Galisteo mission sites. In 1621 San Lazaro, administered from Galisteo throughout the seventeenth century, became a *visita* of either Galisteo or San Marcos. When Father Zambrano went there in 1621,[29] he found the Tanos of San Lazaro and the other Galisteo pueblos publicly practicing idolatry. Having chastised the natives, he learned from one of them that the *encomendero*, Juan Gómez, a fluent Tano speaker, had departed New Mexico bound for Mexico City to seek permission for the

Tanos "to live as before they were Christians."[30] Governor Juan de Eulate had encouraged Gómez in that effort. During his term of office (1618–25), Eulate had engaged in a series of disputes over authority with Father Custos Estéban Perea. Zambrano remained at Galisteo until at least 1632.

During Zambrano's guardianship at Galisteo, he sent a lay brother, Pedro de Vergara, in 1621 to begin mission work at San Cristóbal. The mission work went slowly, and not until 1626 did San Cristóbal have a *convento* and a guardian, Fray Alonso de Estremera. During his tenure at Galisteo, Zambrano had established the convent of San Marcos. The establishment of the Galisteo missions actually began during the Oñate period and intensified under Zambrano between 1621 and 1630. Along the lower Rio Grande mission work begun earlier continued at Zia, and Santo Domingo. Fray Cristóbal de Quiros, its guardian, apparently remained until his death in 1643.[31]

Between 1617 and 1621, San Felipe and Pecos were the only new convents established. In 1621 a new custodian, Fray Miguel de Chavarría, arrived to replace Fray Estéban Perea. Apparently Perea's fight against Governor Juan de Eulate had reached a point where authorities in Mexico decided to send out a peacemaker. Perea viewed Eulate as an obstacle to the mission process and someone who should be removed from New Mexico. Many of the priests supported that view, especially Father Zambrano, who watched his missionary endeavors almost fall into shambles because of Eulate and his *encomenderos'* constant efforts to undermine his work. Sarcastically, Zambrano quipped that Eulate was "a man more suited to a junk shop than to the office of governor he holds."[32] Even less forgiving, Custos Perea wrote the viceroy about Eulate's venal acts, defiant immorality, and crass misuse of the natives. Once again, ecclesiastical privilege, power, and spheres of activity clashed with civil jurisdiction under the traditional Spanish church-state arrangement.

Eulate and his tribute collectors saw it differently; after all, he had been appointed royal governor, the third one since Peralta and Ceballos. Like his predecessors, he had been given a set of instructions to maintain all colonial laws and policies, which included the right and the obligation to collect tribute, a form of taxation, in the name of the king. If the tribute could not be paid by the Indians, he had the customary right to convert the tribute in kind to service. He also had the right to authorize Indian work crews upon request by an *encomendero*, settler, or even a priest, when necessary public works such as the construction of acequias, buildings, or other structures needed to be built or a piece of land needed to be cleared for cultivation. Under the rules of the *repartimiento* (forced labor system under contract policies), Indians were to be paid a minimum wage, were contracted for a particular task and number of days, and were exempted from working on holy days of obligation and prayer. The viceroy's instructions of 1621 were clear: "All levies or repartimientos of Indian laborers were to be limited only to the work of sowing and planting, the number to be called from each pueblo strictly limited."[33] Although some abuses did take place, the Spanish legal system did permit Indians to sue or bring charges for any abuses. Especially during the *residencia* of an outgoing governor, such abuses were reviewed and evaluated by a special official called the *protector de indios*.[34]

The Laws of the Indies prohibited governors, as in Eulate's case, from meddling with the mission process. Governors were also not allowed to collect tribute from mission Indians. By law, mission Indians were exempt from tribute paying and tithing for ten years. The ten-year period represented the period of time required for conversion, rarely achieved and generally extended by mission priests. Specifically, Eulate and future governors as well as the friars were instructed about the policies regarding the collection of tribute. In 1621, on the other hand, the viceroy of New Spain decreed, "In those pueblos already subject to tribute of encomienda, the friars were not to impede the collection of tribute. In pueblos converted in the future, no tributes were to be levied until governor, custodian, and the guardian of the convent had made reports to the viceroy who would decide what was best. In New Mexico, for example, no tributes were collected at the Zúñi and Hopi pueblos, as they were still unconverted."[35] Thus it was to Eulate's advantage not to encourage Indians to participate in the mission process. Indians, on the other hand, found that the mission had at least one advantage: exemption from tribute and payment of tithes. Colonial governors in charge of tribute collection loathed the missionization of Indians because it was an obstacle to the administration of tax collection and public works.

As New Mexico's third royal governor, Eulate had, previous to coming to New Mexico, served in Flanders and in the New Spain Flota.[36] He had also served as governor of the island of Margarita in the Caribbean, north of Venezuela. Contrary to the opinions of the missionaries, civil authorities there held that Eulate had served with distinction. The treatment of Indians at Margarita was not the most ideal. The pearl fisheries, where Indians were forced to dive and stay underwater for long periods of time, were well known. Perhaps such experiences gave Eulate the impression that the friars' views of Indian rights could be discounted in New Mexico, as they had been on Isla de Margarita.³⁷

Eulate clashed with churchmen over other values and matters. He held strong opinions that aggravated the priests, who condemned his views as unorthodox. When he proclaimed that matrimony was better, or more perfect, than celibacy, they were outraged. As regards ecclesiastical jurisdiction, Eulate declared that the king was his superior and that given the choice between obeying the king or obeying the pope, he would obey the king. He did not hide his disdain for clergymen and insulted them in the presence of Spaniards and Indians, often expressing a desire, although never actually doing so, to beat and maltreat the friars. In general, Eulate's behavior proved to be unsympathetic and hostile to the missionaries. In his view their program to convert Indians interfered with his line of authority over the citizens of the province, who were considered by the priests to be laymen of the church. Caught between the two jurisdictions, church and state, the citizenry did not often know where their loyalties should rest. Complicating the situation, Eulate demanded that he had first authority over the citizenry of the province he governed. If Custos Perea had any thought of excommunicating him, Eulate had a solution for that too: he threatened to send Perea to Mexico as a prisoner if the *custos* excommunicated him.³⁸

In many ways it was Eulate's Indian policy, as much as his attitude and opinions about the clergy, that caused much of the conflict between him and the equally strong-headed Father Perea. Although *escoltas* usually helped the friars control the Indians and often meted out the punishments for the priests, Eulate refused to permit his soldiers to do so. He denied military escort for friars who needed to travel between pueblos and remain in hostile Indian villages for periods of time as they did their mission work, and even went as far as to discourage soldiers from doing so on a voluntary basis. Yet he would assign soldiers to escort tribute collectors because he felt it was more in keeping with his instructions and duties as governor. And he discouraged Spanish frontiersmen from assisting the priests in their mission work as well. Often called upon by priests to help in the construction of churches and other buildings, the settlers were intimidated and ridiculed by Eulate for doing so.³⁹

As a result, discipline among mission Indians broke down and the pueblos easily reverted to their old religious practices. When Juan Gómez, *encomendero* at San Lazaro, encouraged the Indians to ignore the priest and to continue their old ways, Eulate exploited the delicate relationship between mission, pueblo, and *encomienda*. He knew that pueblo headmen opposed the presence of friars in their pueblos. He also knew that Indians not in a mission program were subject to tribute payments. It appears that at San Lazaro, at least, the Puebloans chose to keep their old ways by resisting the friars and preferred the liabilities of the *encomienda* to conversion. Earlier Eulate had ordered Captain Pedro Duran y Chaves to inform the Tiwas that they need not obey the friars at all except when the friars called them to mass, and then they should go with them.[40]

Beyond recognizing the obligation of the king's vassals to attend mass, Eulate often sided with pueblo religious leaders against the friars. The priests watched Eulate's exploitation of Indians and his involvement in Indian slavery, as well as his attempts to influence elections of Indian officials who governed the pueblos. Thus, the friars, frustrated in their work because of the lack of support given them by the chief civil authority, turned to Mexico City for relief.[41]

As soon as the friars' grievances could be gathered, Custos Perea sent them on to the Tribunal of the Holy Office of the Inquisition in Mexico City and other officials, who eventually passed them on to the king in Spain. The response from imperial authorities came slowly. On July 29, 1620, the viceregal authorities began their deliberations in the charges brought against Eulate by Perea. Six months later, dispatches were sent to Perea and Eulate. The dispatches not only contained instructions for Governor Eulate to carry out but also reflected a change of policy affecting the fundamental authority of the royal governor. Both ecclesiastical and civil jurisdictions were defined in terms that Perea and Eulate would understand. The dispatch, issued on January 9, 1621, also alluded to the grievance voiced by friars and civilians against Eulate in a series of "letters, memorials, depositions and other documents."[42]

Perea's charges were addressed specifically. Basing his claim to authority on church documents, he said that his "authority and jurisdiction in the province was supreme as well as ordinary" in all ecclesiastical matters. He furthermore claimed his rights from bulls issued by Popes Leo X and Adrian VI that authorized him to "issue any censure and interdict against any persons whatever state, condition, or preeminence that may be, imposing upon them punishments at [his] command," and that the governor "should not and could not decree or determine any matter touching on his said government without first consulting . . . and following the advice" offered by him and his friars in the Custodia de la Conversión de San Pablo. Perea also claimed that his predecessor, Fray Isidro Ordóñez, exercised the same rights against Royal Governors Peralta and Ceballos. In stating that such authority exceeded and contradicted what had been intended by the holy canons and bulls of the papacy and in viceregal cedulas, the viceroy took umbrage at his governors being excommunicated and humiliated by the clergy.[43]

As regards Perea's power as *padre custodio*, the viceroy wrote, "I ask you and I enjoin you that you, the said Father Custodio holding ordinary jurisdiction in those said provinces, employ it and exercise it in conformity with what is right in the matters spiritual and ecclesiastical which may pertain to your Jurisdiction."[44] The viceroy further prohibited Perea from passing judgments against laymen without first making an appeal to the archbishop of Mexico, adding, "You shall not proceed to execute your decisions until my said Audiencia which resides in the City of Mexico may decide whether you shall give them effect or not."[45] Meantime, the archbishop ordered Perea to absolve anyone whom he might have excommunicated and to rescind any interdicts and censures he might have imposed while the *audiencia* considered the judgment. Perea's instructions were clear; his jurisdiction lay only in ecclesiastical matters. But within the sphere of the church-state arrangement the instructions were not as clear as the viceroy believed them to be.

The instructions given to Eulate were detailed but as vague as those given to Perea. The viceroy ordered the governor to grant the assistance Perea had requested for his missionaries earlier. The viceroy, moreover, commanded his governor to consult the *padre custodio*, other experienced friars, and the Cabildo de Santa Fe for their opinion in certain matters, but he alone had the authority to make the final decision. Under such terms, Governor Eulate had to stay away from the pueblos during the days of their elections. Clearly, the law stressed that no representative of church or state should be present at any pueblo on election day, January 1 of every year, so that Indians would be assured of their own leadership. The governor's only role in pueblo elections was to confirm the election results. On feast days, Sundays, and other special holidays, the priests should go to the pueblos where there were churches so that the Indians would not have to travel long distances to hear mass, receive the sacraments, or be instructed in the catechism.[46]

As regards tribute, the instructions in the Real Provisión of 1621 were sufficiently clear.[47] In pueblos already subject to the *encomienda*, the friars were not to interfere with the collection of tribute. However, no tribute could be collected in pueblos yet to be converted without orders from the custodian. Even then, the governor, the *padre custos*, and the missionary must show cause for the imposition of tribute on a pueblo and submit a report to the viceroy, who would decide what would be best. A common justification for tribute had to do with the required Spanish military protection of the pueblos from their enemies. The protection requirement meant that Eulate had to assure that the sacraments be administered in the pueblos and that military escorts be detailed to protect the mission supply trains from Mexico City.[48]

As one of the complaints against Eulate concerned his unlawful employment of Indian labor on a cattle ranch (*estancia*) that he maintained and where he used Indian workers for personal purposes, the viceroy denied him Indian labor in grazing herds for his personal use. The instructions of 1621 specifically stated that the governor was "forbidden to graze herds of livestock for his own account." Additionally, Spaniards were instructed "not to pasture their stock within three leagues of the pueblos, except under certain circumstances."[49] Likewise, neither the friars nor the *custos* would be permitted the illegal use of Indian labor for themselves. At the mission it should be used only "for things necessary for the church and the convenience of the living quarters . . . with the greatest moderation." The instructions of 1621 forbade the employment of Indian women as servants by Spaniards unless "they voluntarily go with their husbands."[50] All authorized *repartimientos* of Indian laborers limited work to sowing and planting, specified the size and number of crews from each pueblo, and required wages paid for the work as prescribed by law. In that same directive, Indian labor in the missions could only be used for "things necessary for the church and the convenience of the living quarters . . . with the greatest moderation."[51] However, the friars continued to complain that Eulate's *encomenderos* did not pay the Indians as they should according to law: *un real cada dia o de comer y medio real* (one real a day, or one meal and half a real a day).

The instructions of 1621 prohibited that Indians be punished by having their hair cut for minor offenses. Such punishments had caused mission

Indians to flee to the unconverted pueblo of Acoma, which meant "returning to idolatry" (*bolviendose a la ydolatría*), because, to the Indian, "it is a very great affliction as it is for them a principal affront."⁵²

By the time Chavarría replaced Perea, the viceroy had identified the fundamental causes of the controversy, which revolved around the question of ecclesiastical jurisdiction in relation to civil authority and Indian policy. Although the viceroy stated that the authority of the governor would predominate, the clergy would continue to press for a more equitable situation.

Chavarría arrived in New Mexico sometime in October 1621. As Perea's replacement, he hoped to ameliorate relations with Eulate just as his superiors had instructed him. He had come to restore harmony with an old friend, for he and Eulate had known each other previously. Perea did not like the situation and appealed to his prelate to let him go to Mexico City, but Chavarría refused to grant him permission. From 1,500 miles away, the viceroy tried to dictate the deportment of Eulate and Perea toward one another, even to the point of prescribing to them how they should greet each other with courtesy. Perea, on principle, would have nothing to do with it. As a staunch protector of the New Mexico church, he must have felt a sense of outrage whenever Custos Chavarría exchanged pleasantries with Governor Eulate. For the next few years, Perea would work to get rid of Chavarría. The rift between Chavarría and Perea was irreconcilable.⁵³

Before returning to Mexico City in 1622, Fray Chavarría appointed Fray Asensio de Zarate as *custodio* and prelate. Fray Asencio served as interim *custodio* from 1622 to 1625.⁵⁴ During Chavarría's absence and Fray Asencio de Zarate's tenure as *custodio* ad interim, the missionary effort in the Conversión de San Pablo picked up. Franciscan missionaries were assigned to Picurís, Taos, Jémez, and Abó. One of the priests who came with Chavarría in 1621, Fray Martín de Arvide, founded the mission of San Lorenzo at Picurís.

Indeed, Father Arvide's tenure as a missionary in New Mexico indicated that he had served at several pueblos.⁵⁵ Of Father Arvide, who had a difficult time with the natives at Picurís, Fray Alonso Benavides in his memorial wrote:

> Here [at Picurís] he converted more than two hundred Indians, suffering great hardships and personal dangers, as these people are the most indomitable of that kingdom. He founded a church and convent large enough to minister to all the baptized. Among the newly converted there was a young man, a son of

one of the principal sorcerers. On a certain occasion, the latter undertook to pervert his son and dissuade him from what the father taught. When the friar was informed of it, he left the convent with a crucifix in his hands and, filled with apostolic spirit, he went to the place where the infernal minister was perverting that soul and began to remonstrate with him saying, "It is not sufficient that you yourself want to go to hell without desiring to take your son also?" Addressing the young man, he said, "Son, I am more your father and I love you more than he, for he wants to take you with him to the suffering of hell, while I wish you to enjoy the blessings of being Christian." With divine zeal, he advanced these and other arguments. The old sorcerer arose, grasped a large club nearby, and struck the blessed father such a blow on the head that he felled him, and then he and the others dragged him around the plaza and ill-treated him cruelly. Miraculously, he escaped from their hands; although very eager to offer his life to its giver, God preserved him for a later occasion.[56]

Brutal though the treatment of Father Arvides turned out to be, Benavides realized that the anti-Spanish factions among the pueblos represented a conservative view that the Spanish were destructive to the Indian way of life. Those who tried to temper the situation realized that they could not overcome Spanish arms and might, so they tried to make the best out of an unfavorable situation. In some places, like Acoma, the Spanish opponents prevailed for a long period of time. Throughout New Mexico, as elsewhere in the Americas, however, incidents of Indian defiance had become increasingly common.

Father Arvides's poor treatment at the hands of Picurís warriors signaled the beginning of the open rebellion at Picurís that lasted seven years. After the incident at Picurís, Arvide became the missionary at the Conversión de los Piros on the lower Rio Grande near Socorro, where he served until 1626. Shortly afterward, he was assigned to Jémez.[57] There he replaced Fray Gerónimo de Zárate Salmerón, who arrived with Chavarría in 1621. Fray Gerónimo had been at Jémez since late 1621 where he founded San José de Jémez near the hot springs. Despite his talents as a linguist and his tireless efforts as a missionary, the independent Jémez residents rebelled in 1623, burned the church, and abandoned the mission. The priest blamed Eulate's policies for the rebellion. Benavides reported that, from 1625 to 1626, Father Arvide had established two pueblos: one at San José de Jémez and another at San Diego de la Congregación. Actually, Arvides's efforts were aided by other factors. The Jémez returned because of increased raids by the Navajo against them and a famine that threatened their lives. San Diego was founded in the principal pueblo of the Jémez.[58] As for Fray Gerónimo de Zárate Salmerón, he achieved fame for his *Relaciones*, which was an "account of all the things that have been seen and learned in New Mexico by sea as well as by land from the year 1538 until the year 1626."[59] As a linguist he wrote a *doctrina*, a catechism in the Jémez language.

Under Chavarría, Fray Pedro de Ortega undertook the conversion of Taos. Ortega, who had been at Pecos, was transferred in 1622 to work among the rebellious Taoseños, who constantly threatened his life. He arrived in New Mexico with Governor Eulate's caravan in 1618.[60] Before going to Taos, he helped establish the mission at Pecos. The Taoseños severely and cruelly tested him. The Indians, he claimed, tried to discourage him from being there by giving him "tortillas of corn made with urine and mice meat, but he used to say that for a good appetite there is no bad bread, and the tortillas tasted fine."[61] Nor would the Taos give him shelter in their pueblo. He lived alone outside the village in a shelter made of branches, a privation that caused him great suffering in the below-freezing temperatures in the winter months of northern New Mexico.[62] By considerable effort and good fortune, Father Ortega succeeded in converting a leading war captain who helped him convert others. Mounting a flat roof with him, he preached to the Indians, and the captain exhorted them also. Before long, Ortega gained a following, and "they gave him a site for a house and church, and with their help he built a convent."[63] Soon afterward, Fray Tomas Carrasco succeeded him at Taos. Meanwhile, Ortega joined Fray Asensio de Zárate in the "miraculous conversion of the Humanas."[64]

Meantime, progress in the Manzano Mountains range had continued since the days of Father Alonso Peinado. Peinado had been at Chililí as early as 1613 and from time to time had received assistance from other priests. In 1622 the "Santo Viejo," as he was affectionately called, reported about the "nations" that had recently been converted. Among them, wrote Peinado on October 4, 1622, were "Taos, Pecos, Jemez and the pueblos of war (pueblos de la guerra) Abó and Penabo [Tenabo]." By January 1626, Fray Francisco Fonte served as Padre Guardian of the Convento de Abó. Three years later, Father Francisco de Acevedo, a newcomer to New Mexico, replaced Fonte.[65]

Much had happened since 1618 when Father Perea took over as custodian of the missions of New Mexico. By 1626 two governors, Ceballos and Eulate, had come and gone, and Perea, too, was recalled to New Spain. However, in 1628, Perea was reassigned to New Mexico with thirty new friars for the missions. In 1626 a new prelate, Fray Alonso de Benavides, who would serve as both commissary of the Holy Office of the Inquisition and custodian of the missions, arrived in New Mexico. By the end of his term, in 1629, he had left in his care twenty-five missions and fifty friars.

12

Benavides's Halation of New Mexico

Pueblo and Great Plains Evangelists

The most important thing is the good example set by the friars. This, aside from the obligation of their vows, is forced upon them because they live in a province where they concern themselves with nothing but God. Death stares them in the face every day! Today one of their companions is martyred, tomorrow another; their hope is that such a good fortune may befall them while living a perfect life

—*Alonso de Benavides, 1634*[1]

Traveling the entire 1,600-mile length of the Camino Real de Tierra Adentro, Fray Alonso and twelve others came with the caravan of 1626. Together with fourteen priests who had come to New Mexico earlier with the Peinado, Ordóñez, Perea, and Chavarría groups, the new Benavides-led group brought the total of friars in the Conversión de San Pablo to twenty-six. Fray Alonso de Benavides's arrival signaled a new beginning for the New Mexican missions. The indefatigable friar, with the titles of custodian and agent of the Holy Office of the Inquisition, not only expanded the mission field but also worked in it and promoted it with his prolific pen, which produced much correspondence and a *memorial*, a major report to the king. The *Memorial* was published in at least five languages before the end of the seventeenth century. Although the New Mexico mission field was an offshoot of the colonial Mexican church, it was not unlike the other mission provinces in the New World. Benavides offered a composite, albeit romanticized, view of the New Mexico missions as well as "the pious tasks of the friars in these conversions" of New Mexico.

Of the few missionaries in New Mexico and their dedication, Benavides wrote, "Since the land is very remote and isolated and the difficulties of the long journeys require more than a year of travel, the friars, although there are many who wish to dedicate themselves to those conversions, find themselves unable to do so because of their poverty."[2] Thus, continued Benavides, the friars do the king's business through their zeal and at great savings to the crown. The few friars that worked the convents were so widely spread out that usually most convents had only one priest to minister to six or more neighboring pueblos.[3] In their midst the friar "stands as a lighted torch to guide them in spiritual as well as temporal affairs." At night, the twenty or so mission Indians that lived with them worked as hard as the friars. They worked as porters, sextons, cooks, bell ringers, gardeners, refectioners, and many other jobs. At night, they prayed together in front of a Christian religious image with great devotion.[4]

Like other missions in the New World, each pueblo in New Mexico eventually had a school taught by the friar that included praying, singing, and playing musical instruments. In his *Memorial* Benavides wrote that at dawn the day began with the ringing of the bell and all assembled in the school rooms of the convent. The dawn bell, known as the "prime," signaled the singers to chant the morning prayer. As disciplinarian, the friar took note of those who failed to perform their duties and reprimanded them. In an orderly fashion, a second bell rang and each "student" began the routine learning of their task.[5] Afterward the priest turned to administering the sacraments. Those who wished to confess their sins in order to receive Holy Communion at mass did so. Those who announced they wished to get married did so in order to begin instructions from the priest in preparation for matrimony. Usually, an hour later, a third ringing of the bell would take place and Holy Mass would be prayed. Those absent would be reprimanded. After praying the Holy Mass, all knelt by the church door and sang the "Salve" in their own tongue. At its conclusion, the priest would say, "Praised be the most holy Sacrament," and dismiss them.[6]

Benavides continued describing the work of the friars by writing that at mealtime, as soon as the cook had prepared the food, the friars would serve them at the porter's lodge. The friars would go to the homes of the old and infirm and feed them. After mealtime, the priests would hear confession and observe the boys who were learning to pray and assist at Holy Mass. The missionaries evaluated each boy for his performance as sextons and their duties to help in the sacristy as well as their proficiency in saying their prayers so that they could serve in the Holy Mass.[7]

Every evening, noted Benavides, the church bell would toll for vespers, which were chanted by singers assigned for that week. Along with the organ music, the hymns were selected for specific feast days or the purpose of the Holy Mass. On feast days the friar went early in the morning to each pueblo in his charge and prayed the Holy Mass, where he administered the sacraments and preached the biblical theme of the day. Two masses were said a day, and depending on the proximity to their pueblo, the mission Indians attended one at their pueblo and a second at the neighboring pueblo.[8]

On certain, slower weekdays the priest devoted his time to baptism, weddings, or funerals. He assured that the names for each event were inscribed in books noted for *bautismos, matrimonios,* or *entierros*. Again, at the end of each day, the friar supervised and looked after everything, the same as in the morning.

Throughout any part of the day, the friars settled disputes among Indians, "for since they look upon him as a father, they come to him with all their troubles, and he has to take pains to harmonize them."[9] Similarly, on property or boundary issues, the friars accompanied them to mark their boundaries and settle their arguments. Benavides explained that aside from the daily chores and duties, the friars also taught them to farm. He noted that it would be important to do "for the support of all the poor of the pueblo." Thus, he wrote,

> the friar makes them sow some grain and raise some cattle, because, if he left it to their discretion, they would not do anything. Therefore, the friar requires them to do so and trains them so well that with the meat he feeds all the poor

and pays the various workmen who come to build the churches. With the wool he clothes all the poor, and the friar himself gets his clothing and food from this source. All the wheels of this clock must be kept in good order by the friar, without neglecting any detail, otherwise all would be totally lost.[10]

Above all, the friars set a good example, lived by their vows, and lived in the Provincia de Nuevo México in dedication to God's works and living a perfect life, even if it meant their death.[11]

This description written by Benavides for the eyes of Pope Urban VIII did not exaggerate but did omit a very important perspective: the Indian view. He failed to note, particularly, those natives who harbored strong resentment against their Spanish intruders and the threat of Christianity to their spiritual beliefs and culture. Their view was often expressed by their maltreatment of the friars because they wished to discourage the missionaries from being in their pueblos. When passive resistance failed, they turned to armed rebellion. The friars, too, worked out a coexistence with the anti-Spanish natives. Although religious orthodoxy was their goal, the friars often settled for an imperfectly converted Christian Indian who practiced the "old ways" in his pueblo.

In his *Memorial* Benavides mentioned little, if anything, about how Indians who served the priests were treated by their fellow Puebloans or tribes such as the Apache and the Navajo. Were those who served as *porteros*, sacristans, cooks, or valets in the *conventos* considered outcasts among their relatives and friends of the pueblo? Benavides's remarks gave too much credit to the priests and not enough to the Indians. As to the "poor of the pueblo," it can generally be said that in Puebloan society, no one ever went hungry, regardless of whether a friar was present or not. After all, Indians were self-sufficient for thousands of years before the arrival of the European. One important point to be made in that regard, however, is that the priest's efforts offered "the poor" an alternative source for food.[12]

In the conversions, missions Indians were considered imperfectly converted and not yet a part of the congregation. Given their mission status, they received five of seven sacraments: Baptism, Penance, Holy Communion, Matrimony, and the last rites, Extreme Unction.[13] The sacraments of confirmation and Holy Orders were excluded. Confirmation represented the completion of, commitment to, and the maturity of baptism in which rebirth and the renewal of a spiritual life could be attained. Holy Orders, that is, the taking of priestly vows, were rarely entered into by Indians, although some served as *donados*, or lay brothers, to assist in the conversion of other Indians, as did the Tlaxcalans, who resided in the Barrio de Analco in Santa Fe. In the early history of the church in New Spain, the prohibition against permitting Indians to take Holy Orders was largely a matter left up to the individual orders.

Although many Indians were recognized for their piety and goodness in Christian terms, the discriminatory practice of denying priesthood became a hotly debated issue among Spanish churchmen. In the sixteenth century the Franciscan Order solved the issue by permitting certain Christian Indians to receive the habit of *donado*. Other orders offered the same privilege to Christianized Indian throughout the empire. *Donados* were used as preachers and teachers because of their linguistic abilities but, more importantly, because of the identity with other Indians. In effect, they were models.

Thus Benavides, by his omissions, communicated the colonial perspective by denying the native viewpoint. In his report to his Holiness, the end justified the means. The viceroy, the archbishop, and other church officials in Mexico City encouraged Benavides in his promotion of the New Mexican Custodio de la Conversión de San Pablo. It suited the state's objectives concerning the pacification of the northern frontier, and it conformed to the church's quest to save souls and spread the good news of the Santo Evangelio.

Fray Benavides served as father custodian from 1626 to 1629. His tenure as prelate coincided with the governorship of Felipe de Sotelo Osorio, who succeeded Eulate in 1625. Governor Sotelo appears to have maintained a friendly relationship with Benavides almost from the very beginning. Both men arrived with the caravan of 1626, but the governor, once along the lower Rio Grande pueblos, rode on ahead, as was the custom, to prepare a reception for the father commissary. The dates for the reception were January 24 and 25, 1626, an auspicious period for Benavides's entry into Santa Fe because the second day fell on the feast day of the Conversion of St. Paul, the patron saint of the province. Benavides arrived in Santa Fe where Governor Sotelo and the Cabildo in full military dress received him with all the proper courtesies for which the Spanish were renowned. After the welcome, the soldiers fired a salute with their harquebuses and artillery, and the prelate was led to his quarters. On January 25 a procession of the town's people and the local officials, led by the governor, accompanied Benavides to the church where Friar Pedro de Ortega, guardian of the church of Santa Fe and the newly appointed notary of the Holy Office of the Inquisition, read the edict of faith.[14]

Although the relationship between Sotelo and Benavides began on a reasonably sound basis, in the long term the friendship between them broke down. The rift between them, however, was not as traumatic as that between the previous prelates and their governors. It seems that the friars felt the governor's hostility toward them, for he often expressed the civil authority's superiority over ecclesiastical rights and immunities. In the end, Benavides, upon his return to Mexico in 1629, delivered the sworn testimony of friars and settlers against Sotelo to the Holy Office, but as in the Eulate case, little, if anything, was done.

During his term as agent of the Holy Office in New Mexico, Benavides tended to pursue cases against the lower classes for such crimes against the church as superstition, witchcraft, and demonology. Sotelo, on the other hand, concentrated on meting out punishments for theft and public immoralities. Aside from the usual royal governor's hostility toward the church and the typical scorn expressed concerning church censures, Sotelo managed to offend the soldier-*encomenderos* of the province, who came to resent his boastfulness and his policies. Finally, it was they, as much as the priests, who pushed for his ouster from the province. According to a story about Governor Sotelo Osorio that flitted about New Mexico decades later, he had so incensed his fellow frontiersmen that no one had anything to do with him to the point where he "was even reduced to the extremity of watering his own horse."[15]

Meantime Benavides had a job to do. He would not only expand the missions to the rest of the frontier pueblos but also put the existing ones on a sound footing. Along with that accomplishment, he would write about them. Moving away from the Camino Real eastward behind the Manzano Mountains, Benavides visited the Salinas pueblos in the vicinity of present Willard. Of all the pueblos he visited, they impressed him the most. Somehow the Salinas pueblos seemed to tantalize his fertile imagination. Perhaps Benavides felt a close affinity to the Salinas pueblos because they had been little worked by the friars. As it turned out, he would claim the conversion of one of its principal pueblos, the pueblo of Las Humanas, a distinction he shared with none other. "I came to convert it," he wrote, "on the day of

San Isidro, archbishop of Seville, in the year 1627, and I dedicated it to this saint on account of the great success that I experienced there on that day."[16] Benavides noted that having converted the pueblo, "our Lord delivered me from the manifest dangers in which I found myself on that day, because these Indian are very cruel. Nevertheless, many leaders were converted, and with their favor, I erected the first cross in this place and we all adored it."[17]

By the time Benavides arrived to serve the Salinas pueblos, Chililí had already been firmly established, and the "fourteen or fifteen pueblos in the area, which must have more than ten thousand souls,"[18] were being served by friars who were working to establish "six very good convents and churches" among them.[19] Moving southward, he visited one of the larger pueblos, today known as Gran Quivira, but Benavides called the pueblo "Las Jumanas" because the Jumanos from the plains came "to trade and barter" there.[20]

The Jumanos—as the Spanish called these people, who consisted of a variety of southern plains groups, largely Apachean, scattered over a wide area in southwestern Texas, southeastern New Mexico, and northern Chihuahua—were first identified by Antonio de Espejo in 1582–83. The name Jumano derived from an Indian word of unknown origin that the Spaniards pronounced and spelled in a variety of ways: Xumana, Jumano, Jumana, Jumanes, Humana, Humanes, Umana, Umanes, Xoman, Sumana, Chouman. Spanish explorers noted that their principal villages were located near Junta de los Rios, the junction of the Rio Conchos and Rio Grande. Eighteen years later Oñate reported seeing "three pueblos" of Jumanos on the fringe of the pueblo world in south-central New Mexico. Later Marcos de Farfan claimed to have visited a group of Jumanos in north-central Arizona. Shortly before that, on the western edge of the Great Plains where the Spaniards found "the great settlement," they saw Indians, probably Wichitas or Quiviras, whom they called Jumanos.

It seems the Spaniards used the term indiscriminately but noted several distinguishing characteristics that they identified among those Indian groups. According to Espejo, Luxan, and Hernan Gallegos, who saw the settlements near the Junta de los Rios, these Indians dressed in deer and buffalo skins, raised maize, beans, and calabashes, and lived in houses constructed of palings plastered with mud.[21] As hunters, their weapons were bows and arrows. These groups, known collectively by the Spaniards as Jumanos, were also known as the Amotomanco (variously Otomoaco), Abriache, and

Pararabuey (variously Patazagueyes). When the Spaniards did not call them by these or the variant derivations of Jumanos, they referred to them as *gente rayada* (the striped people) or *los rayados* or *indios rayados*, probably meaning they were painted or tattooed. In 1598, when Vicente de Zaldívar Mendoza, Oñate's nephew, and a force of sixty soldiers went out to the plains, they passed by rancherias of Indians known as Apache Vaqueros (so-called in reference to them as followers of buffalo herds), who "asked him for aid against the Xumanos, as they call a tribe of Indians who are painted after the manner of the Chichimecos."[22]

Body or facial decorations in the form of tattooing or painting did not necessarily distinguish the Jumanos, primarily because body decoration was a common trait among the Indians north of Mexico. The term *indios rayados* could easily have been applied to a number of groups in the Gran Chichimeca Mexico's Central Plateau or other Plains Indians, such as the Quivirias, Escanjaques, Teyas, Paratebueyes, and others. In 1598 Juan de Oñate noted the existence of three pueblos of Jumanos Rayados on the southeastern edge of the pueblo area in New Mexico. They were Las Humanas, Pueblo Pardo, and Tabira. In his *Memorial* of 1630, Benavides described the "pueblo de las Xumanas," which he claimed to have converted. The origins of the Jumanos pueblos could very well have been the work of Jumano hunting parties who frequented the area and built temporary quarters that in time grew into permanent pueblos. When Benavides mentioned that Las Humanas is so called because Jumanos came in from the plains to trade, in all likelihood he inadvertently referred to a process that had led to the development of that pueblo and still continued through his day.

Las Humanas, as it was sometimes spelled, served as a gathering place for traders, hunters from the plains, and Puebloans from the Rio Grande and surrounding towns. "When I came to convert this pueblo," recalled Benavides, "I found there a Christian Indian woman who had fled to this place. She and the war captain stood by me and assisted me greatly. The Indian woman spoke to all the women and persuaded them well, and the Indian man spoke to the principal captains. If it had not been for him, the sorcerers, who could not bear to see destroyed the idolatry in which their power consisted, would no doubt have killed me on that day."[23]

Doubtless, Benavides antagonized quite a few people at Las Humanas with his disruptive preaching in the middle of a busy day, let alone his priestly presence. He must have laughed about his experience with an Indian religious leader who was obviously put out with the father commissary. Benavides wrote,

> I cannot refrain from telling about the amusing remarks of an old sorcerer who opposed me. I was in the middle of the plaza, preaching to numerous persons assembled there, and this old sorcerer, realizing that my arguments were having some effect on the audience, descended from a corridor with an infuriated and wicked disposition, and said to me: "You Christians are crazy, you desire and intend that this pueblo shall also be crazy." I asked him in what respect we were crazy. He had been, no doubt, in some Christian pueblo during Holy Week when they were flagellating themselves in procession and thus, he answered me: How are you crazy? You go through the streets in groups, flagellating yourselves, and it is not well that the people of the pueblo should commit such madness as spilling their own blood by scourging themselves. When he saw that I laughed, as did those around me, he rushed out of the pueblo, saying that he did not wish to be crazy. When I explained to the people the reason why we scourged ourselves, they laughed all the more at the old man and were more confirmed in their desire to become Christians.[24]

Thus, Benavides had begun the conversion of Las Humanas. Not long after Benavides, Fray Francisco Letrado took up the conversion, baptized the people, and convinced them to build a convent and a church. He named the church San Isidro in remembrance of Benavides's first day at the pueblo on April 4, 1627.

San Isidro de Las Humanas must have been one of the first times that the name of St. Isidore of Seville had been so honored. Although canonized in 1598, Isidro was born about 560 and died in 636. A hardworking missionary who had converted the Visigoths, Isidro was a learned man who founded schools and wrote a history of the Goths. He also compiled *Etymologies*, an encyclopedia of knowledge in his time. Considered an early church philosopher, Isidro became bishop of Seville in 600.

Meanwhile, on the other side of the Manzanos, at Isleta on the Camino Real, a mysterious occurrence, one in which Benavides eventually took a great interest, unraveled. It concerned the appearance of María de Agreda, the mystic from the convent at Soria in Spain who inspired the Jumanos to convert. The perplexing question to which Benavides sought an answer revolved around how a cloistered nun who lived in Spain appeared to the Jumanos. The investigation of the puzzling mystery took up much of his time and travels to solve the mysterious appearance of the Lady in Blue.

It began innocently. For several summers, Jumanos from the plains crossed the large mountain east of the Rio Grande near Isleta and "to beg" Fray Juan de Salas to go to their land and baptize them, as they wanted to become Christians. They knew him from an experience in which he had "come to the rescue of some unfortunate people" that they were mistreating.[25] Because of his courage in standing up to the Jumanos, Fray Juan had earned their respect. He had told his superior about the request, but for lack of friars, none were sent to preach to them.

In 1628 thirty friars made the trans-Atlantic voyage to Mexico. Arriving in the ancient capital, the friars told a story about a rare occurrence in which a nun named María de Jesús de la Concepción of the discalced order of St. Francis, who live in Agreda in the Spanish province of Burgos, had "miraculously transported" herself to New Mexico to preach to the Indians. Having assigned them to New Mexico, the archbishop of Mexico asked these friars to inquire into the apparition, which by now "was common news in Spain."[26] A year later, after the long, arduous trek on the Camino Real from Mexico City to Santo Domingo, the friars delivered a missive to Benavides at Isleta authorizing him to undertake an inquiry. It read:

> I, Don Francisco Manzo y Zuñiga, archbishop elect of Mexico, member of the council of his Majesty and of the Royal Council of the Indies, do hereby urgently recommend this inquiry to the reverend custodian and fathers of the said conversion in order that they may carry it out with the solicitude, faith, and devotion that the case demands, and that they duly inform us concerning its results, so that they may be verified in legal form. This will no doubt redound in great spiritual and temporal advancement to the glory and service of our Lord. Issued in Mexico on May 18, 1628.[27]

Caught off guard by the letter, Benavides and Salas read the letter and agreed that they had no idea that any such visitations had taken place among the Jumanos, as they had never thought to ask them why they sought conversion. "We were in incomplete ignorance of it," remarked Benavides, "nor had we ever heard of Mother María de Jesús."[28] Benavides remarked that so many other Indian groups had similarly asked for a priest, but because of the shortage of clergymen, not all requests were granted. As if dazzled by the letter, Benavides said, "We soon noticed that the great care and solicitude with which the Xumana Indians came to us every summer to plead for friars to go and baptize them must have been through an inspiration from heaven."[29] Almost simultaneously with the arrival of the archbishop's instruction to carry out the inquiry, it happened that the Jumanos had returned to Isleta to make their request, four days sooner than they had usually come in the past.

This time Benavides asked them "their motive in coming every year to ask for baptism with insistence. Gazing at a portrait of Mother Luisa de Carrión in the convent, they said: 'A woman in similar garb wanders among us over there, always preaching, but her face is not old like this, but young.' When asked why they had never mentioned this previously, they answered, 'Because you did not ask us, and we thought she was around here, too.'"[30] The priests were dumbfounded, but they needed to verify the Jumano story.

Soon afterward, Fray Juan de Salas and Fray Diego Lopez, led by Jumanos, departed Isleta walking east toward the mountain beyond the salt beds where commenced the Great Plains that stretch to midcontinent. The priests had no idea where they were going. They traveled for many days across the buffalo plains past the land of the fierce Apache Vaqueros, after which they reached the Jumano country.[31]

Now the priests found some evidence of the visitations they were seeking. When they reached the Jumano rancherias, the people came out "in procession carrying a large cross and garlands of flowers." From these Indians the priests learned that the nun in blue had taught them about the cross, "she had [even] helped them to decorate" it, and had instructed them on the procession.[32] The priests reported that at the rancheria a large number of people had come to ask for baptism and that "the Indian women with suckling babes seized their little arms and lifted them on high, shouting also for baptism for them since they were incapable of asking for it themselves."[33] After working among the Jumanos and some Quiviras and Xapies for several days, instructing them in the catechism and in prayer, the priests set up a large cross and, promising to return, departed the rancheria bound for Isleta to report to Benavides.

Fray Alonso de Benavides eventually returned to Spain. There, in 1630, he was given audience with "the most reverend general of the order, Fray Bernardino de Zena" regarding the New Mexico missions and his *Memorial*.[34]

The discussion turned to María de Agreda, and Fray Bernardino assured Fray Alonso "that it was she, that he had investigated this matter eight years previously . . . and that the nun was miraculously carried to the conversion in New Mexico."³⁵ Zena gave Benavides special permission to visit her personally at Agreda.

On the last day of April 1631, Friar Benavides met Mother María de Jesús, abbess of the convent of La Purísima Concepción in the town of Agreda. Bound by obedience, María de Agreda, in the course of their meeting, would answer all of his questions and reveal all that she knew about New Mexico. Impressed by her presence, Benavides wrote,

> First of all, I must state that Mother María de Jesús, present abbess of the convent of Concepción, cannot be twenty-nine years of age yet. She has a beautiful face, very white, although rosy, with large black eyes. Her habit, and that of all the nuns in that convent they number twenty-nine in all, is just the same as our habit. It is made of coarse gray sackcloth, worn next to the skin, without any other tunic, skirt or underskirt. Over this gray habit come the one white sackcloth, coarse with a scapulary of the same material, and the cord of our father, Saint Francis. Over the scapulary there is a rosary. They wear no sandals or any other footwear except some boards tied to their feet, or some hemp sandals. Their cloak is of heavy blue sack cloth. They wear a black veil.³⁶

She told him "all we know that has happened to our brothers and fathers, Fray Juan de Salas and Fray Diego Lopez in the journeys to the Jumanas,"³⁷ and that she asked them to go and call the priests, which they did.

Perhaps Benavides could not help ask leading questions, but he succeeded in getting detailed descriptions of the priests and Indians she claimed to know. "She told me so many details of this country that I did not even remember them myself, and she brought them back to my mind,"³⁸ he wrote. Indeed, Mother María de Jesús reported that the occurrence of her transportations "by angels" took place "from the 1620 to the present year, 1631 in the Kingdom of Quivira."³⁹ She said that she appeared in New Mexico "so often that there were days when she appeared three and four times in less than twenty-four hours."⁴⁰ This had continued without interruption until 1631. When she told him that "she had been present with me at the baptism of the Pizos [Piros] . . . [and] likewise she had helped Father Fray Cristóbal Quiros with some baptisms, giving a minute description of his person and face."[41] Astounded, Friar Benavides asked more questions.

She said that she knew Father Ortega, guardian of the *convento* at Taos, and that she had saved his life "through the signs he found."[42] Benavides thought back to his plan to convert the nomads from the plains. Could Mother María de Jesús have been referring to Ortega's conversion of an Apache leader called Quinia whom Benavides knew to be "very famous in that country, very belligerent and valiant in war?"[43] The lay brother Fray Gerónimo de Pedraza, considered by his peers to be a fine surgeon and healer, had also gone with Ortega among the Apache. When the two Franciscans found him, Captain Quinia, who favored Christianity, had been shot in the chest with an arrow by one of his tribesmen who opposed the friars. They hastened to his side and cured him by tying a "rather large copper medal with the image of our Lady and that of our father Saint Francis."[44] Because of the miraculous healing, Quinia later converted. This happened sometime before 1627.

In 1629 Ortega and a companion, Friar Alonso Yañes, apparently went out to the plains again to the kingdom of Quivira where their lives were constantly threatened by Plain Indians.[45] Perhaps, in Benavides's mind, Mother María de Jesús referred to that particular instance. Later, Benavides learned that Friar Ortega and a companion, either Fray Juan de Salas or Fray Alonso Yañes, with authority from Father Custodian Estéban de Perea, went out once more, probably in 1632, to the Jumano settlements on the Texas plains. The companion soon returned to the Rio Grande, but Ortega remained there for six months. By now he had come to see himself as the apostle of the Plains people. Under great hardship and constant threat to his life, Ortega preached and catechized the natives. After much suffering and broken in health, he, according to Benavides, worked himself to death. In another instance, Benavides wrote that Friar Ortega received the crown of martyrdom when "those idolatrous Indians . . . poisoned him with the most cruel poison."[46] The work among the Jumanos did not end with Ortega. Later Fray Juan de Salas and Fray Diego Lopez returned there and were said to have "converted more than fifteen thousand souls of the nation of Xumanos, Japies and others."[47]

The story of the Lady in Blue fit perfectly with Benavides's promotion of New Mexico, and the Jumanos, whom he had recently seen at Las Humanas, had played a significant role in the growing support for continuing the work in the missions of the Custodio y Conversión de San Pablo de Nuevo Mexico.

Missionary progress under Father Custos Alonso de Benavides (1626–29) proved to be quite extensive in that not only did the already established missions continue to grow and receive support, but also new *conventos* and *visitas* were founded. Under Benavides, for example, missionaries turned their attention to the Tewa, Manzano Tiwa, and Tompiro pueblos. Benavides also encouraged the resumption of work in the Jémez area, where the Pueblo de la Congregación de San Diego was reestablished. New missions among the Piro and at Acoma, Zuñi, and Hopi were founded as the Franciscans spread their influence to all the New Mexico pueblos. Also during his time in New Mexico, Benavides found time to describe the Indians of the upper Gila River region and their mountain wilderness. In so doing, Benavides became the first white man to write about the Gila wilderness area. He called the Indians there the "Gila Apaches." They could easily have been Sumas. The word "Gila," which he probably learned from them, was written for the first time.

North of Santa Fe, Benavides established a third convent at Santa Clara among the Tewa to complement those at San Ildefonso and Nambé. It is possible that a fourth convent had been established at San Juan during this period. Benavides prided himself in the work accomplished there. "The church at the pueblo of Santa Clara, I founded myself, and, as I am the commissary of the Inquisition, these Tewa Indians prided themselves that I lived among them, and they painted the coat of arms of the Inquisition in the church of the pueblo of Santa Clara where I lived, since they did not wish any other church to have it."[48] Santa Clara was the tenth and last mission founded by Benavides.

Completion of the work begun by Benavides, who had served New Mexico for three years, fell to the new Father Custodian Estéban de Perea, the tireless missionary who served in New Mexico for over thirty years.[49] In 1628 Perea rode back from Mexico City, where he had testified against Eulate, with the yearly mission supply caravan. Obviously triumphant, Perea was reappointed as *custodio* and commissary of the Holy Office. As *custodio*, he would continue to expand and support the mission field off the Camino Real. As agent of the Inquisition, Perea, like his predecessor, had the power to investigate charges of heresy, apostasy, blasphemy, sorcery, and other crimes against the church and to bring offenders and all testimony against them before the Holy Office in Mexico City.

With Perea were thirty new friars and a new governor, Francisco Manuel de Silva Nieto, who succeeded Sotelo. Nieto, according to the friars, seemed to be a contrast to all the previous royal governors. He served until 1632. Governor de Silva Nieto deserves as much credit for the establishment of the missions during Perea's second term as the missionaries themselves.[50] He cooperated wholeheartedly with the friars, assigned them the escorts they needed, and even went on the major expedition to establish the *conventos* at Acoma, Zuñi, and Hopi.

The conversions of Acoma, Zuñi, and Moqui were a grand affair. On June 23, 1629, a large expedition of priests and military escort, led by Governor Francisco Nieto Silva and Father Estéban Perea, departed Santa Fe for the new mission field. With the "ten cars and four hundred cavalry horses," were four priests, Fray Roque de Figueredo, Fray Francisco de Porras, Fray Andrés Gutierres, and Fray Agustin de Cuellar, and two lay brothers, Fray Francisco de San Buenaventura and Fray Cristóval de la Concepción.[51] Father Solicitor Fray Tomas Manso, who later served as *padre custos* after Perea, also participated in that expedition.

At Acoma they were well received and given "free entrance." There they left Father Juan Ramírez, known later as the "Apostle of Acoma." Of the conversion of Acoma, "pueblo of the Infidels," Benavides wrote, "In 1629 Father Fray Cristóbal [Juan] Ramírez, a friar of great courage, whom they received in peace, catechized the pueblo."[52] The turning point in the conversion of the Acomans came when a man who claimed that a "sorcerer" had bewitched his grandchild, a baby girl, who lay dying, brought her to Friar Ramírez. The priest took the child and baptized her. "Scarcely had she received the waters of holy baptism," said Benavides, "when she became well and healthy." The incident, according to Fray Alonso, convinced "those Indians of the truth of holy baptism, which they now believed and which was being preached to them."[53] Acoma, however, did not easily convert. Benavides gave a clue for the resistance at the "Sky City" when he wrote: "There are here more than one thousand residents of this Queres nation, and also of many others, delinquents and apostates, who have sought shelter and made themselves strong there. Great wars have been waged over this place."[54]

Beyond Acoma toward the east lay the province of the Zuñi with "eleven or twelve pueblos." On their way to Zuñi they passed the "Malpais" (badlands of lava flow) "ten leagues of burnt cliffs,"[55] as Father Perea described them, "since by ancient tradition it is said that there a great inundation of fire burst out . . . as we know of some volcanoes of the Indies."[56] At Zuñi the caravan left Friars Figueredo and Agustín de Cuellar and the lay brother Fray Francisco del la Madre de Dios. Benavides states that Father Porras also served at Zuñi, perhaps sometime later. Governor Silva Nieto at once issued an edict "that no soldier should enter a house of the pueblo, nor transgress in aggrieving the Indians, under penalty of his life."[57]

Because of pressing business in the Villa de Santa Fé, Silva did not go to the Hopi. On the return trip, Governor Silva immortalized himself by leaving his inscription at El Morro:

> The Lord and Governor don Francisco Manuel de Silvia Nieto came this far with our Lord King's wagons. With his indubitable arm and valor, he has already overcome the impossible, a thing which he alone accomplished 5 August 1629, so that one may well go to Zuñi and carry the Holy faith.[58]

The initial work of the conversion of Zuñi fell to Fray Roque de Figueredo, Fray Francisco de Porras, and four other friars who arrived in New Mexico in 1629. Apparently, Fray Roque, "very highly thought of and esteemed in the city of Mexico," came to the Conversión de San Pablo with much money, "more than 160,000 escudos,"[59] for him and the thirty friars who were with him to spend on "all that was necessary for the foundation of churches of those conversions."[60] He purchased a house at Zuñi, which served at once as the first church and rectory of the pueblo's early Christian tradition.[61]

Of the land and people in the province of Zuñi, Father Perea left his seventeenth-century impressions. He wrote:

> This country is placid and fertile, abundant in waters, agreeable with green fields, shady with groves of cedars [*encinos*], pines [*pinabetos*], piñon trees, and wild grape vines. All those [Indians] of this colony are very observant of superstitious idolatry. They have their temples with idols of stone, and of wood much painted, where they cannot enter except it be their priests and there by some trap doors which they have on top of the terrace. So likewise they have gods in the mountains [or woods] [*montes*], in the rivers, in the harvests, and in their houses as is recounted of the Egyptians for they give to each one their particular protection. Here they [the Spaniards] saw a notable thing; and it was some enclosures of wood and in them many rattlesnakes that,

vibrating their tongues, giving hisses and leaps, are menacing as the fierce bull in the arena. And [our men] desiring to know the object of having their serpents imprisoned, they told them that with their venom they poisoned their arrows, wherewith the wounds which their opponents received were irremediable. They live with civilized [*politico*] government; their pueblos with streets and continuous houses like those of Spain. The women dress themselves in cotton, and the men in buckskin and hides. The country abounds in maize, beans and squashes, with every kind of hunting and other chase."[62]

The work at Zuñi proved to be difficult and slow as the anti-Spanish faction, led "by the priests of idols," worked against him. "After they had converted almost all the people, the sorcerer priests returned to urge them to revolt. By this event he and his companions suffered innumerable hardships."[63] The Zuñi remained restless throughout the seventeenth century.

Fray Francisco Letrado, who had also worked at the pueblo of Las Humanas, became the most famous martyr among the Zuñi. Letrado, filled with zeal and fervor, had asked Padre Perea to assign him to Father Figueredo's mission. "Here, on February 22, 1632, on Quinquagesima Sunday," related Benavides, "when the converted and baptized Indians were summoned to mass, they all rose in rebellion and attacked him in a body, smashing his head with their clubs."[64] The eighteenth-century Franciscan chronicler Agustín de Vetancourt, in his *Menologio*, told a slightly different version of Letrado's death. "On Sunday of Lent" (February 22, 1632), he wrote, "seeing that some of [the Zuñi] were late in coming to mass, he went out to look for them. He met some of the idolaters, and with fiery fervor began to preach to them, and seeing that they swore to take his life, he fell to his knees holding up as his defense, a crucifix with Christ painted on it which he carried around his neck, and he died preaching [as the Zuñi] shot him with arrows."[65] An expedition that later went there could not find the remains of Letrado but reported an account that his body had been desecrated and his scalp had been taken. On the return trip, the soldiers stopped to rest at El Morro. One of them, Juan Lujan, inscribed his name on the sandstone rock.

Soon after, probably in August of 1629, the friars at Zuñi decided to go to the Hopi district to begin work in those remote pueblos. With their crucifixes and staffs in hand, Fathers Porras, Figueredo, and Andrés Gutiérrez and the lay brother, Cristóbal de la Concepción, accompanied by twelve soldiers, left for the "Province of Moqui."⁶⁶ They arrived there on August 20, the feast day of San Bernardo, who became the patron saint of Hopi. Indeed, the name "San Bernardo," applied to Awotobi and, later, the mission at Shongopavi, also named San Bernardo de Zongopabi. A convent at Háwikuh and another at Halona were established during this period.⁶⁷

Perea later wrote a description of their land in pastoral terms. It is "more temperate but similar to that of Spain in regard to the fruits and seeds that grow here," he began, "they harvest much cotton; the houses are of three stories well planned; and the inhabitants are great land tillers and diligent workers. Among them it is considered a great vice to be intoxicated. For amusement they have certain games, and a race which they run with great speed."⁶⁸

But the Moqui Indians were not elated at their coming, although they appeared polite. "Here they received the Fathers with some lukewarmness,"⁶⁹ said Perea of the friars' first meeting with the Hopis since the days of Oñate. Immediately, they knew that the anti-Spanish faction had been active among the Puebloans, but the friars chose to look at it another way. "The devil was trying in all ways to impede and hinder the promulgation of the Divine law," they said. Actually, an "apostate Indian from the Christian pueblos" had preceded the friars and told the Hopi that the Spaniards were coming "to burn their pueblos, rob their belongings and behead their children."⁷⁰ The word spread that the Franciscans were "deceivers and that they must not consent that they should put water on their heads, because at once they would be sure to die."⁷¹

When the friars arrived at the first Hopi pueblo, the Indians who had summoned their Apache allies were ready. They politely greeted the priests, but generally ignored them. The Spanish soldiers took turns on guard duty. The second night the Spanish sentry heard the murmur of people. He awakened his companions, who prepared their arms and horses. The Hopi approached the Spanish quarters, but the soldiers surprised them by showing themselves. "How [was it] they were not sleeping?" asked a Hopi war captain. One of the soldiers responded, "The soldiers of Spain did not sleep, because they were prepared to defend themselves and injure their enemies."⁷² The next night the Hopi again tested the Spaniards. And again they were ready. This time the soldiers threatened that if any harm came to them and the friars, the governor would send out a force "to lay waste and burn their pueblos and lands."⁷³ The Hopi understood clearly that the Spaniards were aware of their intentions and thereafter left them alone. Relationships between the two groups were shaky at best, and as at Zuñi, the Hopi likewise remained restless and desirous of the isolation they had previously enjoyed. Nonetheless, the Hopi looked for opportunities against the Spaniards. Later Benavides wrote that among the first martyrs there, Father Porras had been killed "secretly with poison" by the Moqui.[74]

During the late years of the Benavides administration, Father Martin Arvide, who had been at Jémez, made some contact with the Apaches de Navajo. "While in that locality," Benavides wrote, "I ordered him to make an expedition to the Apache [de Navajo] Indians and to preach the word of God to them."[75] Arvide did so and wrote to Benavides that those Indians "begged for holy baptism" and that another lady in blue, Mother Luisa de Carrión, had preached to them, and they even knew her name.[76] Later Arvide told the story of Mother Luisa and how she had preached to the Navajo. "This is the same region, on the western border of New Mexico, where the blessed father, Fray Francisco de Porras, performed the miracle of giving sight to the blind boy with the cross originally belonging to the said Mother Luisa de Carrión."[77] Benavides himself had had an earlier encounter with the Navajo. It began with his interest in dealing with the Gila and Perillo Apaches. When he went to Santa Clara Pueblo, Benavides hoped to put a stop to the violence against the Puebloans by the Apaches de Navajo who "killed people every day and waged war on them."[78] At first, he hoped to capture one "in order to treat him very well and talk to him about our Catholic faith, and then send him back a full man to his superiors." Admittedly it could not be done, wrote Benavides, "owing to the great caution with which they live and make their raids."[79]

In September 1629 Benavides embarked on a plan to contact the Apaches de Navajo and convince them to stop their raids. He called together the principal captains and governor of Santa Clara. They discussed the risk of sending a delegation of ambassadors to invite the Navajos to Santa Clara for a parley.[80] Finally, the Tewas agreed to send twelve men and their leader, don Pedro, all of whom spoke Navajo. They made their preparations for the trip to the Navajo country, and they made sure that they had the proper paraphernalia for the sign of peace they would give their enemy. Don Pedro carried "an arrow which had a colored feather at the point instead of a flint, and likewise, they gave him a pipe made of reed, very long and slender, filled with tobacco, lighted and drawing. The arrow was to be shot to the Apaches when the party approached their first ranchería, and the enemy, upon seeing it, should understand, as was their custom, that they came in peace, and the reed with the tobacco, which they use extensively in these parts, was to be smoked ceremonially."[81] As the party set out, Benavides gave don Pedro his rosary as a peace emblem and a message for the Navajo leader expressing the friars' desire for a peace meeting.[82]

After a day and half of travel, the peace party came upon a Navajo ranchería. They approached it with trepidation, and when they got close enough, they shot the arrow. A Navajo picked it up, interpreted it as a sign of peace, and "answered it with another."[83] The peace party approached the ranchería. They greeted the chief "and handed him a reed of tobacco asking him to smoke with him."[84] Then the Tewas gave him Benavides's rosary. When they had explained the reason for their visit to the captain, he abruptly changed the subject and asked them to explain the meaning of all the beads strung on that cord. With unpremeditated subtlety one of the peace party spoke, saying that "the friar, who knows that there are so many captains among you, sends each one of you, through . . . each one of these beads, his word that he will always be your friend and that we will also."[85] When the captain understood this, he remarked that "he was very sorry that they should offer peace at this time when he had made such elaborate preparations for exterminating them all with one stroke."[86] Reconsidering his words, the captain then sent the "reed and arrow" to the "chief cacique" of the tribe with an explanation of the meeting. As for the rosary, the captain, intrigued by it, kept it for himself.[87] Before the peace party departed Navajo land, the captain notified them that he would visit the friar at Santa Clara.

Meantime at Santa Clara, a runner came in to tell Friar Benavides that the Apaches de Navajo were coming to parley. The priest prepared the pueblo and a reception party of "fifteen hundred souls to welcome him." At dusk, the church appeared "beautified with many lighted candles, as night had already fallen. It all looked very holy."[88] For that reason, Benavides had chosen the church as the place for this strange meeting. The two men spoke, and Benavides walked away believing that peace had been achieved, for the captain of the Apaches de Navajo said he was ready to receive a friar. Soon after, Fray Martín de Arvide visited the Navajo. Benavides surmised it would be a tremendous victory to convert them, for "this nation alone has more than two hundred thousand souls belong to this tribe of the Navajo."⁸⁹ Of the peace made with the Apaches de Navajo, Benavides wrote that the people of Santa Clara and their traditional enemy "all embraced one another. I ordered the bells to be rung and the trumpets and flageolets to be sounded . . . [their] arrow I placed on the altar as trophies of the divine word, which had caused it all to happen. Thenceforth the peace became so firm that they communicated with one another, unarmed, visiting each other's country with great pleasure."⁹⁰ For the moment, peace was at hand, but in the long run it did not hold.

As a promoter of New Mexico's mission field, Benavides had no peer. Indeed, in a report titled "Regarding the Truth of the Reports of Father Benavides," his superiors, including the viceroy of Mexico, wrote "letters of credence for the said Fray Alonso to the king of Spain" and offered proof of his credibility.⁹¹ As a strong supporter of the New Mexico missions sponsored by the Catholic Church, Benavides had aspirations that he could become one of its leaders in its hierarchical structure. He had hoped and even proposed that a bishopric be established in New Mexico and headquartered in Santa Fe. Of the necessity of establishing such a bishopric, he argued that it should be done because "of the difficulties of ordination, and of the sacred oils, and confirmation, not being able to travel from Old Mexico to New Mexico without great danger from the barbarous natives as there are 400 leagues between Old and New Mexico."⁹²

Disappointed at the slow and unpromising response, Benavides departed for Lisbon. Born in the Azores, Benavides also spoke Portuguese. One of his colleagues wrote, "Father Benavides, with whom I have often discussed matters pertaining to the church in the Indies, and who had induced me to defer bringing it up until seeing if, on the occasion of the present fleet, he might not find out what difficulties hindered the issuing of the royal decrees; without telling me a word, he left for Lisbon in order to sail from there for Goa as an auxiliary bishop of the church there."⁹³ Benavides died at sea before reaching Goa, probably in a shipwreck. In 1764 Francisco Antonio de Rosa Figuroa offered a note of clarification concerning Benavides's acceptance of an assignment in Portuguese-controlled Goa. He explained, "Thus if any critic should reflect how this venerable father being a Spaniard, was recommended to the holy pontiff as auxiliary bishop of Goa in a diocese belonging to the crown of Portugal, he must remember that Portugal and its territories and bishoprics belonged to the Spanish crown until the year 1640."[94] Rosa Figueroa noted that the recommendation for Benavides's appointment to Goa as auxiliary bishop was made by King Philip IV of Spain to the pope.

Another area, which like Taos, Pecos, and Galisteo formed a part of the triad of pueblos, plains, and province, lay at the south end of the present Manzano Mountains. Benavides had begun and encouraged mission development in the area. His successor, Estéban de Perea, continued the conversion of the pueblos behind the Manzano Mountains. Between Chililí and Abó existed other pueblos, prominent among which were Tajique and Quarai. Sometime after 1626 and before 1628, Tajique became a mission site. Under Peinado at Chililí, Tajique could have been a *visita* and, thus, slowly prepared for conversion. The earliest known guardian of Tajique is Fray Francisco de la Concepción, who is mentioned by Benavides as being there in 1635. Other priests who served there were Fray Jeronimo de la Llana in 1636. After him, a long gap in the chronology follows until 1660, when Fray Diego de Parraga served Tajique as guardian. Later Fray Juan Ramírez resided there in 1660, followed by Fray Francisco Gómez de la Cadena (1671–72) and Fray Sebastian de Aliri in 1672. Little is known about Quarai with certainty until 1628, when Fray Juan Gutiérrez de la Chica, who arrived with Benavides in 1626, became "guardian del convento de Nuestra Señora de la Concepción de Querac [Cuarac, Quarai]."[95] During that period the Quarai mission began, like all the others, either as a room in the pueblo purchased by the priest, which he used as living quarters, classroom, and first church, or as a primitive jacal of mud and poles outside the pueblo until the priest could gain acceptance among the Indians. Quarai may have had a convent as early as 1628 under Gutiérrez's guardianship. The changes there must have been rapid, for in the next decade Fray Estéban Perea served there and carried out his official duties as commissary of the Holy Office of the Inquisition between 1633 and 1638, as he had earlier at Sandia Pueblo.[96]

Possibly, Perea had been at Quarai at an earlier date because Vetancurt states that Perea had converted the Tiguias at Quarai. As Friar Gutiérrez de la Chica had served at Quarai before him, it could mean that Perea had been his immediate successor and merely completed the work begun by Friar Gutierrez de la Chica. Perhaps, too, as there is no record of another friar between Gutiérrez de la Chica and Perea, Quarai could have been without a friar for a short period of time. After Perea, Fray Juan de Salas became commissary of the Inquisition and served at Quarai after 1641. Previously, Salas, no stranger to the Salinas pueblos, had ministered to the Indians of Las Salinas and the Jumanos in 1629.[97]

It appears that the first three priests to serve at Quarai were Gutiérrez de la Chica, Perea, and Salas in succession. Fray Juan Gutiérrez, for example, served there in 1628, as did Fray Estéban Perea between 1633 and 1638. Fray Juan de Salas lived at Quarai as its guardian after 1641. With Perea during those years, Fray Alonso de San Juan, a lay brother who worked at Quarai in 1634, served as a Franciscan notary. Fray Alonso first came to New Mexico in 1603 or 1605. Other priests who served at Quarai after Salas included Salazar in 1668 and Fray Diego de Parraga, who lived at Quarai in the early 1660s and later became guardian in 1672.[98]

The missions at Abó and Tenabo were first mentioned as established in 1622 in a letter from Peinado to the viceroy.[99] In 1626 Fray Francisco Fonte was Abó's first known guardian.[100] Three years later Fray Francisco de Acevedo came to work among the Saline pueblos. Acevedo, whose parents were Gonzalo Garcia del Terrero and Isabel de Vargas from Seville, took the Franciscan vows in 1625 at the *convento* in Mexico City. He accompanied Friar Perea to New Mexico in 1629. Perea assigned Acevedo to the work among the Tompiros.[101] A few years later, as guardian at Abó, he ordered the construction of the church (*hizo la iglesia*) called San Gregorio de Abó. As Acevedo had been a priest for only four years in 1629 and lacked the missionary experience to become guardian, it is likely that he worked among the Tompiros for some time, and Friar Juan de Campo preceded him as guardian at Abó in 1634. It appears that the construction of the San Gregorio de Abó church did not take place until the late 1630s or by 1641. Vetancur erroneously gives Acevedo's death as August 1, 1644. Friar Acevedo, however, still alive in 1660, had resided at the mission of Alamillo since 1659.[102] His contemporaries reckoned him to be between eighty and ninety years old.[103] If so, the old priest, born between 1570 and 1580, was close to sixty years old when he came to New Mexico. He worked in the Conversión de San Pablo for over thirty years, almost all of them among the Tompiros in Salinas. Abó served as the *cabecera* or mission headquarters for Tenabo, Tabira, and Las Humanas during Acevedo's tenure there. Other priests who served at Abó were Fray Antonio Aguado (1639), Fray Joseph de Paredes (1662), Fray Gabriel de Torija (1668), and Fray Ildefonso (or Alonso) Gil de Avila (1672).[104]

The missions of the Saline pueblos were among those founded over a period of sixteen years between 1613 and 1629: Chililí (1613), Abó and Tenabo (1622), Las Humanas (1626), Quarai (1628), and Tajique (1629). It is possible that Tabira had been established about the same time, or soon after Abó and Tenabo. By 1641, however, Tabira served as a *visita* of Abó, which by then had a church and convent.

By the end of the third decade of missionization, Fray Estéban Perea's work, which spanned almost thirty years, had resulted in a truly expanded mission frontier that included almost every pueblo in New Mexico. Between the administrations of Peinado and Perea, mission progress had also depended on the short-lived support of Friar Chavarría and the vision of Friar Benavides. In fact, through their efforts the essential ecclesiastical New Mexico had evolved. Yet Indian New Mexico managed to survive the cultural assault dealt them not only through the ecclesiastical arm of Spanish colonialism but also by the civilian element of the Spanish frontier movement. Somehow the Indians managed to keep their cultures and languages alive, despite the religious and military presence that assailed the very fabric of their Indianness.

13

Governors, Missionaries, Kachinas, and the Holy Office of the Inquisition, 1632–59

> The religious of this province do not know God, nor do they respect the king.
> —*Governor Bernardo López de Mendizábal, 1662*[1]

> The governor's reports contain so many falsehoods about the friars and the citizens of this province.
> —*Thomé Domínguez de Mendoza, 1662*[2]

The creaking *carretas* wended their way northward from waterhole to waterhole along the long Camino Real de Tierra Adentro, reaching New Mexico in spring 1659 after months of travel from Mexico City. One wagon stood out. Quite distinct from the *carretas*, a large *carossa*, a covered wagon with bedding and curtains, carried Governor López de Mendizábal and his wife, doña Teresa de Aguilera de la Rocha. In a separate wagon rode their servants, among them, the mulatta Clarilla and the Black Ana de la Cruz, who would live in the Palace of the Governor in Santa Fe as the governor's servants.[3] His term would be tumultuous and unsettling to the missionaries, settlers, and

Pueblo Indians of New Mexico, each for different reasons. While the Plains tribes appeared peripheral to events in New Mexico at the time, missionaries continued to venture among them, hoping to convert them to Christianity.

Still, the succeeding governors in the Provincia de Nuevo México between 1632 and 1659 would not be as easygoing as Governor Manuel de Silva Nieto had been. While the New Mexico friars had opposed the administrations of the provincial governors in the first decades of the seventeenth century, governors Francisco de la Mora (1632 to 1635), Francisco Martínez de Baeza (1635 to 1637), and Luis de Rosas (1637 to 1641) would test the patience of friars, settlers, and Pueblo Indians. Captain Luis de Rosas, for example, arrived in New Mexico in 1637 after the long and arduous journey northward on the Camino Real de Tierra Adentro. Once in New Mexico, word spread up the Camino Real that the new governor had arrived, and typically each Indian pueblo and Spanish settlement along the Rio Grande received him with the customary courtesies.[4] Once at the Villa de Santa Fé, the settlers came out in procession and greeted him. While the welcome extended to the governor appeared joyous, among the friars and some settlers the rumor flitted about that he was a crony of the viceroy, Marqués de Cadereita, who had given him a free hand to deal with the cantankerous friary of New Mexico. The experienced Rosas, who had been a military commander in Flanders for fifteen years, seemed well prepared to deal with any military and political adversity. He certainly knew what he faced, given the well-known treatment of previous governors by the New Mexican friars.

Almost immediately, Governor Rosas offended the friars when he refused to convene the *residencia*, the official audit, of his predecessor, Martínez de Baeza. The friars hoped that the *residencia* would serve as a means to prosecute the former governor for crimes and abuses charged against him by the friars and their loyal settlers.[5] To everyone's amazement, Rosas let Martínez off without insisting on a strong *residencia*. Governor Rosas has lost no time in serving notice to the clergy that he would not do their bidding.

Charges and countercharges between governor and prelate made their way southward to Mexico City as the civil authorities and the clergy of New Mexico each took a self-righteous stance. The situation finally came to a head with disastrous results. In late 1638 the friars and some settlers met at Sandia Pueblo with the ailing Friar Perea presiding.[6] The members of the meeting at Sandia approved an investigation of Rosas and his followers conducted by

Perea. In their report, they accused Rosas of attempting to destroy ecclesiastical privileges, immunities, and authority. In their testimonies against Rosas, the friars gave example after example of his disdain for the clergy. The anti-Rosas missionaries and settlers received a sharp blow, however, when Friar Perea, commissary of the Holy Office, died during the winter of 1638 and was solemnly buried at Sandia Pueblo. His death temporarily set back the plan to have the Tribunal of the Holy Office of the Inquisition in Mexico City prosecute Rosas as soon as they could collect enough damaging evidence against him. Meanwhile, Perea's office as agent of the Inquisition remained vacant for over two years. In the meantime the Rosas affair reached its climax. For the moment, the ecclesiastical court presided over by the prelate Friar Juan de Salas appeared to be the only power in New Mexico left to the friars.[7]

The situation and its complicated issues worsened through 1639, when Sebastian de Sandoval slandered the priests, who had him excommunicated. Despite their demands, Rosas refused to force Sandoval to make absolution. The governor, furthermore, supported and encouraged Sandoval's barrage of vocal statements against the priests and their supporting settlers. The friars feared for Sandoval's life; in fact one of them predicted he would be killed. Early in January of 1640 Sandoval's body was found.[8]

Immediately, Rosas accused two friars of committing the murder. Shocked at the accusation, the priests denied the charges, and the anti-Rosas settlers supported them. Because Sandoval, the excommunicant, had died without absolution, Friar Salas refused to permit his burial in holy ground. While Friar Antonio de Aranda, guardian of the church at Santa Fe, was temporarily absent, Rosas ordered Sandoval's body buried in the church. A supporter of Governor Rosas, Friar Juan de Vidania, officiated over the requiem, and soon afterward Friar Salas had him arrested. The intrepid Rosas forcibly rescued him and appointed the friar to the post of "royal chaplain."[9]

In defiance of Rosas, the clergymen solicited and obtained the support of some of the frontiersmen who opposed Rosas's heavy-handed administration in which their property rights had been threatened. The Sandoval-Vidania affair had forced their hand to support the friars. Meeting at Santo Domingo, the ecclesiastical capital of New Mexico, the disaffected frontiersmen joined the friars to defy the governor. They fortified the pueblo and challenged the governor's authority over them.[10] The challenge amounted to no more than a standoff, which lasted a year while both sides hurled accusations at one another.

Changes were in the wind. In the spring of 1641, another governor, Juan Flores de Sierra y Valdéz, relieved Rosas. About the time that the anti-Rosas faction gained political control of the Cabildo de Santa Fe, the Holy Office of the Inquisition in Mexico City confirmed Friar Juan de Salas as the commissary of the Inquisition in New Mexico. Salas succeeded the deceased Friar Perea to that office. Shortly after his arrival, Governor Sierra, who was ill when he arrived, died. Immediately the inquisitor, Friar Salas, and the supporting *cabildo* members moved to have Rosas arrested, jailed, and bound over for trial.[11] Rosas's enemies now held control of the civil government. Fearing for his life, the incarcerated Rosas managed to contact Flores's son before he returned to New Spain. Entrusting his last will and testament to him to take to Mexico City, Rosas told him that his enemies intended to kill him.[12]

When it did happen, news of Rosas's death spread throughout Santa Fe and other areas in the province with astounding rapidity. Reports of how Rosas died similarly were widespread. It seems that Nicolás Ortíz, a soldier from Zacatecas who had gone to Mexico in 1637 on business, had returned and learned from certain settlers that Rosas had had an affair with his wife, María Bustillos.[13] Suspecting that she had taken refuge in the house where Rosas was held prisoner, Ortíz persuaded the alcalde and other witnesses to go with him to search Rosas's quarters. The first search proved fruitless, but for some strange reason Ortíz insisted on a second search. This time, they found María in a place that had been previously searched. Enraged, Ortíz seemed uncontrollable. María was taken into custody, and Rosas angrily protested the contrived situation and charges. As a precaution, his guard was doubled. The guard, however, refused to accept responsibility for Rosas's life. Just after midnight on January 25, 1642, a gang of masked swordsmen, one of them Ortíz, overpowered the guards. Apparently Ortíz ran into the room and stabbed Rosas to death with a dozen sword thrusts.[14]

After a quick trial, the anti-Rosas supporters acquitted Ortíz. As soon as he could, Ortíz departed New Mexico, moving fast along the Camino Real southward to Nueva Vizcaya (present Chihuahua). Meanwhile, the pro-Rosas faction dispatched a hard-riding messenger ahead of him to advise the governor of Nueva Vizcaya, Luis de Valdéz, of the case and its outcome. Governor Valdéz posted soldiers along the Royal Road, and when Ortíz came by, they arrested him and took him to Parral. After a second trial Ortíz was found guilty and sentenced to death. He was permitted to appeal the judgment against him. Before the appeal could take place, Ortíz escaped, and the final disposition of his case became clouded by time.[15]

The assassination of the king's governor proved to be the undoing of the anti-Rosas faction. In time, word of the conflict reached the king's court in Madrid, and a new governor, Alonso Pacheco de Herédia (1642–44), arrived in New Mexico with secret instructions to punish those guilty of the murder of the royal governor. Armed with sufficient authority to judge and execute those responsible, Pacheco arrived in Santa Fe in the fall of 1642.[16]

Working quickly, Governor Pacheco opened an inquiry regarding the assassination and conspiracy against Rosas. After months of investigation, Pacheco ordered the execution of eight soldiers, ringleaders in the murder plot. After they were beheaded, their impaled heads were displayed in the plaza of Santa Fe as an object lesson for all. Hoping to bring an end to the tragic affair, Pacheco declared a general amnesty to minor offenders. Much to the dismay of the clergy, Pacheco ordered the remains of the excommunicant Sandoval, which had been removed by clergymen from the church, reinterred in the church cemetery.[17] So ended the Rosas affair, which had led to a brief rebellion and narrowly missed plummeting New Mexico into a civil war.[18]

As the succession of governors in the 1640s and 1650s had locked horns with the friars, many of the pueblos, observing such consternations and sensing disunity among them, became increasingly restless. Although Indian rebellions had occurred throughout the period, they were small and easily put down. The church-state issues cooled down between 1656 and 1659 primarily because Friar Tomás Manso, the *padre custodio*, had been influential in having his brother, Juan Manso de Contreras, appointed governor of the province.[19] The pueblos, however, had sensed the disarray caused by the competing Spanish colonial civilian and ecclesiastical authorities. Two decades would pass before the Pueblo Indians, biding their time, could muster their forces for a successful revolt. The administration of Bernardo López de Mendizábal would leave an indelible mark on the harried relationships between church and state as it related to the Spanish colonial Indian policy in New Mexico.

In 1658 Viceroy Duque de Albuquerque appointed López de Mendizábal to succeed Juan Manso as governor of New Mexico. López de Mendizábal, a member of a distinguished family, was born near Puebla on the Hacienda de San Cosme y San Damian in "la jurisdicción del Pueblo de Chietla" in

New Spain.[20] His father, Captain Cristóbal López de Mendizábal, a Basque who had immigrated to Mexico from Oñate, Spain, the same place where the family of Juan Pérez de Oñate originated, died in 1635. In 1663 López de Mendizábal's mother, doña Leonor de Pastrana, resided in Mexico City. She came from a wealthy family whose father, a merchant from Toledo, Spain, had settled for a while in Chietla, then in Puebla de Los Angeles, and finally in Mexico City.[21] His maternal great-grandfather, Juan Núñez de Leon, had been the only dark spot in the family history, for he had been found guilty of some religious indiscretion by the Holy Office of the Inquisition and had undergone the penitent's auto-de-fé in the Convento de San Francisco in Mexico City on April 20, 1603.[22]

Loyal citizens of Spain and the empire, the family included one member who had served on the powerful Consejo Real de Las Indias (the Council of the Indies). Others had been nuns and abbesses or had belonged to the Military Order of Santiago or had served as lawyers and judges. Two family members had served as regents of Navarre and Seville, another as chancellor of Valladolid, and one had served on the Junta del Supremo del Inquisición. His uncle, Fray Ambrosio de Mendizábal, had been a doctor of theology, and a cousin, Fray Cristóbal de la Carraga, became a bishop. Governor López came from a politically active family.[23]

Before his appointment to the governorship of New Mexico, López de Mendizábal had served in various political, ecclesiastical, and military assignments in the New World for almost fourteen years.[24] In the tradition of his family, who had served the crown in imperial posts, López de Mendizábal had attended the Jesuit colleges at Puebla and Mexico City as well as the Royal University of Mexico, the most renowned of the colonial universities, founded in 1551. Very well versed in classical Latin, he also studied common law and the arts. After completing his studies, he served in the Armada de Galeones and the presidio at Cartagena de Indias in Venezuela. While living in Cartagena, López de Mendizábal acted as a *visitador* of the diocese where his cousin was bishop. Afterward he served as *alcalde mayor* at San Juan de los Llanos and later at the pueblo of Chicontepeque in the Corregimiento de Guayacoctla in New Spain.

At Cartagena, López de Mendizábal married doña Teresa de Aguilera de la Rocha, born in Alexandria de la Palla in the Italian kingdom of Milan. Her father, Maestre de Campo Melchor de Aguilera from Granada, had served the crown for fifty years. Teresa de Aguilera was born when her father served as governor of Alexandria. Years later, when her father took a new post as governor of Cartagena de Indias, Teresa met López de Mendizábal. After don Melchor's stint in Cartagena, he retired to Toledo, Spain, where he died.

Teresa de Aguilera's mother, doña María Rocha, born in Ireland, lived in Madrid in her later life. Doña Teresa's maternal grandfather was the Conde de Rocha, who had been ordered from Ireland to Spain by the king. The Rocha family took pride in moving to Spain to escape English tyranny. Doña Teresa came from a family of high social standing.[25] After their marriage, don Bernardo and doña Teresa moved to New Spain where he served as *alcalde mayor*. There he attracted the attention of the viceroy, and in 1658 don Bernardo López de Mendizábal, then forty years old, received his appointment as *gobernador* and *capitán general* of the Provincia de Nuevo México.[26]

Governor López de Mendizábal had a definite preconception of his role as regent of the remote province of New Mexico. He firmly believed in the superiority of secular authority over ecclesiastical privileges, immunities, and jurisdictions. As a well-educated and politically experienced aristocrat, López de Mendizábal viewed the frontier society of New Mexico and New Spain with a certain contempt. In the end, López de Mendizábal's background would work against him in a land that had historically been filled with disenchantment for previous governors. He failed to realize the relationship between the power of the governors and the old-line families who had been in New Mexico for over two lifetimes.

Toward the end of 1658, López de Mendizábal and his retinue left Mexico City with the yearly mission supply caravan. They were accompanied by a member of the military escort, Miguel Noriega, captain of the cavalry, served López de Mendizábal as his personal secretary. Walking among the teamsters were twenty-four priests and the new *padre custodio*, Friar Juan Ramírez. Waving good-bye to their friends and relatives, the members of the caravan departed the ancient capital.

The journey on the Camino Real de Tierra Adentro was long and arduous. By spring 1659 the caravan had reached Parral on the southern end of Nueva Vizcaya's mining frontier. The rigors of the journey manifested themselves in the desertion of some of the drivers, who had had enough. The deserters were captured and returned to the caravan. López de Mendizábal, however, delivered a tirade against their dereliction of duty and was not about to be quieted.²⁷ The wagon train wended its way from water hole to water hole across the desert until it reached the Conversión de los Mansos y Sumas near El Paso on the Rio Grande. The missionaries there had prepared a reception for the new *padre custodio* and had the Camino Real lined with Indians holding branches to form an archway across the road. This angered López de Mendizábal because as the chief political leader of the province, the honor went not to him but to the ecclesiastical chief, Friar Ramírez. The governor ordered his soldiers to break up the demonstration. Pulling the branches from Indian hands and throwing them to the ground, the soldiers roughed up some of the natives, who, perplexed by the Spanish behavior, became afraid and angry.²⁸ The missionaries and Indians of the *conversión* stepped aside and let the governor and his men pass first. As their new prelate and twenty-four friars were behind the wagon train, the El Paso missionaries and Indians grabbed some extra branches and reformed the arch of welcome for their brothers. López de Mendizábal scoffed at the gesture. The priests, however, would remember the bad example set by the governor before the Indians, who could have used a better Christian model.

Moving northward along the Camino Real de Tierra Adentro, the caravan crossed at El Paso, but not without the archway incident. Proceeding northward along the Jornada del Muerto, they reached Socorro at the extreme end of New Mexico's Río Abajo. On June 30, 1659, they reached the *convento* at Nuestra Señora de Socorro. Friar Benito de la Natividad, the padre guardian of the *convento*, graciously received him. Fray Benito waited until the caravan reached the pueblo, and then with church bells ringing and trumpets blaring, the priest sprinkled holy water on the governor and prelate and received them in the church. Appreciative of the token gesture but unimpressed, Governor López de Mendizábal thought the priests could do a little better in receiving him. Someone thought López de Mendizábal had mumbled a sarcasm. "They should receive [me] like the most Holy Sacrament on the Feast of Corpus Christi," he was thought to have said.²⁹ Before long, everyone in the province was either aghast at the comment or secretly in admiration of his sense of humor. The priests again took note of his indiscretion.

The priests witnessed more sarcasms by the governor and took note of his attitude toward religion. Reaching Socorro, the caravan stopped to camp. That evening one of the settlers invited López de Mendizábal and doña Teresa to supper. Doña Luisa Dias de Betansos y Castro, an eighty-year-old widow but a very spry frontierswoman, and her daughter, doña Isabel de Salazar, had made a dinner in honor of the dignitaries. The conversation at the table turned to religious matters, and López de Mendizábal obligingly let doña Luisa know how he felt about the role of the friars. Turning to doña Isabel, López de Mendizábal asked, "Do you go frequently to mass?" "Yes, we go when we can," she responded. "Lord knows we would like to go everyday," she added, "but oftentimes we can't go because we don't have horses or mules." Flippantly, López de Mendizábal remarked that they were "healthier or better off not going to mass."[30] He suggested that they would be happier not having to be around the friars frequently. López de Mendizábal had made a poor impression among these settlers, who were insulted and shocked by his comments. His caustic words put a damper on the conversation and according to report, doña Luisa and doña Isabel were glad when López de Mendizábal and his wife finally departed their home.

After dinner the party went out to the church. López de Mendizábal, still in a caustic mood, remarked to his courteous hosts, "In these remote lands all that is needed is a jacal and some ornaments" instead of a church.[31] The truculent octogenarian, doña Luisa, had been waiting for López de Mendizábal to make one more insulting comment. Calmly but firmly, she answered with asperity, "Where else but in the temple of God should these precious objects be put to use, for they edify all Catholics and Spaniards as well as Indians." With that López de Mendizábal was silenced.

Up the Rio Grande went the caravan. Everywhere they stopped, López de Mendizábal scandalized the citizenry at haciendas, *estancias*, and missions along the way. When they reached Santa Fe, he refused to participate in the traditional reception that the governor and *cabildo* had arranged for the prelate since the days of Governor Pedro de Peralta. Instead, he persisted in enjoying his newly founded reputation as a persecutor of friars. Governor Bernardo López de Mendizábal's fervent belief in the supremacy of civil authority over ecclesiastical jurisdiction became the cornerstone of his policies, or at least his practice, in dealing with the priests. With that, López de Mendizábal quickly established the theme of his administration. The expedition finally reached Santa Fe, and López de Mendizábal prepared for the required tour of the province.

In November 1660, Governor López de Mendizábal unveiled a part of his Indian policy. The missionaries in the Provincia de Nuevo México were shocked by what happened next. Sitting in the plaza of Isleta Pueblo, Governor Bernardo López de Mendizábal and the Spanish settlers of New Mexico who accompanied him there watched the ritualistic pueblo *catzina* dances with interest. In attendance were Captain Tomé Domínguez de Mendoza, the *sargento mayor* of the Jurisdiction of Isleta and local *estanciero*, and his brother, Juan Domínguez de Mendoza. Near Captain Miguel Noriega, the governor's secretary, stood Juan Griego Navatato, a Tewa who lived among the Spaniards in Santa Fe, and Pedro de Arteaga, López de Mendizábal's indentured servant. The Spaniards watched the dance in the cool morning air of fall 1660.[32]

In cadence, the Indians, dressed as *catzinas*, with hawk's bells jingling and hand gourds rattling, came out dancing and chanting, "Hu! Hu! Hu! Hu!" Through Spanish colonial eyes the Indians in the dance appeared fierce in their dress. They looked "evil," said Tomé Domínguez de Mendoza, "especially the one who wore an ugly guise like a demon with horns on his head, and eyes which hung out an inch and a half from their sockets [it was] a horrible thing, and they chanted in a monotone, Hu! Hu! Hu!" López de Mendizábal turned to his retinue and said, "Look at this! This is nothing more than Hu! Hu! Hu! And the thieving friars say that this is superstitious."[33] All the while, Governor López de Mendizábal knew that the friars considered them diabolical and superstitious and that they had forbidden the Indians to dance them for almost thirty years, since the days of Custodio Estévan de Perea. Now Governor López de Mendizábal gave the Indians permission to dance them. His Indian policy, based on permissiveness, would play havoc with the mission program and would become a source of grievance for the friars in the province.[34] Although Domínguez de Mendoza thought differently, López de Mendizábal was his governor and his *capitán general*; who would dare to contradict him? Still, for Domínguez de Mendoza there was something wrong in watching these dancers which the Pueblo Indians called *catzinas*.

The pueblos, on the other hand, quickly saw an opportunity to practice their cultural values in plain sight of Spanish authorities, missionaries, and settlers. In the context of the times, nevertheless, did implementation of the pronounced policies and orders issued by Governor López de Mendizábal offer legitimate alternatives regarding the treatment of Pueblo Indians not under missionary control as well as their counterpart mission neophytes? Or would the entrenched Franciscan-dominated mission field practices in

New Mexico prevail to dictate sole control over mission and non-mission Indians? In the end, López de Mendizábal and his loyal followers, having made their point, would be prosecuted by the Holy Office of the Inquisition in Mexico City for obstructing the mission program as well as for other religious indiscretions.

Indeed, the shocked friars considered the *catzina* dancers diabolical and superstitious and forbade the Indians to dance them. Despite his opposition to the governor, Father Ramírez, the padre guardian of the New Mexico missions, had allegedly told the governor that he saw nothing wrong with the *catzina* dances and had told him to allow them.[35] Later the Franciscans would bring charges against their own padre guardian, Juan Ramírez, for this and other improprieties.

To López de Mendizábal, the broader issues included questions regarding civil versus ecclesiastical control over Indians that needed to be defined. He strongly declared that ecclesiastical jurisdiction conflicted with his authority as governor of the province. He made his policy manifest in a series of declarations about Indian labor and its relationship to the mission process. He refused to support the friars' demands for the punishment of mission Indians for crimes against the church. López de Mendizábal hoped to instruct the friars in the differences between sins against the church and crimes against the state. In his view, the missionaries only had jurisdiction over mission Indians, not the entire pueblo. Thus, he sought to weaken their position by pronouncing the supremacy of his civil authority over that of the church by discrediting the friars and limiting their work and their role in that frontier society.

López de Mendizábal aimed to prevent the missionaries from exercising their power over Indian pueblos, particularly those that had refused to be a part of the mission program. Not only did he draw the distinction between non-mission and mission Indians; he also drew the line between servitude and paid labor by Indians as well as punishment meted out for sins against the church and crimes against the state. Repeatedly López de Mendizábal made it clear that the civil authorities would no longer assist the priests in punishing Indians for sins against the church. The priests would, under his policies, have to mete out their own punishments and pay Indians for work done at their bidding. To that end, he appointed several of his followers to the office of *alcalde mayor de indios* to carry out his policies. The office of *alcalde mayor de indios*, which had been created in the mid-1640s in New

Mexico, had been introduced to manage large Indian areas that had been divided into eight jurisdictions.[36] One of López de Mendizábal's most faithful followers, Nicolas de Aguilar, played an important role in the implementation of his Indian policy.[37] Like all other *alcaldes mayores de indios* assigned to other pueblo districts, Aguilar, as mandated, resided within the Salinas jurisdiction. His duties included informing Indians of their legal status, and he worked tirelessly to familiarize himself with issues between settlers and Indians within his jurisdiction. In particular, he reported all offenses against Indians. As an *alcalde mayor de indios*, he served unsalaried.

The friars observed that the unsalaried *alcaldes mayores de indios* were lower-class people who were constantly seeking ways to better their interests.[38] Perhaps the status of the office intrigued them and inspired unquestioned loyalty to the governor who had appointed them. Aside from his loyalty to don Bernardo, Aguilar, a rugged frontiersman, did not fear the Franciscan missionaries. He would not have long to prove his worth to his governor. The friars not only challenged López de Mendizábal's policies but also questioned the character of his appointees to the office and gathered information about all of the *alcaldes mayores de indios*.

When they focused on Aguilar, for example, they learned that he, born of mestizo parentage sometime in 1623, hailed from Michoacan.[3] At eighteen years old, he settled as a miner in Parral in present Chihuahua. In 1641 he filed charges against claim jumpers who caved in his mine.[39] One dreadful night in 1654, when confronted by a posse led by his uncle, Hernando de Villagomez, who had charged him with kidnapping two women, Aguilar drew his harquebus and killed him. He fled under cover of darkness without a trace.[40] Apparently, Aguilar had been pardoned for the murder of his uncle by the governor of Nueva Vizcaya. Later, Governor López de Mendizábal said that Aguilar had benefited from a *cedula de indulto*, a general amnesty granted throughout the empire by the king on the occasion of a prince being born to the royal family.[41]

Sometime in the 1650s, Aguilar showed up in New Mexico by way of the Great Plains. Former governor Juan de Samaniego y Jaca (1653–56), for whom Aguilar had served, recommended him to Governor López de Mendizábal, who appointed him *alcalde mayor de indios* of the jurisdiction of Las Salinas in 1659.[42] In any case, Aguilar had earned his way into the graces of New Mexican administrators.

Within the first year of his administration, the Laws of the Indies required that each governor make at least one *visita* of the province and submit a report to the viceroy regarding the status of all Indian pueblos and Spanish settlements in the province.⁴³ The law required the governor to make the *visita* only once during his term of office,⁴⁴ but it did not mean that he could not later return to certain pueblos or consider any other complaints from Indians. The law merely limited the obligation to ensure that, for each administration, the entire province would be seen at least once and that each governor would become familiar with places and situations within his jurisdiction. Particularly, during his inspection of the Indian pueblos, the governor, as required, explained his role as judge and defender of their legal rights.⁴⁵ To that end, López de Mendizábal, as part of purpose of the *visita*, listened to Indian complaints and, as required, would later submit them to the *juezes ordinarios* (ordinary judges) in the Villa de Santa Fé for investigation and, if necessary, prosecution.

In October 1659, López de Mendizábal and his *alcaldes mayores* began the inspection of the province.⁴⁶ Quickly the friars pointed out that the *visita* had been undertaken to investigate them, not the items required by law. After the governor's *visita* at the pueblo of Alamillo near Socorro, the friars felt justified in their concern. At Alamillo, López de Mendizábal announced his intention to implement the Indian policy under his control and take it away from the missionaries. Aware of the antimissionary sentiment at Alamillo, López demonstrated support for Indian causes.

Sitting at a table in the plaza, the bald-headed, bespectacled Governor López de Mendizábal, wearing a black traveler's hat with a tall crown and broad brim, gathered his soldiers, translators, and the Indians around him.⁴⁷ Positing a series of leading questions, he asked the natives if they "supported the missions."⁴⁸ To the missionaries' dismay, he inquired about concubinage among them and punishments they received for it. López de Mendizábal made it clear that the friars could not punish Indians for certain crimes. Philosophically, he felt that the friars would distinguish between sins against God and crimes against the state.⁴⁹ In drawing the line between offenses punishable by friars and those punishable by the civil authority, the governor ordered that Indians could not be placed in stocks or jails without his permission. That, he said, had already been determined by the king of Spain.⁵⁰

Bitterly the friars complained to their superiors. They claimed López de Mendizábal had deliberately encouraged the Indians to make accusations against their minister, the ninety-year-old Friar Francisco Acevedo.[51] One woman stood up and said the friar had "deflowered" her. With impunity, Governor López de Mendizábal ordered one of his men to Father Acevedo's cell to take a *manta* (blanket) from him as an indemnity to be paid to the woman. As the aggrieved woman took the blanket, the pueblo broke into a "loud cacophony,"[52] as if in mockery of their minister. When the friars pleaded with him to defend himself, the old priest, kneeling in prayer, replied that his defense was his old age, his ill health, and his reputation as a simple and holy man who had worked among Indians for more than twenty-eight years. Besides, given the false accusation made against him, he did not wish to make more of it.[53] Acknowledging the damage done to his reputation, Acevedo did not remain at Alamillo. Four decades later, the Franciscan chronicler Fray Agustin Vetancurt, in his *Menologio*, wrote that Acevedo died at Abó and was buried there.[54]

The missionaries were outraged, for the judgment against the old priest assumed guilt on his part, and the public humiliation besmirched his reputation as a clergyman. The missionaries maintained that only their prelate, as the *juéz ecclesiástico* (ecclesiastic judge), had the right to judge them—not the governor. López de Mendizábal countered by saying that he was obligated to make the case public in order to discharge his duty.[55] Already the governor could sense the contradictions between the legal status of Indians, ecclesiastical immunities, and gubernatorial jurisdiction.

After Alamillo, López de Mendizábal visited other nearby pueblos, some of which were in the Salinas jurisdiction. Everywhere he went, the friars met him with distrust, while the Indians come out with curiosity to see him. Within the jurisdiction López de Mendizábal visited Abó, Quarai, Tajique, and Chililí before moving northward to Galisteo and Santa Fe. At each place he visited, he informed the Indians of his duty to administer Indian policies as prescribed by the Laws of the Indies.

At Socorro, his last stop before going to the Salinas pueblos, one of the ministers gave the governor a list of names of Indians to be punished by the *escolta* for concubinage. As customary, the priests handed the governor a written list of offenders, but again López drew the line. He announced that no Indian would be punished for any sin by order of the priests. As he saw it, such punishments were not within the purview of the civil government.

Eventually the governor and his retinue moved eastward across the mountains to the Salinas jurisdiction. At San Gregorio de Abó, Fray Aguado, the guardian, came out of the church sprinkling holy water and blessing López de Mendizábal and his retinue. Years later when the friars sought to prove that the López *visita* of 1659 had been undertaken to investigate them, several of them noted their first meeting with Governor López de Mendizábal. They recalled that cold day in early November when all of them, exhausted from the journey from Socorro over the mountainous terrain, had agreed that, overall, the governor had made a lasting negative impression. When Ray Benito de la Natividad came out of the church to meet him "with pealing of bells and with other musical instruments which the churches in that custodia have and with a large cross," the governor harshly rebuked him. López de Mendizábal told him that he should have "gone out two leagues from the convent to receive him."[56] Soon after, when López de Mendizábal arrived at San Gregorio de Abó, Friar Antonio Aguado suffered the same castigation. From there, López de Mendizábal and his retinue continued the *visita* by stopping at Cuarac, Tajique, and Chililí.

Whether López ever went to Tabira or Tenabo is unknown. After he left Salinas, the entourage went to Galisteo, where he encountered more resistance by the friars to his policies. Indeed, the *visita* of 1659 was revealing in two ways. First, the friars were unwilling to accept any tampering with their mission program by the governor, no matter what legalities he might present regarding the appropriateness of his actions. Second, Governor López de Mendizábal had announced the basic premises of his Indian policy as it concerned the Pueblo Indians. López de Mendizábal stressed that he premised his Pueblo Indian policy on the principle that he would attend only to matters of civil disobedience. As a corollary, he would not cooperate with the friars in meting out any punishments of Indians that were based on "sins committed against the church." He felt that the missionaries would have to carry out the punishments themselves without assistance from his administration, inclusive of the *alcaldes mayores*. Moreover, he encouraged the natives to go directly to him and make their complaints. López de Mendizábal went even further. He made it clear that Indians were no longer to do any work for the priests unless the friars paid them according to the Laws of the Indies. Then he stated that, as in other parts of the empire, Indians could participate in native ceremonies as long as they were not idolatrous. Then López de Mendizábal audaciously pronounced that Indians were not obligated to attend the *doctrina* (catechism classes) or assist at the Holy Mass because both functions adversely influenced them to work for the missionaries without pay and under conditions of forced labor.[57]

As López de Mendizábal ordered, Aguilar immediately executed the governor's policies. At each pueblo he visited, Aguilar, speaking in Spanish and in Tompiro, used a crier to proclaim the new Indian work policy.[58] At other nearby pueblos, Aguilar made similar announcements and went a step further. At Quarai, for example, he told the Indians that they would no longer be permitted to serve the priests without pay, nor would they be allowed to serve as choir members or acolytes.[59]

At Las Humanas one of the priests (probably Friar Santander) said that while construction of the church and convent at the pueblos was underway, López de Mendizábal ordered Nicolas de Aguilar to make sure that, under penalty of death, no Indian worked in that construction. To his confusion, nonetheless, they continued to work on the structures. It seems that the old church of San Isidro was no longer used, and Friar Santander referred to the building of San Buenaventura de las Humanas. The friars argued that the Indians worked because they recognized their obligation as Catholics. Still, López stood accused of criticizing the building of the churches in the pueblos, especially "on the occasion in which the church of Humanas was under construction," he allegedly said. "For what [purpose] were the churches . . . a jacal is enough to say mass in."[60]

In the context of seventeenth-century New Mexico, the question of reforming Indian labor policy at the missions did not have a practical solution. The crisis over Indian labor in the missions and the pueblos was one of jurisdiction, and López attempted to define it. The missionary practice of employing Indians to work for no pay in the fields, care for the herds, and serve the priests as house servants had been a longstanding practice in the missions. The friars considered the premise, that it was done for the good of the mission, to be irrefutable. López de Mendizábal nevertheless demanded that the missionaries pay the Indians one *real* a day according to the Laws of the Indies for their services. Accordingly, he argued that Indians ought not be obligated to work for the priests, nor should they be made to feel morally guilty if they did not, unless a native voluntarily desired to serve the friars, in which case an exception would be made. The friars argued that it had already been defined and that López de Mendizábal's policy debilitated the power of the church in New Mexico.

López de Mendizábal's directives, which had been spun into practice by the *alcaldes mayores de indios*, resulted in a series of altercations at the missions and intensified the struggle between the friars and the governor. To defend their works, the friars turned to documenting every incident involving López de Mendizábal's *alcaldes mayores de indios* so that they could build a case against them and the governor. Aguilar, the most audacious among them, seemed to be their primary target.

One incident that fueled their case occurred at Abó. Father Antonio Aguado reported to his superior that one Sunday Aguilar passed by San Gregorio de Abó on his way to Las Humanas and noticed a large gate to the pueblo had been left open and was in disrepair.[61] As it was a Christian holy day, the Tompiros were in their pueblo enjoying a day of rest. That afternoon, Aguilar ordered some men and women to mix some mud for mortar to repair it. Quickly Fray Aguado challenged Aguilar for having made the natives work on a Christian holy day. The confrontation flared and quickly ended, but Fray Aguado did not forget the occasion and reported the incident to his prelate.[62] As a result, the friars believed that they had found a way to tie the governor's Indian labor policy to a church issue. The Aguado-Aguilar confrontation clearly demonstrated the pitfalls of López de Mendizábal's Indian policy. After all, everyone knew that a Christian holy day was a day of rest.

Before 1659 ended, the friars had met in council at Santo Domingo Pueblo, the ecclesiastical headquarters of the New Mexican mission field. There they drew up a report against López de Mendizábal's policies. They complained to the viceroy that the requirement to pay the Indians for labor in the missions had placed an undue imposition on the already meager earnings of the friars.[63] "The religious of this kingdom, sire," they wrote, "who live by themselves in a convent without the enjoyment of company from his brothers, countrymen and relatives have no other conveniences. [They live] daily at great risk from enemies and even the Christian [Indians], who for one word of reprehension about their views take their lives." The isolation they suffered was exemplified by the fact that they walked "ten, twenty, and thirty leagues one way to the next convent and more for the return trip." Their only "stipend, alms, subvention or collection money at the altar, which they received, came to one hundred and fifty pesos, which the king gives every year to each priest. The money from the royal patronage was often stretched to buy necessities for the church. And, the governor does not want the Indians to serve unless we pay them one real each day . . . as if we had it," wrote the friars.[64]

They explained that mission lands were used to provide food to the Indians, to needy Spaniards, and to travelers who came by their convents. Furthermore, they complained that the governor's order that Indians not serve the priests without pay included the stipulation that they should not assist the ministers in anything. The friars reiterated that the Indians "do not want to help the church and *doctrina* in anything because of this order; we here do not have anything with which to pay them other than the food which they cultivated for us."[65] In their report, issued to Mexico City officials at the start of 1660, the friars demonstrated their need for Indian labor at the missions. They stressed their poverty as a factor in not affording payment for Indian services. To that end, they resolved to fight against the governor's Indian policy that would eliminate the practice of Indian servitude at the missions.

The friars argued that López de Mendizábal's implementation of his Indian policies had gone too far. To prove their point, the friars documented an event that clearly showed how Aguilar, acting on the governor's mandates, had openly obstructed the mission program and attacked the church. Later, in 1663, when the priests from Salinas brought formal charges against him before the Tribunal of the Holy Office of the Inquisition, they cited multiple accusations, all stemming from similar incidents.[66]

One incident occurred with mission Indians as witnesses. The friars reported that, one day when morning mass at Quarai had finished, Friar Nicolas de Freitas began "to teach these poor Indians," who had remained in the church to hear him. Aguilar, who had attended mass, stayed to hear what the priest had to say.[67] Friar Freitas spoke about "the truths of one God, one Church, and one supreme head who governs it." As their teacher, Freitas reminded them of the Ten Commandments, emphasizing the Fourth Commandment: Honor thy father and thy mother. He said they must honor the friars as they would their own parents. "You are obligated," explained Friar Freitas from the altar, "to obey all your priests and ministers, and give them the necessary assistance in operating the missions."[68] The Indians sat motionless as a deep silence pervaded the nave of the church.

Aguilar, "unable to stomach such Catholic truths,"[69] stood up and interrupted the sermon and in a loud voice ordered the Indians, in their language, to leave the church. Freitas, looking to God for help, said a short prayer and continued his sermon. Confused, the Indians looked at him sympathetically, trying to hear him, while at the other end of the church, Aguilar raised his voice even louder and harangued them about their civil obligations. They remained in the church and Freitas continued with his lesson. Afterward Father Freitas went up to his room in the *convento* and Aguilar followed him. In front of another clergyman in the priest's quarters, Aguilar told him that he should "acknowledge the evil deed of the friars [instead of] preaching against what the governor had ordered."[70]

There were other incidents involving Aguilar that were recorded by the missionaries. After the altercations in the church and *convento* at Quarai, Aguilar went to the pueblo of Chililí. There he had an Indian whipped for assisting in singing the mass at Las Humanas. Confronting Aguilar, the priests asked him not to execute López's mandates so rigorously. Father Fernando de Velasco had two other requests to make of the *alcalde mayor*. To the first request, that he permit a certain Indian, Francisco, to accompany one of the visiting friars at the pueblo to his convent at Quarai eight leagues away, and to the second request, that he not order the lashing of an Indian musician who had gone to sing at a mass at Las Humanas, Aguilar replied that he must do what his governor had ordered him to do. He refused to listen to the petitions and angrily told the priest that if he interfered with his duties anymore, he would take him "to the Villa de Santa Fe in a pack saddle."[71] Father Velasco backed off for the moment, but he would commit the incident to memory so that he could report it to the vice *custodio* at first opportunity. At Tajique, Aguilar went a step further. After he had ordered the Indians not to assist the friars there, he waited for an opportunity to demonstrate that he meant what he said. One Saturday afternoon soon afterward, Father Freitas had ridden his horse the "four leagues" from Quarai to Tajique to say mass in the absence of Father Parroga.[72] When he arrived at Tajique, Father Freitas asked Diego Chititi, the Indian fiscal of the pueblo, to have some boys feed his horse some grass (*sacate*) and to have the cook prepare the remaining beans in the kitchen. On that occasion Aguilar heard that Chititi had obeyed Freitas's requests. Whereupon, the priest said, Aguilar grabbed the Indian and beat him with his staff. Outraged by Aguilar's actions and having had nothing to eat, Freitas returned to Quarai, and the people of Tajique went without Sunday mass the next day.[73]

By summer 1660, the friars declared Aguilar and other *alcaldes mayores* to be an enemy of the church. About this time three other events occurred that the friars could use against Aguilar. As if Aguilar's interruption of a catechizing sermon were not bad enough in the eyes of the priests, his stopping Sunday mass at Abó infuriated Father Aguado.[74] As the Tompiros knelt in prayer, Aguilar entered the church of San Gregorio and ordered a number of Indians out to help him cover the doors of some storerooms where salt from the Salinas mines had been stored for Governor López. As the Indians were filing out of the church, Father Aguado protested, "First, let them hear mass." To that Aguilar reportedly responded, "It's orders from my governor and he comes first."[75] After the storeroom doors were covered, the *alcalde mayor* took the Indians to work at some other task elsewhere. His effective surveillance of the Salinas pueblos allowed him to be at each pueblo at "the wrong time," as the priests saw it.[76]

At Tajique, the governor's policies underwent a different test. There Fray Diego de Parraga, having served his ministry at the pueblo for eight years, had collected nearly 600 wooden crosses of variable sizes.[77] The crosses were used for processions that took place every Friday of Lent and on Holy Thursday. During the rest of the year, they were kept in several rooms of the convent. Aguilar said they were fragile, broken, or in bad repair. He claimed that the Indians had even urinated on them.[78]

During the hard winter of 1660–61, when storms ravaged the high elevations of New Mexico and left forty-eight inches of snow in the Manzanos, the crosses became an issue that caused even more hardships for the priests. Given the Apache disdain for mission Indians and anticipating that the distressed missionaries would ask for help from their Christian Indians, Aguilar ordered the people of Chililí, Tajique, Quarai, Abó, and Las Humanas, under penalty of 200 lashes, not to help the friars or "to take the priests one stick of firewood."[79]

That winter, Isabel Baca, a mestiza settler near Tajique, went to Aguilar's house to tell him to have compassion on the priest there. She appealed to him to send him some wood so that he could keep warm and cook his food. The *alcalde mayor* responded that the priest could burn the crosses he had stored, for "whatever purpose the crosses served, it didn't matter if he burned them."[80] When Christian Indians attempted to take the priest firewood, he had them lashed. Seeing this, Father Fernando de Velasco told Aguilar that he would not whip them; "instead they should be given a reward." During that winter, Father Velasco went to the foothills to gather wood. Carrying a large load of wood on his shoulders, the priest passed near the *casa de la comunidad* of Tajique, where Aguilar happened to be, and heard him and some friends laughing at him.[81] This incident would haunt Aguilar, for the comment about the crosses would be construed as an irreverent remark, and his refusal to help the priests with their firewood would at least serve to support the friars' argument that he persecuted them. Three years later, when the priests brought up charges against him to the Holy Office of the Inquisition in Mexico City, there would be fifty-two accusations, all stemming from similar incidents.[82]

In their reports to their superiors, the priests not only construed Aguilar's remarks as irreverent but also interpreted his refusal to help them as persecution. Aguilar defended his actions by noting that Apache raiders had made the area unstable and unsafe. For their protection, he forbade Pueblo Indians within his jurisdiction to leave their villages.[83] He argued that the Apache disdain for mission Indians made it too dangerous for Tiwas and Tompiros to go to the foothills, even to get firewood for the priests.

Opposition to Governor López de Mendizábal's policies, as viewed from the fight between Aguilar and the Salinas friars, took on varied dimensions. The friars understood the impact of the governor's Indian policy on their mission program, for lack of cooperation from Indian officials had became evident.

Cooperation from Indian officials at the pueblo had also become difficult for the friars to get. Despite the existence of the office of *protector de indios*, whereby a Spaniard could be appointed as an attorney for Indian causes, Indian governors and war captains could also be considered to be "judges of Indians."[84] At Tabira, a *visita* of Humanas under Fray Diego de Santander had revealed a case of Indian concubinage (i.e., cohabitation of a man and a women without the sacrament of matrimony), and the war captains of Tabira took the two guilty persons before Aguilar for punishment. The incident at Tabira frightened the friars and demonstrated the debilitating effect of López de Mendizáble's Indian policies on the missions. When the friars exposed a case of concubinage at Tabira, they sought to punish those involved as an object lesson for those who would not abide by the sacrament of matrimony.[47] The friars demanded that the war captains of Tabira take the two guilty persons before Aguilar for punishment. After rebuffing the war captains, Aguilar freed the two prisoners without punishment. Fray Diego de Santander got furiously angry when the war captains explained what had happened. He could foresee the breakdown of mission discipline, especially in the area of matrimony. Aguilar explained to Friar Santander that no Indian would be punished by the civil authorities for concubinage or any other offense related to the mission program. Concubinage was a church matter. Aguilar stood his ground. At Quarai, Aguilar summoned an Indian official, Capitán Mayor Juan Yguany, and had him seized and whipped for having punished two Indian girls for missing mass.[85]

Such actions had a cumulative effect. After noticing that Indian officials had been punished for having carried out punishments ordered by the friars, Pueblo Indians looked at the issue of punishments at the missions with great interest. Some mission Indians, outraged by the change in policy, sided openly with the priests. Other mission and non-mission Indians took the opportunity to disobey requests by the priests. Although Spanish settlers in the Villa de Santa Fé were split on the effects of the governor's policies, they agreed that the policies had weakened the missionaries' grasp on the pueblos.

The effects of López de Mendizábal's policies, especially those regarding the *catzina* dances, continued to be visibly apparent and problematic to the missionaries charged with the conversion of the pueblos. The settlers, however, also knew an earlier history of the *catzina* dances. Under Governor Luis de Rosas (1637–42), the *catzina* dancers were allowed to perform in the pueblos.[86] At that time, they seemed harmless. Indeed, some of the settlers had even participated in them. Later the Franciscan missionaries condemned them as diabolical and were no longer allowed. Whether it had created a dangerous situation for the colonials remained to be seen. Such incidents aided the friars in the inquisitorial case they were building against the governor and his loyal followers. Their basic tenet was that López de Mendizábal worked to undermine mission discipline and obstructed the mission program of conversion. The settlers also took note, for collectively they feared that the governor's permissive Indian policy would create dangerous conditions for revolt.

Governor López de Mendizábal contended that there was nothing wrong with the *catzina* dances. To demonstrate his point to the friars and the settlers, he invited the dancers from Picurís to dance in the plaza of Santa Fe.[87] Hospitably, he allowed the Indians to dress in one of the rooms of the Palace of the Governors. When they were ready, the dancers came out with their masks, chanting. As spectators, the settlers in attendance, standing motionless, were supposedly frightened by their "demonic" appearance.

When the *catzina* dancers were finished, Governor López de Mendizábal, who had enjoyed the dance from his vantage point on the porch in front of his quarters, stood up and in a loud voice proclaimed, "The knavish priests say that this is evil, this is not evil but good."[88] Later López de Mendizábal commented that the dance was similar to the *palo volador* spectacle he had seen in southern Mexico. At another time, he exclaimed that the chanting had no more effect that the Gregorian chant sung by the friars. He did not regard the *catzina* dances as being any different from the popular Spanish dances of his day or, for that matter, any other kind of dances.[89] Intrigued by them, López de Mendizábal had seen native dances in other parts of the Americas. The friars noted and documented the governor's contrary comments.

Before long, other pueblos requested permission of the governor to perform the *catzina* dances in their pueblos. In 1659 the Isletans asked him for permission to perform *catzina* dances for the first time at their pueblo in decades. López de Mendizábal agreed. Soon settlers reported *catzina* dances at the pueblos of Alameda, Sandia, Cochití, Isleta, Picurís, Santa Cruz de la Cañada, Galisteo, San Cristóbal, San Lazaro, La Cienega, Tesuque, Pojoaque, Santa Clara, San Juan, San Ildefonso, Sevilleta, Tajique, Chililí, and Quarai, among others.

With the support of Christian Indian and Spanish settlers, the missionaries condemned the dances as "diabolical and superstitious." They were determined to prove their contentions. One Spaniard, Estevan Peralta, a settler who spoke "the language of Sandia," said that the dance was "evil and superstitious."[90] The friars hoped to use testimonies to assemble their case against López de Mendizábal. The friars welcomed as fact the testimony of anyone who claimed to understand the Indians and their culture and who could testify that they prayed to the devil. Another Spanish settler, Francisco Pérez Granillo, who lived near the mission at Socorro, testified that he understood Piro and that one of the Indians there told him the "dances are evil."[91] Similarly, Juan Barela, who lived near Sandia, said that in the winter of 1661 at the pueblo of Alameda he found the Indians enjoying a *catzina* dance. Barela asked one of them, "Why don't you go and dance?" The man responded, "I don't wish to dance those dances, for they are not good, and I am afraid of the priests, don't you see a demon there?" Afraid to turn his face and look, Barela must have believed the Indian.[92] At Sandia Pueblo the friars observed that the dances there "are held day and night" and that the church at Sandia had been desecrated by permitting two calves in the *capilla mayor*, the main chapel.[93] As did other Spanish appointees of Governor López Mendizábal of the various jurisdictions in New Mexico, Alcalde Mayor Nicolas de Aguilar encouraged the dances within the Jurisdiction of Salinas. Later he said that, on seeing the dances, he had failed to see anything evil about them. Testifying before the Holy Office of the Inquisition in Mexico City, he offered a description of the *catzina* dance as follows:

> They entered the plaza wearing ugly masks. Each one carries in his hand fruit, the kind which in commonly eaten. The fruit is tied with a string and is placed in a circle in the plaza one after another. The masked dancers then form a circle to guard the said fruit, while other dancers masqueraded as old men, walk among the fruit making ridiculous figures. Then other Indians come as strangers and whoever of them dares to enter to take the fruit, enters and snatches what he wants and flees. The masked dances attempt to hold him and hit him with some palmillas [yucca leaves]. Ultimately, in this way all of the fruit is taken. They neither add to the dance anything else in ceremony nor anything diabolic.[94]

Although Aguilar did not see anything evil about the dances, he failed to understand their meaning and symbolism.[95]

Aguilar would further offend the sensitivities of the friars when they heard about the time when the snow at Chililí was deep and the Indians wished to dance the *catzina*. Aguilar had ordered the *catzina* dance despite the snow.[96] With a twist of dark humor, Aguilar pointed to the church rooftop and said to Friar Velasco, "Father, why did you order the Indians to dance the *catzina* on the roof of the church?" Flustered, Friar Velasco denied it, saying it was "false and that he had neither ordered nor encouraged things which were offensive to God, our Lord."[97]

The ultimate insult to the friars occurred at Quarai, when in October 1660 the Indians showed their brashness to an offended Father Freitas. The drama unfolded like a midsummer's nightmare for the friars. Moments before the *catzina* dancers appeared at Quarai, an old man entered the plaza and announced that the *catzinas* were coming. "Be ready for they are our pagan priests," he proclaimed.[98] The *catzina* dancers, who had taken a woman from Quarai out of the pueblo, returned with her. The people of Quarai received them outside of the pueblo. One of them, pretending to be a demon, announced in a loud voice that he had been exiled for some time and that the people should be happy, for he now returned to be among them. Then he gave the woman a small fir tree. She took it from the old man and returned to her house. The old man turned and entered a kiva. Meantime, the *catzina* dancers went all over the pueblo, whooping and hollering as they gathered up earthen bowls, calabashes, and other items necessary to carry out their dance.[99]

Other Spaniards present made remarks about the dances. They quickly spread the word about what they had seen. Most witnesses believed that the ancestral *catzinas* had truly been recalled from the spirit world. Not only was it believable; it eerily felt real, as if they were experiencing one of the spirit's periodic visits to the pueblo. Real or imagined, Governor López Mendizábal had revived a tradition that would be difficult to stamp out. Reaction against the governor's Indian policies began to grow within Spanish communities throughout the province.

Francisco Martín Serrano, whose family had been among the original settlers in New Mexico with Juan de Oñate in 1598, knew the correct statement to make before the Commissary of the Holy Office of the Inquisition. In his response, made in careful and measured terms, he straddled the fine line between the Indian point of view and the friars' position. Martín craftily said,

> The Indians receive great consolation with the freedom and license to dance the *Catzinas*. The dances are idolatrous in that generally the natives of this kingdom place their hopes in them for a good harvest in all that they sow; in the dances they ask for water, good fortune to marry, and for their amours, and they ask their false gods for mantas, health and all of their necessities. With this liberty Governor López placed the kingdom in such danger that the Indians do not pay attention to their ministers. . . . If a remedy is not found fast, it is certain that what is left of the kingdom will be lost.[100]

Not only had the friars demanded an end to the governor's permissive policies, especially in regard to the *catzina* dances; they attempted to coerce conformity to their point of view from everyone in the province. When, in 1660, Father Juan Ramírez, the custodian of the New Mexican missions, presented a different view, the friars sought to remove him from the province. Having attended a *catzina* dance event, Friar Ramírez was not troubled in the least about it. Indeed, looking beyond the religiosity of the dances, Ramírez said he liked the rather festive atmosphere created by the dances and the native foods that were served on those occasions.[63]

Largely out of fear of being condemned by the friars and the Holy Office of the Inquisition, the Spanish settlers conformed to the demands of the church. After sixty-four years of living among the Pueblo Indians of New Mexico, some colonials pretended that they did not understand the cultures around them. Even though some settlers had participated in Indian religious rituals, the majority of them did not wish to admit that they, too, believed in the rich Indian spirit world that the friars had condemned as "demon worship," nor did they defend the sanctity of the Puebloan man-woman relationships that the friars branded as "concubinage."

The friars reacted against every facet of López de Mendizábal's Indian policies. Immediately they condemned them as idolatrous and demonic. Next they confronted López de Mendizábal and his agents as well as the Indians whenever the dances took place. Having openly opposed the dances, which they had forbidden for at least thirty years, the friars filed charges before the Holy Office of the Inquisition against López de Mendizábal and his agents. The friars gloated when López de Menizábal was removed from office, under arrest by the Holy Office of the Inquisition. The friars quickly moved to suppress the *catzinas* once again.

The Pueblo Indian reaction to the suppression of the *catzinas* became a burning grievance, among other causes. The next decade would see an increase in Indian resistance to the missionaries and civil authorities that would culminate in the Revolt of 1680. In the meantime, the Tribunal of the Holy Office of the Inquisition in Mexico City took a different view: the *catzina* dances were not considered demonic and should not be denied the pueblos.[101] The friars had failed to make their point, but Indian resentment over the issue had grown immeasurably. The governor and the friars claimed they had grounds for protest against one another. Although the accusations made by each side bore a semblance of truth, the friars held the upper hand, for they took their accusations to the Inquisition, not a civil court.

The end came quickly, especially after the friars had reported all offenses by López de Mendizábal, Aguilar, and several others to the Inquisition. Juan Manso, a former governor with an ax to grind against López de Mendizábal, was made high sheriff of the Province of New Mexico. Instructed to arrest López de Mendizábal and his followers, he did so and quickly turned them over to Inquisition authorities.¹⁰² As for Aguilar, Diego Romero, and Francisco Gómez, those named on the list of complaints by the friars, they were away from their districts, but a plan evolved to apprehend them when they were all together. Returning from a trip to Moqui and passing by way of Zuñi, the group headed toward the Rio Grande. Anticipating their arrival, Manso moved to apprehend them at Isleta. Manso feared that once Aguilar got beyond Isleta and into the Manzano Mountains, it would be difficult to capture him. Actually, Fray Alonso de Posada, commissary of the Inquisition, arrested Aguilar and imprisoned him at Isleta. Soon afterward he was transferred to a cell at Santo Domingo Pueblo, and finally, after a lengthy investigation, he was sent to Mexico City for trial.

Meanwhile López de Mendizábal prepared his defense against the charges against him "before the tribunal." The main tenet of López de Mendizábal's defense was based on his right as governor to implement policies consistent with Spanish law. Whatever Governor López de Mendizábal's motives, the elements of his policy were in line with the Laws of the Indies. He took a stand against all charges against him. His depositions and testimony were marked by directness. The tribunal gave all of his arguments careful consideration. The main issues before them were whether he and his *alcaldes mayores de indios* had been responsible for obstructing the mission program in New Mexico and whether they had committed acts hostile to the clergy and the church. López de Mendizábal knew that they would have to make a very strong case in their defense in order to offset the evidence against them. In his case particularly, given the massive documentation against him, he would have to overcome the tendency of the Tribunal of the Holy Office of the Inquisition, which was extremely jealous of ecclesiastical rights and privileges, to protect the rights of the church and its churchmen.

Three years after the proceedings began, Governor López de Mendizábal's trial came to an abrupt stop when, at 8:30 a.m. on September 16, 1664, an Inquisition jailer found him dead in his cell in the dungeon of the *carcel secreta*.¹⁰³ As a matter of record, by 3:30 p.m., two Inquisition officials entered cell "number 22" to identify the body, which was indeed that of former governor López de Mendízabal. As customary in those circumstances, even though he had never confessed to wrongdoing in his administration, he was unceremoniously buried in one of the corrals near the Inquisition jail. Apparently López de Mendizábal had been ill for some time when he died.

Inquisition authorities, however, suspended judgment in his case until 1671. At that time, they reviewed his case and declared it closed. After a brief deliberation, they cleared his name for absolution, and his remains were removed for a Christian burial at the Convento de Santo Domingo in Mexico City.[104]

For his abuses against the church and the friars of New Mexico, the Inquisition judges sentenced Aguilar to walk the auto-de-fé and suffer exile from New Mexico for ten years; they also declared him ineligible to hold administrative office for the rest of his life.[105] Having read his sentence, the Inquisitor's gavel came down swiftly with an echoing sound.

New Mexico in the seventeenth century was both a mission field and an area of settlement. It seemed a given that conflicts would arise between civil authorities and Franciscan missionaries over control of sedentary Indian populations. During the period 1598–1659 missionaries not only established themselves among the pueblos but also ventured out to the Great Plains. Throughout the pueblo lands of New Mexico, the missionaries claimed jurisdiction over entire populations. Governors before and after Bernardo López de Mendizábal consistently pointed out that the Franciscans did not have full control over Indian pueblos; therefore, they could only control those Indians under their charge for conversion purposes. Still, the Franciscans argued that the mission comprised the entire pueblo as a program of conversion in progress. Spanish officials did not agree that the entire population of a given pueblo was with the mission jurisdiction; they argued that only the neophytes who agreed to be converted were subject to missionization. In their attempts to sidestep conflict with the clergymen, civil authorities generally attempted to avoid interfering with the mission process and kept their hands off Indians already committed to conversion to Christianity.

While the colonials debated the question of jurisdiction over the natives, the Indians saw the issue differently. First, they wondered why any jurisdiction had to exist at all, except for the exigencies of colonialism. Secondly, once they realized that the colonial structure was part of their reality, the only thing left to them was to master colonial gamesmanship and play all loose ends against the middle. To a degree, that strategy worked. As part of the colonial legal system, the Indians marked their time, for they knew they could be useful witnesses against royal administrators, friars, and settlers in the legal action that usually followed the end of a governor's term or anytime an investigation, ecclesiastical or civil, took place. Within the structure of colonial institutions, the native knew well the corrective path to justice. In the end, the natives realized that rebellion was their only recourse. Similarly, the Hispanic settlers of New Mexico feared that the disputes between civil and ecclesiastical authorities would eventually result in rebellion.

Overall, Governor López de Mendizábal's policies, arrest, and trial had called attention to fundamental issues regarding the protection of Pueblo Indians against colonial abuses—that included the treatment of Indians within a mission program. Furthermore, López de Mendizábal had raised questions concerning the inconsistencies in the execution of church and state policies and the maintenance of balance between the two institutions. While he had made his point through his policies, he also outraged the Franciscan missionaries, who, in the context of the times, accused him, before the Holy Office of the Inquisition, of obstructing the mission process. They too had made their point. Still, while the decisions Holy Office in the cases of all the defendants reestablished the right of missionaries to demand unpaid labor from mission Indians, the rights of governors to ensure politician and economic development, especially as it involved trade with natives within the colony, were correspondingly confirmed.[106] Beyond acknowledging the accusations that the *catzina* dances were demonic, questions regarding the "demonic character" of the dances were not specifically addressed in the resolutions issued by the Holy Office. After López de Mendizábal's removal, Pueblo Indian leaders evaluated his permissive policies against the repression that followed. As had been predicted by colonial naysayers against López de Mendizábal's policies, native patience and frustrations violently exploded two decades later in the Pueblo Revolt of 1680.

Certainly, the Pueblo Revolt revealed changes regarding native independence in several ways, for during the revolt years, for example, the Pueblos reverted to their old native customs while at the same time preserving Christian practices and values. For them, Spanish influences had made their mark on their distinct cultures that had, in part, evolved into a sort of syncretism. After the reestablishment of Spanish New Mexico twelve years later, in 1692, such issues as those that had occupied Governor López de Mendizábal and other seventeenth-century governors gradually disappeared, but were not forgotten. New Mexico in the eighteenth century was a different place, and its civil and religious leaders were concerned with other issues of the day. Still, the struggle for native independence has historically been played out on many frontiers. In the 1890s, for example, the revivalist Ghost Dance performed by Plains Indians was condemned and prohibited, and their participants punished by the US government for fear it would spark an era of violent resistance among various tribes. Inclusive of events leading to the US Army massacre of Lakota Sioux at Wounded Knee on December 29, 1890, the widespread messianic Ghost Dance fueled fear of potential native resistance in the Dakotas.[107] Just as in New Mexico's turbulent seventeenth century, so too had history mirrored similar fears of native resistance throughout the Americas.

14

El Alemán and the New Mexican Inquisition of 1668

He who eats one of these small slips of paper, will, from that hour of this first day to that same hour of the second day, be free from any harm, whether it be caused by knife or shot.

—*Bernardo Gruber, Christmas Day, 1667*[1]

This Bernardo Gruber ... I found to have been imprisoned ... since the nineteenth of April of the year 1668. ... Fray Juan de Paz has not sent him to the Holy Tribunal; and at present it is almost impossible to send him for ... the whole land is at war with the ... Apache Indians, who kill all the Christian Indians they can find and encounter. No road is safe.

—*Fray Juan Bernal, April 1, 1670*[2]

The German pulled some slips of paper from his pocket, and on eleven of them he and Juan Martín also wrote the letters +ABNA+ADNA+.

—*Testimony by Joseph Nieto, Santo Domingo Pueblo, 1667*[3]

As relationships between Spanish colonial authorities and Pueblo headmen flared throughout the seventeenth century, the Holy Office of the Inquisition in New Mexico continued to harass Hispanic members of the congregation. Given its demand for conformity in the name of religion, Inquisition officials had sharply defined and curtailed the behavior of Hispanics in New Mexico in regard to anything religious. In the dwindling decades of the seventeenth century, the province faced one of the last cases of the Holy Office of the Inquisition. By the end of the century officials in Mexico City clarified the role of the Inquisition in provincial areas such as New Mexico and reminded Inquisition officials there of its limited powers. In the wake of cases such as those against López de Mendizábal, Nicolas de Aguilar, and others, the case against Bernardo Gruber sharply defined the role of provincial chapters of the Inquisition, which could only make arrests and investigate cases, not try them. Thus, between 1668 and 1670 the Holy Office of the Inquisition investigated one of its last cases in seventeenth-century New Mexico. Facing charges of superstition, Bernardo Gruber, a German trader from Sonora, suffered an ordeal at the hands of frontier Inquisition authorities that cost him his life. Aware of the mistreatment of Gruber, officials of the Holy Tribunal in Mexico City moved to lessen the powers of local agents of the Holy Office in outlying provinces like New Mexico. By that time, Gruber was dead and his case closed. Along the dry wastelands north of El Paso, two place-names, Jornada del Muerto and Alemán, survived to remind New Mexicans of Bernardo Gruber's final test.

On the cold Christmas morning of 1667 at Quarai, on the southern edge of the Manzano Mountains, Juan Nieto, a nineteen-year-old mulatto, stood inside the kiva at Quarai as the older Indian men gathered curiously about him and watched him place a *papelito* (small slip of paper) with mysterious lettering in his mouth and swallow it.[4] Holding an awl so that everyone could see it, he brought its sharp point down swiftly on his hand and again on his wrist. In awe, they were amazed that no blood flowed from his partially mutilated arm.

Soon afterward Nieto entered the *casa de comunidad*, a lodging house in the pueblo. His wife, Magdalena Montaño, and two other people stood by him. Calmly, he swallowed another *papelito*, grabbed a dagger, and began to stab at his legs. Later he explained his bizarre behavior by saying that he did not believe the *papelitos* would protect him and that he only pretended to stab himself with the dagger in order to fool those who saw him do it.⁵ At the moment, Nieto did not realize that this hoax would spell serious trouble for Bernardo Gruber, also known as El Alemán (the German). For Gruber, Nieto's actions precipitated a two-year nightmare.

Earlier, before Juan Nieto's strange feats of "magic," Bernardo Gruber and his New Mexican friend Juan Martín Serrano were inside Nuestra Señora de la Purísima Concepción, the church of Quarai Pueblo, attending Christmas mass. As Fray Francisco de Salazar began to sing the Gospel Acclamation, Gruber and Martín Serrano climbed up the choir loft ladder and stood near the chorus members. Whispering to them, Gruber said, "He who eats one of these *papelitos* will, from that hour of this first day to that same hour of the second day, be free from any harm, whether it be caused by knife or shot."⁶ Nodding to them with assurance, he took some *papelitos* from his pocket and on eleven of them he and Martín wrote "+ABNA+ADNA+." Nieto stepped forth and asked for one.

Martín Serrano, who had witnessed Nieto's stabbing actions, acknowledged that the act of swallowing the slips of paper was one of superstition. He questioned the act and the power of the *papelitos* and challenged Gruber to test his belief in the power of the *papelitos*. As Martín Serrano drew his sword, El Alemán unsheathed his weapon and, with a wild voice, yelled out, "This is how the test should be made!"⁷ As Nieto looked on, Martín Serrano backed down. Three days later, encouraged by his wife, Nieto reported his behavior and the activities of Gruber to Fray Joseph de Paredes, the *ministro guardian* of San Buenaventura de las Humanas. By that time, the threat of a widespread practice of swallowing *papelitos* had passed, for according to witnesses, Gruber had said the charm could only be worked on the first day of Christmas. Nonetheless, Father Paredes began the investigation of Bernardo Gruber's claim concerning the *papelitos*.⁸

As cold winter weather set in throughout January and February 1668, Gruber remained in the protected valley of the Manzano Mountains where he could graze his livestock and trade with the people of Quarai and Abó. By early spring, Fray Juan de Paz, *comisario de Nuevo México*, the agent of the Holy Office of the Inquisition, who presided at the northern mission of Santo Domingo along the Rio Grande, demanded that Gruber remain in the area and warned him not to flee.⁹ Undoubtedly, the apprehensive German weighed the consequences of remaining in New Mexico any longer.

Meanwhile Father Paz made a decision that would begin the severe testing of Bernardo Gruber. On April 19, 1668, just after 7:00 p.m., Captain Joseph Nieto, the *alcalde mayor* of the Salinas jurisdiction, armed with a writ of arrest by order of the Holy Office, departed Abó for Quarai to arrest Gruber.[10] The captain was accompanied by Fray Gabriel Toríja, the Franciscan minister of San Gregorio de Abó, who also served as the notary for the Inquisition, along with the brothers Juan and Joseph Martín Serrano.

At twilight, as the dark of night surrounded them, the four men walked through one of the many small valleys of the Salinas jurisdiction that led from Abó to Quarai. About three hours later, they reached Quarai. Entering the pueblo's *casa de comunidad*, they found the unsuspecting Gruber, who had coincidentally entered the room through another door. In the dim candlelight the blue-robed Fray Gabriel saw that the unsuspecting German was unarmed and held a *jícara de agua* (gourd of water) in his hands. Behind him was another man, Manuel Valencia, a visitor to Quarai.[11]

Stepping forward, Captain Nieto told Gruber that he was under arrest "by order of the Holy Office of the Inquisition." Gruber responded, "Very well," and submitted without a struggle. Next the captain asked him to surrender his weapons, an harquebus and a sword, which were leaning against one of the walls. A brief, tense moment followed when the quiet German pulled a knife from his pocket but cautiously handed it over to the sharp-eyed Captain Nieto. Valencia was then told to leave, which he did without speaking a word.[12]

Preparing to return to Abó that night, Captain Nieto and Fray Gabriel went out to saddle Gruber's horses, enough for all of them to ride. Meanwhile, Joseph and Juan Martín Serrano stood guard over El Alemán. Watching their silent prisoner, they observed his fine clothing, typical of the period. Gruber wore a *jubón*, or doublet, and pantaloons with woolen stockings. To keep warm, the German wrapped himself with an elk-skin overcoat. In a short while, Captain Nieto returned and told them to mount the horses.[13] In the wee hours of the night, sometime after midnight, the small party arrived at Abó with their prisoner. Gruber was escorted to a small room for detention. Because the room lacked security, Gruber's guards, Joseph and Juan Martín Serrano, were ordered to watch the room day and night until a more suitable place could be found.

Later that day Captain Nieto opened the door to Gruber's cell. Fray Juan de Paz, agent of the Holy Office of the Inquisition, quickly stepped into the room. Gruber recognized him, for they had met once before. Following Fray Juan, Captain Nieto and Juan Martín Serrano entered behind him. Father Paz explained that he was there as a matter of routine to ask Gruber a few questions and to take inventory of his property.[14] That done, Father Paz read the list to Gruber for verification: ten mules, thirteen stallions, five mares, three oxen, three Apache servants (two of them female, and one of them a fourteen- or fifteen-year-old male, all of them non-Christians), 105 pairs of assorted woolen socks, an embroidered pillow, fourteen pairs of understockings, two beautifully painted elk skins, and, of course, a sword, an harquebus, one knife, a powder belt, and a small ax. The list continued with eighty-eight elk skins, one tent made from several buckskins, three buckskin bags, two old saddles, one mule bridle, seven harnesses with ropes, and packsaddle pads. Before he approved the inventory, Gruber presented Paz with notes signed by seven individuals who owed him a total of ninety-two pesos. One of his guards, Juan Martín Serrano, owed Gruber thirty-two pesos. Gruber double-checked the list to make sure it was correct.[15]

Looking at Paz, the German made several requests, the first of which named Sargento Mayor Francisco Valencia, *alcalde mayor* of the jurisdiction of Isleta, as the executor of his property. Paz agreed. Gruber also asked that a representative be named to collect his debts. Confidently, Gruber requested that his case be expedited so that he could get back to his business. Offering to pay the salaries of two guards, the German proposed that, as required, he be sent to Mexico City as soon as possible so that the Holy Tribunal of the Inquisition could hear his case.[16]

Weeks later, on May 14, Father Paz reported to the Holy Tribunal that Gruber had been held at Abó for nearly a month. He noted that the cell in which he was held did not have the necessary facilities to ensure his incarceration. Notably, his guards, under pain of excommunication, watched the cell door and window every moment of the day. As Abó lacked a room large enough for the Inquisition to hold hearings on the matter, Father Paz negotiated with Captain Francisco de Ortega, owner of the *estancia* of San Nicolás in the jurisdiction of Sandia Pueblo, to use his house.

Four days later, the shackled Gruber was taken under heavy guard northwestward over a mountain trail that descended westward toward the Rio Grande. Following the river northward they reached Ortega's ranch. The captain met him at the door and politely offered all his hospitality in accordance with Spanish custom. Gruber was led to a room that had one window with heavy wooden bars and one door. For the next twenty-five months the small room, albeit an improvement over his cell at Abó, would be his prison.[17]

Gruber was fully aware of the damning testimony taken in March against him regarding the *papelitos*. By that time Juan Nieto, the leading witness, had confessed to the hoax and affirmed the powerlessness of the formula that Gruber had given him. One witness shrugged off the incident by saying that Gruber had been drunk at the time. But to Paz the damning ingredients of the German's magic could not be put aside. After all, Gruber had promised immortality to Juan Nieto on a holy day inside a church while mass was being said, and he had used a mysterious formula with crosses to work his charm. There would be no pardon for Gruber; he was remanded to his cell at Ortega's house under the custody of the Inquisition.[18]

If the officials of the Holy Office had any case against El Alémán, they had failed to present it. Almost two years passed without any action from the Inquisition authorities in New Mexico. No new evidence or testimony had surfaced. Later, after harsh criticism from the Holy Tribunal in Mexico City about the inability of Friar Paz to bring the case to trial, his replacement, Fray Juan Bernal, responded that due to drought, famine, and Apache raids it was difficult to transfer Gruber to Mexico.[19]

Throughout the entire ordeal, the German had languished in his little cell at Ortega's ranch while his herds, trade items, and Apache servants seemed to have gradually disappeared. During his imprisonment Gruber's property was loaned out to different individuals. Too weak to survive the winters of New Mexico, his stock began to die. Indians hired to care for his herds reported that five horses and one mule had died. In June of 1668, Gruber's teenage Indian servant, Atanasio, who had been given to the widow María Martín of the Salinas jurisdiction, ran away. Father Toríja made every effort to find him but failed.[20]

After two years of confinement, a desperate Gruber began to plot his escape. Somehow he had managed to enlist two accomplices. One of them was his guard and debtor, Juan Martín Serrano. The other was Atanasio, who had secretly returned to help his master. Martín Serrano smuggled supplies and a weapon to Gruber while Atanasio implemented the getaway plans. In the meantime Gruber would complete his part of the plot.[21]

A few days before the daring escape, Gruber called to his guards and complained of a sharp pain on his right side. He said he had some sort of liver ailment. In order to make him more comfortable the guards agreed to remove his shackles. The astute German further convinced his keepers of his failing health by refusing to eat for three days. As soon as he was alone, he worked to loosen the wooden bars to his prison window. With his shackles removed and the heavy wooden bars loosened somewhat, Gruber waited for his accomplices to act.[22]

For three nights before the escape, a servant of Captain Ortega named Nicolasillo, from the Humanas nation, observed Juan Martín Serrano ride his horse to the smithy on the Ortega ranch, dismount, and tie his horse to an iron ring. Soon after, Nicolasillo testified that he had witnessed Martín Serrano going to Gruber's window and handing him supplies. A loaf of sugar, a small bag with toasted ground maize, a bag of gunpowder, and three rounds of shot were passed to him through the bars of his jail. On the last night, the German received the harquebus of Captain Ortega, who lay asleep near the cell. Martín Serrano and Atanasio, according to Nicolasillo and other observers, had completed their parts of the plan.[23]

At midnight on Sunday, June 22, 1670, Atanasio made his way into Ortega's corral, saddled two horses, and separated three others for the escape. Sneaking past the sleeping guard, Atanasio reached Gruber's window. Quietly they worked to remove the bars. The German handed his supplies to the waiting Apache, then climbed out. It had taken longer than they had anticipated. By the time they led their horses out of the corral, it was nearly three in the morning.[24]

Quickly riding south along the Rio Grande through the bosque of the Sandia jurisdiction, the two horsemen followed the Camino Real de Tierra Adentro. Several leagues away from Ortega's ranch house, they came to a fork in the road. One trail led to the house of Thomé Domínguez de Mendoza, an *encomendero* of the area, nearly a league away. Approaching the outskirts of Isleta Pueblo, El Alémán's heart must have skipped a beat: he saw a rider coming toward them! Francisco, son of Thomé, drew near and the two men greeted each other. Quickly and nervously Gruber said, "Don't tell anyone you have seen me." The good-natured Francisco agreed, then offered them better riding horses. Gruber refused, saying, "I appreciate your offer, but we'd best get on, it's getting late."[25] In the pale light of dawn Francisco watched as Gruber and Atanasio rode away.

Meanwhile, at the *estancia* of San Nicolás, Ortega awakened from his slumber hours after Gruber's daring escape. Passing near Gruber's cell, he noticed the broken window bars. Quickly he opened the cell door and saw that Gruber was gone. After a fruitless search of the general vicinity, a nervous Ortega sent a hard-riding messenger over the Manzano Mountains to Captain Alonso de García, *alcalde mayor* of the Sandia jurisdiction, informing him of the escape. Running his horse at a gallop, Ortega went southward to the Camino Real, where he picked up Gruber's trail. Following it, he approached Francisco Valencia's hacienda, where he stopped to alert him of Gruber's escape. Riding hard from there, Ortega followed the trail leading to Thomé Domínguez de Mendoza's house. A short while later a tired Ortega arrived at don Thomé's doorstep and told him about Gruber. Thomé listened but refused to aid in the search. Domínguez de Mendoza believed that Gruber had suffered enough. Angry, Ortega mounted his jaded horse and returned to his ranch. Without Domínguez's horses and supplies he could not pursue Gruber into the hot, waterless terrain that lay to the south.[26]

Two days after Gruber's escape, on June 24, Ortega went to Pecos to confer with Fray Juan Bernal, the commissary of the Inquisition. Riding northeast, he arrived at the mission four days later. Meeting with Bernal, Ortega explained that Gruber had escaped from his house near Sandia Pueblo and that he had followed the trail as far south as Domínguez de Mendoza's ranch. Hopes for catching Gruber had been dashed by don Thomé's refusal to help. After listening to Ortega, Friar Bernal offered an idea. In a few days messengers were sent south to the agents of the Holy Office in present Chihuahua and Sonora advising them to apprehend Gruber should he enter their jurisdictions. After his conference at Pecos, Ortega went to Santa Fe to tell Governor Juan de Medrano y Mesia (1668–71) about Gruber's flight into the *despoblado* of southern New Mexico. Nine days had passed since the German's escape when Captain Cristóbal de Anaya, under the governor's orders to pursue the fugitive as far as El Paso del Norte, led eight soldiers and forty Christian Indians southward.[27]

Many miles and days away, it appeared that Bernardo Gruber's life had already come to an end. A lone Atanasio rode into Mission Senecú, not far from Socorro. There he was apprehended by Anaya. Atanasio confessed his story to Fray Francisco Nicolás Hurtado, *ministro de doctrina* of the Convento de Senecú. The Apache picked up the narrative at the fork in the Camino Real after they had left Francisco Domínguez de Mendoza. Riding day and night through Tuesday, June 24, they passed the feast day of San Juan on the trail somewhere near Senecú. That night they camped at a place called Fray Cristóbal. The next day they pulled their tired horses through the hot wasteland to Las Peñuelas, which was waterless. They arrived there at about 4:00 p.m., when the sun was still high. Exhausted, thirsty, and dusty, Gruber, unable to travel any further, sent young Atanasio in search of water. "Bring it back in a *jícara*," he said hoarsely. In case of danger he gave his harquebus to the Apache, who traveled a full day to the water hole at San Diego, reaching it at midday on Thursday.[28]

At the water hole, he filled the *jícara* and rode back toward Las Peñuelas. But on the way the *jícara* broke, and Atanasio returned to San Diego for water. The only way to carry water back to his master, he reasoned, was to soak his *sudador* (saddle blanket). When Atanasio finally arrived at Las Peñuelas on Friday morning, Gruber was gone! He had taken only one horse south along the Camino Real; the other three were still there. The youth spent the rest of Friday and Saturday unsuccessfully searching for El Alémán. Returning to Senecú, Atanasio reported Gruber's disappearance to Fray Francisco.[29]

Soon afterward Fray Francisco ordered four Indians to take Atanasio to Pedro de Leyba, the *alcalde mayor* of the jurisdiction of Senecú in Socorro. From there, he was transferred to Sandia Pueblo, where he was interrogated by Fray Pedro de Ayala and Padre Bernal. At first Atanasio claimed to be the sole accomplice in the escape of Bernardo Gruber. But Fray Pedro, who was aware of Nicolasillo's testimony, was able to implicate Juan Martín Serrano as well. Soon after his interrogation Atanasio ran away. Father Ayala believed that he had returned to Sonora. Later it would be said incorrectly and without proof that Atanasio had killed Gruber.[30]

Meantime, Leyba and seven Indians searched the *despoblado* in vain for Gruber before calling off the search. Quite by accident, what were believed to be the German's remains were found by another group of men near a point that would later bear the place-name Alemán. New Mexican lore would commemorate the trail as La Jornada del Muerto (The Dead Man's Journey). Almost three weeks after Gruber's escape, five traders on the way to Parral in Chihuahua passed between Las Peñuelas and El Perillo. One of them, Captain Andrés de Peralta, strayed from the group, then called out to his companions that he had found something. Francisco del Castillo Betancur, who knew Bernardo Gruber well, was with them. In September 1670, writing from Parral to a friend in New Mexico, Castillo described what he had seen:

I went to him and found a roan horse tied to a tree by a halter. It was dead and near it was a doublet or coat of blue cloth lined with otter skin. There were also a pair of trousers of the same material, and other remnants of clothing that had decayed. I examined them, and it seemed that they belonged to Bernardo Gruber, the fugitive. I made a search which did not result in vain, for I found at once all of his hair and the remnants of clothing which he had worn. I and my companions searched carefully for the bones, and found in very widely separated places the skull, three ribs, two long bones, and two other little bones which had been gnawed by animals. This, sir, occurred on Wednesday the thirtieth of the month of July of this present year. It is supposed that an Indian who was traveling with Bernardo Gruber killed him.[31]

Castillo and his companions took Gruber's remains to El Paso del Norte. There, outside a mission called La Conversión de los Mansos y Sumas, the bones were buried by the resident priest. Nine years later, after Gruber's case was officially closed, the fiscal of the Holy Tribunal in Mexico ordered that his property, which was still in New Mexico, be sold at an auction and that from the proceeds "mass might be said for the soul of the said Bernardo, and that his bones might be given an ecclesiastical burial."[32]

Gruber's was the last Inquisition case investigated in the jurisdiction of Salinas. In retrospect, the Gruber case had significant consequences for the history of the Inquisition in New Mexico and other similar frontier areas. In condemning Friar Paz's conduct, characterized as "gross ignorance and lack of attention to the obligations of his office," the Holy Tribunal in Mexico City decreed that the local commissaries of New Mexico and other areas no longer had authority to make arrests without express orders from the Holy Office of the Inquisition.[33] Consequently, only one other Inquisition case was prosecuted in New Mexico during the decade prior to the Pueblo Revolt of 1680.

15

Revolt and Reconquest

New Mexico in 1680–92

That all the publos break up and burn the images of the Holy Christ, the Virgin Mary and the other saints, crosses, and everything pertaining to Christianity and that they burn the temples, break up the bells, and separate from the wives whom God had given them in marriage.

—*Popé, 1680*[1]

According to . . . reports . . . on the thirteenth day of August of the past year 1680 the rebellious Indians, by prearranged conspiracy, fell upon all the pueblos and farms at the same time with such vigor and cruelty that they killed twenty-one missionaries . . . and more than three hundred eighty Spaniards, not sparing the defenselessness of the women and children.

—*Viceroy Conde de Paredes, 1681*[2]

Long live our king, Carlos the Second! May God spare him! King of Spain and all this New World, and of the realm and provinces of New Mexico, and of these subjects newly won and conquered!

—*Diego de Vargas, September 1692*[3]

Four months had passed since the pueblos of New Mexico had rebelled, and now the Spaniards were back in an attempt to reconquer their lost land. By mid-December 1680, Governor Antonio de Otermín and a small army were camped on high ground along the Rio Grande in view of the pueblos of Alameda, Sandia, and Puaray, all near present Albuquerque. The north wind blew gusts of cold air, causing the loose ends of their tents to flap incessantly, and the snow-bearing clouds reflected a pale light throughout the night across "the fields and sierras all covered with snow."[4] Otermín and his men hoped to understand the immediate causes of the revolt that stemmed from long-range issues revolving around Spanish sovereignty and Indigenous territoriality.

In that bitterly cold land Otermín hoped to find out how the rebellion had, in secrecy, occurred. Ten days earlier, the Spaniards had attacked Isleta Pueblo and taken a captive, Spanish-speaking Pedro Naranjo, a Keres from San Felipe Pueblo. Standing before Otermín and a board of inquiry, Naranjo said he knew the reasons for the rebellion. Naranjo recounted how the pueblos had planned the rebellion for years and had "always kept in their hearts" the desire to drive out the Spanish settlers. During the years leading to the attack, the pueblos had united under an Indian leader named Popé. "It happened in a kiva of the pueblo of Los Taos," swore Naranjo, "there appeared to the said Popé three figures . . . called Caudi, another Tilini and the other Tleume."[5] Still in awe, Naranjo told them how Popé "saw these figures emit fire from all the extremities of their bodies."[6] They told him to make a cord of maguey fiber "and tie some knots in it which would signify the number of days that they must wait for the rebellion."[7] The cord was passed from one pueblo to the next, each of which accepted the righteousness of the revolt. The mandate to rebel, explained Naranjo, had come from the three spirits who then "returned to the state of their antiquity."[8]

Later Juan Domínguez de Mendoza recalled that when the rebels were asked why they had rebelled, they responded that it was not because of the friars but because of certain individuals, including Governor Otermín. They "all said and stated that by no means had they rebelled on account of the friars nor any one in particular, rather, they found consolation in the friars since there were many who paid the tribute for them in order to be free from vexations. [They said] that the reason why they rebelled was [the conduct of] the governor don Antonio de Otermín, because he never did them justice."[9]

Historiographically, the Pueblo Revolt of 1680 has been viewed as an isolated event in New Mexico. As elsewhere in the Americas, the revolt represented an accumulation of Indian resentments against a Spanish colonial occupation that had assumed total sovereignty over them (see appendix B). In New Mexico longstanding grievances caused by an oppressive economic system and a suppressive Indian policy had worked to undermine the religious, political, and social traditions of the pueblos. Although colonial native relationships were often adversarial, they were not exclusively antagonistic. In the eighty years since Oñate's establishment of New Mexico, intermarriages and religious kinships (*compadrazgo*) had been established. Familial friendships and social associations had been formed among Spanish settlers and their Indian counterparts. Indeed, during the Pueblo Revolt, twelve families remained to live among their pueblo relatives. But such relationships were not enough to thwart Indian resentment against the injustices of colonialism.

Between 1650 and 1680, pueblo grievances and resentments against Spanish rule and colonial attitudes had seethed to a boiling point. Indignation against Spanish authority and its Indian policies and practices had, over the decades, surged and receded, but not been forgotten. This time, in 1680, the pueblos were organized and ready for an all-out, highly organized fight that would result in ridding themselves of Spanish sovereignty over them. In the wake of the revolt and his investigation concerning its immediate causes, pueblo informants told Otermín about the underlying and overt reasons for the revolt. Pedro García, a pueblo warrior, told Otermín that the Tanos from Galisteo had planned to rebel "for more than twelve years . . . because they resented greatly that the friars and Spaniards should deprive them of their idols, their dances, and their superstitions."[10] Two brothers, Juan and Francisco Lorenzo, who lived with their mother and an older brother on a small ranch near San Felipe Pueblo, explained that the people of San Felipe had rebelled because three Spaniards, Francisco Javier, Luis Quintana, and Diego López Sambrano, "would not leave them alone, and burned their *estufas* [kivas]."[11] Later another Indian, named Josephe, reported that Francisco Javier, Diego López Sambrano, and Luis Quintana were among those who mistreated the natives, for they often "beat them, took away what they had, and made them work without pay."[12] Indeed, when Popé had made contact with the three spirits in the kiva at Taos, he was hiding from Francisco Javier, who sought to punish him for his sorcery.¹³ It seemed that recent events had combined with longstanding grievances to inspire the rebellion.

Spanish officials in New Mexico were well aware of the grievances and the several previous attempts by the pueblos to liberate themselves of colonial rule. Red-haired Diego López Sambrano, who was lucky to survive the revolt with his wife and six children, for example, said that he had witnessed attempted Indian revolts and Spanish punishments of them "since the time of the government of Don Fernando de Arguello [1644–47], who hanged and lashed and imprisoned more than forty Indians."¹⁴ Furthermore, López Sambrano recalled that in 1650, during the administration of Governor Hernándo de Ugarte y la Concha (1649–53), another plot to rebel had been discovered and quelled. López Sambrano surmised that plot was different because the pueblos had attempted to unite with Apaches against the Spaniards. In the conspiracy of 1650, recounted López Sambrano,

> the sorcerers and chief men of the pueblos had arranged with the enemy Apaches, and for that purpose the Christians [Indians] under the pretext that the enemy was doing it, turned over to them in the pastures the droves of mares and horses belonging to the Spaniards, which are the principal nerve of warfare. They had already agreed with the said apostates to attack in all the districts on the night of Holy Thursday, because the Spaniards would then be assembled. The said rebellion was discovered because of Captain Alonso Vaca and other soldiers having followed a drove of mares which the Indians were driving off, and the aggressors being overtaken, they declared that the Christians of the pueblos of Alameda and Sandia had turned them over to them, and that they were all plotting and conspiring with all the said Apaches to rebel and destroy the whole kingdom, and to be left in freedom as in ancient times, living like their ancestors. The Spaniards returned with this news and with a knife belonging to a Christian Indian of the pueblo of Alameda, to the presence of the alcalde mayor of the said district, who was Captain Juan García Olgado.¹⁵

Spanish justice was swift. Upon completion of the investigation of the conspiracy, "many Indians" from most of the pueblos in the province were arrested. Nine leaders from Isleta, Alameda, San Felipe, Cochití, and Jémez were found guilty and hanged, and many others were "sold as slaves for ten years."¹⁶

López Sambrano told about other acts of violence against Spanish settlers, one of which took place near Socorro during the term of Governor Fernando de Villanueva (1665–68). He recalled that a Piro warrior named El Tanbulita and six Christian Indians joined a band of Apaches in the "Sierra de Madalena" (Magdalena Mountains), where they ambushed and killed six Spaniards. El Tanbulita and five others were captured and hanged, and several others "were sold and imprisoned."[17]

Of the several uprisings, one of the most serious was led by the Spanish-speaking don Estéban Clemente, governor of the Tanos and Salinas pueblos, whom "the whole kingdom secretly obeyed." Clemente was extremely influential among Spaniards as well as Puebloans. He spoke several Indian tongues and could read and write Spanish. López Sambrano said that Clemente had organized a "conspiracy which was general throughout the kingdom."[18] Clemente's plot had many of the characteristics that had played out in other rebellions. For example, he gave orders to the Christian Indians that they should drive all the Spanish horse herds in all of the jurisdictions to the sierras and leave the Spaniards afoot. This they should do on the night of Holy Thursday during Holy Week while the settlers were in their churches preparing for Good Friday and Easter. Clemente hoped to strike, "not leaving a single religious or Spaniard" alive.[19]

Clemente's plot, which took place sometime during the administration of Governor Fernando de Villanueva y Armendaris (1665–68), was discovered. Clemente was quickly apprehended, tried, convicted, and hanged while the pueblos looked on with great futility. With Clemente gone, no one of his stature dared step forward to conspire against the Spaniards. López Sambrano recalled that the colonials, who had trusted Clemente without reservation, were surprised by "this treason." After his execution, when the Spaniards sequestered Clemente's property, they found in his house "a large number of idols and entire kettles full of idolatrous powdered herbs, feathers, and other trifles."[20]

In the 1670s Spanish officials continued to suppress the Indian religious practices. During the administration of Governor Juan Francisco de Treviño (1675–77), for example, charges were made claiming that the Indians had continued "their abuses and superstitions." López Sambrano recalled that, in 1674, the Indians "had bewitched the father preacher, Fray Andrés Durán," guardian of the *convento* of San lldefonso, along with his brother and wife, and an Indian interpreter named Francisco Guiter, "who denounced the said 'sorcerers.'"[21] Of the forty-seven Tewa Indians arrested, four admitted to the "witchcraft" worked against Friar Durán and his companions. According to López Sambrano, the four were sentenced to death for the "above crimes and for other deaths which were proved against them."[22] One was hanged at Nambé, another at San Felipe, a third *hechicero* (sorcerer) "hanged himself while alone," and the fourth man was hanged at Jémez.[23]

The 1674 witch trial did not end there. López Sambrano explained how the execution and suicide of the four "sorcerers," along with the detention of the remaining forty-three men, almost started a spontaneous rebellion. Of the forty-three *hechiceros*, Governor Treviño ordered some released with a reprimand, and others "he condemned to lashings and imprisonment." Among the forty-three was an angry headman named Popé, whose resentment against the Spaniards grew.[24]

Soon after the sentences were announced and the hangings had taken place, the Palace of the Governors was besieged by "more than seventy protesting Pueblo warriors armed with *macanas* [clubs] and leather shields." Filling two rooms, the protesters entered the governor's office. Hoping to gain a pardon for the arrested forty-three convicted *hechiceros*, the warriors hoped to placate Governor Treviño. As a sign of peace, they brought gifts, "some eggs, chickens, tobacco, beans and some small deerskins." The governor at first refused the gifts, whereupon one of the Indians in the second room called out, "Leave it there if he does not want it."[25] Wisely the governor ordered López Sambrano to accept the gifts. Quickly the Indians got to the point. They asked the tough-minded governor to release the prisoners to them, "that he should pardon them; and that they would make amends." The colonial governor responded condescendingly, "Wait a while, children; I will give them to you and pardon them on condition that you forsake idolatry and iniquity."[26] As a magnanimous gesture, Governor Treviño gave them some woolen blankets and released the prisoners. The Indians were satisfied and withdrew from his office.

The seriousness of the matter was soon revealed. A few days later López Sambrano saw some of the Indians who had pleaded for the prisoners with the governor. With an air of friendliness, López Sambrano asked them to "come and tell me why so many of your people came armed to see the governor." One of them replied, "We came determined to kill him if he did not give up the said prisoners, and on killing him, to kill the people of the villa as well."[27] Furthermore, they explained, an ambush had been left in the nearby hills to support their escape. López Sambrano asked them where they would have gone, for the Apaches would kill them in the sierras. The pueblo warriors let López Sambrano know how seriously determined they felt about the injustice with the chilling reply that "in order to defend the sorcerers whom they asked for they would have gone to the sierras even though the Apaches would kill them."[28]

The pueblos and their warriors had learned much from their past challenges to Spanish rule. The lessons of past attacks, conspiracies, and rebellions, albeit not successful, were not lost on the pueblo warriors. Their collective memories, on the other hand, had taught them four important ingredients for a successful revolt as follows: first, deprive the Spaniards of their horses; second, unite the pueblos; third, form alliances with the Apaches; fourth, and maintain absolute secrecy in order to surprise the Spaniards. At least one of the four elements had been present in past rebellions. Popé knew them all, and he had five years to plan and pull them all together into one successful revolt. Absolute secrecy would be required if he was to catch the Spaniards off guard.

Popé knew that his persecution by certain Spaniards would continue. Fleeing harassment from Captain Francisco Javier, Popé hid in one of the kivas at Taos Pueblo. There he communicated with the spirits Caudi, Tleume, and Tilini and formulated his plan. Convinced that secrecy was of utmost importance, Popé was known to have killed his brother-in-law, Juan Bua, because Bua had threatened to tell the Spaniards of the plot. Bua was not alone in his misgivings. Other Puebloans thought the plan insane and refused to support it; others warned their Spanish friends and relatives to prepare for a general rebellion. While total unity for the rebellion was demanded, some Pueblo Indians did not support it. When the rebellion occurred, some Indians helped Spaniards escape; others fled with them.

On the feast day of San Lorenzo, August 10, 1680, the rebellion began with full fury. Curly-haired Pedro Hidalgo, who bore a scar on his neck, had often assisted the friars as a military escort when they traveled to minister to the pueblos. At dawn that morning, he and Friar Juan Bautista Pío set out from the Villa for mass at Tesuque Pueblo.[29] At sunrise they arrived at the pueblo and found it abandoned. As Father Pío had come to say mass for the inhabitants, he decided to search for them. Not far from the pueblo, the priest and his guard caught up with them. Approaching the Indians, Hidalgo noticed that they were armed with bows, arrows, lances, and shields and wore war paint.[30] Holding a shield, Friar Pío walked toward them, saying, "What is this . . . are you mad? Do not disturb yourselves; I will help you and die a thousand deaths for you."[31] Both men tried to persuade them to return to the pueblo. The friar followed the Puebloans into a ravine while Hidalgo rode over the ridge of it to intercept the people on the other side.

At the entrance to the ravine Hidalgo saw two Indians coming at him on the run. One of them, named El Obi, carried the shield Friar Pío had taken into the ravine; the other, named Nicolás, painted with clay, had blood splattered on his person.[32] Moving quickly, the two warriors grabbed the reins of Hidalgo's horse and tried to pull him down. Holding on to his sword and hat, Hidalgo managed to stay on his mount. Spurring his horse down the hill, he broke away, dragging along those who clung to him.[33] As he made his getaway, arrows zipped past him. Looking back, he saw several other warriors, who had reached the struggle too late, shoot at him. Riding hard through outlying Spanish settlements, Hidalgo warned his fellow colonials along the way and at the Villa. He was the first to spread the alarm of the Pueblo Revolt.

Unknown to Hidalgo, Governor Antonio Otermín had received warnings the day before of a possible rebellion. The governor had begun an investigation into the matter and had devised a plan of attack should an uprising occur. But now it was too late. The rebellion had begun, and the slaughter of Spanish women, children, friars, and other frontiersmen had started to take on horrific proportions. Where possible, settlers along the Rio Grande in northern New Mexico fled to the walled Villa de Santa Fe. By chance, Otermín had ordered the gates repaired eight days before. The rebel Indians surrounded the Villa and clamored for vengeance, especially against Maese de Campo Francisco Javier.[34]

The Apaches, too, would have liked to get their hands on him. Shortly before the revolt, Javier had seized a number of Apaches at Pecos Pueblo who were under his protection and promised safe conduct while they traded there. Betraying their trust, he distributed some of his captives among his troops and sent others to Parral for sale. The Apaches were outraged, as were the Pecoseños, who feared the Plains Indians and depended on their trade. For them, the planned revolt offered a chance for revenge. When the revolt broke open, the Pecoseños joined the besiegers of Santa Fe, shouting "give us Francisco Javier, who is the reason we have risen, and we will remain in peace as before."³⁵

Other pueblo warriors also wanted Javier, Luis de Quintana, and Diego López Sambrano. Otermín would not turn them over. The siege of Santa Fe lasted from August 12 to August 21, 1680. Otermín attempted to round up some stray cattle, but he was driven back to the safety of the Villa's walls. Over a thousand settlers had sought refuge in the overcrowded fortress. The pueblo warriors taunted them, saying all Spaniards on the Río Arriba and the Río Abajo had been slain. The Spaniards in the Villa believed it, as did the besieged settlers on the Río Abajo, for the day had seethed with death and destruction.

Everywhere, in August 1680, families experienced the full fury of the Pueblo warriors. Like many others who were taken by surprise, for example, Cristóbal de Anaya Almazán, his wife Leonor Domínguez de Mendoza, daughter of Captain Tomé Domínguez de Mendoza, and their five children were slain in their home, and their bodies were stripped of their clothing. Two adult sons survived and were taken captive, and another was left for dead.³⁶ The attack took place south of San Felipe Pueblo at Angostura. In all, the slain—over 400 men, women, and children—accounted for 15 percent of New Mexico's total non-Indian population. That included twenty-one members of the clergy.³⁷

Far to the south on the Río Abajo on August 10, 1680, Alonso García, lieutenant general of the Río Abajo, rallied the settlers to defend themselves. As soon as he learned of the general rebellion, he and eight men rode hard to rescue Captain Luis Granillo at Jémez and several others at Jémez and at Zia. As night fell on August 10, García heard that three friars and four Spaniards had died at Santo Domingo. Moving north of Sandia, he discovered the bodies of Captain Agustín Carbajal and his family in their house. Farther along the trail he found the bodies of Cristóbal Anaya, with his two sons, his wife, and three children in their home. Between Santo Domingo and San Felipe, García, working into the night, found six other dead Spaniards. By dawn, he was convinced that all the other Spaniards between Sandia and Taos had been slain, including the governor and the settlers in the Villa. The Indians had falsely told him so, hoping to rattle him and cause him to lose heart, but now he believed the report to be true.

Turning back, García determined to remove the refugees in his charge southward, away from danger. Reinforced by his six sons, García and over 1,000 bedraggled Spaniards decided to abandon the Río Abajo and head south toward the safety of El Paso. By September 6 they had passed Senecú and were near a campsite on the Camino Real called Fray Cristóbal, "beyond the jurisdiction of the settled part of the kingdom."[38]

Meantime, a letter to García sent by Otermín, still besieged at Santa Fe, never reached him. Later Otermín explained:

> I found myself with scarcely three men who could carry the first news to the nearest jurisdictions, where it was most urgently required, not having been able to send it to the lieutenant general of the Río Abajo because the person who was carrying it was killed on the way.[39]

The pueblos had succeeded not only in becoming a united force but also in surprising the Spanish settlers.

Fighting his way out of the siege of Santa Fe on August 21, Otermín and his soldiers broke the siege. The rebel pueblo warriors took heavy casualties. With Santa Fe behind them, Otermín led more than 1,000 settlers to Isleta with whatever provisions they could carry. From there they proceeded down the Río Abajo to Alamillo. Governor Otermín, still wondering where García could be, sent hard-riding messengers ahead. On receiving news of his governor's march, a much relieved García, who thought Otermín dead, set out with reinforcements and a herd of animals to resupply him.

At first Otermín considered arresting García for desertion, but later exonerated him when it was learned that García had been led to believe that everyone north of Cochití Pueblo had been slain in the revolt. Furthermore, he learned that García was without adequate munitions, supplies, and soldiers to attempt going past Santo Domingo. For those reasons García had decided, after consulting with all survivors under his charge, to retreat to the nearest garrison, hundreds of miles to the south.[40] Fortunately for the refugees, Isleta Pueblo and the Piros farther south did not join the revolt. Other Indians joined the Spaniards in their retreat. Save for some Spaniards who remained as captives of the pueblos in revolt, the Río Arriba and the Río Abajo down to El Paso had been abandoned by the colonials.

By mid-September the two refugee groups, one led by Otermín and the other by Garcia, had united and, fatigued, shocked, and mourning their losses, proceeded to El Paso. There they regrouped and rested. Otermín reported to the viceroy that 2,500 settlers had made it to safety. About 400 settlers had been killed in the revolt. Within two months, Otermín led a small army of 130 soldiers and 112 Indian allies along with several priests north into the destruction. It was the first of many sorties to attempt the reconquest of New Mexico. Otermín and his small army crossed over the Jornada del Muerto and headed northward along the Rio Grande. Once into the settlement areas, they surveyed the destruction from Socorro to Cochití.

A day's ride south of Senecú, Otermín's scouts found signs of Apache horses. Upon reaching Senecú they found the pueblo abandoned, with signs that the Apaches had raided the pueblo, causing its people to flee. The church and *convento* had been burned. Friar Francisco de Ayeta found that the altar had been thrown into the Rio Grande along with other religious items. All around them were household items strewn about, signs that the mission had been ransacked purposefully.[41] Passing on to Socorro, they found similar destruction by Apache raiders, and at Sevilleta more of the same. Most Puebloans had fled before the Apaches; others went northward to join the revolt.

By early December, Otermín was within sight of Isleta Pueblo. Finding it fortified and unfriendly, he and seventy soldiers attacked the pueblo and took it with little resistance. Once the plaza was taken, Otermín asked the Indians to lay down their arms. They did so, explaining the reason for their hostile behavior was that the Apaches had caused so much strife that they mistook the Spaniards for them.[42] As Otermín did not want any more trouble, he accepted their explanation.

The expedition proceeded northward past the valley of present-day Albuquerque and Atrisco to Alameda and Sandia. Near there they established a base camp and began an inquiry into the extent of the destruction and the causes of the revolt. They took captives and interrogated them, and they accepted the surrender of others. Indian informants came to their camp and answered questions regarding how the revolt had fared for the Indians.

Not long afterward a second expedition sallied northward to the rebel-held lands. Juan Domínguez de Mendoza and sixty picked mounted men and a number of Indian allies proceeded north to reconnoiter the *tierra de guerra* (land of war) north of Sandia Pueblo. They took Indians from Isleta to prove that the Spaniards had not killed Isletans or mistreated them in anyway. It seems that the rebel Indians had spread the rumor that the Spaniards had killed all of the Isletans in their attack on the pueblo. Stopping at Isleta, Domínguez de Mendoza next moved northward, visiting the pueblos of San Felipe, Santo Domingo, and Cochití. He found resistance at all three places.[43]

Otermín learned later that the Isletans were relieved that the Spaniards under Domínguez de Mendoza had returned. The Spanish presence had saved Isleta from an all-out attack by the pueblos of the north, which were in revolt. It seems that a famine had struck the northern pueblos and much suffering had occurred. Otermín was told that the rebels had planned to attack Isleta and raid its granaries. The date of the anticipated attack by Otermín's calculations would be December 12, 1680.[44] Perhaps the Spanish presence had saved Isleta, but likely it was a combination of Spanish troops and bad weather. Snow had recently fallen, and freezing temperatures had slowed down even the heartiest of men.

Despite the cold and snow, Juan Domínguez de Mendoza, with his soldiers and Indian allies, spent time reconnoitering the land north of Sandia Pueblo.[45] They had departed Isleta on December 8 and had camped at Domínguez de Mendoza's old hacienda at Atrisco in the Albuquerque area. All day they had been dogged by "extreme cold, deep snow, and wind."[46] Their stay at Atrisco was short, lasting part of the night, so that his soldiers could warm themselves. Given their situation, Domínguez de Mendoza gave orders to conceal their fires. In the dead of night he ordered his men to move out toward Alameda. Proceeding with "all vigilance and secrecy," Domínguez de Mendoza and his men arrived at the pueblo of Alameda at dawn, surrounding and besieging it. After they had cautiously entered the pueblo, they found it deserted. During a quick search of the houses, the soldiers found in one of them "a lone Indian who had hanged himself," perhaps in despair, for he had been left behind, so they thought, or possibly killed by the rebels.

In another house the soldiers found an old, blind Indian woman. Speaking in Spanish, she told Domínguez de Mendoza that the people had gone to the sierra. Weeping, the old woman told the Spaniards of another very old man who had been left outside the pueblo of Alameda. Domínguez de Mendoza sent the soldiers to look for him.[47] The old man was from Sandia Pueblo. Domínguez de Mendoza surmised that his people had left him to die in the fields, for the freezing temperatures alone would have done in the old man. When found, the old man did tell the Spaniards that the people of Sandia had likely gone to the "upper pueblos." Before the Spaniards left, Domínguez de Mendoza put the two elderly Indians together in a house with water, a fire, and a meal.

Like most other pueblos they saw, the Alameda church had been burned. Most of the church fixtures, furniture, and religious paraphernalia had been taken by the Indians. In some of the houses the Spaniards found some things belonging to the church. It appeared that the Indians had been respectful of religious items. Domínguez de Mendoza noted that a box with a chalice and paten and a holy figure of Christ was found in one house; in another was found a small picture of Our Lady, which had been stolen from a house belonging to Spaniards. The Indians had become accustomed to things Spanish, for practical items such as tools were found in the houses. Plowshares, axes, large hoes, and other implements had been gathered by the Indians. Domínguez ordered some of the items buried so that "the enemy might not take them."[48]

Departing Alameda, Domínguez de Mendoza led his men to the pueblo of Puaray to investigate the shouts of an Indian who was on horseback on a hill. When the soldiers approached him, he turned his horse around and galloped away. A short while later they observed him sending up smoke signals to other Indians near Sandia Pueblo. They arrived at Puaray on December 9, 1680. From a distance a smoldering fire appeared to be coming from ruins of the mission The fire was recent, and Domínguez de Mendoza sent his men to investigate it. They returned to report that "it was a corral which was burning." After a quick search, they determined that the pueblo had been abandoned. They visited all the quarters, house by house, and found many "things that [the Indians] had stolen from the Spaniards." They found a silver lamp, "a carpet which they call Turkish," and other items taken from houses of Spaniards.[49] Perhaps the most disturbing part of their search was the discovery of many masks used for dances of *catzina* and *losse*. Domínguez de Mendoza must have sensed that the Pueblo Revolt ran deeper than a mere desire to expel the Spaniards from the province.

Moving northward the next day, they went to the ruined mission of San Francisco de Sandia. There they saw the Chapel of San Antonio burning. Like Alameda and Puaray, the pueblo had been abandoned. Of the convent, Domínguez de Mendoza concluded that "only three cells remained, which it appeared that they left with particular care for their diabolical dances."[50] One room had been converted into a smithy, for a forge had been set up in it. The other two rooms were used as storage, for a large number of masks were found hanging in them. The rest of the convent had been demolished, and the main church had been burned. In the pueblo they came upon a blind man who told them that all of the people had fled to the Sierra de Sandia.[51] As at the previous pueblos, Domínguez de Mendoza's men searched the houses of the Indians and found many Spanish items. In the cemetery they found the church bells "broken and in pieces, which they did by heating them and then breaking them with stones."[52] The work of the friars had, with exception, been for naught.

Next, the expeditionary force proceeded to San Felipe Pueblo. It too was depopulated. There they met an old Indian named Francisco. He told them that his people had fled to La Cieneguilla or to the pueblo of Cochití. Going through the houses, they recovered many church items, an incensory of silver, a common censer, small boxes of holy oils, broken crosses, and other such things. In most of the houses in the middle plaza they found a great number of masks, and in the plaza were piles of stones "where they worshipped their idols." The church was unroofed, and the convent had been demolished. The Spaniards also learned that the church bell had been dumped by the river. The Indians had attempted to break it up but succeeded only in tearing a hole in it.[53] It must have struck Domínguez de Mendoza as a curiosity that some of the religious paraphernalia of the Christians had been kept by the Indians. Perhaps the influence of the friars on the Puebloan cultures, in that regard, did have a double edge.

Daringly, they moved northward toward the more populated areas held by the rebels. By mid-December Domínguez de Mendoza and his men were camped a short distance from the rebel stronghold at Cochití Pueblo. There they hoped to speak with the rebellious factions composed of many warriors from different pueblos. Among them was Alonso Catiti from San Felipe.[54] Catiti was referred to as a *"coyote"* by the Spaniards because he was part Indian and part Spanish.[55] Domínguez de Mendoza had gone through Catiti's house at San Felipe and had found there and in the house of another warrior, named Diego el Zapatero, most of the religious items had once been in the church and offices of the convent. The Spanish commander and the priest, Antonio Guerra, knew that they could manipulate Catiti. As soon as the principal warriors from Taos, Picurís, Pecos, Jémez, and Acoma and those from the Tanos, Keres, Tiwas, and Tewas had gathered to parley with the Spaniards, Friar Antonio Guerra and Domínguez de Mendoza reminded them of the many crimes that had been committed. Alonso Catiti was told of his crimes, "for which he was already condemned to the infernal regions." Fray Antonio Guerra exhorted him with a spiritual discourse that would have made the most valiant warrior flinch.[56]

Moved by the accusations, Catiti "replied, weeping so loudly that the whole camp heard him. He begged me, for the love of God and the most holy Virgin, and the saints, and by the life of the king, our lord, that I grant them peace," said Domínguez de Mendoza. The contrite Catiti "kissed the feet of the said reverend father" and told Domínguez de Mendoza that they had rebelled because of "the *maestre de campo*, Francisco Javier, and the *sargentos mayores*, Luis de Quintana and Diego López [Sambrano]." He promised that he would bring down from the sierra the people of Cochití, San Felipe, and Santo Domingo.[57] It appeared that peace was in the making, but the rebel warriors wanted no part of it.

Against Alonso Catiti's willingness to talk peace, another faction of warriors demonstrated hostility to the Spaniards. Waiting for them to drop their guard, the pueblo warriors planned to attack the small Spanish force. First, they would take their horses, and then they would attack them as they tried to leave the area. The Spanish commander was too sage. Cochití was a heavily armed camp, and the Spaniards were outnumbered. Although Domínguez de Mendoza did consider a plan "to attack them before they could do it to me," he thought better of it. By December 19, after eleven days in hostile territory, Domínguez de Mendoza turned his little army around and rejoined the main force led by Antonio de Otermín.[58] He had much to report to his governor.

Governor Otermín had moved his force northward. Camped at a place south of Sandia Pueblo where he could also watch Alameda and Puaray, a disappointed Otermín learned how the peace talks at Cochití had broken down and how the Spaniards, hearing from their Indian allies that the rebel warriors planned to ambush them, decided to leave that place. Otermín had caught his first glimpse of the northern edge of the province since the revolt. Seeing little promise in regaining their lost land, the army of the *reconquista* broke camp for now and turned their horses southward.[59] They would be back.

Along the way to El Paso, Otermín and his army stopped at Isleta and set up camp opposite the pueblo. Close to 400 loyal Isletans spoke to the governor about their safety, for the rebel pueblo warriors had threatened them and Apache raiders had attacked them. Otermín removed them to a place near El Paso, which came to be known as Isleta del Sur. Senecú del Sur had its beginnings in a similar way. At that time, Isleta was abandoned. Typical of any retreating army, Otermín ordered that all food stores be burned.[60] He was determined not leave Isleta for the rebel warriors to use. Joseph de Leiva Nevares testified that "all the grain was set afire, destroying more than a thousand *fanegas* of maize besides the beans, of which there was a quantity, all being burned along with the houses and other buildings, a whole day being spent in doing this."[61]

Retaking Spanish New Mexico occurred in stages. Owing to manpower shortages, logistics involving the movement of people and things such as military equipment, supplies, and other planning efforts for warfare purposes, the reconquest of New Mexico would take nearly the entire decade to achieve. Given the lack of resources, their ability to secure the area for resettlement would be slow and difficult. Between 1684 and 1691, several raids were made by Spanish forces into the Río Abajo. In effect, the Spaniards were able to move freely along the lower river, generally up to San Felipe and sometimes to Cochití. Aside from attacks against Zia Pueblo or some other sortie against another pueblo, the Spaniards were not confident of holding their regained territory for resettlement.

Little by little, returning armies saw the pueblo alliance weakening. As one pueblo warrior somberly predicted in 1681, "In the end, the Spanish must come and gain the kingdom, because they were sons of the land and had grown up with the natives."[62] So too were the observations of returning Spanish armies into the area. From some of the houses they had seen, the Spaniards reported that some of the rebels had taken items from the churches and homes of settlers for their own use. In some cases, religious artifacts had been used to create small altars in the homes of some Indian families. Nearly four generations of Spanish rule had made a mark on the pueblos.

The pueblo alliance had problems. Once the fighting had subsided, Popé aggravated the situation by declaring himself leader of the pueblos of the Rio Grande. He toured the pueblos as the Spanish governors of yore had done and, like them, demanded tribute.[63] Popé called for the destruction of all things Spanish and forbade Christian religious practices, going as far as to prohibit the use of seeds introduced by the Spanish settlers. When Popé lost power, Luis Tupatú of Picurís had, by 1681, become the leader of the pueblos.⁶⁴ He held power until 1688, when Popé again resumed leadership of the pueblos. After Popé's death, Tupatú again resumed leadership of the pueblos. During his leadership, Tupatú, with other leading pueblo warriors, distributed the large herds of livestock once owned by the settlers.⁶⁵ By 1682, Otermín had detected infighting among the pueblos and had heard about an epidemic that had also weakened pueblo unity.

Finally, in the summer of 1692 the newly appointed governor, don Diego de Vargas, led a small army northward along the Rio Grande from El Paso to Santa Fe.⁶⁶ His sole objective was to retake New Mexico from Indian rebels who had held the province since 1680. The march up the river through the pueblos of the Río Abajo was uneventful, primarily because all the pueblos of that region had been abandoned. Apache raiders had driven some Puebloans out, and rebel warriors from the northern pueblos had intimidated others to join them or leave. But the constant sorties by invading Spanish armies through their land had made the area unsafe. Consequently, Vargas and his men saw very few Indians along the trail of the Río Abajo. By mid-September Vargas had laid siege to Santa Fe, and before nightfall of the first day the natives had surrendered without much of a fight. The next day Spanish priests absolved the rebel Indians of their apostasy, and children, most of whom had been born after the revolt had begun, were presented for baptism. With the aid of Luis Tupatú, the most powerful of the rebel chieftains, Vargas was able to persuade many of the pueblos to submit to Spanish sovereignty once again. Although Santa Fe appeared wrested from rebel hands, Vargas's work was only beginning. The Spanish presence sparked new revolts, for the Pueblo Revolt died slowly. Still, it would take several years before New Mexico lay comfortably in Spanish hands.

It was, nonetheless, the beginning of a new era for the Spanish colonial province of New Mexico. Vargas's *reconquista* was propitious. By that time Popé had died (in 1688) and the alliance that he had created against all odds was gone. Vargas took advantage of the situation and negotiated peace with willing pueblos and otherwise made a military show of strength at others or attacked pueblos who threw out a challenge. In December of 1692 Vargas returned to El Paso for settlers to recolonize New Mexico. By 1694, the Spaniards under Vargas had made a triumphant *entrada* into Santa Fe. The pueblos on the Camino Real de Tierra Adentro and those along the Rio Grande had been the scene of much history. As the seventeenth century came to an end, a new era was at hand, for despite a rocky beginning, the pueblos and the Hispanic settlers, in contrast to pre-1680 New Mexico, would settle into a more peaceful relationship. New Mexico in the eighteenth century was, indeed, a different place. The triad of pueblos, plains, and province would take on a new history of its own.

APPENDIX A

An Overview of Salinas Pueblo Missions National Monument

It should be noted that themes, issues, and events that occurred in the Provincia de Nuevo México during the colonial period were commonly repeated throughout the colonial worlds of Spain, France, England, and Portugal. In that regard, New Mexico's history is a shared history throughout the Americas. In writing about Spanish colonial New Mexico, especially in regard to issues related to church and state disputes as well as Indian policies during the seventeenth century, historians have tended to focus on the problems and events within the province, thus giving the impression that such historical episodes were isolated and unique to the province. New Mexico's early years are among the most studied, especially in detailed fashion. The historiography, however, has produced other images of early New Mexico. For example, in *The Cities That Died of Fear: The Story of the Salinas Pueblos*, originally published in 1916, Paul A.F. Walter initiated a renewed interest in the history of the pueblos that constituted the seventeenth-century Salinas jurisdiction under Spain.¹ The title of his book not only created an impressionistic theme to the history of the area but also suggested a type of lore

DOI: 10.5876/9781646420957.c016

that resulted in an image of the distressed pueblos and missions that were abandoned, historically, in the 1670s, because of drought, famine, and Apache raids that gripped all of New Mexico's Hispanic settlements and Indian pueblos alike. The history of the Salinas pueblos is not only braided in lore, but its depth lies in the Spanish colonial archival collections in Spain, Mexico, and New Mexico that document its history from the early years of European contact to the last decades of the seventeenth century. To that end, the US Congress established Salinas National Monument in December 1980 "to set apart and preserve for the benefit and enjoyment of the American people the ruins of prehistoric Indian pueblos and associated seventeenth century Franciscan Spanish mission ruins."[2] In 1988 Salinas National Monument was renamed Salinas Pueblo Missions National Monument to reflect the incorporation of the remains of surviving portions of the churches at three sites: Gran Quivira, San Gregorio de Abó, and Nuestra Señora de la Purísima Concepción (Quarai), along with their adjacent pueblo ruins representing what existed in the seventeenth century.[3] The legislative history of the creation of Salinas National Monument began earlier, in 1909, when Congress established Gran Quivira National Monument, which preserved and protected only one of the three sites, Las Humanas. That site contained ruins of two early mission churches and the adjacent pueblo. Throughout much of its modern history in the nineteenth and twentieth centuries, Abó and Quarai alternated between total neglect and ownership by private individuals or the University of New Mexico or the Museum of New Mexico. In time, they were designated and managed as state monuments.

Salinas Pueblo Missions National Monument tells the story of both prehistoric pueblos and their contact with the European world. Its story is embedded in the seventeenth-century history of New Mexico, for during the period 1598 to 1679 Spanish settlers and Franciscan missionaries brought religious and other changes to them, which interrupted their ancient traditions and introduced European traditions, laws, governance, language, and technology into the entire area. Interpretive themes vary at each site, but the overall story of Spanish colonialism and its effects is the overshadowing theme at Salinas Pueblo Missions National Monument. Indeed, the National Park Service recognized that without the broader history of seventeenth-century Spanish colonial New Mexico, the Salinas pueblo history would suffer in both context and detail. In regard to the complexity of overall interpretation

Appendix A: An Overview of Salinas Pueblo Missions National Monument

of historical themes at Salinas National Monument, National Park Service planners appropriately cautioned that:

> Much of the story at Salinas consists of themes common to all of the sites, including cultural change processes on a regional basis as well as economic and social relationships among the three sites, throughout the Salinas Basin, and in the large contexts of the Province of New Mexico and the Spanish New World Empire. Without interpretation of these overall themes, the individual sites would become isolated ruins without a context . . . interpretation of these overall themes would have to be extremely simplified, leading to an incomplete understanding of the Salinas story.[4]

One other site, among other possible related ruins in the region, Tabira (also known as Pueblo Blanco), is owned by the US Forest Service.[5] Although it is not a part of Salinas Pueblo Missions National Monument, related aspects of its story are interpreted by the National Park Service.

The history of the missions and pueblos at Salinas Pueblo Missions National Monument is linked to that of the Great Plains, for the pueblos and Spanish haciendas of the lower Rio Grande were often stopping places for expeditions entering or leaving the province. The pueblos at Taos, Pecos, Galisteo, and Salinas were gateways to the Great Plains. Like the pueblos on the Rio Grande, they were sometimes the stages of events that developed swiftly on the troubled frontier of the Provincia de Nuevo México. The interval between 1598 and 1610 was one of exploration and incipient settlement and missionization of the upper Rio Grande. The period from 1610 to 1659 was one of numerous expansion projects, the occupation of new frontiers, especially along the lower Rio Grande between Cochití and Socorro, as well as the lands east of the Manzano Mountains and those to the west toward Acoma and Zuñi. Intense missionization characterized the period as Santo Domingo on the Rio Grande became the ecclesiastical headquarters of New Mexico after 1610. From Santo Domingo the line of missions spread southward past Sandía and Isleta to Senecú near Socorro and, finally, to the El Paso area, where the Conversión de Mansos y Sumas (Mission to the Manso and Suma Indians) was begun toward the end of the period. To the east of Santo Domingo, Franciscan friars worked the pueblos of the Galisteo Basin, and from there they began a chain of missions that ran south from Chililí to Tajique, Quaraí, Abó, Tenabó, Tabira, and San Buenaventura de las Humanas.

In 1909 Congress established Gran Quivira National Monument, and its boundaries were fixed in 1919. The site, known in the Spanish period as the Pueblo de las Humanas, included the ruins of the two churches that were constructed early in the Spanish period and the excavated prehistoric mounds of the pueblo. The first church, San Isidro, was mentioned by Father Alonso de Benavides in 1626 when he visited the pueblo. San Isidro was completed in 1635. Today all that remains of the church is the stone foundation that outlines where it once stood. The second church, San Buenaventura, was constructed about 1659.[6] The site was abandoned in 1671 during a period of famine that hit the entire Provincia de Nuevo México. Its colossal ruins stand proudly among the ruins of San Isidro and the Pueblo de las Humanas that it once served. Las Humanas has prehistoric beginnings as recorded by excavations done in between 1965 and 1967 by Alden Hayes, a National Park Service archaeologist, his colleagues, and a crew from the local area. They excavated and stabilized 226 rooms of the site known as Mound 7, the largest of the pueblo mounds at Gran Quivira.[7]

Early excavation of the Las Humanas site began in 1923. Ten years later, in 1933, the School of American Research, assisted by the National Park Service, undertook a partial excavation and study of the ruin. Archaeologists found small reservoirs and irrigation ditches in the fields near the pueblo. Additionally, they studied the buildings of the large church and found them to be six feet thick. The adjoining *convento* (monastery) measured 160 feet to the south. Some the timbers for the structure were believed to have come from the mountains sixteen miles away.[8]

The other two mission churches—at Abó, eleven miles west of Mountainair, and at Quarai, about eight miles north of Mountainair—fell under different owners. In 1913 the private owners of Quarai transferred their interest to the Museum of New Mexico. Twenty-four years later, in 1935, Quarai became a State of New Mexico monument. In 1937 the University of New Mexico (UNM) acquired Abó and initiated excavation of the site. A year later, UNM transferred Abó to the Museum of New Mexico as a state monument. Of the complex transfer of San Gregorio de Abó by private owners to the University of New Mexico, Joseph H. Toulouse Jr., an archaeologist, wrote:

> In 1937, through the negotiations of Mr. Pearce Rodey, of Albuquerque, the picturesque ruins of San Gregorio de Abó and the adjacent Indian pueblo

were purchased from private owners by alumni of the University of New Mexico and presented to that institution. Subsequently, ownership was vested jointly in the University, the Museum of New Mexico, and the School of American Research. Thus, after several decades of neglect and vandalism, these ruins came under the protection of institutions which have devoted themselves to the acquisition, protection, and preservation of early Franciscan Missions of New Mexico. In the latter part of 1938, Mr. Fred Cisneros of Abó Viejo donated sufficient land to include the apsidal portion of the church which was not embraced in the original purchase. Declaration of the tract as a State Monument was made in August 29, 1938.[9]

Throughout the 1930s, the Museum of New Mexico carried out a series of excavations of the church ruins and the pueblos at both Quarai and Abó.

Like Gran Quivira and Quarai, Abó lay dormant for over 140 years. In 1815 Spanish sheep herders attempted to return to the area, but the Apaches pushed them out in 1830. Settlers would permanently return in 1865. The site attracted interest for its cultural significance—in 1938 Abó became a New Mexico State Historic Monument and was later excavated by the University of New Mexico and School of American Research. In 1962 Abó was designated a National Historic Landmark, and by 1980 the ruins became part of the Salinas Pueblo Missions National Monument, which the National Park Service administers. Today, roughly 40 percent of the original pueblo buildings remain as ruins—many still unexcavated. Skeletal red sandstone walls of the San Gregorio de Abó church stand as reminders of the Spanish and Catholic influence in the American Southwest.

Interest in creating Salinas Missions National Monument was voiced in 1941 when, well ahead of his day, archaeologist Erik Kellerman Reed proposed the creation of a Salinas Missions National Monument that would include all three major mission ruins at Abó, Quarai, and Gran Quivira along with their associated pueblos. His hope was not only to connect the history and archaeology of the sites and other related prehistoric ruins in the area but to preserve and protect them from intrusions and vandalism. Although the idea had promise, it did not come to fruition at the time. Meanwhile, Abó and Quarai became National Historic Landmarks in 1962. Soon after, the National Park Service undertook a feasibility study and proposed their designation as national monuments. The next year the National Parks, Historic

Sites, Building and Monuments Advisory Board proposed the establishment of Salinas National Monument. While the proposal planted the seed for their inclusion in the National Park system, in 1966, the Advisory Board placed Abó and Quarai on the National Register.

After a decade of consideration, the National Park Service maintained that the two units were meritorious of National Monument designation. Finally, in 1974, the State of New Mexico agreed to transfer Abó and Quarai to the National Park Service. Three years later, in 1977, Congress passed Senate Bill 1864 to establish Salinas National Monument.[10] In 1980 Public Law 96-550 affirmed the designation. Pending an agreed-upon General Management Plan between the State of New Mexico and the National Park Service, Abó and Quarai became national monuments in 1981. On October 28, 1988, Congress abolished Gran Quivira National Monument, incorporated Abó and Quarai with Gran Quivira, and renamed the monument Salinas Pueblo Mission National Monument.[11]

The site known as Gran Quivira is the largest of the abandoned pueblos once occupied by Piros.[12] In the historic period it was known as Las Humanas because an Apachean tribe, the Jumanos, were said to be living there among the Piros. Known as the "great pueblo of the Jumanos," Friar Alonso de Benavides wrote that it was so called because the Jumanos went there "to trade and barter."[13] Possibly, however, some had remained to live there. Often portrayed in touristic literature as "The Cities That Died of Fear," the pueblos of Abó, Quarai, and Las Humanas were abandoned in the 1670s because of a famine that spread, not only to the Spanish population living in Tajique and Chililí but also to the western Great Plains, causing Plains tribes to raid those pueblos and others for food. The people of Las Salinas fled to the Rio Grande pueblos for protection. Some went to Galisteo, others as far south as the El Paso missions where they established towns that still exist today.

The second unit of the Salinas Pueblo Missions National Monument mission church site and its attendant pueblo is Nuestra Señora de la Purísima Concepción de Cuarac, commonly known as Quarai and historically called Cuarac. The mission and pueblo of Quarai were, like Abó and Las Humanas, part of the Spanish colonial administration of the area called La Jurisdicción de las Salinas, which encompassed the Salinas Valley. The Jurisdicción de las Salinas included a wide area from Abo, eastward to Quarai thence northward to the Tajique-Chililí area and, from there southeasterly to Las Humanas.

Beyond present-day Willard are the salt beds called Las Salinas, from which source the Salinas Pueblos derived their name, today as in the past.

Located on the east side of the Manzano Mountains, the Salinas Valley was the homeland of many peoples and cultures for hundreds of years. The pueblos managed by the National Park Service at Salinas Pueblo Missions National Monument, inclusive of Las Humanas, Abó and Quarai, which were three of several Piro and Tompiro settlement sites, evolved over time. The prehistorical period of the area began as early as the tenth century A.D. when Mogollon and Ancestral Puebloan groups established pueblos in the valley that served as major centers of trade between the people of the Rio Grande region and the Plains Indian tribes. Early Puebloan peoples moved into the Salinas Valley around the 1200s.

The pueblo of Quarai lay in a rich, fertile area at the time, with several other pueblos nearby, including Tajique and Chililí. Tiwa speakers likely occupied these pueblos. Neighboring Abó, Gran Quivira, and Tabira were Tompiro-speaking communities. Based on artifacts found at Quarai, people were living there by 1250. The people of the settlement had most likely left it uninhabited by 1400, as there is no evidence to indicate that a permanent population lived at the pueblo from 1400 to around 1600. The consensus is that the reoccupation of the pueblo likely occurred before the Spanish initially made contact in the late sixteenth century.

When Spanish exploration of the valley began in the late sixteenth century, Franciscan missionaries saw its potential as a missionary field and later returned to build large mission churches. The pueblo of Quarai contains the best preserved of these churches. Mission Nuestra Señora de la Purísima Concepción de Cuarac was completed ca. 1629. In 1633 Friar Esteban de Perea, the commissary of the Holy Office of the Inquisition for New Mexico, was stationed at the mission at Sandia Pueblo. That year he moved to the struggling mission at Quarai in the Manzano Mountains. During the period when Commissary Perea used the convent at Quarai as his residence, the site officially served as the seat of the Spanish Inquisition in New Mexico. There and at the mission at Sandia Pueblo whenever he would return, Perea held inquisitorial investigatory proceedings, as he was required to do by the Tribunal in Mexico City until sometime before his death in 1638.[14]

Today Quarai is a National Historic Landmark within the Salinas Pueblo Missions National Monument. The site contains a variety of settlements from

1250 through the colonial period. The pueblo and mission remains at Abo, Quarai, Las Humanas, Tabira, and Tenabo reflect the early period of Pueblo-Spanish interaction, the conflicts between the Spanish church and state, and their overall effects on native culture in the Southwest. Visitors should not miss exploring the impressive structures on a trip through central New Mexico.

Early Spanish explorers learned about the pueblos of the Salinas Valley and several of its pueblos as early as 1540. The Spanish had already successfully established missions at Chililí and Abó, and in 1625 Fray Juan Gutiérrez de la Chica became the first missionary at Quarai. Upon his arrival, Gutiérrez de la Chica met little resistance from the native population and soon began planning for a new church and *convento*.

In terms of its construction, which began in 1627 and was completed in 1632, Nuestra Señora de la Purísima Concepción de Quarai measures about 108 feet long and 28 feet wide.[15] The walls are all made of local red sandstone and average 4.5 feet thick—though many measure up to 10 feet at their bases in order to support the tall structure. Today, the wall ruins still stand roughly 20 feet tall, but it is likely the walls once towered around 40 feet. The outline on the ground of the existing ruins of the church show its basic plan as a Latin cross. The red sandstone *convento* rooms surrounded a central plaza. A square kiva is located inside the north *convento* of the mission and presents a seemingly unanswerable riddle, as it not only is located near the mission church but also seems to have been built at the same time as the church and convent. Such a scheme would not have been allowable under the missionary rule. Still, kivas are an important part of many pueblo religious practices. The kiva's presence within the Spanish complex raises interesting questions about how, over time, traditional tribal religion beliefs and practices intermingled and syncretized with Catholic traditions.

Due to a number of hardships during the early 1670s, Quarai, along with Abó and Las Humanas, was abandoned. The causes for the abandonment include a series of droughts that severely diminished the food supplies throughout the Indian pueblos and Hispanic settlements of New Mexico. Apache attacks increased and hit hard at the mission sites and farms in the Salinas Valley. The people of Las Humanas, Abó, and Quarai were forced to flee to the Rio Grande pueblos. Hard-pressed for food on the Great Plains, the Apache, too, were starving and raided to survive. By 1678, all of the Salinas Valley pueblos and their missions were no longer inhabited. Not only had the

Native Americans abandoned the area; so, too, had the Hispanic settlers deserted their farms and ranches in Tajique and Chililí for settlements along the Rio Grande. Nearly a century and a half had passed when, in 1815, Hispanic settlers returned to Quarai and established the Casa Colorado land grant, a village called Manzano, not far from the mission site. Sometime later the church at Manzano was constructed. The Manzano Land Grant was established in 1829–30. Today the Hispanic descendants of those early settlers at Manzano and neighboring towns still live there.

The Abó Unit of Salinas Pueblo Missions National Monument sits west of the town of Mountainair, New Mexico, and contains approximately 370 acres. Access to the site of the ruins and the pueblo is through the Salinas Pueblo Missions National Monument, which offers interpretive tours and self-guided walks through the ruins of Abó, Quarai, and Gran Quivira. Recent stabilization efforts at Abó have made it possible for visitors to walk directly around and within the old walls of the Abó mission church and through the largely unexcavated pueblo structures.

Early Spanish *entradas* into the Manzano Mountains and the Salinas Valley began in the sixteenth century. The men of the expedition led by Francisco Vazquez de Coronado in 1540 were cognizant of the pueblos on the east side of the Sandia-Manzano ranges. Meanwhile, Oñate's nephews, Maese de Campo Juan de Zaldívar and Sargento Mayor Vicente de Zaldívar, explored the nearby pueblos northeast of the camp. Doubtless those pueblos and the salt beds to the east of the mountains were seen by Sánchez Chamuscado in 1581 as well as by Antonio de Espejo in 1582. Sixteen years later, in spring 1598, as the expedition led by Governor Juan de Oñate wended its way northward, his nephews, Vicente and Juan de Zaldívar, leading an advance scouting party, saw large mountains they called the Sierra Morena (the Manzano Mountains) and wondered what lay beyond them. Indians along the Rio Grande had told them that there were other pueblos in the mountains. Where present-day Abó Pass—which the Spaniards later called *el portuelo* (the little gateway)—comes into view from the river, the small scouting party turned east. At the southern end of the Manzano Mountains, they found the mountain pueblos. Upon returning to make their report to Governor Oñate, the Zaldívars told him about the many pueblos on the other side of the mountains. One of them, they said, had the fascinating name of "Aboó,"[16] doubtless the site of the present day ruins at Abó.

The history surrounding Salinas Pueblo Missions National Monument did not end with the abandonment of the area. Indeed, the site continued to have visitors from time to time. During the years 1751–54, Spanish soldiers and their Indian auxiliaries were from time to time stationed at a place they called "Coara" and Tajique. Later, in the early 1800s, Hispanic New Mexicans return there and resettled lands near Quarai and Abó. In 1846 US troops under the command of Lieutenant J. W. Abert passed through the Salinas area and stopped at Quarai. His report is believed to be the first English-language report of the Salinas ruins.[17] Seven years later, in 1853, Major James H. Carlton and his California troopers also visited Quarai. His report, "Diary of an Excursion to the Ruins of Abó, Quarra, and Gran Quivira in New Mexico," was published 1854.[18] One of the most famous visitors to Quarai, Adolph F. Bandelier, visited Quarai in late December 1882 and described the ruins. He returned a year later to take measurements of certain walls of the ruins.[19] Thus, the history of the pueblos and missions at Salinas Pueblo Missions National Monument, which is narrated in thepreceding chapters, has spilled into the modern era, appropriately commemorated by the National Park Service as a part of our national story.

APPENDIX B

Contested Lands in Perspective
Acoma, the Jumano War, and the Pueblo Revolt

Did I fear the Great White Chief? No. He was my enemy and the enemy of my people. His people desired the country of my people. My heart was strong against him. I said he should never have my country.
 —*Geronimo to President Theodore Roosevelt, 1905*[1]

Like all other European claims to the Americas inclusive of French, English, and Portuguese settlements, the Spanish colonial establishment of the Western Hemisphere had, indeed, been traumatic on Native American populations. The Indian rage caused by the brutality of conquest and occupation in the early decades of European occupation would not and could not be forgotten by the many tribes in North and South America as well as the Caribbean. In general, the tribes viewed the Spanish intrusion into their territories, which they themselves had defined since time immemorial through war with other tribes and their own justifiable claims and occupations of certain lands, as intolerable. The Spanish intrusions, either by force of arms or intimidation, into their claimed homelands; the settlement of missionaries

DOI: 10.5876/9781646420957.c017

in their midst without their consent, which threatened the disintegration of their cultures and beliefs; the presence of settlers and explorers who made demands for provisions from their dwindling food supply; as well as the encroachment on tribal sovereignties by demands that they swear loyalty to the king of Spain added to a number of grievances that formed a list of causes for their constant warfare against their unwelcome visitors. In general, native peoples, on the other hand, viewed European contact, whether it be Spain, England, France, Portugal, or any other budding nation-state, not as benign but as a threat to their homelands, cultures, and territorial boundaries. Across the Americas, native tribes saw their actions as a war against intruders, not a rebellion against a foreign sovereign who claimed all lands, people, and resources.

From the earliest Indian resistance against the men of Christopher Columbus in the Caribbean to the last outbreak in North America at Wounded Knee in 1890, the Indian world was at war with all intruders. From their point of view, rebellion took a back seat to invasion and defense of homeland. The Indian world was at war with all intruders. Perhaps Geronimo said it best in 1905, when he met President Theodore Roosevelt. In explaining why he fought to protect his homeland, Geronimo began with a traditional greeting and said these words, "Great Father. . . . Did I fear the Great White Chief? No. He was my enemy and the enemy of my people. I said that he should never have my country."[2] Gerónimo answered the age-old question, "What would you have done?"

One of history's oddities is the misconception and misnomers of Indian wars as "rebellions." From the Indian point of view, the tribes across the Americas and the Caribbean did not view their attacks against colonial powers as rebellions. They saw it as plain and simple war. In their view resistance to invasions or incursions into their territories was enough to wage war. Once settlers moved into Indian country, there was no other alternative. Settlers, miners, soldiers, missionaries, and other colonials with their Indian allies posed a threat to their way of life. In contrast, nearly all colonials justified their punitive expeditions against "rebelling" tribes as a "just war."

On the other hand, tribes that saw intrusions into their way of life also resented those who willingly entered the missions. Apaches, for example had a disdain for mission Indians throughout New Mexico. Mission documents throughout the Americas are replete with examples of attacks on missions and mission Indians. In 1677 missionaries in Nueva Vizcaya reported that "rebellious Indians . . . attacked the *doctrina* called Zape and killed some of the reduced Indians and many children, and our minister had not appeared; that they did the same in the *doctrina* of Santa Catalina, [and] that in many parts of the roads of that province trade could not be carried on because they are cut off by the Indians who have risen and are committing robberies and atrocities."[3] Thus, war was justified by both colonials and warriors.

In her study, Ida Altman similarly noted the difference between a "rebellion" and "war," which took place over a large geographic area known as Nueva Galicia and was referred to as the *"tierra de guerra"* (land of war) by Spanish colonials. Nueva Galicia included the present Mexican states of Jalisco, Colima, Nayarit, Aguascalientes, and Zacatecas. Of the Mixton War that spread from western Jalisco to Zacatecas during the years from 1540 to 1542, Altman wrote: "The conflict, today known as the Mixton War, often has been depicted as a spontaneous uprising. There is, however, evidence of considerable planning, organization, and effective communication before the rebellion, as people had been meeting and fortifying and supplying high mountainous strongholds, known as *peñoles*, for some time without the knowledge of Spanish settlers and officials."[4] Indeed, the Spanish victory was largely due to the role of their Tlaxcalan and other Nahua-speaking allies from central Mexico. Having ensured the Spanish victory, the Indian allies, as they would in other conflicts, including those in New Mexico, helped open Nueva Galicia to settlement. Altman concluded, "Not only did the diverse peoples of western Mexico pay the price for their defeat in terms of loss of lives and communities, but after the war they witnessed the arrival of waves of Indigenous migrants from central Mexico who came to settle in their midst."[5] Significantly, neighboring tribes north of Zacatecas as well as throughout Nueva Galicia clearly saw the Spanish threat to their homelands.

In general, European colonials in North and South America preferred to rule through intimidation, not through force of arms. Rebellion, revolt, uprisings, and other similar words assume that many of the tribes within European colonial control had surrendered their sovereignty. From a colonial viewpoint those words reflected that those tribes had agreed to live peacefully, convert spiritually, linguistically, and culturally. In reality, the natives did not initially view their compliance as surrender but rather as a mode of survival. In the end, they gave in to colonial intimidation, but in the first few centuries after contact, many tribes saw their plight as a long-drawn-out war against all European invaders.

Spain was not alone in the dealings and treatment of the tribes with whom they came into contact. Indeed, from the days of Columbus to the long periods of Spanish, English, French, and Portuguese colonial occupations, the tribes of the Americas, from Alaska and Canada to Argentina and Chile, waged a series of wars of attrition—albeit rarely unified, but separately in their own territories—against European invaders. For nearly 400 years the many theaters of war ranged from the Patagonia region of southern South America to Brazil, Chile, Peru, Central America, Mexico, and the Caribbean and across Canada and the United States, where war was common beginning with the founding of Jamestown in 1607 to Custer's Last Stand in 1876 and the debacle at Wounded Knee in 1890. So too are the annals of US history filled with legendary chieftain names like Powhatan, Opecancanough, Pontiac, Crazy Horse, Sitting Bull, Black Hawk, and others. Throughout the colonial centuries, Indian peoples of the Americas, as First Peoples, shared one thing in common: the lands of their ancestors, and all that they implied, were sacred to them. It seemed that everywhere the Europeans, principally the Portuguese, French, German, Dutch, English, and Spanish, landed, a new nightmare for Native Americans began. It would be a collective nightmare that would never go away. Thus, in perspective, the battle of Acoma in 1599 and the Pueblo Revolt of 1680 were part of a long series of acts of Indian resistance that spread north within the mining frontier areas along the Camino Real de Tierra Adentro in Guanajuato, Durango, Zacatecas, Santa Barbara, and beyond to New Mexico.

In perspective, when seen against the backdrop of Indian resistance such as that demonstrated by the pueblos of the Rio Grande against Francisco Vázquez de Coronado and his men in 1540–42, the battle at Acoma in 1599, for example, was not an isolated case nor was it merely a rebellion against Spain, as it has been portrayed by historians who have written about it. Neither, until the advent of history books, was it buried deep in the lore of Acoma. The battle at Acoma was reawakened after nearly three centuries when early US historians rediscovered the story. Since that time, they have written about it as a rebellion, sometimes from a nationalist pen with an anti-Spanish, Black Legend viewpoint.[6] Too, tourist guides at Acoma interpret their version gleaned from history books with enhanced or misrepresented facts surrounding the causes, the combat, and the results of the battle. Between sense and sensibility, the search for objectivity through historical analysis suffers from repetitive and simplified narratives in the interpretation of events found in written histories that distort actual events for convenience or to suit the needs of the narrator.

Historically, the people of Acoma were not alone in their fight for their homeland. For decades prior to the 1590s, other Indians tribes along the northern frontier of New Spain defied Spanish governance in Nueva Vizcaya (Chihuahua), Coahuila, Sonora, and New Mexico, but Spanish forces were often sufficient to quiet them. One of the earliest rebellions against Spanish colonial rule by the Ximenes in northern Mexico occurred in 1599. Rebellions south of New Mexico along the Camino Real de Tierra Adentro flared up from time to time. In 1601, in Nueva Vizcaya, the Acaxées, numbering nearly 5,000 warriors from the mountains of Topia and San Andreas, attacked Spanish settlements and mining camps.

Similarly, the Indian wars of Nueva Vizcaya and New Mexico tell of continuous warfare between tribes and Spanish colonial intruders on their lands that began early, by the end of the sixteenth century. In New Mexico, the farthest northern point of settlement beyond Nueva Vizcaya, Acoma "rebelled" against such intrusions; later, in 1680, a united effort resulted in the Pueblo Revolt. But the war had earlier already begun to the south of there. Beginning in 1599 and stretching for nearly a hundred years, a series of "rebellions" rocked the northern frontier, particularly the areas known as Nueva Vizcaya and New Mexico.

The seemingly isolated but widespread rebellions, tantamount to all-out war, can be easily viewed against a broader historical background in northern Mexico as evident in the Mixton War, 1540–42. In addition to battles at Acoma in 1599 and 1613 and other rebellions in New Mexico between 1645 and 1675 that led to the Pueblo Revolt of 1680, numerous uprisings against Spanish rule occurred in northern New Spain beginning in the sixteenth century (see table A.1).

Such "rebellions" were clearly acts of war aimed at ridding the land of intruders. In the seventeenth century, the last of the "rebellions" took placed in 1690 in the land of the Tarahumaras, which extended from southern Chihuahua northward along the Sierra Madre Occidental across to eastern Sonora. That rebellion, the Spaniards learned from informants, had ties to the Pueblo Revolt. Indeed, the Pueblo Indians of New Mexico may have

TABLE A.1. *Uprisings against Spanish rule in Northern New Spain*

Date	Native American Wars and Rebellions	Location
1540–42	Tarahumaras, Tepehuanes, etc.	Mixton War, Nueva Galicia
1540	Tiguex War (Coronado Expedition)	Albuquerque Valley
1565	Opatas resist Francisco de Ibarra	Sonora
1599–1601	Ximene	NW and W Durango
1599	Acoma	W New Mexico
1601	Jumanos (sporadic warfare, 1599–1601)	New Mexico
1601–3	Acaxces	NW Durango, Topia
1610	Ximene	W and NW Durango
1613	Acoma	New Mexico
1616–18	Tephuanes with some Tarahumaras and Acaxces	W and NW Durango
1621–22	Tarahumaras with some Tepehuanes Tobosos, and Conchos	W and E Durango, S Chihuahua
1630s	Tobosos, Tepetucanes, Salineros, Masames	Durango and Chihuahua
1644–75	Pueblo Rebellions	Socorro, Jémez, Cochití, Nambé, San Felipe, Isleta, etc.
1645–52	Tobosos, Conchos; Tarahumaras (ca. 1648)	E and NW Durango, SW Texas, N and S Chihuahua
1660s	Salineros, Conchos, Tobosos, some Tarahumaras; El Tanbulita Rebellion	S and NE Durango, S and W Chihuahua, SW Texas, New Mexico
1670s	Pueblos and Clemente Revolt	New Mexico
1680–1700	Pueblo Revolt (1680), Conchos, Tarahumaras, Chizos, Sumas, Mansos, Tanos, Tobosos, Julimes, and Opatas	New Mexico; Sonora, Texas, all of Chihuahua and Durango

Inclusive of notes in this chapter, other sources for the chart include Jones, *Nueva Vizcaya*, 99. Other rebellions, such as the Mixton War (1540–42), Tiguex War (1540), Tepetucanes, Salineros, and Masames revolts (1630s), Pueblo rebellions (1644–75), Opata rebellions (1565 and 1681–82), Acoma rebellions (1599 and 1613), and the Jumano War (1601), were added to the list. Also see "A Report by Licenciado Diego de Medrano, Priest of the City of Durango, Capital of the Kingdom of Nueva Vizcaya, which Describes the State of the Kingdom Resulting from the Riots and Ruin Wrought by the Rebellious Indians. Durango, August 31, 1654," in Naylor and Polzer, *Presidio and Militia*, 411–13.

influenced other "rebellions." There is no doubt that the Pueblo Revolt of 1680 influenced the Tarahumara, who had watched the Pueblo Revolt unfold. Did New Mexico's Pueblo Indians influence other rebellions?

Sixty-four years before the Pueblo Revolt of 1680 on a fateful November day the Tepehuan Revolt of 1616 began in Sinaloa south of Tarahumara country. Tepehuan warriors had sent settlers, miners, and missionaries scurrying for safety as they all but destroyed the Jesuit mission system there for several years. In those six decades of warfare, many had been killed on both sides, and a large pattern of destruction had taken place.

Still, the Tepehuan Revolt of 1616 left behind another legacy, a form of millenarianism, in which it was supposed that a messiah would come again to organize and lead the Tepehanes to victory and rid their land of the invading Spaniards. That legacy pervaded future rebellions in Nueva Vizcaya. Historian José de la Cruz Pacheco Rojas explains the origins of millenarianism in the Tepehuan Revolt of 1616. He offers the documentary dialogue that ensued the end of the revolt. In the interrogatory that followed the rebellion, the Spaniards wondered if, in fact, during Lent of one of the previous years, an idol in the form of a badly formed cross had been carried by an Indian who traversed the land to incite them, saying that God had sent him to exhort them to rebel against and kill all the priests and Spaniards in the area. He said that all Indians killed in the rebellion would be "resurrected on the seventh day."[7]

The follow-up response to the interrogatory was chilling. Captain Martín de Olivas said that the rebellion was instigated by an Indian from New Mexico who had, indeed, passed through several villages with a small crucifix with the figure of Jesus Christ. The "Cristo" was "girded with a silk-like belt, and in two folded letters," both looking rather official. The two missives served as testimony, verifying that Christ was the "true son of God. The Indian also said that the son of God would descend from the heavens and would come to visit and console them, and he would visit all of the world, particularly the poor people whom he loved throughout all of this land which the Spaniards had usurped and all they had served them as if they were their slaves."[8] Olivas also said that the New Mexican Indian had told them that "God, the Father" had authored the letters, telling them that abusive Spaniards and missionaries were corrupt and that the time for change was nigh. He exhorted them to rebel against the Spaniards and drive them out. He said that God had told them to rebel many times before; this time, if they did not do it, he would "destroy them and cast them into the fires [of hell]."[9] The New Mexican Indian explained the two letters contained that message from God. He exhorted his listeners to select the wisest man among them to carry the Christ and the two letters from one pueblo to the next, preaching the message, until they reached the settlements at Guadiana. Before long, he had a large following.[10] After a ritualistic ceremony revolving around the Cristo and the two letters, the New Mexican Indian left the area. Later the messianic message surfaced in other small rebellions of other tribes in Nueva Vizcaya. Thus, the seed for a rebellion, coordinated by certain leaders in various pueblos, was planted. Many of the warriors in the region began constructing and stockpiling bows, arrowheads, and shafts for the coming rebellion.

Later, in his history, published in 1645, the Jesuit priest Andrés Pérez Ribas confirmed that there was, indeed, an influential person who fanned the flames of rebellion. Ribas wrote that "a sorcerer" made several disguised apparitions among the Tepehuan, the Acaxee, and the Xixime nations, exhorting them to rebel.[11] Attributing the rebellion to the devil and his lying ways, Ribas wrote that an old Indian

> entered the pueblos of Santiago, Tunal, and Tenerapa, which were all near Durango, he preached perversely against our Holy Faith, with the harmful intention of inciting those people to abandon their Faith and rebel against God and the king. . . . He told them that this was the God whom he and his companions worshiped. Afterwards, however, he went to the aforementioned pueblo of baptized Tepehuan, called Tenerapa, which was not far from Santiago Papasquiaro. There he ordered that his idol be worshiped, and through his lies and tricks he convinced these Indians that both he and his idol were angry and offended because he had assigned the Spaniards a homeland in kingdoms on the other side of the ocean in Spain, and yet they had come to these parts without his permission, settling in his lands and introducing the Christian law. He wished to free them of this, and in order to do so, as well as to placate their true gods, they would have to cut the throats of all long-time Christians, particularly the priests and fathers who instructed them, as well as all the Spaniards in the region. . . . if they obeyed him, he promised them safety for their own lives, their women and children, and victory over the Spaniards. Even if some of them should die in battle, he promised them that within seven days they would be resurrected.[12]

The sojourn of the New Mexican Indian left a lasting imprint of the Tepehuans. Historian Pacheco Rojas wrote that the Tepehuanes eventually developed a philosophic premise that formed a legacy within their culture and theology. They firmly believed, through their evolving seventeenth-century ceremonies and rituals, that a recurring theme reinforced their conviction that the "true savior is the *tlacatexista* or 'Cristo' that they had carried with them from pueblo to pueblo as the New Mexican Indian had charged them to do. They had learned well that the 'Cristo' had come to their land to look after them as they suffered the tyranny and exploitation by Spaniards. Even though the Jesuits had taught them about the 'Cristo,' they nonetheless viewed them as members, or at least supporters, of the exploiters. Instead, they adopted this 'Cristo' as their own in their religious ideologies and formed their own beliefs that the 'Cristo' had come to save them."[13] Indeed, in at least one way, the broader story came full circle: from the defense of ancestral lands and the honor of the spirits of their ancestors, their descendants found a way to sustain their way of life through a useful syncretic union of old and new beliefs. While "millenarianism" would appear philosophically profound, the historic survival of the tribes depended on both war that worked as a short-term solution and surrender as an initial phase of the long term.

When taken individually, the "rebellions" seem to direct attention to a small confined area and a small population of Spanish settlers who "caused" the problems. When viewed against the broader history of the northern Spanish frontier, such events were not isolated to small regions but were, in fact, an expression shared by all tribes in those far-ranging regions. Obviously, Native Americans did not coordinate their attacks with other tribes, but their sentiments against European intruders were shared in spirit across the land. Neither were Native American communications restricted to small pockets of Indian settlements but were far-ranging. When the Tarahumara Rebellion occurred, the communications ranged far to the west across the Sierra Madre Occidental and to the east across the Sierra Madre Oriental into Coahuila and north to New Mexico. Each "rebellion" was not only viewed by Spanish authorities but closely monitored by neighboring tribes. The perspective from the earliest rebellions in the sixteenth century to the nineteenth century across North America is that Indian America was at war.

Notes

Chapter 1: Introduction

1. See Sánchez, *Comparative Colonialism*.
2. An excellent study that demonstrates the complexity of Native American views related to territoriality is Pekka Hamalainen's *The Comanche Empire*. Hamalainen notes the extent of Comanche claims before and after their expansion into lands held by other tribes and those claimed by Europeans.
3. I define the historical process as an occurrence, a state of, or phenomenon that has to do with the evolution of a concept that ties to an event or a series of events in the context of values associated with the cultural, ethnic, and linguistic identities that represent the time period in which they occurred. The historical process is a function of the relationships within and interactions of the affairs of humankind with time, events, the sequence, and continuities of events, causes, effects, and the change or changes that develop as a consequence. The historical process may provide directionality. In summary, the historical process is evident in the questions, who are we, where do we come from, and where are we going? In the historical dialectic, the historical process is best defined as an unanswerable paradox that can never be completed because it is something that is in a perpetual state of becoming.

4. See section 1 of the National Historic Preservation Act, Pub. L. 89-665, as amended by Pub. L. 96-515.

5. Section 1 of the National Historic Preservation Act reads as follows:

> (b) The Congress finds and declares that (1) the spirit and direction of the Nation are founded upon and reflected in its historic heritage; (2) the historical and cultural foundations of the Nation should be preserved as a living part of our community life and development in order to give a sense of orientation to the American people; (3) historic properties significant to the Nation's heritage are being lost or substantially altered, often inadvertently, with increasing frequency; (4) the preservation of this irreplaceable heritage is in the public interest so that its vital legacy of cultural, educational, aesthetic, inspirational, economic, and energy benefits will be maintained and enriched for future generations of Americans; (5) in the face of ever-increasing extensions of urban centers, highways, and residential, commercial, and industrial developments, the present governmental and nongovernmental historic preservation programs and activities are inadequate to insure future generations a genuine opportunity to appreciate and enjoy the rich heritage of our Nation; (6) the increased knowledge of our historic resources, the establishment of better means of identifying and administering them, and the encouragement of their preservation will improve the planning and execution of Federal and federally assisted projects and will assist economic growth and development; and (7) although the major burdens of historic preservation have been borne and major efforts initiated by private agencies and individuals, and both should continue to play a vital role, it is nevertheless necessary and appropriate for the Federal Government to accelerate its historic preservation programs and activities, to give maximum encouragement to agencies and individuals undertaking preservation by private means, and to assist State and local governments and the National Trust for Historic Preservation in the United States to expand and accelerate their historic preservation programs and activities.

6. Sánchez, *Comparative Colonialism*.

7. Hoig, *Came Men on Horses*, 208; also see 172, 188–89, 216.

8. For example, see Hoig, *Came Men on Horses*, chapters 4–9 and 19. The alleged history of brutality by Sir Walter Raleigh, early founder of the Virginia colony and a contemporary of Oñate, for example, is brushed aside. Unlike US historians, Irish

historians see Sir Walter Raleigh differently. It was said that he lined the path to his tent with the impaled heads of Irish rebels. His participation in the Smerwick massacre, his deforestation of the Blackwater plantation, and the horrific executions in O'Neill's Rebellion (1573) and Desmond's Rebellion (1579) are part of other accusations made against him. See Teresa R. Richardson and Erwin V. Johanningmeier, *Race, Ethnicity and Education: What Is Taught in Schools* (Greenwich, CT: Information Age Publishing, 2003), 33. Also see www.historyireland.com/early-modern-history-1500. Also see Wikipedia entry as follows: /sir-walter-ralegh-in-ireland/ and https://en.wikipedia.org/wiki/Siege_of_Smerwick, last consulted on January 18, 2018.

9. See *Recopilación de las Leyes de los Reynos de las Indias* (Madrid, 1681), vol. 2. For examples, see Que cerca de las Reducciones no haya estancias de Ganado, libro VI, titulo III, Ley XX; Que entre los Indios no vivan Españoles, Mestizos, ni Mulatos aunque hayan comprador tierras den los Pueblos, libro VI, titulo III, Ley XXI. Living in pueblos was prohibited, libro VI, titulo III, Ley XXII; Que no se den tierras en perjuicio de los Indios, y las dadas se vuelvan a sus dueños, libro IV, titulo XII, Ley IX; Que las estancias para ganados se den apartados de Pueblos y Sementaras de Indios, libro IV, titulo XII, Ley XII.

10. See Treaty of Guadalupe Hidalgo: Findings and Possible Options Regarding Longstanding Community Land Grant Claims in New Mexico, a Report to Congressional Requesters by the United States General Accounting Office (GAO-04-60), June 2004, Joseph P. Sánchez, consultant/researcher, 26–27; see also 214, 215, 230, 231, 234–36. Historic seventeenth-century Spanish land grants ceded to Native American Pueblos in New Mexico and confirmed by the United States in 1858: Pueblo de Acoma, Pueblo de Cochiti, Pueblo de Isleta, Pueblo de Jémez, Pueblo de Laguna, Pueblo de Nambé, Pueblo de Pecos, Pueblo de Picuris, Pueblo de Pojoaque, Pueblo de San Felipe, Pueblo de San Ildefonso, Pueblo de San Juan, Pueblo de Sandia, Pueblo de Santa Ana, Pueblo de Santa Clara and Cañada de Santa Clara, Pueblo de San Cristóbal: failed to pursue; Pueblo de Santo Domingo, Pueblo de San Felipe, Pueblo de Taos, Pueblo de Tesuque, Pueblo de Zia, and Pueblo de Zuñí; Pueblo de Quemado failed to pursue land grant. See also Joseph P. Sánchez, Jerry Gurulé, and Mario Milliones, trans., *El Tratado de Guadalupe Hidalgo: Hallazgos y opciones posibles con respecto a los reclamos de larga duración de mercedes de tierras comunitarias en Nuevo Mexico* (GAO-04-60) (Washington, DC: Government Accounting Office, June 2004).

11. As noted, some of the many publications by France V. Scholes, Charles Wilson Hackett, Herbert E. Bolton, and Hubert Howe Bancroft were utilized in the writing of the present study and are included in the bibliography.

Chapter 2: Pueblos, Plains, and Early Spanish Explorers

1. Gallegos, Relación of the Chamuscado Rodríguez Expedition, in Hammond and Rey, *The Rediscovery of New Mexico*, 8.
2. Simmons, *Last Conquistador*, 111.
3. See Sánchez, "Bernardo Gruber."
4. "The Itinerario de Juan de Oñate," in Pacheco, Cárdenas, and Torres de Mendoza, *Colección de Documentos Inéditos*, 16:254–56.
5. Hammond and Rey, *Don Juan de Oñate*, 1:319.
6. Simmons, *Last Conquistador*, 96.
7. Hammond and Rey, *Don Juan de Oñate*, 1:320.
8. Ibid.
9. Cyclone Covey, trans. and ed., *Adventures in the Unknown Interior* (Albuquerque: University of New Mexico Press, 1961), offers a translation of Cabeza de Vaca's Relación. Morris Bishop, *The Odyssey of Cabeza de Vaca* (New York: Century, 1933), presents a popular biography of Vaca and his route. Also consulted for this study was the transcript copy of the original manuscript titled Alvar Núñez Cabeza de Vaca, La Relación que Dió Alvar Núñez Cabeza de Vaca de lo Acaecido en las Indias en la Armada donde Yua (Iba) por Governador Pamphilo de Narváez (Valladolid, 1555), which is located in the New York Public Library, New York.
10. Hammond and Rey, *Don Juan de Oñate*.
11. Marcos de Niza, "Relación del Descubrimiento de las Siete Ciudades," in Pacheco, Cárdenas, and Torres de Mendoza, *Colección de Documentos Inéditos*, 3. For an early translation see Hallenbeck, *Journey of Fray Marcos de Niza*; "Report of Fray Marcos de Niza, August 26, 1539," in Hammond and Rey, *Narratives of the Coronado Expedition*, 63–82.
12. Marcos de Niza, "Relación del Descubrimiento." Also see Hammond and Rey, *Narratives of the Coronado Expedition*, 60.
13. Marcos de Niza, "Relación del Descubrimiento." Also see Hammond and Rey, *Narratives of the Coronado Expedition*, 76, 160, 177–78, 197–99.
14. Hallenbeck, *Journey of Fray Marcos de Niza*, 6.
15. Ibid.
16. Ibid.
17. Ibid.
18. Chávez, *Coronado's Friars*, 49–53.
19. Two excellent studies on early New Mexican setters are Chávez, *Origins of New Mexico Families; A Genealogy of the Spanish Colonial Period*; and Snow, *New Mexico's First Colonists*.

20. "Entran los capitanes, Castaño y Bonilla sin orden," in Juan villagutierre Sotomayor, La Conquista, Perdida, y Restuaración del Reino y Provincia de la Nueva Mexico de America Septentrional (1711), No 2759, Libro II, Capitulo 4, folio 100, Biblioteca Nacional de Madrid, Spain.
21. Gallegos, Relación. See Hammond and Rey, *Rediscovery*, 81–82.
22. Ibid., 82.
23. Ibid., 82.
24. Ibid., 82.
25. Ibid., 83.
26. Ibid., 83.
27. Ibid., 84.
28. Ibid., 84.
29. Ibid., 86.
30. Ibid., 87.
31. Ibid., 87.
32. Ibid., 94–96.
33. Ibid., 62, 137.
34. Ibid., 137.
35. Ibid., 107.
36. Ibid., 111.
37. "Antonio de Espejo and the Mexican Inquisition, 1571–1586," in Riley, *Inquisition in Colonial Latin America*, 59.
38. Ibid., 70.
39. Ibid., 63.
40. Ibid., 67, 71, 75.
41. Ibid., 59.
42. Ibid., 73.
43. Ibid., 73.
44. "The Espejo Relación," in Pacheco, Cárdenas, and Torres de Mendoza, *Colección de Documentos Inéditos* (A), 15:101–26, 163–89. See Hammond and Rey, *Rediscovery*, 214.
45. Bolton, *Spanish Exploration*, 163–64.
46. Diego Pérez de Luján's Relación, AGI, Patronato 22. Hammond and Rey, *Rediscovery*, 170.
47. Hammond and Rey, *Rediscovery*, 171.
48. Ibid., 173.
49. Ibid., 172.
50. Ibid., 173.
51. Ibid., 177.

52. Ibid., 179.
53. Ibid., 183.
54. "The Espejo Relación, in Pacheco, Cárdenas, and Torres de Mendoza," *Colección de Documentos Inéditos*, 15:180.
55. Bolton, *Spanish Exploration*, 184, cites a third Indian named Antón, from Guadalajara. Hammond and Rey, *Rediscovery*, 186.
56. Hammond and Rey, *Rediscovery*, 204–6.
57. Ibid., 206–7.

Chapter 3: Strangers on New Mexico's Eastern Plains

1. Memoria del Descubrimiento que Gaspar Castaño de Sosa hizo en el Nuevo Mexico, siendo teniente de Governador y Capitán General del Nuevo Reino de León, vol. 70, expediente 1543, Real Academia de la Historia. Hereafter cited as Castaño de Sosa Memoria, RAH, vol. 70, expediente 1543.
2. Ibid.
3. Ibid.
4. Hammond and Rey, *Rediscovery*, 297.
5. Instrucciones a Juan Morlete, AGI, México, 220.
6. Castaño de Sosa Memoria, RAH, vol. 70, expediente 1543.
7. Ibid.
8. Ibid.
9. Ibid.
10. Ibid.
11. Ibid.
12. Ibid.
13. Ibid.
14. Ibid.
15. Ibid.
16. Ibid.
17. Ibid.
18. Ibid.
19. Ibid.
20. Ibid.
21. Ibid.
22. Ibid.
23. Ibid.
24. Ibid.
25. Ibid.

26. Ibid.
27. Ibid.
28. Ibid.
29. Temkin, *Gaspar Castaño de Sosa*, document 18, 240.
30. Ibid., document 9, 230.
31. Thoma, *Historia Popular*, 49; Bolton, *Spanish Exploration*, 201.
32. "Declaration of Jusepe to Juan de Oñate," in Hammond and Rey, *Rediscovery*, 323.

Chapter 4: The Land of Disenchantment

1. Hammond and Rey, *Don Juan de Oñate*, 1:47.
2. Hammond and Rey, *Don Juan de Oñate*, 2:674.
3. Bolton, *Spanish Exploration*, 201.
4. Ibid.
5. Hammond and Rey, *Rediscovery*, 238n1.
6. Bancroft, *History of Arizona*, 119.
7. The number of people on the expedition cannot be satisfactorily known because not all people were listed. Generally, "essential" Spanish settlers are listed, but information regarding the accountability of servants and other personnel is scant. The best study, Snow's *New Mexico's First Colonists*, accounts for 560 people and identifies as many of them as possible by name. Some estimates, which may include unaccounted-for Nahua-speaking allies, number as high as 800. In his study Snow diligently attempts to account for desertions that took place during and after the settlement reached New Mexico and suffered through the starvation period, 1598–1602.
8. Sánchez, *Río Abajo Frontier*, 54.
9. "The Itinerario de Juan de Oñate," in Pacheco, Cárdenas, and Torres de Mendoza, *Colección de Documentos Inéditos*, 16:242.
10. Ibid., 244.
11. Ibid. The date was May 4, 1598.
12. Ibid., 244–45. The date was May 11, 1598.
13. Ibid., 235. The date was May 11, 1598.
14. Ibid., 247. The date was May 22, 1598.
15. Ibid., 248. The date was May 23, 1598.
16. Ibid., 249.
17. See Sánchez, "Bernardo Gruber."
18. "The Itinerario de Juan de Oñate," in Pacheco, Cárdenas, and Torres de Mendoza, *Colección de Documentos Inéditos*, 16:251.
19. Ibid., 252.
20. Ibid., 252–53.

21. Ibid., 253.
22. Ibid., 256.
23. Ibid., 254.
24. Ibid., 256.
25. Ibid., 254–56.
26. Ibid.
27. *Recopilacion de las Leyes de los Reynos de las Indias* (Madrid, 1681), vol. 2, Libro V, Título II, Ley XXI, "Que ningún Governador, Corregidor, ó Alcalde mayor visite su distrito mas de una vez . . ."
28. "The Itinerario de Juan de Oñate," in Pacheco, Cárdenas, and Torres de Mendoza, *Colección de Documentos Inéditos*, 16:254–56.
29. Ibid., 258.
30. Ibid.
31. Ibid.
32. Ibid.
33. Ibid.
34. Ibid., 228–76.
35. Ibid.
36. Ibid.
37. Ibid., 263.
38. Ibid., 264.
39. Ibid.
40. "Act of Obedience and Vassalage by the Indians of San Juan Bautista," in Hammond and Rey, *Don Juan de Oñate*, 1:342–47.
41. Ibid.
42. Ibid., 342–43.
43. Ibid., 343.
44. Ibid., 344.
45. Ibid., 345–46.
46. Ibid., 346.
47. "Fray Francisco de Escobar's Diary of the Oñate Expedition to California, 1605," in Hammond and Rey, *Don Juan de Oñate*, 2:1013–31. Also see Ronstadt Milich, *Relaciones*, 64.
48. Ibid.

Chapter 5: Death on the Great Plains

1. Hammond and Rey, *Don Juan de Oñate*, 1:417–18.

2. Ibid., 1:59.
3. "Juan de Oñate to Viceroy, Conde de Monterey, March 2, 1599," in Bolton, *Spanish Exploration*, 213.
4. "Declaration of Jusepe to Juan de Oñate," in Hammond and Rey, *Rediscovery*, 323.
5. "Declaration of Jusepe to Juan de Oñate," in Hammond and Rey, *Rediscovery*, 323.
6. Ibid., 324.
7. Ibid.
8. Ibid.
9. Ibid.
10. Hammond and Rey, *Don Juan de Oñate*, 2:650–51.
11. Bolton, *Spanish Exploration*, 237.
12. "Account of the Discovery of the Buffalo, 1599," in Bolton, *Spanish Exploration*, 229n3.
13. "Declaration of Jusepe to Juan de Oñate," in Hammond and Rey, *Rediscovery*, 326. Also see Bolton, *Spanish Explorations*, 224.
14. "Account of the Discovery of the Buffalo, 1599," in Bolton, *Spanish Exploration*, 224.
15. Ibid., 225.
16. Ibid.
17. Ibid., 229.

Chapter 6: The Big Clash

1. Hammond and Rey, *Don Juan de Oñate*, 1:461–62.
2. Ibid., 465.
3. Ibid., 2:650.
4. Ibid., 696.
5. Typically a *fanega* equals approximately 1.6 bushels. Therefore, 50–60 *fanegas* would be about 80–96 bushels.
6. Hammond and Rey, *Don Juan de Oñate*, 2:696.
7. Simmons, *Last Conquistador*, 152.
8. Bolton, *Spanish Exploration*, 233–34.
9. See Encinias, Rodríguez, and Sánchez, *Historia*, 169.
10. Ibid., 165–69.
11. Bancroft, *History of Arizona and New Mexico*, 141–42.
12. Bancroft, *History of Arizona and New Mexico*, 142.

13. Hammond and Rey, *Don Juan de Oñate*, 1:464.
14. Ibid., 465.
15. Ibid., 466.
16. Bancroft, *History of Arizona and New Mexico*, 142.
17. Encinias, Rodríguez, and Sánchez, *Historia*, 217–21.
18. Ibid., 197–98.
19. Taxio's testimony also confirmed the details of the death of Juan de Zaldívar and some of his men. Hammond and Rey, *Don Juan de Oñate*, 1:465–66.
20. Encinias, Rodríguez, and Sánchez, *Historia*, 209–12.
21. Bancroft, *History of Arizona and New Mexico*, 142.
22. Ibid.
23. Ibid.
24. Encinias, Rodríguez, and Sánchez, *Historia*, 223.
25. "Testimony of Alonso Sánchez, February 28, 1599," in Hammond and Rey, *Don Juan de Oñate*, 1:427.
26. "Instructions to the Sargento Mayor for the Punishment of Acoma," in Hammond and Rey, *Don Juan de Oñate*, 1:456–59.
27. Ibid.
28. Ibid.
29. Ibid.
30. "Proceedings at Acoma," in Hammond and Rey, *Don Juan de Oñate*, 1:460.
31. Ibid.
32. Ibid.
33. Ibid.
34. "Testimony of Captain Villagrá," in Hammond and Rey, *Don Juan de Oñate*, 1:470.
35. "Proceedings at Acoma," in Hammond and Rey, *Don Juan de Oñate*, 1:461, 470.
36. The twelve men were Cristóbal Sánchez, Francisco Sánchez, Captain Alonso de Quesada, Juan Piñeiro, Francisco Vázques, Manuel Francisco Cordero, Juan de Pedraza, Martín Alonso Naranjo Carrasco, Juan Rodrigues, Leon de Ysasti, Bernabé de las Casas, and Alonso Gómez Montesinos. Defienden los Yndios el fingido Asalto del segundo Peñol mantienen los doçe castellanos la Guerra en el primero Villagutierre Sotomayor, La Conquista, Perdida y Restoración del Reyno de la Nueva Mexico en la America (1711), capítulo 9, fol. 198r, Archivo del Palacio Real, Madrid. Also see "The Salazar Inspection Muster Roll," in Hammond and Rey, *Don Juan de Oñate*, 1:280–300. The Palacio Real version appears older than the second version in the Biblioteca Nacional, Madrid: Juan de Villagutierre Sotomayor, Historia de la Conquista, Perdida y Restoración del Reyno y Provincia de la Nueva Mexico en la America Septentrional (1711), Manuscritos de America, 2.823.

37. "Proceedings at Acoma," in Hammond and Rey, *Don Juan de Oñate*, 1:462.
38. Ibid. Also see Hammond and Rey, *Don Juan de Oñate*, 2:471, 473, 474, 476, 478.
39. "The Valverde Investigation," in Hammond and Rey, *Don Juan de Oñate*, 2:649.
40. Ibid., 650. "Zaldívar Inquiry," in Hammond and Rey, *Don Juan de Oñate*, 2:784.
41. "Proceedings at Acoma," in Hammond and Rey, *Don Juan de Oñate*, 1:464–68. Indian testimony and other accounts are presented.
42. Ibid., 466–67.
43. Ibid.
44. Ibid., 466.
45. Ibid., 469.
46. Ibid., 477–79. Also see Hammond and Rey, *Don Juan de Oñate*, 2:889, 1127.
47. "Proceedings at Acoma," in Hammond and Rey, *Don Juan de Oñate*, 1:477.
48. Ibid., 477–78.
49. Ibid., 2:615.
50. Ibid., 2:1109, 1114, 1127–28.
51. Simmons, *Last Conquistador*, 151.
52. Hammond and Rey, *Don Juan de Oñate*, 2:650, 862.
53. Simmons, *Last Conquistador*, 150–51.
54. Hammond and Rey, *Don Juan de Oñate*, 2:650. Simmons, *Last Conquistador*, 151.
55. Hammond and Rey, *Don Juan de Oñate*, 2:650
56. Ibid.
57. Ibid., 2:651. Simmons, *Last Conquistador*, 151.
58. Hammond and Rey, *Don Juan de Oñate*, 2:651.
59. Ibid.
60. Ibid.
61. Ibid.
62. Simmons, *Last Conquistador*, 151.
63. Hammond and Rey, *Don Juan de Oñate*, 2:704.
64. Ibid., 705.
65. Ibid. He took it upon himself. See ibid., 795, 793. Zaldívar provided horses and mules to the men. Ibid., 795, 801, 799. Zaldívar led by common agreement. Ibid., 803, 945.
66. Ibid., 708. 706. Also see ibid., 746, 798–99.
67. Simmons, *Last Conquistador*, 151
68. Hammond and Rey, *Don Juan de Oñate*, 2:705; see also 793, 791–92.
69. Ibid., 804.
70. Ibid., 799.
71. See ibid., 787, 789, 792, 793–94, 796. Also see 795–96, 804, 806–7 on Zaldívar's injuries.

72. Ibid., 808.
73. Ibid., 792–93, 796, 806–7.
74. Ibid., 1110, 1115.
75. Ibid., 705.
76. Ibid., 792.
77. Ibid., 803.

Chapter 7: Oñate's Exploration of the Great Plains, 1601

1. Hammond and Rey, *Don Juan de Oñate*, 2:853.
2. Juan de Oñate to Viceroy, Conde de Monterey, March 2, 1599, in Bolton, *Spanish Exploration*, 213.
3. Simmons, *Last Conquistador*, 161.
4. Hammond and Rey, *Juan de Oñate*, 2:951.
5. "True Account of the Expedition of Oñate toward the East, 1601," in Bolton, *Spanish Exploration*, 250–51.
6. Rondstat Milich, *Relaciones*, 58.
7. Bolton, *Spanish Exploration*, 223n5. Bolton noted that Jusepe had declared "that five or six leagues beyond the Pecos, the Humaña party had encountered a great quantity of plums." It appears that Vicente de Zaldívar had also reached the same area in 1599.
8. Rondstat Milich, *Relaciones*, 58.
9. Ibid.
10. Ibid., 58–59.
11. Ibid., 59.
12. Ibid., 49. Bolton, *Spanish Exploration*, 201.
13. Rondstat Milich, *Relaciones*, 59.
14. "True Account of the Expedition of Oñate toward the East, 1601," in Bolton, *Spanish Exploration*, 258. Rondstat Milich, *Relaciones*, 59.
15. "True Account of the Expedition of Oñate toward the East, 1601," in Bolton, *Spanish Exploration*, 258.
16. Ibid., 259.
17. Ibid.
18. Ibid., 261–62. Also see Thoma, *Historia Popular*, 49; Bolton, *Spanish Exploration*, 201.
19. Rondstat Milich, *Relaciones*, 60.
20. "True Account of the Expedition of Oñate toward the East, 1601," in Bolton, *Spanish Exploration*, 262.

21. Ibid., 262–63.
22. Ibid., 263.
23. Ibid.
24. Ibid., 264.
25. Ibid.
26. Rondstat Milich, *Relaciones*, 59–61.
27. "True Account of the Expedition of Oñate toward the East, 1601," in Bolton, *Spanish Exploration*, 267.
28. Ibid., 263.
29. Rondstat Milich, *Relaciones*, 60. Also see Bolton, *Spanish Exploration*, 264n3. Bolton's note reads: "His name was Miguel. He was a captive and according to his own statement a Tancoa. In Mexico he told much about gold, and he drew a map for the factor Vergara, a copy of which from the original, I have in my possession. Father Zárate tells of a map drawn by him in the possession of the Duke of the Infantado, Spain. According to Zárate, his reports induced the king to order the expedition of one thousand men, one-half furnished by a private individual, to be sent to the north country. The viceroy of Monterey, did not think much of Miguel's testimony."
30. Hammond and Rey, *Don Juan de Oñate*, 2:876.
31. Ibid., 874. Also see Bolton, *Spanish Exploration*, 264n3.
32. Hammond and Rey, *Don Juan de Oñate*, 2:848.
33. Ibid., 872.
34. Ibid., 873.
35. Ibid., 874.
36. Ibid., 876.
37. Ibid., 875.
38. Ibid.
39. Ibid., 876.
40. Ibid., 872, 874.
41. Ibid., 875.
42. Ibid., 874.
43. Ibid., 873.
44. Ibid., 874.
45. Ibid., 876.
46. Ibid., 877.
47. Rondstat Milich, *Relaciones*, 61. Zárate Salmerón, "Relaciones."
48. Rondstat Milich, *Relaciones*, 61.

Chapter 8: The Case against Juan de Oñate and Vicente de Zaldívar

1. Simmons, *Last Conquistador*, 194.
2. William H. McNeill, "Mythhistory, or Truth, Myth, History, and Historians," *American Historical Review* 91 (February 1986): 134.
3. Simmons, *Last Conquistador*, 194.
4. Ortiz, "Cruelty Abounds."
5. See Sánchez, *Comparative Colonialism*.
6. Simmons, *Last Conquistador*, 194.
7. Ibid., 195. For a description and history of the route see Sánchez, "La Ruta de Oñate."
8. Simmons, *Last Conquistador*, 195.
9. Cohen, "Little Ice Age." While Cohen discusses the effects of the Little Ice Age on Europe, her model fits New Mexico and the Americas as well.
10. Hammond and Rey, *Don Juan de Oñate*, 2:693.
11. Ibid., 651.
12. Ibid., 651–52.
13. Ibid., 808.
14. Generally, the *cabildo* opened its meetings by announcing its purpose and naming its officials. For example, the Cabildo of San Gabriel of 1603 open its meeting by stating, "Sepan cuanto" that the "Cabildo Justicia Regidores de la Villa de San Gabriel del Nuevo México estando juntos y congregados; en nuestro cabildo, según que lo habemos de vos y costumbre de vos de juntas para tratar cosas locales a cumplideras al dicho cabildo especialmente este estando presente de Capitán Francisco Rascón Alcalde ordinario y hermano de hinojos, y Antonio Gutiérrez, y Gonzalo Hernández y Pedro Sánchez Monroy, y Juan de Medel, Regidores, ya con licencia del Señor Don Juan de Oñate Gobernador Capitán General y el adelantado de éstos Reinos y provincias por su Majestad. Poder otorgado por el Cabildo de la Villa de San Gabriel a favor del Maestre de Campo Vicente de Saldivar y Capitán Gaspar de Villegas," Biblioteca Nacional de Antropología e Historia, Mexico City, Serie Documentos, CA 199.
15. Ibid., 2:697.
16. Ibid., 701.
17. Ibid., 656.
18. Ibid.
19. Ibid., 654.
20. Ibid., 653.
21. Simmons, *Last Conquistador*, 165.
22. Ibid., 653.
23. Ibid., 704.

24. Ibid., 710.
25. Ibid., 698.
26. Ibid., 709.
27. Ibid., 710.
28. Ibid.
29. Ibid., 712.
30. Ibid., 768–69.
31. Ibid., 893.
32. Ibid., 1109.
33. Ibid., 1112–13.
34. Ibid., 1110–11.
35. Calloway, *One Vast Winter Count*, 477n110.
36. Kessell, *Spain in the Southwest*, 84.
37. In her query, Patricia Ortiz supports Kessell's statement by asking, how absolute is the historical judgment that has been passed down historiographically, that is in history books, as opposed to the documentation that is left unclear? See Ortiz, "Cruelty Abounds." Like Kessell, Patricia Ortiz questions the act: "Wasn't it the toes that were cut off, or were the Acoma even mutilated at all? They were able to escape and make their way back home from San Juan Pueblo to Acoma: that was quite a distance to travel in those days."
38. "Plano del puerto de San Francisco situado en la costa de California septentrional . . ." (1793), Museo Naval, Madrid, Spain. Copy in Spanish Colonial Research Center Collection, Center for Southwest Research, Zimmerman Library, University of New Mexico.
39. "Zaldívar Inquiry, 1602," in Hammond and Rey, *Don Juan de Oñate*, 2:796.
40. Ibid.
41. Ibid., 649–50.
42. "The Valverde Investigation," in Hammond and Rey, *Don Juan de Oñate*, 2:650. Also see "Zaldívar Inquiry, 1602," in ibid., 784.
43. "Fray Francisco Pérez Huerta. Relación que el padre predicador Fray Francisco Pérez Guerta de la orden de San Francisco guardian del convento de Galisteo hizo el Reverendismo Comissario General de la dicha orden de la Nueva España de las cosas succedidas en el Nuebo Mexico por los encuentros que tubieron don Pedro de Peralta governador de la dicha provincia y Fray Ysidro Ordoñez, comisario de los frailes de la dicha orden de San Francisco que residen en ella" (ca. 1617), AGN, Inquisición 316 Copy in Center for Southwest Research, Zimmerman Library, University of New Mexico.
44. By way of balancing the historical judgment against Oñate, Ortiz wrote: "Oñate brought the first European settlements to northern New Mexico in what

is today the United States. Simultaneously, he did not exterminate the Natives or exile them as the English did on the East Coast. Oñate also introduced Christianity, still practiced to this day by the Pueblo Indians. Regardless of Oñate's 16th/17th-century cruelties, some of his many credits are that the Pueblos are still in ancient lands where the Spanish found them, he allied with the Pueblos during attacks by nomadic marauding Indians; he introduced Spanish blood, kin, names, traditions and customs, and merged them all into a Pueblo identity; and he practiced human rights more than any other European during the 1600s. Records of that day show that Pueblo Indians were not united and not all were anti-Spanish, with all the introductions the Spanish brought." Ortiz, "Cruelty Abounds."

45. His death is referenced in a series of documents beginning with Poder que dio Juan de Oñate, Adelantado de las Provincias de Nuevo México, visitador General de Minas de España a Andrés de Carrasquilla, su secretario para que tomase el asiento de rendimiento, trabajos y administración de todas las minas del Reino descubierto y por descubrir 1625–1627, AGS, Contadurias Generales 852.

46. Información de la Genealogia y Limpieza de el Maese de Campo Vicente de Zaldívar Vecino de Zacatecas, Archivo Histórico Nacional, Inquisición 1367. Also see Arbol de la Generación de el Capitan General de esta Nueva España que con todo claridad se vee el grado de parentesco, en que se halla cada uno de los que litigan este vinculo formal, AGN, Vínculos 110.

Chapter 9: Pedro de Peralta and the Founding of Santa Fe, 1609–13

1. Pérez Huerta, Relación Verdadera, AGN Inquisición 316.
2. Pérez Huerta, Relación Verdadera, AGN Inquisición 316.
3. Hammond and Rey, *Don Juan de Oñate*, 2:1040.
4. Ibid., 1076.
5. Ibid., 1043.
6. Ibid., 1043.
7. Ibid., 894–95, 969.
8. Ibid., 1040, 1042.
9. Ibid., 1048.
10. Ibid., 1050.
11. Ibid., 1051.
12. Ibid., 1051.
13. Ibid., 1092.
14. Ivey, "Viceroy's Order," 101.
15. For example, the series of laws and ordinances in tomo II, libro IV, titulo VIII, "De las Ciudades, y Villas," stipulate that villas, for example, would be seats

of superior government and their exemptions and privileges would be preserved. *Recopilación de Leyes.*

16. Instrucciones de el Virrey don Luis de Velasco a Pedro de Peralta, 30 de Marzo de 1609, AGI, Audiencia de Mexico 27; and Hammond and Rey, *Don Juan de Oñate*, 2:1087–1091.

17. Instrucciones de el Virrey don Luis de Velasco; and Hammond and Rey, *Don Juan de Oñate*, 2:1087–88.

18. Instrucciones de el Virrey don Luis de Velasco; and Hammond and Rey, *Don Juan de Oñate*, 2:1088.

19. Instrucciones de el Virrey don Luis de Velasco; and Hammond and Rey, *Don Juan de Oñate*, 2:1087.

20. Instrucciones de el Virrey don Luis de Velasco; and Hammond and Rey, *Don Juan de Oñate*, 2:1088–89.

21. Instrucciones de el Virrey don Luis de Velasco; and Hammond and Rey, *Don Juan de Oñate*, 2:1089.

22. Instrucciones de el Virrey don Luis de Velasco; and Hammond and Rey, *Don Juan de Oñate*, 2:1090.

23. Instrucciones de el Virrey don Luis de Velasco; and Hammond and Rey, *Don Juan de Oñate*, 2:1090.

24. Instrucciones de el Virrey don Luis de Velasco; and Hammond and Rey, *Don Juan de Oñate*, 2:1090.

25. Hammond and Rey, *Don Juan de Oñate*, 2:1090.

26. Fray Francisco Pérez Huerta, Relación verdadera que el padre predicador Fray Francisco Pérez Guerta de la orden de San Frencisco guardian del convento de Galisteo hizo al Reverendisimo Comisario General de la dicha orden de la Nueva España de las cosas succedidas en el Nuebo Mexico por los encuentros que tubieron don Pedro de Peralta governador de la dicha provincia y Fray Ysidro Ordoñez, comisario de los Frailes de la dicha orden de San Francisco que residen en ella (ca. 1617), AGN, Inquisición 316. Also see the pioneering historical work by Scholes, *Church and State in New Mexico*.

27. Pérez Huerta, Relación verdadera, AGN, Inquisición 316.

28. Ibid.

29. Ibid.

30. Ibid.

31. Ibid.

32. Ibid.

33. Ibid.

34. For the rest of the seventeenth century in New Mexico, see Scholes, *Troublous Times.*

35. Pérez Huerta, Relación verdadera, AGN, Inquisición 316.
36. Ibid.
37. Ibid.
38. Ibid.
39. Scholes and Bloom, "Friar Personnel and Mission Chronology."
40. Peinado to the Viceroy, Chililí, October 4, 1622, AGI, Civil 77, exp. 4.
41. Pérez Huerta, Relación verdadera, AGN, Inquisición 316.
42. Ibid.
43. Ibid.
44. Ibid.
45. Ibid.
46. Ibid.
47. Ibid.
48. Ibid.
49. Ibid.
50. Ibid.
51. Ibid.
52. Ibid.
53. Ibid.
54. Ibid.

Chapter 10: Showdown in Santa Fe

1. Pérez Huerta, Relación verdadera, AGN, Inquisición 316.
2. Ibid.
3. Chávez, *Origins of New Mexico Families*, 105.
4. Pérez Huerta, Relación verdadera, AGN, Inquisición 316.
5. Ibid.
6. Ibid.
7. Ibid.
8. Ibid.
9. Ibid.
10. Ibid.
11. Ibid.
12. Ibid.
13. Ibid.
14. Ibid.
15. Ibid.
16. Ibid.

17. Ibid.
18. Ibid.
19. Ibid.
20. Ibid.
21. Ibid.
22. Ibid.
23. Ibid.
24. Ibid.
25. Ibid.
26. Ibid.
27. Ibid.
28. Ibid.
29. Chávez, *Origins of New Mexico Families*, 28–29.
30. Pérez Huerta, Relación verdadera, AGN, Inquisición 316.
31. Ibid.
32. Chávez, *Origins of New Mexico Families*, 110; Pérez Huerta, Relación verdadera, AGN, Inquisición 316.
33. Pérez Huerta, Relación verdadera, AGN, Inquisición 316.
34. Ibid.
35. Ibid.
36. Ibid.
37. Ibid.
38. Ibid.
39. Ibid.
40. Ibid.
41. Ibid.
42. Ibid.
43. Chávez, *Origins of New Mexico Families*, 63.
44. Pérez Huerta, Relación verdadera, AGN, Inquisición 316.
45. Ibid.
46. Chávez, *Origins of New Mexico Families*, 95.
47. Pérez Huerta, Relación verdadera, AGN, Inquisición 316.
48. Ibid.
49. Ibid.
50. Ibid.
51. Ibid.
52. Ibid.
53. Ibid.
54. Ibid.

55. Ibid.
56. Ibid.
57. Ibid.
58. Ibid.
59. Ibid.; Chávez, *Origins of New Mexico Families*, 87.
60. Pérez Huerta, Relación verdadera, AGN, Inquisición 316.
61. Ibid.
62. Ibid.
63. Ibid.
64. Ibid.
65. Ibid.
66. Ibid.
67. Ibid.
68. Ibid.
69. Chávez, *Origins of New Mexico Families*, 14.
70. Pérez Huerta, Relación verdadera, AGN, Inquisición 316.
71. Ibid.
72. Ibid.
73. Ibid.
74. Ibid.
75. Ibid.
76. Ibid.
77. Ibid.
78. Ibid.
79. Ibid.
80. Ibid.
81. Ibid.
82. Ibid.
83. Ibid.
84. Ibid.
85. Ibid.
86. Ibid.
87. Ibid.
88. Ibid.
89. Ibid.
90. Ibid.
91. Ibid.
92. Ibid.
93. Ibid.

94. Ibid.
95. Ibid.
96. Ibid.
97. Ibid.
98. Ibid.
99. Ibid.
100. Ibid.
101. Ibid.
102. Ibid.
103. Scholes, *Church and State in New Mexico*, 38.

Chapter 11: La Custodia de la Conversión de San Pablo

1. Bloom, "Esteban de Perea," 226.
2. Pérez Huerta, Relación verdadera, AGN, Inquisición 316.
3. Ibid.
4. Ibid.
5. Ibid.
6. *Recopilacion de Leyes*. See tomo II, libro VI, titulo IX, Ley XI: Que ningún Encomendero tenga casa en su Pueblo ni este en el mas de una noche.
7. Pérez Huerta, Relación verdadera, AGN, Inquisición 316.
8. Ibid.
9. Ibid.
10. Ibid.
11. Ibid.
12. Ibid.
13. Hodge, Hammond and Rey, *Fray Alonso de Benavides' Revised Memorial of 1634*, 126–37. Forrestal, *Benavides' Memorial of 1630*, x–xi.
14. See Hubert Howe Bancroft, *History of Arizona and New Mexico, 1530–1888* (San Francisco: The History Company, 1889), 133, 145. Also see Miguel Encinias, Alfred Rodríguez, and Joseph P. Sánchez, eds. and trans., *Historia de la Nueva México: A Critical and Annotated Spanish/Edition by Gaspar Pérez de Villagrá* (Albuquerque: University of New Mexico Press, 1992), 298–99.
15. Simmons, *Last Conquistador*, 173. "Journey of Juan de Oñate to California by Land by Gerónimo Zarate Salmeron," in Bolton, *Spanish Exploration*, 278. "Fray Francisco de Escobar's Diary of the Oñate Expedition to California, 1605," in Hammond and Rey, *Don Juan de Oñate*, 2:1013–31.
16. Report of the Inquistion of Llerna, Spain, October 28, 1630, AGN, Inquisición 268, exp. 5.

17. Pérez Huerta, Relación verdadera, AGN, Inquisición 316.
18. For a summary of Friar Perea's career in New Mexico, see Scholes, "Church and State in New Mexico," 146–65, 283–303; and Scholes, "First Decade of the Inquisition," 195–228.
19. See Scholes, "Church and State in New Mexico," 146–65, 283–303; and Scholes, "First Decade of the Inquisition," 195–228.
20. Ibid.
21. Ibid.
22. Ibid.
23. Hodge, Hammond, and Rey, *Fray Alonso de Benavides' Revised Memorial*, 256–70.
24. Pérez Huerta, Relación verdadera, AGN, Inquisición 316.
25. Pérez Huerta, Relación verdadera, AGN, Inquisición 316.
26. Ibid.
27. Ibid.
28. Declaración de Fray Pedro Zambrano Ortiz, August, 18, 1621, AGN, Inquisición 356. Also see Scholes, "Church and State in New Mexico," 167–69.
29. Hodge, Hammond, and Rey, *Fray Alonso de Benavides' Revised Memorial*, 268. Hereafter cited as *Revised Memorial*.
30. Declaración de Fray Pedro Zambrano Ortiz, August, 18, 1621, AGN, Inquisición 356. Also see Scholes, "Church and State in New Mexico," 169.
31. Hodge, Hammond, and Rey, *Revised Memorial*, 256–70.
32. Fray Pedro de Zambrano Ortiz to Viceroy, October 7, 1622, AGN, Inquisición, 356.
33. Scholes, "Church and State in New Mexico," 155.
34. "De los Protectores de Indios," *Recopilación de Leyes*, tomo II, libro VI, titulo 6, fol. 217.
35. Scholes, "Church and State in New Mexico," 155.
36. Ibid., 146.
37. Ibid., 145–62.
38. Ibid.
39. Ibid.
40. Ibid.
41. Ibid.
42. Ibid.
43. Ibid.
44. Ibid.
45. Ibid.
46. Ibid., 154–55.
47. Ibid.

48. Ibid., 145–62.
49. Ibid., 155.
50. Ibid.
51. Ibid.
52. Ibid.
53. Ibid., 156–60.
54. Ibid., 160.
55. Hodge, Hammond, and Rey, *Revised Memorial*, 250, presents a biographical sketch of Father Arvide in New Mexico.
56. Ibid., 78.
57. Ibid., 78–79.
58. Ibid.
59. See Rondstat Milich, *Relaciones*.
60. Editorial notes in Hackett, Bandelier, and Bandelier, *Historical Documents*, 3:283.
61. "Life and Happy Death of the Blessed Father, Fray Pedro de Ortega," in Hackett, Bandelier, and Bandelier, *Historical Documents*, 3:97.
62. Ibid.
63. Ibid.
64. Ibid., 98, 283. Also see Scholes and Bloom, "Friar Personal and Mission Chronology."
65. Scholes and Bloom, "Friar Personal and Mission Chronology."

Chapter 12: Benavides's Halation of New Mexico

1. Hodge, Hammond, and Rey, *Revised Memorial*, 100.
2. Hodge, Hammond, and Rey, *Revised Memorial*, 100.
3. Ibid.
4. Ibid., 101.
5. Ibid.
6. Ibid.
7. Ibid., 102.
8. Ibid.
9. Ibid.
10. Ibid.
11. Ibid., 103.
12. Ibid., 102.
13. Sánchez, "El Farol Indiano," 53.
14. Hodge, Hammond, and Rey, *Revised Memorial*, 127–29, 97–99.
15. Ibid., 104.

16. Ibid., 65–66.
17. Ibid.
18. Ibid., 65.
19. For a representation of friars at the Salinas missions see Vetancurt, *Menológio*, 278–79.
20. Hodge, Hammond, and Rey, *Revised Memorial*, 66.
21. See "Diego Pérez de Luxan's Account of the Antonio de Espejo Expedition into New Mexico, 1582," in Hammond and Rey, *Rediscovery*, 157–69.
22. Rondstat Milich, *Relaciones*, 58–59.
23. Hodge, Hammond, and Rey, *Revised Memorial*, 66–67.
24. Ibid., 66.
25. Ibid., 92.
26. Ibid., 93.
27. Ibid., 93–94.
28. Ibid., 94.
29. Ibid.
30. Ibid.
31. Ibid.
32. Ibid.
33. Ibid.
34. Ibid., 95.
35. Ibid.
36. "Tanto que sacó de una carta, May 15, 1631. This much was extracted from a letter that the Reverend Father Fray Alonso de Benavides, former Custodian for New Mexico, sent to the friars of the Holy Custodia of the Conversion of Saint Paul in the said Kingdom [of New Mexico], Madrid 1631," in Hodge, Hammond, and Rey, *Revised Memorial*, 138.
37. Ibid., 140–41.
38. Ibid., 141.
39. Ibid., 140.
40. Ibid.
41. Ibid.
42. Ibid., 141.
43. Hodge, Hammond, and Rey, *Revised Memorial*, 88–91.
44. Ibid., 89–90.
45. Roque de Casaus, secretario de guerra y gobernación, Villa de Santa Fe, a 8 dias del mes de octubre de 1629, Biblioteca Nacional, Madrid, ms. 3048, fols. 71–73.
46. For both views on Ortega's death see Hodge, Hammond, and Rey, *Revised Memorial*, 99, 164.

47. Ibid.
48. Forrester, *Benavides Memorial of 1630*, 46.
49. See Bloom, "Estaban de Perea."
50. Ibid., 222.
51. Ibid.
52. Hodge, Hammond, and Rey, *Revised Memorial*, 72, 241.
53. Ibid., 73.
54. Ibid., 72.
55. Bloom, "Estaban de Perea," 227.
56. Ibid., also 213.
57. Ibid., 228.
58. For referenced annotations and translations of Spanish inscriptions at El Morro National Monument see Joseph P. Sánchez, Jerry L. Gurulé, and Larry D. Miller, "Paso por Aquí." (unpublished manuscript on file at El Morro National Monument, National Park Service, 2003), Governor Silva Nieto's inscription is on panel number JJ-3.
59. Hodge, Hammond, and Rey, *Revised Memorial*, 74.
60. Ibid.
61. Ibid., 214.
62. Bloom, "Estéban de Perea," 227. Also see Hodge, Hammond, and Rey, *Revised Memorial*, 213–14.
63. Hodge, Hammond and Rey, *Revised Memorial*, 75.
64. Ibid., 77, 301. See also original Spanish version of the following translated quotations in Benavides Memorial de 1634, Biblioteca de la Universidad y Provincia de Zaragoza, no. 2969. Copy in Center for Southwest Research Zimmerman Library, University of New Mexico. Hereafter cited as Benevides Memorial, no. 2969.
65. Hodge, Hammond, and Rey, *Revised Memorial*, 300–301. Benavides Memorial, no. 2969.
66. Hodge, Hammond, and Rey, *Revised Memorial*, 298. Benavides Memorial, no. 2969.
67. Hodge, Hammond, and Rey, *Revised Memorial*, 75, 298. Benavides Memorial, no. 2969.
68. Hodge, Hammond, and Rey, *Revised Memorial*, 217. Benavides Memorial, no. 2969.
69. Hodge, Hammond, and Rey, *Revised Memorial*, 217. Benavides Memorial, no. 2969.
70. Hodge, Hammond, and Rey, *Revised Memorial*, 300–301. Benavides Memorial, no. 2969.

71. Hodge, Hammond, and Rey, *Revised Memorial*, 217. Benavides Memorial, no. 2969.

72. Hodge, Hammond, and Rey, *Revised Memorial*, 217–18. Benavides Memorial, no. 2969.

73. Hodge, Hammond, and Rey, *Revised Memorial*, 218. Benavides Memorial, no. 2969.

74. Hodge, Hammond, and Rey, *Revised Memorial*, 77. Benavides Memorial, no. 2969.

75. Hodge, Hammond, and Rey, t *Revised Memorial*, 79. Benavides Memorial, no. 2969.

76. Hodge, Hammond, and Rey, *Revised Memorial*, 89. Benavides Memorial, no. 2969.

77. Hodge, Hammond, and Rey, *Revised Memorial*, 79. Benavides Memorial, no. 2969.

78. Hodge, Hammond, and Rey, *Revised Memorial*, 86. Benavides Memorial, no. 2969.

79. Hodge, Hammond, and Rey, *Revised Memorial*, 86. Benavides Memorial, no. 2969.

80. Hodge, Hammond, and Rey, *Revised Memorial*, 86. Benavides Memorial, no. 2969.

81. Hodge, Hammond, and Rey, *Revised Memorial*, 87. Benavides Memorial, no. 2969.

82. Hodge, Hammond, and Rey, *Revised Memorial*, 87. Benavides Memorial, no. 2969.

83. Hodge, Hammond, and Rey, *Revised Memorial*, 87. Benavides Memorial, no. 2969.

84. Hodge, Hammond, and Rey, *Revised Memorial*, 87. Benavides Memorial, no. 2969.

85. Hodge, Hammond, and Rey, *Revised Memorial*, 87. Benavides Memorial, no. 2969.

86. Hodge, Hammond, and Rey, *Revised Memorial*, 87. Benavides Memorial, no. 2969.,

87. Hodge, Hammond, and Rey, *Revised Memorial*, 87. Benavides Memorial, no. 2969.

88. Hodge, Hammond, and Rey, *Revised Memorial*, 87.

89. Ibid., 89. Benavides Memorial, no. 2969.

90. Hodge, Hammond, and Rey, *Revised Memorial*, 88. Benavides Memorial, no. 2969.

91. Hodge, Hammond, and Rey, *Revised Memorial*, 198.

92. Ibid., 197.
93. Ibid., 199.
94. Ibid., 204.
95. Ibid., 257.
96. Ibid., 257.
97. Ibid., 257.
98. Ibid., 257.
99. See ibid., 249.
100. Ibid., 264.
101. Ibid.
102. Ibid.,
103. When Governor Bernardo López Mendizábal visited Alamillo, Acevedo's contemporaries reckoned he was ninety years old. See documents on López Mendizábal's inspection tour of 1659 in Fray Miguel de Guevara's corroborating testimony against Cristóbal de Anaya, and testimony of Francisco Gomez in Primera Audiencia de don Bernardo López de Mendizábal, 1662, AGN, Inquisición 593. Capitulaciones, capítulo 31, El Fiscal contra López de Mendizábal, 1663, AGN, Inquisición 594; corroborating testimony of Francisco Gomez, El Fiscal contra López de Mendizábal, AGN, Inquisición 593. Capitulaciones, capítulo 32 and 33, El Fiscal contra López de Mendizábal, 1663, AGN, Inquisición 594. Capitulaciones, capítulo 31, El Fiscal contra López de Mendizábal, 1663, AGN, Inquisición 594.
104. Hodge, Hammond, and Rey, *Revised Memorial*, 264.

Chapter 13: Governors, Missionaries, Kachinas, and the Holy Office of the Inquisition, 1634–59

1. Proceso contra Mendizábal, 1662, AGN, Inquisición, 593.
2. Proceso contra Mendizábal, 1662, AGN, Inquisición, 593
3. Proceso contra Mendizábal, 1663, AGN, Inquisición 594.
4. Scholes, *Church and State in New Mexico*, 115.
5. Información hecha en las Provincias del Nuebo Mexico en virtud de Patente del Reverendísimo Padre, fray Juan de Prada, Comisario General de las Provinicas de Nueba España, por el Padre Predicador, fray Tomas Manso, Custodio, sobreagravios hechos a los religiosos de San Francisco que estan en dicho Nuebo Mexico por el Governador d. Luis Rosas, Año 1644, AGI, Patronato 244, ramo 7. Also see Scholes, *Church and State in New Mexico*, 117.
6. Scholes, "Church and State in New Mexico," 297–340.
7. Scholes, *Church and State in New Mexico*, 134.
8. Ibid., 135–36.

9. Ibid., 136.
10. Ibid., 137–38.
11. Ibid., 155.
12. Ibid. Also see Scholes, "Church and State in New Mexico," 336–37.
13. Death of Governor Rosas at the hands of Nicolás Ortíz, AGI, Patronato 244. Copy in Spanish Colonial Research Center Collection, Center for Southwest Research, Zimmerman Library, University of New Mexico, Microfilm Roll 1, frames 246–47. Scholes, *Church and State in New Mexico*, 155. Also see Scholes, "Church and State in New Mexico," 337.
14. Scholes, *Church and State in New Mexico*, 163. Also see Scholes, "Church and State in New Mexico," 337–40.
15. Scholes, *Church and State in New Mexico*, 163.
16. Scholes, "Church and State in New Mexico," 83–84.
17. Ibid., 82–83, 93–94.
18. Ibid., 84–86.
19. Scholes, *Troublous Times*, 2.
20. López Mendizábal Genealogy, Primera Audiencia, Proceso contra Mendizábal, AGN, Inquisición 594, fols. 1–2.
21. Ibid.
22. Ibid., fol. 3.
23. Ibid.
24. Ibid., fol. 1.
25. Ibid., fol. 3.
26. Ibid., fol. 1.
27. Ibid.
28. Proposción 5, Proceso contra López de Mendizábal, AGN, Inquisición 593, fol. 252.
29. Testigo de Fray Benito de la Navidad, Proceso contra López de Mendizábal, AGN, Inquisición 593, fol. 208.
30. Testigo de Luisa Diaz de Betansos y Castro, Socorro, April 30, 1662, Proceso contra Mendizábal, AGN, Inquisición 593.
31. Ibid.
32. Capitulo 181, Proceso contra López de Mendizabal, AGN, Inquisición 594. Also Sacada para el Proceso de Francisco Gomez, AGN, Inquisición 593.
33. Sacada para el Proceso de Francisco Gomez, AGN, Inquisición 593. Declaration of Joseph Nieto, Santo Domingo, January 19, 1667, AGN, Inquisición 666, fol. 375. The entire case against Governor Bernardo López de Mendízabal is found chiefly in AGN, Inquisición 593 and 594. Other Inquisición records repeat similar information or testimonies. Also see Proceso contra Aguilar, 1661–1665, AGN,

Inquisición 512. The acknowledged pioneering authority on seventeenth-century New Mexico is France V. Scholes. See Scholes, *Church and State in New Mexico*, and *Troublous Times in New Mexico*. The present study follows a similar story line to that in *Troublous Times* but differs in the opinion presented by Scholes, who followed what can be construed as biased arguments made by seventeenth-century Franciscan missionaries against López Mendizábal, Aguilar, and others.

34. Sacada para el Proceso de Francisco Gomes, AGN, Inquisición 593. Declaration of Joseph Nieto, Santo Domingo, January 19, 1667, AGN, Inquisición 666, fol. 375.

35. Capitulo 180, Proceso contra Mendizabal, AGN, Inquisición 594. Also see Proceso contra Ramirez, AGN, Inquisición 502, for the many charges brought against him, including the testimony of Don Bernardo López de Mendízabal against Fray Juan Ramírez del Orden de Señor San Francisco, whose testimony in his defense was admitted against Fr. Ramírez.

36. Scholes, "Civil Government," 93. Also see Scholes, *Troublous Times*, 40.

37. As a companion to the present essay and for a fuller account of Aguilar's actions and the inquisitorial case against him, see Joseph P. Sánchez, "Nicolas de Aguilar y la Jurisdicción de las Salinas, 1654–1661," *Revista Complutense de Historia de America* 22 (1996), 139–59.

38. Scholes, "Civil Government," 93. Also see Scholes, *Troublous Times*, 40.

39. Causa de denunciación por querella que dió Nicolas de Aguilar contra Sebastian de la Canal y otras personas sobre averlo derrumbado un pilar de su mina, 11 de marzo de 1641, Archivo Historico de Parral, Sección Causas Criminales, año 1641.

40. Causa criminal contra Nicolas de Aguilar por homicidio cometido en la persona de Germando de Villagomez en San Diego de Minas Nuevas, Archivo Historico de Parral, Sección Causas Criminales, año 1654.

41. Causa criminal contra Nicolas de Aguilar por homicidio cometido en la persona de Germando de Villagomez en San Diego de Minas Nuevas, Archivo Historico de Parral, Sección Causas Criminales, año 1654.

42. Causa criminal contra Nicolas de Aguilar por homicidio cometido en la persona de Germando de Villagomez en San Diego de Minas Nuevas, Archivo Historico de Parral, Sección Causas Criminales, año 1654.

43. Información hecha en las Provincias del Nuebo Mexico en virtud de Patente del Reverendísimo Padre, fray Juan de Prada, Comisario General de las Provinicas de Nueba España, por el Padre Predicador, fray Tomas Manso, Custodio, sobreagravios hechos a los religiosos de San Francisco que estan en dicho Nuebo Mexico por el Governador d. Luis Rosas, Año 1644, AGI, Patronato 244, ramo 7.

44. *Recopilación de Leyes*, tomo II, libro V, titulo II, Ley X.

45. Ibid., tomo II, libro V, titulo II, Ley XV and Ley XXI.

46. Ibid.

47. Fray Miguel de Guevara, corroborating testimony against Cristóbal de Anaya, and testimony of Francisco Gomez in Primera Audiencia de don Bernardo López de Mendizábal, 1662, AGN, Inquisición 593. Capitulaciones, capítulo 31, El Fiscal contra López de Mendizábal, 1663, AGN, lnquisición 594, and corroborating testimony of Francisco Gomez, El Fiscal contra López de Mendizábal, AGN, Inquisición 593. Capitulaciones, capítulo 32 and 33, El Fiscal contra López de Mendizábal, 1663, AGN, Inquisición 594. Capitulaciones, capítulo 31, El Fiscal contra López de Mendizábal¡, 1663, AGN, lnquisición 594.

48. AGN, Inquisición 593.
49. AGN, Inquisición 593.
50. AGN, Inquisición 593.
51. AGN, Inquisición 593.
52. AGN, Inquisición 593.
53. AGN, Inquisición 593.
54. Vetancurt, *Menológio*, 260.
55. Vetancurt, *Menológio*. Fray Miguel de Guevara, corroborating testimony against Cristóbal de Anaya, and testimony of Francisco Gomez, Primera Audiencia de don Bernardo López de Mendizábal, 1662, AGN, Inquisición 593. Also see Capitulaciones, capítulo 31, El Fiscal contra López de Mendizábal, 1663, AGN, lnquisición 594, and corroborating testimony of Francisco Gomez, El Fiscal contra López de Mendizábal, AGN, Inquisición 593. Capitulaciones, capítulo 32 and 33, El Fiscal contra López de Mendizábal, 1663, AGN, Inquisición 594. Capitulaciones, capítulo 31, El Fiscal contra López de Mendizába¡, 1663, AGN, lnquisición 594.

56. Hackett, Bandelier, and Bandelier, *Historical Documents*, 3:147.

57. These and other alleged pronouncements by López Mendizábal formed the complaints against him by the friars as discussed in Proceso contra Mendizabal, AGN, Inquisición 593 and 594.

58. Declaración de Fray Nicolas de Freitas, Proceso contra Nicolas de Aguilar, AGN, Inquisisción 512.

59. Declaración de Fray Nicolas de Freitas, Proceso contra Nicolas de Aguilar, AGN, Inquisisción 512.

60. Proceso contra Mendizábal, AGN, Inquisición 593, fol. 182. Scholes, *Troublous Times*, 54.

61. Acusaciones, capitulo 4, Proceso contra Nicolas de Aguilar, AGN, Inquisición 512.

62. Ibid.

63. Declaración signed by Fray Jacinto de Guebara, Juan Ortis de los Heros, Fr. R° de Medenilla, Proceso contra Mendizábal, AGN, Inquisición 593.

64. Declaración (presented on February 28, 1660) signed by Fray Jacinto de Guebara, Juan Ortis de los Heros, Fr. R° de Medenilla, Proceso contra Mendizábal, AGN, Inquisición 593.

65. Declaración signed by Francisco Monte, Escribano Real, February 26, 1660, Proceso contra López de Mendizábal, AGN, Inquisicion 593, fol. 254.

66. All charges listed in Proceso contra Nicolas de Aguilar, AGN, Inquisición 512.

67. Acusaciones, capitulo 6, (also see Contestaciones, capitulo6), Proceso contra Aguilar, AGN, Inquisición 512. Letter from Fray Nicolas de Freitas to Fray Garcia de San Francisco, visecustodio del Nuevo México, June 15, 1660, Quarac, Proceso contra Aguilar, AGN, Inquisición 512; and Proposiciones y Hechos que se han de calificar, tercera proposición, signed by Dr. don Juan Saenz de Mañozca, July 29, 1661, Proceso contra Aguilar, AGN, Inquisición 512.

68. Acusaciones, capitulo 6, Proceso contra Aguilar, AGN, Inquisición 512.

69. El Fiscal contra Aguilar, Proceso contra Aguilar, AGN, Inquisición 512, fols. 4 and 108; and Acusaciones, capitulos 6–8, Proceso contra Aguilar. See Fray Nicolas de Freitas to Fray Garcia de San Francisco, vise-custodio del Nuevo México, June 15, 1660, Quarac, Proceso contra Aguilar, AGN, Inquisición 512.

70. Acusaciones, capítulo 7; El Fiscal contra Aguilar, Proceso contra Aguilar, AGN, Inquisición 512, fol. 108.

71. Acusaciones, capítulo 8; El Fiscal contra Aguilar, Proceso contra Aguilar, AGN, Inquisición 512, fol. 108.

72. Testigo 5, capítulo 22, Proceso contra Aguilar, AGN, Inquisición, 512, fol. 146.

73. Ibid.; and Acusaciones, capítulo 9, Proceso contra Aguilar, AGN Inquisición 512.

74. Testigo 7, capítulo 2, El Fiscal contra Aguilar, Proceso contra Aguilar, AGN, Inquisición 512, fol. 146. Testigo 8, capítulo 22, El Fiscal contra Aguilar, Proceso contra Aguilar, AGN, Inquisición, 512, fol. 147.

75. Testigo 7, capítulo 2, El Fiscal contra Aguilar, Proceso contra Aguilar, AGN, Inquisición 512, fol. 161. Testimony of Juan Manso, Proceso contra Aguilar, AGN, Inquisición 512, fol. 19. Declaración de Juan Manso, Thursday, January 13, 1661, Proceso contra Aguilar, AGN, Inquisición 512.

76. Capítulo 9, Proceso contra Aguilar, AGN, Inquisición 512, fol. 179. Also Sentencia de Nicolas de Aguilar, Secretario Ibañez, El Fiscal contra Aguilar, Proceso contra Aguilar, AGN, Inquisición 512, fol. 210.

77. Testificación de Ysabel Baca, Proceso contra Aguilar, AGN, Inquisición 512. Also see Declaración de Fray Fernando de Velasco, Proceso contra Aguilar, AGN, Inquisición, 512, fol. 4. Also see Testigo 3, capítulo 1, El Fiscal contra Aguilar, Proceso contra Aguilar, AGN, Inquisición 512, fol. 142.

78. Testificación de Ysabel Baca, Proceso contra Aguilar, AGN Inquisición 512. Also see Declaración de Fray Fernando de Velasco, Proceso contra Aguilar, AGN,

Inquisición, 512, fol. 4. Proceso contra Aguilar, Testigo 18, capítulo 14, AGN 512, fol. 176.

79. Declaración de Fray Fernando de Velasco, Proceso contra Aguilar, AGN, Inquisición, 512, fol. 4.

80. Ibid.

81. Testigo 2, capítulo 4, Proceso contra Aguilar, AGN, Inquisición 512, fol. 141.

82. Capítulo 9, Proceso contra Aguilar, AGN, Inquisición 512, fol. 179. Also Sentencia de Nicolas de Aguilar, Secretario Ibañez, El Fiscal contra Aguilar, Proceso contra Aguilar, AGN, Inquisición 512, fol. 210.

83. Testigo 9, capítulo 14, Proceso contra Aguilar, AGN Inquisición 512, fol. 164; Also see Testigo 2, capítulo 1, Proceso contra Aguilar, AGN, Inquisición 512, f 156; and Testigo 2, capítulo 7, Proceso contra Aguilar, AGN, Inquisición 512, fols. 156–57.

84. The "protector y defensor de naturales cristianos" for the New Mexico pueblos under López de Mendízabal was Antonio Gonzáles. See various references to Gonzáles for October 5–29, 1661, in AGN, Sección Tierras 3268.

85. Declaración de Fray Nicolas de Freitas, Monday, February 21, 1661, Proceso contra Aguilar, AGN, Inquisición 512. Also see capítulo 23, Proceso contra Aguilar, AGN, Inquisición 512.

86. Capitulos 175–76, Proceso contra López de Mendízabal, AGN, Inquisición 594.

87. Corroborating testimony taken from Proceso contra Doña Theresa de Aguilera de la Rocha, Proceso contra Mendízábal, AGN, Inquisición 593. Also see Fray Nicolas Chaves, San Buenaventura, Proceso contra Mendízábal, AGN, Inquisición 593.

88. "Disen estos Picaros friales que esto es malo no es malo sino muy bueno," said López Mendízábal. Proceso contra Mendízabal, AGN, Inquisición 593.

89. Declaración de Fray Diego de Santander, Proceso contra Mendízabal, AGN, Inquisición 593, fol. 172.

90. Declaración del Capitán Juan Griego, November 1, 1661, Proceso contra Mendízabal, AGN, Inquisición 593, fol. 202.

91. Declaración de Juan Pérez Granillo, April 22, 1662, Proceso contra Mendízabal, AGN, Inquisición 593, f 238.

92. Declaración de Capitán Juan de Barela, Proceso contra Mendízabal, AGN, Inquisición 593, f.145.

93. Ibid.

94. Declaración de Nicolas de Aguilar, Proceso contra Aguilar, AGN, Inquisición 512, ff.103–4.

95. Capítulo 3, Proceso contra Aguilar, AGN, Inquisición 512.

96. Declaración de Fray Fernando de Velasco, Proceso contra Aguilar, AGN, Inquisición 512, fol. 5. Capítulo 11, Proceso contra Aguilar, AGN, Inquisición 512.

97. Declaración de Fray Fernando de Velasco, Proceso contra Aguilar, AGN, Inquisición 512, fol. 5.
98. Declaración de Francisco de Valencia, Proceso contra Aguilar, AGN, Inquisición 512, fol. 58. Also see capítulo 17, Proceso contra Aguilar, Inquisición 512.
99. Declaración de Francisco de Valencia, Proceso contra Aguilar, AGN, Inquisición 512, fol. 58.
100. Declaración de Capitán Hernando Serrano, March 6, 1662, Proceso contra Mendízabal, AGN, Inquisición 593, fol. 221.
101. Scholes, *Troublous Times*, 129.
102. A separate case was filed against López Mendizábal's wife, Doña Teresa Aguilera y Rocha. See González and Levine, "In Her Own Voice."
103. Certificacion del fallecimiento de Don Bernardo Lopez de Mendízábal, Proceso contra Mendizábal, AGN, Inquisición 594. Also see *auto* signed by Dr. D. Pedro Medina Rico. He also noted that López Mendízábal had regularly confessed his sins to a priest on a weekly basis and had done so just before his death. That he had done so—that is, died pure of sin—likely helped in his posthumous exoneration in the review of his case in 1671.
104. Certificación de la muerte de Don Bernardo Lopez y de a donde está enterrado, Proceso contra Mendizabal, AGN, Inquisición 594. Also see Certificación de haverse enterado los guesos de Don Bernardo Lopez de Mendízábal en sepultura eclesiastica, Proceso contra Mendizábal, AGN, Inquisición 594. Sánchez, *Río Abajo Frontier*, 95. Also see Sánchez, Spude, and Gómez, *New Mexico*, 54.
105. Sentencia de Nicolas de Aguilar, Proceso contra Aguilar, AGN, Inquisición 512, fol. 195.
106. Also see Galgano, *Feast of Souls*, 115–16.
107. Brown, *Bury My Heart at Wounded Knee*, 406–12.

Chapter 14: El Alemán and the New Mexican Inquisition of 1668

1. Declaración of Juan Martín Serrano, AGN, Inquisición 608.
2. Auto sent by Fray JuanBernal to Mexico City, April 1, 1670, AGN Inquisición 608.
3. Testimony of Joseph Nieto, January 19, 1670, Santo Domingo Pueblo, AGN, Inquisición, 666.
4. Declaración de Joseph Nieto, Santo Domingo, January 19, 1667, AGN, Inquisición 666, fol. 375. Also see Sánchez, "Bernardo Gruber."
5. Declaración de Joseph Nieto, Santo Domingo, January 19, 1667, AGN, Inquisición 666, fol. 375.
6. Declaración de Juan Martín Serrano, Santo Domingo, January 9, 1667, AGN, Inquisición 608, fol. 435.

7. Contestación, Cuarac, February 8, 1668, AGN, Inquisición 608, fol. 436.
8. Declaración de Juan Martín Serrano, AGN, Inquisición 666, fol. 380. Inquiry signed by Fray Joseph de Predes, Abo, June 21, 1668, AGN, Inquisición 666, fol. 387.
9. Testimonios de Fray Gabriel Torja, Joseph Martín Serrano, and Juan Martín Serrano, AGN, Inquisición, 666.
10. Ibid. Writ of Arrest, Abo, April 19, 1668, AGN, Inquisición 608, fol. 390.
11. Testimonios de Fray Gabriel Torja, Joseph Martín Serrano, and Juan Martín Serrano, AGN, Inquisición, 666. Also see Writ of Arrest, Abo, April 19, 1668, AGN, Inquisición 608, fol. 390.
12. Testimonios de Fray Gabriel Torja, Joseph Martín Serrano, and Juan Martín Serrano, AGN, Inquisición, 666. Also see Writ of Arrest, Abo, April 19, 1668, AGN, Inquisición 608, fol. 390.
13. Testimonios de Fray Gabriel Torja, Joseph Martín Serrano, and Juan Martín Serrano, AGN, Inquisición, 666. Also see Writ of Arrest, Abo, April 19, 1668, AGN, Inquisición 608, fol. 390.
14. Inventory of Gruber's sequestered property, AGN, Inquisición 608, 666.
15. Ibid.
16. Ibid.
17. *Autos* sent by Fray Juan Bernal to Mexico City, AGN, Inquisición 608, fol. 333, and 666, fol. 406.
18. Ibid.
19. Ibid. Also see AGN, Inquisición 590, for similar commentary.
20. Declaración de Fray Gabriel de Torja, June 9, 1668, Cuarac, AGN, Inquisición 666, fol. 399.
21. Declaración de Atanasio Sandia, July 8, 1670, AGN, Inquisición 666, fol. 411.
22. Testigo de Capitán Francisco de Ortega, Pecos, June 30, 1670, AGN, Inquisición 666, fol. 406.
23. Ibid.
24. Undated letter of Fray Juan Bernal, AGN, Inquisición 666, fol. 404.
25. Ibid.
26. Declaración de Atanasio Sandia, July 8, 1670, AGN, Inquisición 666, fol. 411.
27. Declaración de Fray Juan Bernal, June 30, 1670, AGN, Inquisición 666, fol. 408.
28. Declaración de Atanasio Sandia, July 8, 1670, AGN, Inquisición 666, fols. 411–12.
29. Ibid.
30. Francisco del Castillo Betancur to Dr. Juan de Ortega, El Parral, September 1, 1670, AGN, Inquisición 666, fol. 402.
31. Ibid.
32. Ibid.
33. Scholes, *Troublous Times*, 321.

Chapter 15: Revolt and Reconquest

1. Hackett and Shelby, *Revolt of the Pueblo Indians*, 2:247–48
2. Carta del conde de Paredes, virrey de México, al rey, 28 de febrero 1681, AGI, Audiencia de Guadalajara 138.
3. Diego de Vargas to the Viceroy, October 16-18, 1692, Spanish Archives of New Mexico (SANM), II, no 54a.
4. Antonio de Otermín to Juan Domínguez de Mendoza, Isleta, December 10, 1681, in Hackett and Shelby, *Revolt of the Pueblo Indians*, 2:223.
5. Declaration of Pedro Naranjo of the Queres Nation, Place of the Río del Norte, December 19, 1681, in Hackett and Shelby, *Revolt of the Pueblo Indians*, 2:246.
6. Ibid.
7. Ibid., 247.
8. Ibid.
9. Scholes, Simmons, and Esquibel, *Juan Domínguez de Mendoza*, 264–65.
10. Statement of Pedro Garcia, Place of El Alamillo, September 6, 1680, in Hackett and Shelby, *Revolt of the Pueblo Indians*, 2:62.
11. Declaration of Juan Lorenzo and Francisco Lorenzo, Place of the Río del Norte, December 30, 1681, in Hackett and Shelby, *Revolt of the Pueblo Indians*, 2:249.
12. Declaration of Josephe, Spanish-speaking Indian, Place of the Río del Norte, December 19, 1681, in Hackett and Shelby, *Revolt of the Pueblo Indians*, 2:239.
13. Declaration of Pedro Naranjo, in Hackett and Shelby, *Revolt of the Pueblo Indians*, 2:246.
14. Declaration of Diego López Sambrano, Hacienda of Luis de Carbajal, December 22, 1681, in Hackett and Shelby, *Revolt of the Pueblo Indians*, 2:299.
15. Ibid.
16. Declaration of Lieutenant General of Cavalry, Place of the Río del Norte, December 20, 1681, in Hackett and Shelby, *Revolt of the Pueblo Indians*, 2:266.
17. Declaration of Diego López Sambrano, in Hackett and Shelby, *Revolt of the Pueblo Indians*, 2:299.
18. Ibid.
19. Ibid., 300.
20. Ibid.
21. Ibid.
22. Ibid.
23. Ibid.
24. Ibid.
25. Ibid.

26. Ibid.
27. Ibid.
28. Ibid.
29. Declaration of Pedro Hidalgo, Soldier, Santa Fe, August 10, 1680, in Hackett and Shelby, *Revolt of the Pueblo Indians*, 1:6.
30. Ibid.
31. Ibid.
32. Ibid.
33. Ibid.
34. Autos tocantes al Alsamiento de los Yndios de la Provincia de la Nueva México, Santa Fe, 1690, in Hackett and Shelby, *Revolt of the Pueblo Indians*, 1:3–5.
35. Opinion of Fray Francisco de Ayeta, Hacienda de Luis de Carbajal, December 23, 1681, in Hackett and Shelby, *Revolt of the Pueblo Indians*, 2:305.
36. Chávez, *Origins of New Mexico Families*, 4. Scholes, Simmons, and Esquibel, *Juan Domínguez de Mendoza*, 388.
37. Scholes, Simmons, and Esquibel, *Juan Domínguez de Mendoza*, 380 and 30.
38. Order of arrest against the person of Lieutenant General Alsonso Garcia, Place of El Alamillo, September 6, 1680, in Hackett and Shelby, *Revolt of the Pueblo Indians*, 1:62.
39. Antonio Otermín to the Viceroy, Paso del Río del Norte, October 20, 1680, in Hackett and Shelby, *Revolt of the Pueblo Indians*, 2:207.
40. Notification and arrest, Place of El Alamillo, September 6, 1680, in Hackett and Shelby, *Revolt of the Pueblo Indians*, 1:63–65.
41. Hackett and Shelby, *Revolt of the Pueblo Indians*, 1:cxxvii.
42. Ibid., cxxcii.
43. Ibid.
44. Ibid., cxxcvii.
45. Declaration of the Lieutenant General of the Cavalry, in Hackett and Shelby, *Revolt of the Pueblo Indians*, 2:257–266.
46. Hackett and Shelby, *Revolt of the Pueblo Indians*, 2:258-259.
47. Ibid., 2:258.
48. Ibid., 259.
49. Ibid.
50. Ibid.
51. Ibid., 260.
52. Ibid., 260.
53. Ibid.
54. Ibid., 261.
55. Scholes, Simmons, and Esquibel, *Juan Domínguez de Mendoza*, 227n6.

56. Declaration of the Lieutenant General of the Cavalry, in Hackett and Shelby, *Revolt of the Pueblo Indians*, 2:261.

57. Ibid., 262.

58. Ibid., 264–65.

59. Ibid., 358.

60. Ibid.

61. Ibid.

62. Declaration of the Indian Juan, December 18, 1681, in Hackett and Shelby, *Revolt of the Pueblo Indians*, 2:235.

63. Espinosa, *Crusaders of the Rio Grande*, 22–23.

64. Reply of the Fiscal, Mexico, June 25, 1682, in Hackett and Shelby, *Revolt of the Pueblo Indians*, 2:382. Espinosa, *Crusaders of the Rio Grande*, 22–23.

65. Sánchez, "Spanish-Indian Relations," 144–45.

66. Kessell and Hendricks, *By Force of Arms*.

Appendix A

1. Walter, *The Cities That Died of Fear*.

2. National Park Service, *Proposal/Environmental Assessment*, 3. Also see the enabling legislation for the establishment of Salinas National Monument, Pub. L. 96-550.

3. For the renaming of Salinas National Monument to Salinas Pueblo Missions National Monument see Pub. L. 100-559, title I, §101, October 28, 1988.

4. National Park Service, *Proposal/Environmental Assessment*, 103.

5. Ivey, *In the Midst of a Loneliness*, 2; also see note 2.

6. Hewett and Mauzy, *Landmarks of New Mexico*, 96. The authors write that construction began in 1659. Also Ivey, *In the Midst of a Loneliness*, 31. Specifically, Ivey states that "in the winter of 1659–60, [Friar] Santander evaluated the site he had selected for the church and convent" (185). Ivey uses the date 1660 as the construction date for the church and convent (96).

7. The history of the excavation of Mound 7 and its findings is told in Hayes, Young, and Warren, *Excavation of Mound 7*.

8. Hewett and Mauzy, *Landmarks of New Mexico*, 96.

9. Toulouse, *Mission of San Gregorio*, 1.

10. National Park Service, *Proposal/Environmental Assessment*, 2–6, 24–27. The proposal contains a legislative history marking the way for the creation of Salinas National Monument.

11. Salinas Pueblo Missions National Monument, NM, enabling legislation and legislative acts include "Gran Quivira National Monument, New Mexico [Monument abolished and funds made available to Salinas National Monument by Pub.

L. 96-550, title VI, §601(b), Dec. 19, 1980, 94 Stat. 3231/ Salinas National Monument redesignated Salinas Pueblo Missions National Monument by Act of October 28, 1988, Pub. L. 100-559, title I, §101, Oct. 28, 1988, 102 Stat. 2797]," U.S.C. (2006), suppl. 1, p. 416.

12. One of the earliest uses, if not the first, of the name Gran Quivira for the site is Carleton, "Diary of an Excursion." Carleton's report is also published in 33 Cong., 2d sess., Senate Miscellaneous Document no. 24, 1854. Carleton visited the site in 1853.

13. Hodge, Hammond, and Rey, *Revised Memorial*, 315.

14. Sánchez, *Río Abajo Frontier*, 104.

15. For a complete analysis of the seventeenth-century construction of the church at Quarai see Ivey, *In the Midst of a Loneliness*, 125–55.

16. "The Itinerary of Juan de Oñate's Expedition," in Pacheco, Cárdenas, and Torres de Mendoza, *Colección de Documentos Inéditos*, 16:228.

17. Abert's report is published in 30 Cong., 1st sess. House Executive Document no. 41, 1847.

18. Carleton, "Diary of an Excursion."

19. Hurt, *The 1939–1940 Excavation Project*, 2, 4, 5.

Appendix B

1. Angie Debo, *Geronimo: The Man, His Time and Place* (Norman: University of Oklahoma Press, 1989), 420.

2. Debo, *Geronimo: The Man, His Time and Place*, 420.

3. "Royal Cedula of Approbation of the Succor," in Hackett, Bandelier, and Bandelier, *Historical Documents*, 3:300.

4. Altman, *Contesting Conquest*, 61, appropriately, for example, titles chapter 3, "Insurrection and War." Altman treats the Mixton War, 1540–42, as a defining event in the conquest of northern Mexico.

5. Ibid., 96.

6. See Sánchez, *Comparative Colonialism*; Powell, *Tree of Hate*; and, Juderías y Loyot, *La Leyenda Negra*. Also see Juderías y Loyot, *La leyenda negra y la verdad histórica*.

7. Pacheco Rojas, *Milenarismo tepehuán*, 110.

8. Ibid., 110–11.

9. Ibid., 111.

10. Ibid.

11. Reff, Ahern, and Danford, *History of the Triumphs*, 595.

12. Ibid., 594–95.

13. Pacheco Rojas, *Milenarismo tepehuán*, 114.

Bibliography

Archives

Archivo General de Indias (AGI), Seville.
    Sección Audiencia de México, legajos 27, 220.
    Sección Audiencia de Guadalarara 138.
    Sección Civil, legajo 77.
    Sección Justícia, legajos 336, 1021.
    Sección Patronato, legajos 22, 244.
Archivo General de la Nacion (AGN), Mexico City.
    Sección Inquisición, tomos 268, 316, 356, 512, 587, 593, 594, 608, 666.
    Sección Vinculos, tomo 110.
    Seccion Tierras tomo 3268.
Biblioteca Nacional, Madrid.
    Manuscritos de America.
Biblioteca Nacional de Antropología e Historia, Mexico City.
    Serie Documentos, CA 199.
Biblioteca Nacional de España, Madrid.
Palacio Real, Madrid.
    Manuscritos.
Real Academia de la História, Madrid.
    Colección Carlos Muñoz, tomo 70, expediente 1543.

Books, Articles, and Miscellaneous Publications

Altman, Ida. *Contesting Conquest: Indigenous Perspectives on the Spanish Occupation of Nueva Galicia, 1524–1545*. University Park: Pennsylvania State University Press, 2017.

Bancroft, Hubert Howe. *History of Arizona and New Mexico*. Vol. 17. San Francisco: The History Company, 1889.

Bloom, Lansing B., trans. "Esteban de Perea, Verdadera Relación de la Grandiosa Conversión que ha avido en el Nuevo Mexico." *New Mexico Historical Review* 8 (1933): 211–35.

Bolton, Herbert E. *Spanish Exploration in the Southwest, 1542–1706*. New York: Charles Scribner's Sons, 1908.

Brown, Dee. *Bury My Heart at Wounded Knee*. New York: Henry Holt, 1971.

Calloway, Colin Gordon. *One Vast Winter Count: The Native American West before Lewis and Clark*. Lincoln: University of Nebraska Press, 2005.

Carleton, James Henry. "Diary of an Excursion to the Ruins of Abó, Quarra, and Gran Quivira in New Mexico, under the Command of Major James Henry Carleton, U.S.A." In *Ninth Annual Report of the Board of Regents of the Smithsonian Institution*, 296–316. Washington, DC, 1855.

Chávez, Fray Angélico. *Coronado's Friars*. Washington, DC: Academy of American Franciscan History, 1968.

Chávez, Fray Angélico. *Origins of New Mexico Families: A Genealogy of the Spanish Colonial Period*. Rev. ed. Santa Fe: Museum of New Mexico, 1992.

Cohen, Jennie. "Little Ice Age, Big Consequences." *History*, January 31, 2012. http://www.history.com/news/little-ice-age-big-consequences. Last consulted September 29, 2017.

Dussenberry, William H. *The Mexican Mesta*. Urbana: University of Illinois Press, 1963.

Encinias, Miguel, Alfred Rodríguez, and Joseph P. Sánchez, eds. and trans. *Historia de la Nueva México, 1610: A Critical and Annotated Spanish/English Edition*. By Gaspar Pérez de Villagrá. Albuquerque: University of New Mexico Press, 1992.

Espinosa, José Manuel. *Crusaders of the Rio Grande: The Story of Don Diego de Vargas and the Reconquest of New Mexico*. Chicago: Institute of Jesuit History, 1942.

Forrestal, Peter P., trans. *Benavides' Memorial of 1630*. Washington, DC: Academy of Amrican Franciscan History, 1954.

Galgano, Robert C. *Feast of Souls: Indians and Spaniards in the Seventeenth-Century Missions of Florida and New Mexico*. Albuquerque: University of New Mexico Press, 2005.

González, Gerald T.E., and Fran Levine. "In Her Own Voice, Doña Aguilera y Rocha and Intrigue in the Palace of the Governors, 1659–1662." In *All Trails Lead to Santa Fe: An Anthology Commemorating the 400th Anniversary of the Founding of Santa Fe, New Mexico, in 1610*, 179–208. Santa Fe: Sunstone Press, 2010.

Hackett, Charles Wilson, Adolph F.A. Bandelier, and Fanny R. Bandelier, eds. *Historical Documents Relating to New Mexico, Nueva Vizcaya, and Approaches Thereto, to 1773*. 3 vols. Washington, DC: Carnegie Institutions of Washington, 1937.
Hackett, Charles Wilson, and Charmion Clair Shelby, eds. and trans. *Revolt of the Pueblo Indians of New Mexico and Otermín's Attempted Reconquest*. 2 vols. Albuquerque: University of New Mexico Press, 1942.
Hallenbeck, Cleve. *The Journey of Fray Marcos de Niza*. Dallas: University Press, 1949.
Hamalainen, Pekka. *The Comanche Empire*. New Haven, CT: Yale University Press, 2008.
Hammond, George P., and Agapito Rey. *Don Juan de Oñate: Colonizer of New Mexico, 1595–1628*. 2 vols. Albuquerque: University of New Mexico Press, 1953.
Hammond, George P., and Agapito Rey, eds. and trans. *Narratives of the Coronado Expedition, 1540–1542*. Albuquerque: University of New Mexico Press, 1940.
Hammond, George P., and Agapito Rey. *The Rediscovery of New Mexico, 1580–1594*. Albuquerque: University of New Mexico Press, 1966.
Hayes, Alden C., Jon Nathan Young, and A. H. Warren. *Excavation of Mound 7, Gran Quivira National Monument, New Mexico*. Publications in Archeology, no. 16. Washington, DC: National Park Service, 1981.
Hewett, Edgar J., and Wane L. Mauzy. *Landmarks of New Mexico*. Albuquerque: University of New Mexico Press and School of American Research, 1953.
Hodge, Frederick Webb, George P. Hammond, and Agapito Rey, trans. *Fray Alonso de Benavides' Revised Memorial of 1634*. Albuquerque: University of New Mexico Press, 1945.
Hoig, Stan. *Came Men on Horses: The Conquistador Expeditions of Francisco Vázquez de Coronado and Don Juan de Oñate*. Boulder: University Press of Colorado, 2013.
Hurt, Wesley R. *The 1939–1940 Excavation Project at Quarai Pueblo and Mission Building: Salinas Pueblo Missions National Monument, New Mexico*. Santa Fe: Southwest Cultural Resources Center, National Park Service, 1990.
Ivey, James E. *In the Midst of a Loneliness: The Architectural History of the Salinas Missions, Salinas Pueblo Missions National Monument Historic Structures Report*. Southwest Cultural Resources Center Professional Papers, no. 15. Santa Fe: National Park Service, Southwest Regional Office, 1988.
Ivey, James E. "The Viceroy's Order Founding the Villa of Santa Fe: A Reconsideration, 1605–1610." In *All Trails Lead to Santa Fe: An Anthology Commemorating the 400th Anniversary of the Founding of Santa Fe, New Mexico, in 1610*, 97–108. Santa Fe: Sunstone Press, 2010.
Jones, Oakah. *Nueva Vizcaya*. Albuquerque: University of New Mexico Press, 1988.
Juderías y Loyot, Julián. *La Leyenda Negra: estudios acerca del concepto del Espana en el extranjero*. Barcelona: Casa Editorial Araluce, 1917.
Juderías y Loyot, Julián. *La leyenda negra y la verdad histórica: contribución al estudio del concepto de España en Europa, de las causas de este concepto y de la tolerancia

política y religiosa en los países civilizados. Madrid: Tipografía de la Revista de Archivos, Bibliotecas y Museos, 1914.

Kessell, John L. *Spain in the Southwest: A Narrative History of Colonial New Mexico, Arizona, Texas, and California*. Norman: University of Oklahoma Press, 2002.

Kessell, John L., and Rick Hendricks, eds. *By Force of Arms: The Journals of Don Diego de Vargas, 1691–1693*. Albuquerque: University of New Mexico Press, 1992.

Klein, Julius. *La Mesta: Estudio de la Historia Económica Española, 1273–1836*. Madrid: Alianza Editorial, 1985.

National Park Service. *Proposal/Assessment General Management Plan. Proposed Salinas National Monument, New Mexico*. Santa Fe: US Department of the Interior, National Park Service, Southwest Regional Office, 1978.

National Park Service. *Proposal/Environmental Assessment/General Management Plan: Development Concept Plan, Salinas National Monument, New Mexico*. Santa Fe: US Department of the Interior, National Park Service, Southwest Regional Office, 1983.

Naylor, Thomas H., and Charles W. Polzer. *The Presidio and Militia on the Northern Frontier of New Spain: A Documentary History*. Tucson: University of Arizona Press, 1986.

Ortiz, Patricia. "Cruelty Abounds throughout Recorded History." *Albuquerque Journal*, November 10, 2017.

Pacheco, Joaquin F., Francisco de Cárdenas, and Luis Torres de Mendoza, eds. *Colección de Documentos Inéditos Relativos al Descubrimiento, Conquista y Organización de las Antiguas Posesiones Españoles de América y Oceanía*. 42 vols. Madrid, 1864–84.

Pacheco Rojas, José de la Cruz. *Milenarismo tepehuán: Mesianismo y Resistencia Indígena en el Norte Novohispano*. Mexico City: Siglo XXI, 2008.

Powell, Philip Wayne. *Tree of Hate: Propaganda and Prejudices Affecting United States Relations with the Hispanic World*. New York: Basic Books, 1977.

Recopilacion de Leyes de los Reynos de las Indias. 4 vols. Madrid, 1681.

Reff, Daniel T., Maureen Ahern, and Richard K. Danford, trans. *History of the Triumphs of Our Holy Faith amongst the Most Barbarous and Fierce Peoples of the New World*. By Andrés Pérez de Ribas. Tucson: University of Arizona Press, 1999.

Report to Government Requesters. Treaty of Guadalupe Hidalgo: Findings and Possible Options Regarding Longstanding Community Land Grant Claims in New Mexico. A Report to Congressional Requesters by the United States General Accounting Office (GAO-04-60), June 2004, Joseph P. Sánchez, consultant/researcher.

Riley, James D., ed. *The Inquisition in Colonial Latin America: Selected Writings of Richard E. Greenleaf*. Berkeley, CA: Academy of American Franciscan History, 2010.

Ronstadt Milich, Alicia, trans. *Relaciones: An Account of Things Seen and Learned by Father Jerónimo de Zárate Salmeron from the year 1538 to year 1626*. Albuquerque: Horn and Wallace, 1966.

Sánchez, Jane C. "Spanish-Indian Relations during the Otermín Administration, 1677–1683." *New Mexico Historical Review* 58 (April 1983): 133–51.

Sánchez, Joseph P. "Bernardo Gruber and the Mexican Inquisition." In *Salinas: Archaeology, History, and Prehistory*, ed. David Noble, 26–31. Exploration, Annual Bulletin of the School of American Research. Santa Fe: School of American Research, 1982.

Sánchez, Joseph P. *Comparative Colonialism, the Spanish Black Legend, and Spain's Legacy in the United States: Perspectives on American Latino Heritage and Our National Story*. Albuquerque, NM: National Park Service / Spanish Colonial Research Center, 2013. http://npshistory.com/publications/american-latino-heritage.pdf.

Sánchez, Joseph P. "El Farol Indiano: The Administration of Sacraments to the Natives of New Spain, 1713." In *Seeds of Struggle, Harvest of Faith: The Papers of the Archdiocese of Santa Fe Catholic Cuarto Centennial Conference on the History of the Catholic Church in New Mexico*, ed. Thomas J. Steele, Paul Rhetts, and Barbe Awalt, 53–68. Albuquerque: LPD Press, 1998.

Sánchez, Joseph P. "La Ruta de Oñate: Early Parages of Northern Chihuahua and Southern New Mexico along the Camino Real de Tierra Adentro." *Southern New Mexico Historical Review* 24 (January 2017): 11–24.

Sánchez, Joseph P. "Nicolas de Aguilar y la Jurisdicción de las Salinas, 1654–1661." *Revista Complutense de Historia de America*, no. 22 (1996): 139–59.

Sánchez, Joseph P. *The Río Abajo Frontier, 1540–1692*. Albuquerque, NM: Albuquerque Museum of History, 1989.

Sánchez, Joseph P., and Bruce A. Erickson. *From Mexico City to Santa Fe: A Historical Guide to the Camino Real de Tierra Adentro*. Albuquerque, NM: Rio Grande Books, 2011.

Sánchez, Joseph P., Jerry L. Gurulé, and Larry Miller. "Paso por Aquí: Hispanic New Mexican Spanish Colonial, Mexican and Early Anglo-American Period Inscriptions at El Morro National Monument." 2006, unpublished manuscript.

Sánchez, Joseph P., Jerry Gurulé, and Mario Milliones, trans. *El Tratado de Guadalupe Hidalgo: Hallazgos y opciones posibles con respecto a los reclamos de larga duración de mercedes de tierras comunitarias en Nuevo Mexico* (GAO-04-60). Washington, DC: Government Accounting Office, June 2004.

Sánchez, Joseph P., Robert L. Spude, and Art Gómez. *New Mexico: A History*. Norman: University of Oklahoma Press, 2013.

Scholes, France V. "Church and State in New Mexico, 1610–1650." *New Mexico Historical Review* 11, no. 1 (January 1936): 9–76; no. 2 (April 1936): 145–78; no. 3 (July 1936): 283–94; no. 4 (October 1936): 297–349.

Scholes, France V. *Church and State in New Mexico, 1610–1650*. Albuquerque, Historical Society of New Mexico, 1937 (1936).

Scholes, France V. "Civil Government." *New Mexico Historical Review* 10, no. 2 (1935): 71–111.

Scholes, France V. "The First Decade of the Inquisition in New Mexico," *New Mexico Historical Review* 10 (July 1935): 195–241.
Scholes, France V. *Troublous Times in New Mexico 1659–1670*. Albuquerque, Historical Society of New Mexico, 1942 (1937).
Scholes, France V., and Lansing B. Bloom. "Friar Personal and Mission Chronology, 1598–1629." *New Mexico Historical Review* 19 (1944): 319–36.
Scholes, France V., Marc Simmons, and José Antonio Esquibel, eds. *Juan Domínguez de Mendoza: Soldier and Frontiersman of the Spanish Southwest, 1627–1693*. Albuquerque: University of New Mexico Press, 1937.
Snow, David H., ed. *New Mexico's First Colonists: The 1597–1600 Enlistments for New Mexico under Juan de Oñate, Adelantado & Gobernador*. Albuquerque: Hispanic Genealogical Research Center of New Mexico, 1998.
Temkin, Samuel, ed. and trans. *Gaspar Castaño de Sosa: Conquistador, Explorador, Fundador*. Saltillo: Escuela de Ciencias Sociales, Universidad Autónoma de Coahuila, 2015.
Thoma, Francisco de. *Historia Popular de Nuevo México*. New York: American Book Company, 1896.
Toulouse, Joseph H., Jr. *The Mission of San Gregorio de Abó: A Report on the Excavation and Repair of a Seventeenth-Century New Mexico Mission*. Albuquerque: University of New Mexico Press, 1949.
Vetancurt, Fray Agustín. *Menológio*. Vol. 4 of *Teatro Mexicano: Descripición breve de los sucessos exemplares de la Nueva España en el nuevo mundo occidental de las Indias*. Madrid: José Porrua Turanzas, 1960–61. First published in 1698.
Walter, Paul A.F. *The Cities That Died of Fear: The Story of the Salinas Pueblos*. Santa Fe: El Palacio Press, 1931.
Weddle, Robert S. *San Saba Mission: Spanish Pivot in Texas*. Austin: University of Texas Press, 1964.
Zárate Salmerón, Gerónimo de. "Relaciones de todas las cosas que en el Nuebo Mexico se han visto y savido, assi por mar como por tierra." Transcription by Aaron C. Taylor of Mss. 6882, Biblioteca Nacional de España, Madrid. Berkeley: Cibola Project, Research Center for Romance Studies, Institute of International Studies, University of California, Berkeley. https://escholarship.org/uc/item/65g7j2kr.pdf. Last consulted January 28, 2018.

Index

A
Abendano, Simon, 123
Abo Pass, 57, 74, 263
Abo, 31, 57, 84, 86, 162, 171, 194–196, 210, 213, 216, 230, 231, 256, 258–264. *See also* Salinas Pueblo Missions National Monument
Aboó, 57, 263
Acequias, 6, 13, 101, 163
Acoma, 15, 31, 36, 52, 65, 72, 74–82, 87, 100, 102, 108–110, 145–146, 169–170, 186–187, 250, 257, 268–270
Aguacane, 94, 96
Agualagu, 84–86
Aguilar, Nicolas de, 208, 212–218, 220, 222–224, 228
Aguilar, Pablo, 108
Ahijados (Aijados), 90, 93
Alameda, 219, 238, 240, 247–249, 251
Alamillo, 195, 209–210, 246
Alcaldes Mayores de Indios, 208, 209, 211, 213, 215, 223
Alcaldes Ordinarios, 115, 116, 130, 135, 141, 148
Albuquerque, 21, 29, 35, 57, 101, 238, 247–248, 270
Alemán, El. *See* Gruber, Bernardo
Alvarado, Hernando de, 36
Anaya, Cristóbal de, 234
Angostura, 245
Archuleta, Asencio, 127, 129, 131, 136, 137, 142, 155
Arenal, 35, 47
Arizona, 7, 19, 24, 25, 37, 65, 75, 82, 179
Atanasio, 232–235
Atrisco, 247, 248

B
Baca, Alonso, 134, 142
Barela, Alonso, 134, 142
Barela, Juan, 219
Barela, Pedro, 134
Baum, Frank L., 7
Betancur, Francisco del Castillo, 235
Biruega, Diego de, 43
Bonilla, Francisco Leyba de, 50, 67–71, 87, 88

320   INDEX

Braba, 59. *See also* Taos Pueblo
Buffalo Plains, 18, 26, 27, 30, 35, 36, 38, 69–71, 87–89, 95, 96, 122, 126, 127, 133, 179, 180, 183

C
Cabeza de Vaca, Alvar Núñez, 7, 19, 22, 23, 27
Cabildo, 9, 12, 15, 100, 103, 105, 112–115, 126, 135, 146, 167, 177, 200, 205
Cabrillo, Juan Rodríguez, 26
California, 7, 17, 19, 24, 26, 65, 110, 158, 264
California Gold Rush, 6
Calloway, Colin Gordon, 109
Camino Real de Tierra Adentro, 8–10, 19, 20, 38, 55, 59, 101, 114, 115, 141, 142, 151, 152, 160, 173, 178, 182, 186, 197, 198, 200, 203, 204, 233–235, 246, 253, 268, 269
Caoma, 75, 79
Carbajal, Agustín, 243
Carbajal, Luis de, 41
Carlsbad, 40, 42
Carretas, 53, 57, 102, 197
Carrizozo, 34
Carvajal, Juan de Victoria, 142
Casa de Comunidad, 217, 228, 230
Castañeda, Juan de, 83
Castañeda, Pedro de, 26
Cat-Ticati, 75, 79
Catiti, Alonso, 250, 251
Catzina (Kachina), 197, 206, 207, 218–222, 225, 249
Caudi, Tilini and Tleume, 238, 243
Caucachi, 79
Chamuscado, Francisco Sánchez, 27, 29, 30, 31, 33, 34, 40, 50, 52, 57, 69, 263
Chapel of San Antonio, 249
Chihuahua, 8, 19, 22, 27, 38, 40, 53, 54, 68, 81, 101, 140, 179, 200, 208, 234, 235, 269, 270. *See also* Nueva Vizcaya
Chililí, 31, 121, 152, 156, 159, 160, 171, 179, 194, 196, 210, 211, 215, 216, 219, 220, 257, 260–263
Cíbola, 24, 25, 54
Cicuye. *See* Pecos Pueblo
Cieneguilla, 250
Clemente, Esteban, 241, 270
Cochiti, 64, 219
Colorado, 7, 19, 26, 65, 263

Columbus, Christopher, 11, 26, 63, 266, 268
Compadrazco, 239
Concha, Hernando de Ugarte y la, 240
Contreras, Juan Mansos de, 201
Conversión de San Pablo, 15, 63, 154, 157–159, 167, 169, 173, 177, 185, 188, 195
Coronado, Francisco Vázquez de, 23, 25–27, 35–38, 47, 50, 60, 69, 263, 268, 270
Cortéz, Hernán, 60
Cristóbal, Sánchez, 56
Cuarác. *See* Quarai; Salinas Pueblo Missions National Monument
Culiacán, 23
Cuyamungue, 45

D
Dead Man's Journey. *See* Jornada del Muerto
Despoblado, 24, 27, 234, 235
Diezmo, 15, 133
Dios, Juan de, 60
Domínguez de Mendoza, Francisco, 234
Domínguez de Mendoza, Juan, 206, 238, 247–251
Domínguez de Mendoza, Thome, 197, 206, 233, 234, 245
Donayre de las Misas, Juan, 130, 131
Donis, Juan Pérez de, 54
Duran, Pedro, 123, 166

E
El Obi, 244
El Paso, 10, 21, 31, 34, 54, 59, 63, 101, 152, 204, 228, 234, 236, 246, 247, 251–253, 257, 260
El Perillo, 56
El Portuelo, 57, 74, 263
El Morro, 6, 36, 65, 66, 75, 173, 188, 189
Encomienda, 14, 52, 104, 115, 116, 166, 168
Encuche, 95, 96
Escanjaques, 89–93, 180
Escarramad, Juan, 133–135, 144, 146, 151, 160, 161
Escoto, Nicolas, 49
Espejo, Antonio de, 32–38, 40, 50, 52, 57, 60, 69, 179, 263
Espejo, Pedro de, 33
Estanque del Peñol. *See* El Morro

Estebaníco, 22–24. *See also* Zemmouri, Mustafa
Excasi, 79
Extremadura, 158

F

Fanega, 14, 73, 104, 105, 155, 252
Farfán, Marcos de, 75, 179
Francavila, 31
Fresno, Villanueva de, 158
Friars: Acevedo, Fray Francisco, 171, 195, 210, 301(n103); Aguado, Fray Antonio, 195, 210, 211, 213, 216; Aliri, Fray Sebastian de, 194; Aranda, Fray Antonio de, 199; Arvide, Fray Martín, 169, 170, 191, 192, 179; Ayala, Fray Pedro de, 235; Bautista, Friar Andrés, 120, 121, 159; Beltrán, Fray Bernardino, 32, 33, 36, 37; Benavides, Fray Alonso de, 169, 170–189, 191–194, 196, 258, 260; Bernal, Fray Juan, 234, 235; Burgos, Fray Agustín de, 120, 146, 156, 159; Carrasco, Fray Tomas, 171, 284; Chavarría, Fray Miguel de, 163, 173, 196; Chica, Fray Gutiérrez de la, 194, 195, 262; Concepción, Fray Cristóval de la, 187, 189; Cuellar, Fray Agustín de, 187, 188; Escalona, Fray Juan de, 73, 102, 103, 106; Estremera, Fray Alonso de, 163; Figueredo, Fray Roque de, 187–189; Fonte, Fray Francisco, 171, 195; Gutierres, Fray Andrés, 187, 189; Hurtado, Fray Francisco Nicolas, 231; Letrado, Fray Francisco, 181, 189; López, Fray Diego, 160, 183–185; López, Fray Francisco, 47; Madre de Dios, Fray Francisco de la, 188; Manso, Fray Tomás, 201; Martínez, Fray Alonso, 58, 63; Natividad, Fray Benito de la, 211, 204; Fray Niza, Marcos de, 23–25; Ordóñez, Fray Isidro, 119, 154, 155, 259; Oróz, Fray Pedro de, 60; Ortega, Fray Pedro de, 162, 171, 178, 185; Padilla, Fray Juan de, 25, 26; Paredes, Fray Joseph de, 195, 229; Paz, Fray Juan de, 227, 229–232, 236; Pedraza, Fray Gerónimo de, 138, 140, 144, 185; Peinado, Fray Alonso, 115, 117, 118–121, 140, 141, 151, 152, 156, 158–160, 171, 173, 194–196; Perea, Fray Estevan de, 140, 144, 147, 154, 157–163, 165–167, 169, 171–173, 185–190, 194–196, 198–200, 206, 261; Pérez Granillo, Fray Francisco, 112, 219; Pérez Huerta, Fray Francisco, 118, 119, 126, 127, 131, 132, 135, 138, 140, 141, 148–150, 155–159, 161; Perguer, Fray Andrés, 126, 134, 135, 137, 159; Pio, Fray Juan Bautista, 243; Porras, Fray Francisco de, 187–189, 191; Posada, Fray Alonso de, 223; Quiros, Fray Cristóbal de, 119, 120, 147, 148, 160, 161, 163, 184; Ramírez, Fray Juan, 187, 194, 203, 204, 207, 221; Rodríguez, Fray Agustín, 31, 35–37, 47, 57; Salas, Fray Juan de, 120, 146, 149, 157, 160, 182–185, 194, 195, 199, 200; Salazar, Fray Cristóbal de, 56, 62; San Buenaventura, Fray Francisco, 187; San Juan, Fray Alonso de, 161, 195; Santa María, Fray Juan de, 30, 35, 36; Santander, Fray Diego de, 212, 217, 218; Tirado, Fray Luis, 118, 121–124, 128–140, 142, 144, 147–152, 156–159; Torija, Fray Gabriel, 195; Vetancurt, Fray Agustín, 194, 210; Vidania, Fray Juan de, 199; Zambrano Ortiz, Fray Pedro de, 162, 163; Zárate, Fray Asencio de, 169; Zárate Salmerón, Fray Gerónimo, 90–93, 97; Zena, Fray Bernardino de, 183, 184

G

Galisteo, 29, 30, 37, 38, 46, 59, 60, 65, 70, 74, 82, 88, 121, 134, 149, 151, 156, 159, 160, 162, 163, 194, 210, 211, 219, 239, 257, 260
Gallegos, Hernán, 18, 29–32, 52, 179
García Alonso de, 234, 245, 246
Gila Apaches, 186, 191
Gil de Avila, Fray Ildefonso, 195
Glorieta Pass, 45
Goa, India, 193, 194
Gómez, Juan, 162, 166
Governors of New Mexico: Arguello, Fernando de, 240; Baeza, Francisco Martínez de, 198; Ceballos, Bernardino de, 141, 142, 149, 150–152, 154, 156, 157, 163, 167, 171; Eulate, Juan de, 162–171, 177, 178, 186; Flores de Sierra y Valdez, Juan, 200; Heredia, Alonso Pacheco de, 201; Manso de Contreras, Juan, 201, 202, 222, 223; Medrano y Mesia, Juan de, 234; Mendizábal, Bernardo López de, 197, 201–

214, 217–225; Mexico City, 17, 19, 20, 22, 23, 25, 27, 32, 34, 40, 41, 49, 59, 60, 68, 88, 92, 93, 96, 97, 102, 103, 107, 115–117, 120, 129, 142–144, 146, 149, 152, 157, 160–162, 166, 168, 169, 177, 182, 186, 195, 197–200, 202, 203, 207, 214, 217, 220, 222–224, 228, 231, 232, 236, 261; Mora y Ceballos, Francisco de la, 198; Oñate, Cristòbal de, 114; Oñate, Juan Pérez de, 10, 11, 16, 18, 20, 21, 27, 50–68, 70–71, 73–77, 79–84, 87–94, 98–114, 116, 117, 122, 133, 142, 143, 145, 148, 158, 159, 163, 179, 180, 190, 202, 221, 239, 263; Otermín, Antonio de, 238, 239, 243–248, 251–253; Peralta, Pedro de, 100, 112, 114–147, 149–156, 158, 160–163, 167, 205, 289; Rosas, Luis de, 198–201, 218; Samaniego y Jaca, Juan, 208; Silva Nieto, Francisco Manuel de, 187; Treviño, Juan Francisco de, 241; Vargas, Diego de, 237, 253; Villanueva y Armendaris, Fernando de, 241
Gran Quivira, 69, 82, 179, 256, 258–261, 263, 264
Great Plains, 6, 7, 16, 19, 21–23, 25–27, 30, 31, 37–40, 46, 50, 52, 59, 60, 65, 67–71, 73, 80, 82, 87–89, 91–97, 102, 105, 107, 111, 112, 122, 162, 173, 179, 183, 208, 224, 257, 260, 262
Gruber, Bernardo, 228–236
Guadalajara, 23, 37
Gutiérrez, Alonso, 134
Gutiérrez de Quiros, Bernardo, 127

H
Halona, 190
Háwikuh, 24, 25
Hechicero, 242
Hidalgo, Pedro, 243, 244
Hoig, Stan, 10
Hopi, 65, 75, 164, 186, 189–191
Humaña, Antonio Gutiérrez de, 50, 67–69, 71, 88, 90, 91
Humaña, Jusepe Gutiérrez de, 50, 66, 68–71, 88

I
Iglesia de Nuestra Señora de la Asunción, 58
Indehe, 106
Inquisition, Holy Office of the, 14, 32, 33, 41, 127–130, 132, 135, 144, 148, 152, 160, 172, 173,

178, 186, 194, 195, 197, 199, 200, 202, 207, 214, 217, 220–225, 227–232, 234, 236, 261
Inscription Rock. *See* El Morro
Isleta Pueblo, 65, 74, 143, 144, 146, 149, 157, 159, 160, 181–183, 206, 219, 223, 231, 233, 238, 240, 246–248, 251, 252, 270

J
Jacona, 45
Jamestown, 6, 11, 100, 111, 268
Jaramillo, Juan de, 26
Javier, Francisco, 239, 243, 244, 248, 251
Jémez Pueblo, 171
Jim Crow Laws, 12
Jornada del Muerto, 21, 56, 101, 152, 204, 228, 235, 246
Juárez, Andrés, 148, 149
Jumanos, 15, 71, 72, 82–84, 86, 102, 103, 109, 110, 179–183, 185, 195, 260, 265, 270
Jusepe. *See* Humaña, Jusepe Gutiérrez de

K
Kachina. *See* Catzina
Keres, 58, 117, 120, 238, 250
Kessell, John l., 109, 110

L
La Cienega, 219
La Joya, 31
La Mesa, 31
Las Humanas, 26, 52, 64, 82, 171, 178, 180, 181, 185, 189, 195, 196, 212, 213, 215–217, 229, 233, 256–262. *See also* Salinas Pueblo Missions National Monument
Las Vueltas del Río, 34
Los Puertos, 54
Luján, Diego Pérez de, 34–38
Luján, Juan, 131, 137, 139, 142, 189

M
Malpais, 34, 36, 187
Manzano Mountains, 29, 31, 57, 64, 70, 82, 110, 121, 134, 152, 159, 162, 171, 178, 181, 186, 194, 216, 223, 228, 229, 234, 257, 261, 263
Margarita, Island of, 164, 165
Márquez, Gerónimo, 81, 86, 103, 105, 122, 133, 134, 142, 161

Martín Serrano, Francisco, 221
Martín Serrano, Joseph, 230
Martín Serrano, Juan, 227, 229–233, 235
Martínez, Baltazar, 94
Martínez de Montoya, Juan, 113, 114
Mazaque, 36
Memorial of 1630, 174, 176, 180, 183
Miguel, el indio, 92–97
Moho, 35, 47
Montero, Juan, 143
Montesinos, Alonso Gómez de, 79, 80, 106
Morlete, Juan, 41, 42, 48–50, 55, 58
Moros y Cristianos, 62
Mountainair, 31, 258, 263

N
Nahua allies. *See* Tlaxcalans
Nambé, 45, 123, 124, 159, 160, 186, 242, 270
Naranjo, Pedro, 238
Narvaez, Panfilo de, 22
National Historic Preservation Act (1966), 3, 4, 276(n5)
National Park Service, 6, 9, 256–261, 269
Nevada, 7, 19
Nevares, Joseph de Leiva, 252
Nicolasillo, 233, 235
Nieto, Joseph, 229, 230
Nieto, Juan, 228, 229, 232
Nueva Almaden, 41, 42, 48
Nueva Sevilla, 57–59
Nueva Vizcaya, 19, 38, 40, 50, 53, 106, 200, 208, 267–272. *See also* Chihuahua
Nuevo León, 40, 48

O
Ohkay Owingeh, 21
Opecancanough, 11, 268
Organ Mountains, 55
Ortega, Francisco de, 231–234
Ortiz, Pedro Zambrano, 162
Ortiz Mountains, 59, 159

P
Pacheco Rojas, José de la Cruz, 17
Parages, 20
Parral, 200, 203, 208, 235, 244

Paz, Diego de, 49
Pecos Pueblo, 6, 26, 30, 37–41, 42–46, 48, 52, 60, 61, 68, 70, 123, 162, 163, 171, 194, 234, 244, 245, 250, 257
Pedrosa, Martín de, 32
Peñalosa, Francisco de Sosa, 51, 54
Peralta, Andrés de, 238
Pérez, Andrés, 43
Pérez, Gaspar, 123, 124, 140
Pérez, Miguel, 67
Pérez, Simon, 133, 134, 141, 142
Pérez de Lujan, Diego, 34, 35
Pérez Ribas, Andrés, 272
Peru, 23, 53, 125, 268
Picuris Pueblo, 30, 59, 60, 123, 125, 134, 162, 169, 170, 218, 219, 250, 252
Piro, 28, 29, 34, 57, 170, 184, 186, 219, 241, 246, 260, 261
Pojoaque, 45, 123, 219
Popé, 237–239, 242, 243, 252, 253
Powhatan War, 11, 268
Práctica Criminal Eclesiástica, 144, 151
Protector de Indios, 164, 217
Puaray, 29–31, 35–37, 47, 48, 57, 58, 61, 74, 84, 238, 249, 251
Pueblo Pardo, 180

Q
Qualacu, 56, 64
Quaquina, 36
Quarai, 31, 64, 159, 194–196, 210, 212, 215, 216, 218–220, 229, 230, 256, 258–264. *See also* Cuarác; Salinas Pueblo Missions National Mounument
Querechos, 80
Queres, 72, 78, 187
Quintana, Luis de, 239, 245, 251
Quivira, 69, 82, 89–91, 179, 183–185, 256, 258–261, 263, 264. *See also* Salinas Pueblo Missions National Monument

R
Rascón, Francisco de, 86
Real Provisión de 1621, 168
Reconquista, 64, 281
Repartimiento, 14, 164, 168

324 INDEX

Rivers: Arkansas River, 26, 71, 89, 90; Canadian River, 70; Gila River, 65, 186; Pecos River (Cicúye), 38, 40, 42, 70; Río Arriba, 45, 46, 58, 62, 117, 245, 246; Río Chama, 16, 58, 73, 93, 100; Río Conchos, 20, 179; Río Florído, 20, 21, 34, 53; Río Grande, 5, 7, 19–23, 25–31, 34–38, 40–42, 45, 46, 52–56, 58, 59, 61, 68–70, 73, 74, 82, 93, 100, 101, 114, 117, 120, 158–160, 162, 163, 170, 177, 179, 180, 182, 185, 198, 204, 205, 223, 229, 231, 233, 238, 244, 247, 252, 253, 257, 260–263, 268; Río Nuestra Señora, 36; Río Salado, 42; Río Turbio, 34
Rodríguez Nieto, Juan, 43
Romero, Bartolomé, 105, 106, 128, 136, 137
Ruiseco, 31
Ruíz de Rios, Pedro, 124
Ruíz de Caceres, Juan, 142, 143, 151

S
Salazar, Martín de, 43
Salazar, Fray Francisco de, 160, 195, 229
Salinas Pueblo Missions National Monument, 16, 30, 31, 57, 64, 65, 70, 74, 82, 84, 86, 121, 134, 151, 159, 178, 179, 194–196, 208, 210–220, 228–230, 232, 236, 241, 255–264
Sambrano, Diego López, 239–243, 245, 251
San Agustín, alias Filipinas, 110
San Buenaventura de las Humanas. *See* Salinas Pueblo Missions National Monument
Sánchez, Alonso, 90, 106
San Cristóbal Pueblo, 59, 64, 70, 122, 163, 219
Sandia Mountains, 29, 30, 35, 46, 58, 70, 82, 84, 151, 250, 263
Sandia Pueblo, 117, 119, 140, 143–147, 149, 157, 158, 160, 161, 194, 198, 199, 219, 231, 233–235, 238, 239, 245, 247–251, 261
Sandoval, Sebastian de, 199, 201
San Felipe Pueblo, 36, 64, 160, 163, 228, 239, 240, 242, 245, 248, 250–252, 270
San Felipe (near San Marcial), 28, 34
San Francisco de Sandia. *See* Sandia Pueblo
San Gabriel, 61, 65, 66, 73, 74, 84, 86, 92–94, 100, 102, 103, 105, 107, 110, 112–115
Sangleyes, 49
San Ildefonso, 58, 68, 69, 121, 123, 125, 134, 159, 160, 186, 219

San Isidro, 179, 181, 217, 258
San Juan Bautista: church, 62; village, 61, 62
San Juan de los Caballeros, 9, 58, 59, 70–76, 88, 93, 100, 101
San Juan Pueblo, 21, 45, 68, 124, 125, 159, 160, 186, 219, 234. *See also* Ohkay Owingeh
San Lazaro, 134, 135, 159, 160, 166, 219
San Marcial, 21, 28, 34, 56
San Marcos, 46, 162, 163
San Mateo, 29, 30
San Miguel, 28, 59, 93
Santa Barbara, 101, 140, 146, 148, 268
Santa Cruzada, 15
Santa Cruz de la Cañada, 219
Santa Fe, 14, 20, 21, 29, 31, 45, 100, 101, 112, 114–118, 120, 121, 123, 124, 126–128, 130, 131, 133, 134, 135, 137, 140–144, 146–152, 156, 159, 160, 162, 167, 177, 178, 186, 187, 193, 197–201, 205, 206, 215, 218, 234, 244–246, 253
Santo Domingo, Dominican Republic, 23
Santo Domingo Pueblo, 46–49, 58, 61, 64, 79, 80, 117, 119, 120, 122, 123, 128, 130, 135, 138–152, 157, 160, 163, 182, 199, 213, 223, 224, 227, 229, 245, 246, 248, 251, 257
Scholes, France V., 16, 17
Senecú, 234, 235, 246, 247, 252, 257
Sevilleta, 57, 219, 249
Sierra de Madalena, 241
Sierra de San Lázaro. *See* San Lazaro
Sierra del Olvido. *See* Organ Mountains
Sierra Madre Occidental, 22, 38, 269, 273
Simmons, Marc, 98, 99
Socorro, 21, 25, 56, 57, 170, 204, 209–211, 219, 234, 235, 241, 247, 257, 270
Sombrerete, 41, 55, 107
Sonora, 24, 25, 38, 228, 234, 235, 269, 270
Sosa, Alonso de, 108
Sosa, Gaspar Castaño de, 37, 41–50, 55
Sotelo Osorio, Felipe de, 177, 178, 187
Soto, Hernando de, 26

T
Tabira, 196, 211, 217, 257, 261, 262
Tajique, 31, 152, 159, 194, 196, 210, 211, 215–217, 219, 257, 260, 261, 263, 264
Tanbulita, El, 241, 270

Tancoa, 94–96
Tanos, 117, 162, 163, 239, 241, 250, 270
Taos Pueblo, 25, 30, 58–60, 122–128, 162, 169, 171, 185, 194, 238, 239, 243, 245, 250, 257
Tayberon, 59. *See also* Taos Pueblo
Tenabo, 171, 195, 196, 211, 262
Tesuque, 45, 219, 243
Tewa, 186, 206, 242
Texas, 7, 10, 19, 22, 26, 38, 41, 70, 179, 185, 270
Tierra Adentro, 22, 23, 27, 28, 30, 32, 38, 40–42, 52, 54, 68
Tierra de Guerra, 247, 267
Tiguas, 29, 31, 35, 64, 72, 78
Tiguex, 27, 47, 270
Tiwa, 29, 84, 117, 120, 121, 158–160, 166, 186, 217, 250, 261
Tlaxcalans, 21, 77, 78, 79, 177, 267
Tompiro, 84, 162, 186, 212, 213, 216, 217, 261
Tupatú, Luis, 252, 253
Tusayan, 75
Tzanoa, 96

U
Urraca, 45, 46

V
Vaca, Alvar Núñez Cabeza de. *See* Cabeza de Vaca, Alvar Núñez
Valencia, Francisco de, 231, 234
Valencia, Manuel, 230
Valenciano, Miguel Sánchez, 33, 34
Valverde y Mercado, Francisco, 93, 94, 96
Velarde Investigation, 103, 104
Valle de San Gregorio, 33
Valley of San Bartolomé, 34, 38, 53
Viceroys: Albuquerque, Duque de, 201; Cadereita, Marqués de, 198; Conde de Paredes, 237; Fernández de Cordova, Diego (Marqués de Guadalcázar), 107, 141, 146; Marqués de Villamanrique, 41; Mendoza, Antonio de, 23, 25; Suárez de Mendoza, Lorenzo, 138, 139, 159; Velasco, Luis de, 41, 49–53, 113, 114, 115; Zuñiga y Acevedo, Viceroy Gaspar de (Conde de Monterrey), 53, 68, 103, 108
Villagrá, Gaspar Pérez de, 56, 81
Virginia, House of Burgesses and General Assembly, 100
Vyana, 96

W
Whitman Mission National Historic Site, 6
Women: Agreda, María de, 181–184 Anaya, Casilda de, 33, 34; Bustillos, María, 200; Carrión, Mother Luisa de, 183, 191; Castro, Luisa Diaz de Betansos, 204; Clarilla, 197; Cruz, Ana de la, 197; Doña Ines, 59, 60; Jesús, Mother María de, 182, 184, 185; López Robledo, Lucía, 137; Martín, María, 232; Montaño, Magdalena, 228; Ortiz, Patricia, 99; Rocha, Teresa de Aguilera de la, 197, 202, 203; Salazar, Isabel de, 205; Vargas, Isabel de, 195
Wounded Knee, 6, 11, 111, 226, 266, 268

X
Xunusta, 75, 79

Z
Zacatula, 31
Zaldívar, Juan de, 56, 57, 59, 65, 74–76
Zaldívar, Vicente de, 53, 56, 57, 70, 71, 74–81, 84–89, 91, 93, 94, 98, 106, 107, 109, 110, 111, 113, 263
Zemmouri, Mustafa, 22. *See also* Estebaníco
Zia, 36, 61, 72, 78, 142, 145–147, 149, 150, 160, 252
Zongopabi, San Bernardo de, 190
Zumárraga, Juan de, 23
Zuñi, 24, 26, 27, 31, 36, 37, 52, 65, 75, 182, 186–189, 191, 223, 257
Zuñiga, Francisco Manzo y, 182

www.ingramcontent.com/pod-product-compliance
Lightning Source LLC
Chambersburg PA
CBHW060550080526
44585CB00013B/510